The Miles Kelly
Book of
British
History

The Miles Kelly

Book of British History

Written by Philip Steele
and Fiona MacDonald

Miles Kelly
PUBLISHING

First published in 2007 by
Miles Kelly Publishing Ltd
Bardfield Centre, Great Bardfield, Essex, CM7 4SL

Copyright © Miles Kelly Publishing Ltd 2007

Some of this material first appeared in the *Encyclopedia of British History*

2 4 6 8 10 9 7 5 3 1

Editorial Director Belinda Gallagher
Art Director Jo Brewer
Editor Amanda Askew
Editorial Assistant Carly Blake
Designers Jo Brewer, Simon Lee, Candice Bekir, Rick Caylor
Indexer Jane Parker
Picture Researcher Laura Faulder
Production Manager Elizabeth Brunwin
Reprographics Stephan Davis, Liberty Newton, Ian Paulyn

ISBN 978-1-84236-857-2

Printed in China

British Library Cataloguing-in-Publication Data
A catalogue record for this book is available from the British Library

www.mileskelly.net
info@mileskelly.net

Contents

Raiders and Settlers AD 446–1066

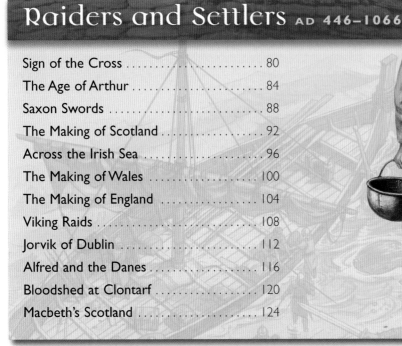

Castles and Knights 1066–1509

The Modern Age 1901–2007

History-makers

The Ancient Islands

500,000–700 BC

THE WORLD AT A GLANCE

ELSEWHERE IN EUROPE

c.12,000 BC
Cave paintings in France and northern Spain.

c.7200 BC
Dugout canoes are being made in the Netherlands.

c.6500 BC
Farming reaches the Balkan peninsula from Asia.

c.3200 BC
Wheeled vehicles in use in Eastern Europe.

c.2300 BC
Start of the European Bronze Age.

c.1900 BC
Rise of Minoan civilisation on the island of Crete, palaces and script.

c.1400 BC
Rise of Mycenaean civilisation in southern Greece, walled citadels.

c.900 BC
Rise of Etruscan civilisation in northern Italy, fine statues.

ASIA

10,500 BC
Pottery being made in southern Japan.

c.8350 BC
Foundation of Jericho, the world's oldest known walled city.

c.6400 BC
The wheel is invented in Mesopotamia, in the Middle East.

c.6250 BC
Town of Çatal Hüyük is founded, southern Turkey.

c.3250 BC
Writing is invented in Mesopotamia.

c.2500 BC
Rise of civilisation in Indus valley, at Mohenjo-Daro and Harappa.

c.2300 BC
Sargon of Akkad founds first Asian empire.

c.1500 BC
Shang emperors rule China, slaves, bronze weapons, silk.

AFRICA

c.12,000 BC
Grindstones used for making flour from wild seeds.

c.8500 BC
Start of rock art in the Sahara region, which was still fertile.

c.7500 BC
Decorated pottery being made in the Sahara region.

c.6000 BC
Start of farming in the Nile valley, Egypt.

c..4000 BC
Sailing boats being used in Egypt.

2530 BC
The Great Pyramid is raised at Giza in Egypt.

1325 BC
Egypt's young ruler, Tutankhamun, is buried in the Valley of the Kings.

c.1000 BC
Growth of the kingdom of Kush, in southern Nubia.

"The earliest history of Britain and Ireland is written in stone, bone, wood and clay…"

NORTH AMERICA

c.18,000 BC
One of several possible dates for the first peopling of the Americas.

c.16,800 BC
Possible date of tools found at Cactus Hill site in Virginia.

c.5000 BC
Maize is being grown in Mexico.

c.2300 BC
Earliest pottery in Central America.

c.2000 BC
A wave of Inuit migrations through the Arctic region.

c.1200 BC
Olmec civilisation in Central America, carved stone and temples.

c.1000 BC
Rise of Adena culture in eastern woodlands of USA, burial mounds.

c.800 BC
Zapotec civilisation in Mexico, first writing in the Americas.

SOUTH AMERICA

c.12,500 BC
Possible date for human occupation of Monte Verde, Chile.

c.8600 BC
Beans, gourds and peppers are grown in Peru.

c.3500 BC
Llamas are being used as pack animals, to transport goods.

c.3200 BC
Maize is first grown in South America.

c.3200 BC
Dead bodies made into mummies, Chile.

c.2800 BC
Villages built in the Amazon river basin.

c.2500 BC
Cloth is woven using looms, irrigation of fields.

c.1500 BC
The first metal-working in Peru.

c.900 BC
Rise of Chavín civilisation in the Andes, stone temples.

OCEANIA

c.50,000 BC
Aborigines settle in Australia, migrating from Southeast Asia.

c.28,500 BC
Humans settle the land now known as New Guinea.

c.10,000 BC
New wave of Aboriginal settlement in Australia, tame dogs.

c.7000 BC
Taro root is grown as a food crop in New Guinea.

c.5000 BC
Rising sea levels, New Guinea and Tasmania become islands.

c.1500 BC
Ancestors of the Polynesians start to migrate eastwards across the Pacific Ocean by canoe.

c.1000 BC
Stone settlements built in southeastern Australia.

c.1000 BC
Polynesian ancestors reach Tonga and Samoa.

c.500,000 BC
Homo erectus living in western Europe.

c.250,000 BC
Neanderthal people living in western Europe.

The Lonely Hunters

The British Isles are a group of small islands lying in shallow waters off the northwestern coast of Europe. The two largest islands are called Great Britain and Ireland. Today these lands are green, with a moist and mild climate. Fifteen thousand years ago, they were in the grip of Arctic weather conditions. Great Britain was roamed by reindeer and bears and by prehistoric hunters. It was still part of the European mainland and the River Thames flowed into the Rhine. There were no villages or towns and humans were very few and far between. The population of the whole world in 15,000 BC was probably about the same as that of Scotland today.

IN THE BEGINNING

We find out about human-like creatures and early ancestors of humans by studying the remains of fossilized bones and stone tools.

c.500,000–400,000 years ago
Site: Boxgrove, Sussex, England
Type: Heidelberg Man

c.250,000 years ago
Site: Swanscombe, Kent, England
Type: human ancestor

c.230,000 years ago
Site: Pontnewydd cave, northeast Wales
Type: Neanderthal

c.70,000 BC
Start of the last great Ice Age.

c.59,000 BC
A warmer period (interglacial) interrupts the Ice Age.

➡️ *Neanderthal people were living in Britain by 250,000 years ago. Their skull shape indicates that they had sloping foreheads with heavy brow ridges. They probably died out by about 30,000 years ago.*

➡️ *True humans did not appear in Europe until about 35,000 years ago. They were very similar to modern humans but with marginally bigger jaws and noses, and more rounded braincases.*

⬇️ *Herds of woolly mammoths were hunted during the Ice Age in northern Europe and Asia. They were a kind of elephant that had adapted to cold weather conditions.*

THE FIRST INHABITANTS

We do not know when the first human-like creature known as *Homo erectus* (upright man) first appeared in the British Isles, but most European remains date from 500,000–200,000 years ago. Some finds from this period may be very early ancestors of humans. At times the hunters were driven away from Britain by severe Ice Ages. However during warmer periods called interglacials (between the ice), they had returned.

THE LONELY HUNTERS 13

c.37,000 BC
Another interglacial period affects northern Europe.

c.35,000 BC
True human beings living in Britain. Great advances in making tools and weapons.

Flint and Stone

Between about 35,000 and 8500 BC, the peoples of western Europe learned to produce fine tools and weapons. They were nomadic hunters and used all the parts of the animals they killed – meat for food, skins to make clothes, gut to make thread, bone to make needles and other tools, and fat to make grease and lamp fuel. These people took shelter in caves or made tents of hide and timber. They also made paintings of wild animals on the walls of caves and studied the stars.

⬇️ *Careful chipping could turn a flint into a razor-sharp tool or weapon.*

TOOLS OF THE OLD STONE AGE

The earliest period of settlement in Britain is called the Palaeolithic (Old Stone) Age. Tools and weapons were made of chipped and flaked stone, bone and wood.

▲ *Flints were used to make knives, axes and spearheads.*

▼ *Flint scrapers could be used to scrape the flesh off the hides of wild animals.*

▶ *People became more and more skilled at making weapons of stone, bone and wood.*

c.30,000 BC
Neanderthal people disappear from Britain and become extinct.

c.24,000 BC
Ritual burial at Paviland, South Wales.

THE 'RED LADY' OF PAVILAND

In 1823 a man called William Buckland discovered a skeleton in a cave on the Gower peninsula in South Wales. He thought it was that of a Roman lady. Because it was covered in red ochre (a type of earth) the find became known as the 'Red Lady' of Paviland. Modern scientists now know that the skeleton was actually that of a young man who had been alive in about 24,000 BC.

→ *The Paviland burial was carried out with great care. The pouring of red ochre onto the body tells us that people at this time carried out funeral ceremonies and must have believed in gods or spirits.*

c.11,000 BC
Cave art, Cresswell Crags, Derbyshire.

c.10,000 BC
Changes in vegetation. Broadleaved trees gain
a foothold in northern Europe.

↓ *Saws were made from about 12,000 BC, and had flint 'teeth' held in place by resin.*

EARLY SAWS

Flint workers discovered how to make very small flint flakes. They fixed the flakes like teeth in a straight handle of wood or bone. If the teeth broke, they could fix new ones. Saws were used to cut through tough bones as well as wood.

HUNTING TECHNOLOGY

Flint was an excellent stone for making tools. It was very hard and yet could be chipped and flaked until it was razor-sharp. As the Palaeolithic or Old Stone Age merged into the period we call the Mesolithic or Middle Stone Age, the flint work became increasingly fine and precise. One reason for this was that new tools and weapons were needed. The climate was warming and the environment was changing. New forests of birch, hazel and pine grew up in this warmer climate and herds of red deer and other smaller, quick-running animals were moving into them.

↑ *In 2003–4 amazing rock carvings were found in caves at Creswell Crags, in Derbyshire, England. They date from about 11,000 BC. This one shows the outline of a stag.*

c.8500 BC
Evidence of a hunter-gatherer encampment at Crammond, near Edinburgh.

c.7150 BC
Estimated date of human remains found in Gough's cave, Cheddar Gorge.

↑ *Gough's Cave in England's Cheddar Gorge hase offered up hundreds of tools made of stone, bone and antler, and even some amber from the Baltic region of Europe.*

← *A hunting band in the later years of the Old Stone Age goes about its daily work. Hunters bring in game they have killed. Others bring in fuel, sew clothes made from animal skins, or play a flute made from bone.*

IN THE CHEDDAR GORGE

Hunters still needed to live nomadic lives. They set up camps as they travelled but still used natural shelters such as caves. Remains of an adult male found at Gough's Cave in the Cheddar Gorge in 1903 have now been dated to about 7150 BC. Amazingly, his genetic pattern or DNA has been found to match that of people living in the same area today.

c.8500 BC
Start of the Middle Stone Age in the British Isles.

c.8300 BC
Melting of the last glaciers in Britain.

The Rising Sea

Along the western coasts of Wales, Cornwall, the Scilly Isles and Brittany, there are ancient folk tales of lands lost beneath the sea. It could be that these are distant memories of real floods, for between 8000 and 3000 BC sea levels rose rapidly. As the climate warmed, the water expanded, spilling over coastal plains and filling channels. By about 6500 BC, the strip of land joining England to mainland Europe had been swallowed up by the sea for the last time.

After the mammoths had gone, people learnt how to hunt smaller animals such as deer. Hunters camped on high ground to spy out the dense forests, or by lakes and shores that offered a good supply of fresh fish.

c.8000 BC
New waves of hunters cross into Britain from the European mainland.

c.5000 BC
Oak forests now cover much of northwestern Europe.

THE RIDDLE OF THE SNAKES

Why are there no snakes in Ireland? An old tale claims that snakes were banished by a miracle carried out by St Patrick, the Christian saint. In fact, snakes entered Britain when it was still linked to France by a strip of land. However Ireland was already an island at that time, and snakes could not swim across the Irish Sea.

MESOLITHIC LIFE

The Mesolithic (Middle Stone) Age is the name given to the prehistoric period just before the coming of agriculture. As the climate warmed, forests of oak, ash and elm extended across Britain. The human population grew and spread north. Hunters travelled by boat from Scotland to Ireland. Arrowheads are made with tiny crafted flints called 'microliths'.

⬇ Hunters now crossed by boat from Scotland into Ireland. Tools and weapons were still of stone, bone or wood, but were made with much greater precision.

c.7600 BC
Star Carr in Yorkshire has a population of about 250 people.

c.7600 BC
A wooden paddle from Star Carr, first evidence of boats in Britain.

STAR CARR SETTLERS

A typical Mesolithic encampment from about 7600 BC has been found at Star Carr in Yorkshire, England. It was built in birch forest beside a lake and boggy land along the River Derwent. The settlement was home to about 250 people, with a territory of about 25 square kilometres. The people of Star Carr killed red deer, boar, elk and big wild cattle called aurochs. They paddled canoes and wore headdresses made of deer antlers.

➡ *Archaeologists excavating the site at Star Carr found 21 red deer antlers and skull parts. They had been bored with holes so that they could be tied onto the head. They may have been used as headdresses during religious rituals or dances.*

⬇ *Rising sea levels made Great Britain an island. This would affect its history in many ways for the next 8500 years.*

c.7600 BC
Skull of dog at Star Carr, first evidence of tame animals in Britain.

c.6500 BC
Britain completely isolated by rising sea levels.

Middle Stone Age hunters tamed dogs and used them for chasing red deer.

The First Farmers

Few discoveries changed the way people lived more than farming. In southwest Asia, grain crops were being grown and sheep were being raised as early as 9000 BC. Farming soon spread into North Africa and westwards across Europe. It was first brought to southern Britain by invaders and traders from the European mainland, about 6000 years ago. They brought with them seed for planting and livestock.

⬇ *The first wheat crops needed improving, to produce better yields of grain. Farmers did this by only choosing seed from the very best plants.*

A SETTLED LIFE

People no longer had to live as nomads, hunting for their food. They were able to stay in one place, building permanent settlements and storing up grain to use for future food. They could exchange any extra produce they made for other goods. In the Old Stone Age, every man, woman and child had been a food producer. Now, a surplus of food allowed some people to specialise as traders, craft workers, labourers – or rulers.

c.4000 BC
Farming spreads through the British Isles.

c.3200 BC
New Stone Age Settlement at Skara Brae, Orkney.

↑ *New Stone Age living rooms can be seen at Skara Brae. There are wall alcoves, dressers, stone beds and a central, smoky hearth.*

SKARA BRAE

In 1850 a severe storm battered the coast of Orkney, an island off the north coast of Scotland. When it was over, the ruins of a New Stone Age settlement were revealed in the shifting sands. Skara Brae had been inhabited from about 3200 to 2300 BC. Its people were fishermen or herders of sheep and cattle, for crops would not have grown well on this bleak and windy shore. The houses were built with stone blocks, and the roofs were made of turf and whalebone. The houses were linked by covered passages.

THE NEW STONE AGE

Farming spread throughout the British Isles from about 4000 BC. Field patterns from about 3000 BC can be seen today at Céide Fields, above high cliffs near Ballycastle, on the west coast of Ireland. They have been excavated from layers of peat bog. The arrival of farming marks the beginning of the period known as the Neolithic (New Stone) Age. In order to grow crops, clearings had to be cut from the forests of oak that now covered large areas of the country.

↑ *The first sheep in Britain were tough and wiry creatures, rather like today's Soay breed.*

THE FIRST FARMERS   **23**

c.3500 BC
Simple wooden ploughs being used in the south of England.

c.3000 BC
Grimes Graves flint mines, Norfolk, England.

MEDICINAL PLANTS

Stone Age people relied on nature to help cure sickness or ailments. Centaury was used to help heal wounds and treat snakebites. Henbane made the patient drowsy and relieved aches and pains. Rose hips, from the dog rose, were used to boost the immune system and ward off colds.

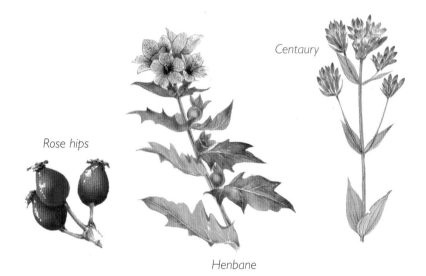

Centaury

Rose hips

Henbane

Stone hand mills, or querns, were used for grinding wheat. The central hole was filled with grain and then the top stone was turned, or ground, against the bottom one. Flour spilled out between the stones.

MAKING THINGS

New Stone Age peoples were skilled craftworkers. They produced baskets, jewellery and, from about 4500 BC, pottery. Wood was used to make farm tools. Stone was used to make hand mills called querns, for grinding grain into flour. Stone was also polished and ground to make axes for clearing the forest. In stony areas, axe-heads were produced at factory sites and exported right across the British Isles – from Northern Ireland to the southeast of England, from Cornwall to the northeast of England.

THE FIRST MINES

By about 4000 BC, flints were being mined underground. Over 360 mine shafts have been found at the Grimes Graves flint mine in Norfolk, England. It dates back to 3000 BC.

Down the shaft
Miners climbed down timber ladders or ropes.

Flint beds
Flints are balls of hard stone found in layers of chalk.

Cutting tools
Miners used picks made of deer antlers to dig out flints.

Baskets of flint
Flints were carried to the surface to be chipped and flaked.

c.3300 BC
The first stone circles are erected in the British Isles.

c.2700 BC
A henge is in use at Llandygai, North Wales.

Stones of Mystery

In the years between about 3200 and 1500 BC, massive pillars of stone or timber were raised in the British Isles and other parts of northwestern Europe. Some were placed on their own, others were arranged in long avenues. They are called standing stones and may have been used to mark tribal borders or ceremonial routes. Some pillars were arranged within oval, ditched enclosures called henges. These seem to have been observatories, used to mark the appearance of the Sun at midsummer or midwinter, or to track the movement of the stars. They must have been sacred places where religious rituals were carried out.

c.2700 BC
Silbury Hill, an artificial mound, is built near Avebury, Wiltshire, southern England.

c.2250 BC
85 stones are transported to Stonehenge from southwest Wales.

ARTIFICIAL MOUND

Silbury Hill in southern England (not far from Stonehenge) is the biggest mound made by prehistoric people in Europe. Over 3000 years old, the mound is 40 metres high and covers an area the size of three football pitches. In 1970, a burial mound, or barrow, was discovered inside.

↑ *Castlerigg in Cumbria is one of the most beautiful stone circles in Britain. It is also thought to be one of the earliest, and dates from around 3000 BC. The circle is made up of 38 stones, all of differing shape and size.*

← *Stonehenge towers over the grasslands of Salisbury Plain in Southern England. It was built in several stages and was in use from about 3200 to 1100 BC.*

Megaliths could weigh as much as
26 tonnes. They were quarried by
being being cracked with stakes,
fire, water and hammers.

The base of each pillar was placed
over a post-hole. Ropes and timber
scaffolding were then used to raise
the pillar to an upright position.

c.1800 BC
Stones of Callanish, Outer Hebrides, Scotland.

c.1500 BC
End of megalithic building in the British Isles.

⬇ *The builders of Stonehenge transported massive blocks of stone all the way from the Preseli Mountains of southwest Wales, a distance of over 215 kilometres.*

SUMMER SOLSTICE

It is believed that the arrangement of the giant megaliths of Stonehenge was such that the sun shone into the main entrance on the morning of the longest day of summer – the summer solstice. The solstice would have been the most important festival for farmers. People may have prayed for crops to thrive before harvesting.

PEOPLE OF THE MEGALITHS

Archaeologists call the monuments of this period megaliths (great stones). The builders of Stonehenge must have been very organised, with a large workforce. They were powerful and wealthy, trading across a large area of northwestern Europe. They had advanced technology and a knowledge of astronomy.

Massive stones such as this would have been transported on wooden sleds and timber rollers hauled by ropes. These were pulled by perhaps as many as 1000 men.

STONES OF MYSTERY **29**

c.3700 BC
First phase of Wayland's Smithy long barrow, Oxfordshire, England.

c.3200 BC
Passage grave at Newgrange, Boyne Valley, Ireland.

Places of the Dead

The builders of henges and stone circles also used the great stones we call megaliths to build burial chambers. All over the British Isles, these stone slabs have survived long after the simple huts of their builders have disappeared.

➡ *Le Dehus burial chamber on Guernesy was built between c.3500–2000 BC. It was excavated between 1837 and 1847 and contained well-preserved human remains.*

⬆ *Megalithic tombs such as Newgrange are older than the pyramids of Egypt.*

NEWGRANGE

The Brú Na Bóinne area of eastern Ireland includes three megalithic tombs – Dowth, Newgrange and Knowth. The Newgrange tomb was built in about 3200 BC and is made up of a huge mound over a passage grave. A slit in the roof allows the rising sun to creep into the gloomy burial chamber at midwinter. Many of the stones are decorated with swirling spiral patterns. Later peoples believed that the Newgrange site must have been made by the gods.

BURIAL AND CREMATION

During the New Stone Age, bodies were often placed in burial chambers once they were already skeletons, or else cremated. Some burial sites could hold the remains of up to 50 bodies.

➡ *The Creevykeel tomb in Sligo, Ireland, dates from between c.4000–2500 BC.*

c.2500 BC
Barclodiad y Gawres passage grave, North Wales.

c.2500 BC
West Kennet long barrow no longer used.

c.2200 BC
Round barrows raised by new settlers, southwest England.

c.2100 BC
Bryn Celli Ddu passage grave, North Wales.

DESIGNS FOR THE DEAD

New Stone Age people were often buried under narrow mounds called long barrows. Some of these were just made of earth, but others covered megalithic burial chambers. Some megalithic tombs are called passage graves. Here the chamber is reached by an underground passage, beneath a rounded hump of earth. After 2200 BC new peoples arrived in the British Isles and built round barrows for single burials.

Long barrow

Long barrow exposed

Passage grave

A MAGIC POTION

At Barclodiad y Gawres, an Irish-style passage grave on Anglesey, in North Wales, archaeologists found cremated bodies. A magic potion had been used to put out a fire. It included the bones of mice, snakes, toads and eels as well as seaweed and limpet shells.

Toad

Seaweed

The passage

A central passage led to the burial chambers. Its entrance was sealed by massive stones.

The mound

The mound was made of chalk rubble, soil and turf. It was about 100 metres long.

← *The passage grave of Bryn Celli Ddu is on the Isle of Anglesey, in North Wales. It was built on the site of an earlier henge. The excavated site revealed a hearth, a fire-pit and an ox-burial, as well as human remains and arrowheads. The grassy mound is a modern reconstruction. The original mound would have been larger.*

↓ *West Kennet long barrow in Wiltshire, England was in constant use from 3600 to 2500 BC. The barrow was used to bury at least 46 adults and children.*

Burial chambers
Five burial chambers were built from upright slabs and cap-stones.

East-West
Long barrows were lined up east to west, to face the sunrise.

c.2500 BC
Copper working reaches British isles from southeast and southwest Europe.

c.2200 BC
Early 'beaker' burials in British Isles.

Metal and Pottery

The building of stone monuments outlasted the New Stone Age, for builders of the later megalithic monuments and round barrows used metals.

Copper was worked in southeast Europe and western Asia by about 6000 BC. Within about 3000 years, smiths in these areas began to make alloys (mixtures of metals). The most useful alloy was bronze, a combination of tin and copper. Bronze-working reached the British Isles by about 1700 BC. Bronze tools and weapons were sharper than those made of stone and harder than those made of copper.

⬇ *Bronze needed to reach a temperature of about 900°C before it could be poured into moulds and left to cool and harden. It was then hammered and polished.*

MAKING BRONZE

About 5500 years ago, metal workers invented bronze by smelting copper ores and tin ores together. They used the bronze to make hard, sharp swords, spearheads and axe heads.

INTO THE FURNACE

Metal workers had to heat the mined rocks until the ore melted. This process is called smelting. The smelted metals were then mixed, with just under 1 part of tin to 9 parts of copper, and placed in a pot called a crucible. Blow pipes or simple bellows were used to make the fire burn hotter and hotter.

→ *Molten bronze would be poured into moulds, perhaps made of sandstone. The inside of the mould was smeared with soot and grease, to give a smooth finish. When the bronze had cooled and hardened, the mould could be knocked away.*

Open mould
Simple one-piece moulds like this could be used to make axes, daggers and other simple shapes. This sandstone mould is seen sideways on.

Mould
Viewed from above, the axe-shape cut into the mould can be clearly seen. Molten bronze was poured into the hollow.

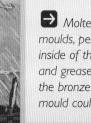

→ *One of the biggest sources of copper in Britain was a mine on the headland of the Great Orme, at Llandudno in North Wales. It has been suggested that 1700 tonnes of copper ore were extracted from the mine during the Bronze Age. Tunnels have been dated to the years between 1860 and 600 BC.*

METAL AND POTTERY 35

c.1600 BC
Manufacture of bronze in Scotland and Ireland.

c.1400 BC
Decline of the 'Wessex' culture of central southern England.

WEAPONS AND ORNAMENTS

Bronze was used to make spearheads, daggers, swords and axes. The designs varied over the ages. Axes were joined to the wooden hafts (handles) in various ways – wedged through a hole, mounted in a metal socket, inset and bound or fitted over a projecting strip of wood. Rings, jewellery, tweezers, cauldrons and harnesses for horses have also been found. Most Bronze Age objects have been found in the graves of chieftains, for gold, bronze and copper were used to show off the wealth and power of their owners.

⬇ *Bronze axes were so precious that they were often only used in ceremonies. Some were used in battle, but stone axes continued in everyday use for a long time.*

⬇ *Gold is quite soft, and early goldsmiths beat it into a variety of shapes, and made patterns of hammered indentations on its surface.*

Blade
This blade has been fitted to the handle in the simplest way possible – by being forced through a slit in the handle.

Haft
The axe handle would have been made of hard wood. Only metal parts survive for the archaeologist to find.

ORES AND MINES

The British Isles were rich in ores (rocks containing raw metals). Ireland had gold and copper, Cornwall had tin and exported it far and wide. Copper was also to be found in western and northern Britain. Mining became an industry in these areas and Scotland and Ireland became major centres of bronze manufacture.

c.700 BC
Bronze workshop finds, Heathey Burn cave,
Durham, England.

c.600 BC
End of the Bronze Age in the British Isles.

THE BRITISH ISLES AND THE BEAKER PEOPLE

The technology and customs of the Beaker People may have originated in Spain, a region rich in metals, before spreading through Europe. Beaker sites are found in both Great Britain and Ireland.

NORTH SEA

IRELAND

IRISH SEA

GREAT BRITAIN

ENGLISH CHANNEL

Areas of concentration

Beaker Extent

↓ *Pottery had been made in Britain since the fifth millennium BC. However the beakers of the early Bronze Age belong to a different tradition, which is also found in Spain and the Rhineland region of Europe. The beakers, probably used for drinking mead, are thought to have been symbols of wealth and power.*

WHO WERE THE BEAKER PEOPLE?

At about the time that metals first appeared in the British Isles, there was a change in the way in which the dead were buried. Personal possessions were now often placed in single graves, along with pottery containers called beakers. These burial customs began to spread to the British Isles from mainland Europe. It is possible that new invaders or traders arrived by sea around this time, and that it was they who introduced the skills of metal working. By this period of history there was a Europe-wide network of trading routes by land and sea.

METAL AND POTTERY

37

Celts and Romans

700 BC–AD 410

THE WORLD AT A GLANCE

ELSEWHERE IN EUROPE

c.700 BC
Rise of Celtic civilisation in Central Europe.

509 BC
Rome expels kings and becomes a republic.

432 BC
The Parthenon temple is built in Athens, golden age for Greece.

52 BC
Romans finally defeat the Gauls (Celtic tribes living in France).

27 BC
Rome becomes an empire under the rule of Augustus.

AD 9
Germanic tribes under Arminius (Hermann) defeat the Romans.

AD 285
The Roman empire splits into two halves, east and west.

AD 410
Visigoth warriors sack the city of Rome.

ASIA

c.660 BC
Jimmu, legendary first emperor of Japan.

c.563 BC
Birth of religious teacher Gautama Siddhartha (the Buddha) in Nepal.

550 BC
Cyrus the Great founds the Persian empire.

334 BC
Alexander the Great begins the Greek invasion of Western Asia.

322 BC
The Mauryan empire is founded in India.

221 BC
Chinese empire unites under Qin Shi Huangdi.

c.AD 30
Possible date for the crucifixion of Jesus Christ in Jerusalem.

AD 132
Jews rebel against Roman rule and are scattered into exile.

AFRICA

600 BC
Meroë in Nubia (Sudan) becomes a powerful city.

c.500 BC
Bantu-speaking peoples start to spread out from West Africa.

c.450 BC
Rise of Nok civilisation in Nigeria, iron working, terracotta heads.

c.400 BC
Phoenician city of Carthage, North Africa, at height of power.

331 BC
Greeks found city of Alexandria, Egypt.

AD 44
Romans now rule North Africa from Egypt to Morocco.

AD 50
Kingdom of Axum, in Ethiopia, rises to power.

AD 429
The Vandals, a Germanic people, found kingdom in North Africa.

> *"Iron swords are drawn — for the tribe or for the empire?"*

NORTH AMERICA

c.500 BC
Picture writing (hieroglyphs) at Monte Albán, Mexico.

c.310 BC
Chiefdoms in America's eastern woodlands — the Hopewell culture.

c.100 BC
The Hohokam people of the American South irrigate their crops.

c.AD 1
North Pacific coastal villages, carving and building in cedarwood.

c.AD 1
Villages being built in the American Southwest.

c.AD 1
Possible date for first Arawak settlement of the Caribbean islands.

c.AD 50
The city of Teotihuacán is built in Mexico, massive pyramids.

c.AD 300
Height of the Maya civilisation in Mexico, great cities.

SOUTH AMERICA

c.700 BC
Rise of the Parácas civilisation in Peru.

c.400 BC
The great temples of Chavín de Huantar, Peru.

c.200 BC
Rise of the Nazca civilisation in Peru.

c.200 BC
Nazca people scratch ceremonial lines across the desert, Peru.

c.200 BC
Decline of the Chavín civilisation.

c.AD 1
The Moche people of northern Peru, gold working and pottery.

c.AD 100
Growth of the city of Tiwanaku, near Lake Titicaca.

c.AD 400
Powerful chiefdom on Marajó island at mouth of the River Amazon.

OCEANIA

c.700 BC
Pacific trade in obsidian, a black stone used to make weapons.

c.300 BC
Polynesian settlement of Ellice Islands (Tuvalu).

c.200 BC
Later burials at Aboriginal site of Roonka Flat, Australia

c.200 BC
Polynesians reach the Marquesas Islands.

c.AD 1
Large increase in the Aboriginal population of Australia.

c.AD 150
Egyptian geographer Ptolemy suggests 'unknown southern land' — perhaps Australia.

c.AD 400
Polynesians reach Easter Island, in the eastern South Pacific.

c.AD 400
Polynesians reach the Hawaiian Islands, in the Central Pacific.

Masters of Iron

Copper and bronze continued to be used for making all sorts of tools, weapons and jewellery. However a new metal was being worked in Europe. Iron-working was first mastered in western Asia, between 2000 and 1500 BC. By about 600 BC, smiths were hammering out glowing bars of iron in the British Isles, too.

THE ANCIENT CELTS

One group of Europeans became expert at working the new metal, iron. The ancient Greeks called them 'Celts'. Their ancestry may have been the same as that of the Beaker People. The Celtic homeland was in Central Europe, southern Germany and the Alps, but after about 700 BC their influence spread across a vast area of Europe, from Turkey to Spain, from northern Italy through France to the British Isles. They raided and looted and

they settled and farmed new lands. Trading and travel led to their way of life being adopted by other peoples, too. Northwest Europe was dominated by three main Celtic groups. Gauls lived in what is now France. Britons lived in Great Britain and Gaels lived in Ireland.

THE CELTIC PEOPLES 1ST CENTURY BC

The British Celts, like the Gaels, formed many different tribes. Some were new invaders from the European mainland, others were native peoples who took up the Celtic way of life.

c.600 BC
Celts from Germany settle in northeast Scotland and spread north and west.

c.400 BC
Iron now common throughout the British Isles.

The Celts were brilliant metal workers who often decorated their work with birds, animals and interlacing patterns. Bronze mirrors such as these were used after 100 BC by the Belgae, Celtic tribes who had settled in southern England.

SMITHS AND FORGES

Iron was much harder and tougher than copper or bronze. It proved ideal for making swords and spears, or hammers and axes. Some people believed iron was magical, and horseshoes are still a symbol of good fortune. The blacksmith's forge was at the centre of Celtic village life.

and Ireland.

CELTIC SOCIETY

The ancient Celts never saw themselves as one people and were rarely united. Celtic tribes were ruled by kings and by queens, too, for women held considerable power. Warriors came from noble families and prided themselves on being brave, heroic fighters and skilled hunters. They loved feasting and drinking. Both British and Gaelic tribes fought endlessly amongst themselves, quarrelling and raiding each others' cattle. The poorer members of the tribe were farmers, toiling on the land, raising animals and cutting the hay. They served as charioteers and fort-builders. Prisoners of war and lawbreakers were treated as slaves.

↑ The Celts wove their clothes from linen and wool and wore cloaks fastened at the shoulder.

↑ The ancient Celts were famed for their love of gold and jewellery. Nobles wore splendid brooches, rings, armbands and torcs (ornate metal collars).

c.150 BC
Fifteen Celtic tribes ('Belgae') invade England from Gaul.
Celtic way of life at its greatest extent in Europe.

c.100 BC
Celts increasingly under attack in mainland Europe.

POTTERY MAKERS

Britain had many areas with good quality clay. The Celts made fine pottery on the wheel, firing the clay in kilns. Some of the best work was produced in southern Britain, especially in areas occupied by the Belgic Celts, who also made glass and enamel.

CELTIC LANGUAGES

Most of the languages spoken today in lands from Western Europe to northern India share a common origin. They are called Indo-European. Some languages still spoken in modern times came down to us from the ancient Celts. The language of the Britons turned into Welsh, Cornish and Breton (spoken in Brittany, France). The language of the Gaels gave us Irish, Scottish Gaelic and Manx (spoken on the Isle of Man). In Britain, no fewer than six rivers are called Avon. Why? It is simply a Celtic word for 'river'.

← Celtic potters made all sorts of items including jugs, storage jars, bowls, funeral urns and loom weights. Many items were beautifully decorated.

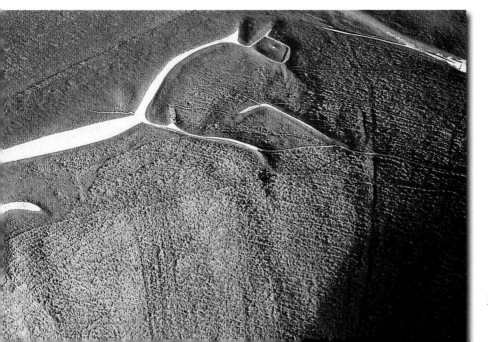

← This ancient white horse design is carved into the chalk at Uffington, Oxfordshire, England. Its date is uncertain. By the Iron Age, horses had become very important. The Celts mostly rode small, stocky ponies, but probably bred larger, more powerful horses too.

The Celts at Home

Forts had been built in the British Isles before the Iron Age. They were large enclosures protected by earthworks and walls, and were sited on hilltops and headlands. They often enclosed dwellings that were occupied in peacetime as well as war. New enclosures were raised by the Celts. Within Tre'r Ceiri hillfort in North Wales, the walls of 150 huts built in about 200 BC can still be seen today. Farming villages were often built on less protected lowlands, wherever the soil was good. In Ireland and Scotland, some villages were built on artifical islands in lakes. The last of the Celtic invaders, the Belgae, built towns, such as St Albans and Colchester.

ROUND HOUSES

Royal enclosures may have included large, rectangular halls, but most ordinary people in the western lands of the Celts lived in round huts that were about 15 metres across. The roofs were cone-shaped with a heavy thatch. The walls were normally built of timber and wattle-and-daub (interlaced sticks covered in clay). Stone was used in areas where timber was scarce.

On the floor
Floors were of beaten earth or slabs. They could be strewn with sweet-smelling rushes or grasses.

c.100 bc
Lake village at Glastonbury, Somerset, England.
Beautifully decorated hand mirrors become popular.

c.90 bc
First British coins, southern England.

↓ *Inside the Celtic roundhouse, smoke drifted up to the rafters from the central hearth. The timber posts may have been carved with ornate decorations. People slept on the ground in the cubicles, beneath warm animal skins.*

Livestock
Farm animals were kept in pens or even in the same huts as the villagers. They included sheep, goats, pigs, cattle and horses.

CELTIC FOOD

A big cauldron steamed over each hearth and the Celts were famous for enjoying their food. They might eat beef, mutton or pork, cheese or buttermilk. Bread and porridge were made from wheat, barley, rye or oats. Hunting and fishing provided boar, venison (deer meat) or salmon. Southern Europeans were amazed by the large amounts of alcohol drunk by Celtic men and women – imported wine, home-brewed ale and mead, a drink made from honey.

Apples

Wild boar

Honey

Nuts

The loom
Farm animals were kept in pens or even in the same huts as the villagers. They included sheep, goats, pigs, cattle and horses.

Compartments
Farm animals were kept in pens or even in the same huts as the villagers. They included sheep, goats, pigs, cattle and horses.

The hearth
A wood fire in the centre of the hut was used for cooking and heating.

THE CELTS AT HOME **45**

Warrior Heroes

The Celts were famed as fighters through most of Europe. Far to the south of the British Isles, Celtic warrior bands were storming into Rome and Greece between 387 and 279 BC. Celtic tribes did take part in large pitched battles, but they preferred single combat, where champions from each army came out to fight each other. They belonged to an age that admired individual bravery more than organisation or discipline. In the royal halls, warriors would boast of their exploits and drink to their dead companions.

➡ *Maiden Castle in Dorset, England, was already an important site during the New Stone Age. From about 450 BC, it was a major hillfort and the capital of a Celtic tribe called the Durotriges.*

Timber defences
Heavy timbers were used to build fences and gates, the last line of defence against invaders.

High earthworks
The banks were staggered so that it was impossible to launch a direct attack on the gates. The fort was finally taken by the Romans.

RATHS, DUNS AND BROCHS
Some forts were large defended settlements, but others were smaller and built more like castles. The remains of stone 'duns' may still be seen in Scotland and royal 'raths' in Ireland. The Picts, ancient inhabitants of northeastern Scotland who adopted the Celtic way of life, built 'brochs' – big stone towers that could be used as shelter in wartime.

The settlement
The settled area covered 18 hectares. Finds here have included Iron Age pots, sickles, combs made of bone and the skeletons of warriors who died in battle.

→ *The Celtic warrior could use throwing spears and stabbing spears. His deadliest weapon was his long sword, which he whirled around his head and brought crashing down on the enemy.*

WEAPONS AND WARRIORS

Most Celts went into battle unprotected by helmets or armour. They often fought without any clothes at all, preferring to strip naked. Later, Celts on the European mainland did design very effective armour to use against the Romans. They may even have been the inventors of chain mail – armour made from linked rings of iron. Celtic warriors carried mostly long- or oval-shaped shields, spears, daggers and long slashing swords made of iron. Hillforts were defended with a hail of pebbles hurled from slings. Some Celtic warriors used lime to dress their hair into spikes and tattooed their skin with a blue dye, called woad – the name 'Picts' comes from the Latin for 'painted people'.

Body patterns
Some Iron Age warriors decorated their bodies with blue dye from the woad plant.

Shield
Celtic shields of this period were made of oak, probably covered in hide or felt, and a central strip of iron.

Sword
Long swords with iron blades were used in battle. The hilt was usually beautifully decorated.

WARRIOR HEROES   **47**

CELTIC CHARIOTS

A new wave of Celtic warriors reached the British Isles in about 250 BC. With them came the light war chariot. Built of wood, it had iron-rimmed wheels and was pulled by two tough ponies, bred for their speed. It was driven by a non-fighting charioteer and was used to carry a fully armed warrior into battle. Some warriors who died were buried in their chariots.

⬇ *Celtic war chariots were made of wood, with iron-rimmed wheels. They carried warriors into battle.*

⬅ *By about 300 BC, the Celts were producing beautiful shields decorated with bronze and colourful enamel. Some, like this one found in London, may have been used in religious ceremonies.*

CÚ CHULAINN, CHAMPION OF THE GAELS?

Some tales told by the ancient Celts were written down many centuries later, during the Middle Ages. The Irish tales tell of Sétanta, nick-named Cú Chulainn ('the Hound of Culain'), a legendary hero of Ulster in northern Ireland. As a boy he kills a fierce hound. As a youth he is trained in fighting by a female warrior called Scáthach. He has a magic spear and as a man takes on the invading army of Queen Medb of Connaught single-handed. Cú Chulainn represents all the things a Celtic warrior wished to be. He is a cattle-raider, a warrior and a champion – swift, cunning, tireless and brave.

➡️ *When Cú Chulainn was mortally wounded by Lugaid, he tied himself to a stone pillar in order to keep standing and fight to the death. He only died when the Morrigan, goddess of death, alighted on his shoulder in the form of the battle-raven, Badhbh.*

Druids and Mistletoe

The landscape was sacred to the ancient Celts, with holy mountains, mysterious woods and magical waters. Offerings were thrown into lakes and left by springs and wells. In parts of Ireland, Scotland and Cornwall today, it is still believed to be lucky to tie ribbons to trees near certain springs. Groves of sacred trees formed places of worship. There were important religious enclosures called nemetons, although we do not know how they were used. Birds, snakes, fish and animals such as boars and stags were believed to have magic powers. Celtic tales are peopled with gods turning into animals, animals changing shape or becoming human.

Hen-dŷ head, Anglesey

THE FIRES OF BELTAIN

Celtic festivals were held throughout the year. On Beltain, 1 May, the dark hills were ablaze with bonfires. Lughnasa, for two weeks after 1 August, was a harvest festival in honour of Lugh. At Samhain, on the eve of 1 November, spirits from the other world were believed to walk the Earth. Imbolc, on 1 February, honoured the powerful goddess known as Brigit or Brigantia.

↑ *The Celts made many sculptures of human heads in stone or wood. Some were double or triple heads. Celts believed that the human soul lived inside the head. Celtic warriors cut off the heads of their enemies and displayed them in halls and shrines. This custom may be the origin of the pumpkin and turnip heads people place in their windows at Hallowe'en.*

The goddess Brigantia

c. AD 50
First evidence of the Celtic calendar – a bronze plate from Gaul.

c. AD 500s
Druidism finally dies out in British Isles.

GODS AND MYSTERIES

The oldest form of worship in the British Isles honoured the Earth Mother, bringer of fertility to the land. She was still honoured by the ancient Celts, under various names. They also believed in other gods and goddesses. Some belonged to a particular tribe or place. Irish gods included the Dagda, or supreme god, the goddess Dana, the shining Lug, Nuada of the Silver Hand, Morrigan, the terrifying raven goddess. Gods of the British Celts included a giant called Bran the Blessed, the powerful warrior Gwydion, Llew of the Strong Hand and the goddess Arianrhod. The Celts believed in other worlds, too, home of gods and the dead. Sometimes these were described as a happy island beneath the setting sun, sometimes as a mysterious fairy-world beneath the ground.

➔ *Cernunnos, was one of the most important Iron Age gods. He was worshipped throughout the Celtic world and is often shown surrounded by sacred animals. Later, Christians identified him with the devil.*

A MURDER MYSTERY

In 1984 a body was discovered in Lindow Moss, Cheshire, England. It had been preserved beneath the bog for over 1900 years. The dead man wore an armband of fox fur. His stomach contained traces of burnt bread and mistletoe pollen. He had been hit over the head with an axe, strangled with a rope and cut across the throat. His hands were well cared for, so this was no warrior or labourer. Archaeologists have guessed that he was a druid who was sacrificed to the gods.

Sacrifice of Lindow Man

Roman Invasion

After about 100 BC, the Celts in mainland Europe came under attack from German and Central European warriors. From Italy, too, Roman armies marched northwards to conquer the Gauls. In August 55 BC the Roman general Julius Caesar landed near Deal, in Kent, with 10,000 troops. He met with furious resistance, but returned the following year with at least 30,000 foot soldiers and 2000 cavalry. This time they crossed the River Thames and invaded the tribal lands of the Catuvellauni, Belgic Celts who had settled around St Albans. The Britons of southeast England were forced to pay tribute to Rome, and Caesar withdrew.

Aquila
Each legion had an eagle standard. This was carried at parades and served as a rallying point in battle. The standard bearer defended the eagle with his life.

Animal skins
Standard bearers wore animal skins over their helmets, with the upper jaw resting on the helmet.

Armour
Shirts of mail armour provided protection.

The aquilifer (standard bearer) carrying an eagle standard. Each legion had an eagle standard. Units of cavalry and auxiliaries carried standards of other animals.

JULIUS CAESAR
The conqueror of the Gauls and southern Britons was one of the most brilliant generals the world has known. Born in about 100 BC, his military campaigns made him the most powerful man in Rome. He made many enemies and was stabbed to death in 44 BC.

↑ A Roman warship. The war fleet of 54 BC was much bigger than the previous invasion. It included 28 warships and hundreds of other ships to carry troops, horses, weapons, equipment and stores.

↑ These coins are marked 'Cunobelin'. They show the wealth of the Catuvellauni just before the Roman conquest.

THE CONQUEST BEGINS

In the years following Caesar's death, the Romans found out more about Britain. They heard of rich prizes, such as tin mines. They sent merchants to spy, who reported that the Catuvellauni were growing powerful under a new king called Cunobelinus. Then in AD 41, Cunobelinus died. Some rival British kingdoms called for the Romans to teach the Catuvellauni a lesson. In AD 42 the emperor Claudius raised an army that was 40,000 strong. It aimed to bring the whole of Britain under Roman rule.

BRITONS ATTACKED

Roman troops, under general Aulus Plautius, landed in Kent in AD 43. They defeated two sons of Cunobelinus – Caratacus and Togodumnus. The biggest battle was fought by the River Medway, where the Romans broke through the massed tribes. Advancing into Essex, the Romans captured Camulodunum (Colchester). It was there that the emperor Claudius, on a fortnight's visit, took surrender of 11 tribes.

CARATACUS THE REBEL

Eleven British rulers immediately allied themselves with the Roman invaders. However Caratacus waged a fierce guerrilla campaign. Defeated, he sought refuge with Cartimandua, queen of the Brigantes, but she handed him over to the Romans. He was taken to Rome in chains, but in the end he was pardoned. He died in AD 52.

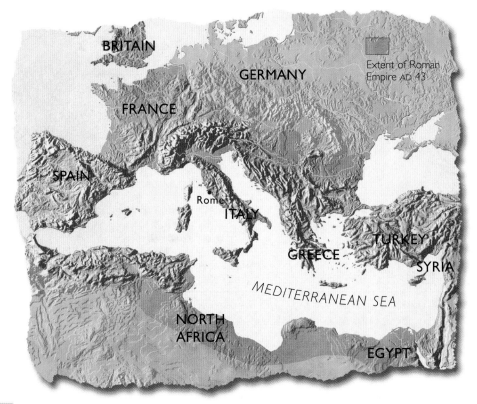

THE ROMAN EMPIRE AD 43

The Roman invasion of AD 43 brought Britain into a vast empire that stretched from Spain into Western Asia, and southwards into North Africa. Its capital was Rome. Britain marked the northern limits of Roman rule. The Romans never conquered the far north of Scotland and Ireland too remained free.

AD 51
Caratacus taken to Rome as a prisoner.

AD 60
An uprising against the Romans, lead by Boudicca, queen of the Iceni, begins in East Anglia.

RESISTING THE INVADERS

Many tribes tried to resist the Romans. It took about four years for the invaders to finally gain control over southern England, and another 30 years for them to conquer all of the West Country and the mountains and valleys of Wales. The battle for Yorkshire and the remainder of northern England was still underway in AD 70, when a tribe called the Brigantes rose in rebellion.

The Britons fought bravely, but the Roman troops were better equipped, better trained and highly disciplined. The Romans had experience of fighting in many parts of their empire.

The Romans sometimes used elephants to trample the enemy in battle. The emperor had some brought to Britain to impress the natives.

THE ATTACK ON MONA

As the Romans advanced, many Britons fled into Wales. The island of Mona (Anglesey) was a holy centre of the druids, and must have been a major centre of resistance. The Romans attacked in AD 60. As they crossed the water, druids cursed them, women dressed in black screamed abuse and warriors hurled spears. The Romans slaughtered them and burned down the sacred groves of oak trees.

➡ *Boudicca's rebellion was savage and many Roman citizens died in the flames of London. The revenge of the legions was merciless. About 80,000 British warriors were killed and Boudicca committed suicide by taking poison.*

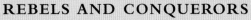

REBELS AND CONQUERORS

Just as the Romans were attacking Mona, they had to march back to southeastern Britain where a rebellion was breaking out. It was led by Boudicca, queen of the Iceni. When her husband, Prasutagas, died, the Romans had broken their word by annexing his kingdom and had wronged his family. The tribes joined Boudicca. Colchester and London were destroyed. Eventually the Romans caught up with the rebels and massacred them. Boudicca took her own life. By the AD 70s the Romans had control of the north and in AD 84 they defeated the tribes of what is now southern Scotland at Mons Graupius, near Inverurie. Calgacus, the defeated leader, said bitterly, 'They make a wilderness and call it peace'.

The Iron Legions

Once the native resistance had been broken, the Romans imposed their government on the island of Britain. The limits of their rule were marked by the Irish Sea to the west and by a series of defences to the north. The farthest of these was the Antonine Wall, built in AD 142, but this was later abandoned in favour of the earlier Hadrian's Wall, built in AD 122. Large forts were built across Britain. Roman rule was maintained through the second century AD by the iron grip of its army, which was highly mobile and ruthlessly efficient.

BRITANNIA
(GREAT BRITAIN)

MARE
ORIENTALE
(NORTH SEA)

MARE
HIBERNIAE
(IRISH SEA)

Luguvalium
Carlisle

Eboracum
York

Segontium
Caernarfon

Deva
Chester

Lindum
Lincoln

Ratae
Leicester

Camoludunum
Colchester

Glevum
Gloucester

Verulamium
St Albans

Isca Silurum
Caerleon

Londinium
London

Venta Belgarum
Winchester

Dubris
Dover

Isca Dumnoniorum
Exeter

MARE AUSTRUM
(ENGLISH CHANNEL)

ROMAN BRITAIN

The new Roman province was called Britannia. London soon outgrew Colchester as the most important town. Important bases for the legions were built at Chester and York in northern England, and Caerleon in South Wales. After about AD 213, Britannia was divided into two regions – Upper and Lower.

↑ *When storming a hill fort, Roman soldiers would form a close unit, crouching with shields covering their heads and their sides. This formation was called a 'testudo', or tortoise. Hillforts were also attacked with huge catapults.*

THE ROMAN ARMY

When the Britons were called to arms, their organisation suffered from tribal rivalries and lack of military planning. In contrast, the Roman army was completely professional. It was organised into legions, military units that at the time of the conquest numbered about 5500 troops each. Each legion was divided into ten sections called cohorts. The backbone of the legion was formed by 59 middle-ranking officers called centurions. Support troops who were not Roman citizens were known as auxiliaries.

← *Horses were used by officers and by separate cavalry units. These were armed with long swords and spears.*

Throwing spear

The legionary's spear was a weighted javelin, made of wood and iron.

Marching baggage

The legionary marched with a heavy bundle slung over his shoulder. It included all sorts of digging tools, buckets and clattering tins as well as his basic food rations – biscuits, cheese and bacon.

Hand-fighting

The legionary carried a short sword in a scabbard and also a dagger.

Armour

Caesar's legions wore armour of mail, but by the time of Claudius, Roman foot soldiers wore armour made of metal plates.

Sandals

Sandals were made from leather and the soles were studded with iron for the long marches.

A SOLDIER'S LIFE

The Roman legionary was a paid, professional soldier. Recruits were given very hard training. They learned parade-ground drill and battle formations. They were forced to march very long distances. They were taught how to fight with swords and throw javelins, how to pitch camp and dig defences. Punishments for disobedience were harsh. At the time of the conquest of Britain, legionaries were not allowed to marry whilst in service. After 25 years, however, they could retire. Many then settled around military camps and towns, often marrying a British woman and raising a family.

Shield

Roman shields at this time were rectangular. They were made of wood, leather and linen, with a boss (central stud) of iron or bronze.

← *The Roman legionary was soldier, builder, engineer and labourer all in one.*

HADRIAN'S WALL

Hadrian's Wall stretched from the Solway Firth in the west to the river Tyne in the east, a distance of 177 kilometres. Much of it still stands today, and offers us a fascinating glimpse of military life on the Roman frontier at the time of the wall's construction in AD 122, The wall took its from the emperor Hadrian (AD 76–138). The wall served several purposes. It divided the rebellious Caledonians (the tribes from the far north of Britain) from the tribes to the south. It provided a route for rapid movement of troops and supplies, and traded goods.

A Roman patrol brings in two Picts ('painted people') from beyond the wall, for questioning.

Roman Camps and Forts

Place names today that include the words 'caster', 'chester' or 'caer' generally signify the presence of a camp or fort in Roman times. During a military campaign, Roman soldiers would build temporary camps of leather tents. However more permanent forts were soon needed. These varied in size. Along Hadrian's Wall there were small fortlets built every 1500 metres (a Roman mile). Bigger fortresses might be built elsewhere to protect signal stations or harbours from attack.

Fort
Forts were built on rising ground in defensible positions.

ROMAN ARMOUR

Roman armour was made of metal strips. At the height of the Roman Empire, around AD 50 to 250, legionaries wore armour called *lorica segmentata*. It was made up of strips of metal that were bent to fit the body, and held together by straps and buckles.

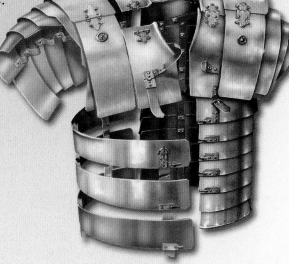

⬇ *Having been drilled on the parade ground, Roman troops march out from their fort at the start of a new military campaign.*

Equipment

Troops carried camping equipment as well as weapons. Soldiers were expected to march up to 30 kilometres a day.

⬆ *Fitted plate armour like this was worn by legionaries from about AD 50 to 250. It was held together by straps and buckles. Examples have been discovered at Hadrian's Wall.*

THE MILITARY BASES

The biggest Roman forts included a principia (military headquarters), officers' quarters, barracks for the troops, a parade ground, cookhouse, toilet blocks, baths (outside the walls), wells, stores for grain, stables and religious shrines. Buildings might be of timber and tiles, or sometimes of stone. The fort was defended by walls, ditches and ramparts.

All Roads Lead to Rome

The Romans did not conquer Britain just for the glory, or simply to protect their territories in mainland Europe. They wanted to make a profit. The island had precious metal ores, fertile lands for farming and a large labour force. It could also provide a new market for goods produced in Italy or Gaul. Imports into Britain included pottery from Gaul and wine from southern Europe and the Rhineland. Exports included woollen cloaks, lead, silver, the black stone called jet, oysters and hunting dogs.

Lead and silver being mined in southwest England.

The Roman town of Londinium (London) is founded on the River Thames.

SHIPS AND CARGOES

Creaking, square-sailed wooden ships carried cargoes and merchants across the choppy waters of the North Sea and the English Channel. London, on the River Thames, became Britain's biggest port.

▶ *Roman ships followed coastlines whenever possible.*

◀ *Layers of broken flint and crushed stone were laid as foundations. The surface was generally of gravel, but sometimes paved. The roads were built by the army using troops or slaves as labour.*

THE GROWING TOWNS

Celtic life had mostly been based in the country, but Roman life was centred on towns with about 5000 inhabitants. The Romans rebuilt many of the old British settlements with straight streets and drainage. They built large town halls, law courts, markets, shops, bakeries, restaurants and bars, even public toilets. Smaller towns grew up around military camps and forts, or wherever there was a need to trade.

ROMAN ROADS

Most roads were made using whichever stone was available locally. The route was carefully surveyed and forest was cleared well back from the verges, to prevent ambush.

ALL ROADS LEAD TO ROME **65**

BRITAIN'S ROMAN ROADS

The Romans built over 9000 kilometres of roads in Britain. Some roads were built to be over 12 metres wide, others were minor routes. Transport included horses and mules, carts and heavy wagons pulled by oxen. The first road workers and bridge builders were legionaries, but later city councils took over responsibility for building new roads and repairing old ones.

▲ *Official courier on horseback.*

Ermine Street
Linked London and York, joining Dere Street northwards to Scotland.

Watling Street
Ran through Kent to London, then northwest across the English Midlands to Chester.

From Exeter people could travel eastwards to London or join the Fosse Way which led northeast to Lincoln.

York

Chester

Lincoln

London

Dover

Exeter

Ox-cart

Mule-cart

ROMAN TRANSPORT

The most important travellers on the roads were the official messengers, who rode on horseback. They travelled at speed, obtaining fresh horses from wayside inns. Some travellers used fast, lightweight carts pulled by mules, while others rode in slower, horse-drawn carriages. Heavy goods were carried in wooden wagons hauled by teams of oxen.

A COMMUNICATIONS NETWORK

The Roman road network was centred upon Londinium (London). From there, main roads went out to the chief army towns – Dubris (Dover), Camulodunum (Colchester), Noviomagus (Chichester), Isca Dumnoniorum (Exeter), Viroconium (Wroxeter) and Eboracum (York). A cross-country route from Exeter to Lindum (Lincoln) marked the temporary frontier of the advancing Romans in AD 47. Some sections of these routes still carry traffic today.

➡️ *Stone pillars (milestones) were erected to show distances between towns in Roman miles. Many of them showed which emperor was ruling at the time. This milestone bears the name Victorinus, who came to power in AD 269.*

ALL ROADS LEAD TO ROME

Roman Peace

British rebels were sold into slavery, but local rulers and nobles who supported Rome prospered. Many of them adopted Roman ways and dress. They learned to speak Latin, the language of Rome. Roman rule was often harsh, but it did bring a period of peace to large areas of Europe.

↑ *The baths at Aquae Sulis (Bath) had changing rooms and lockers, hot baths, warm baths and cold baths – but no soap. Bathers oiled their bodies and then scraped themselves clean.*

BRITISH AND ROMAN

Romans who stayed in Britain for more than a few years were influenced in turn by the Celts. Although Romans worshipped their own gods and goddesses, they were also prepared to honour many of the Celtic gods. When the Romans built luxurious new public baths at Bath, in western England, these were dedicated both to the Celtic goddess Sulis and the Roman goddess Minerva.

C.AD 90
A Roman theatre is built at Canterbury, Kent.

C.AD 90
Large town houses being built in Britain for the first time.

LIVING IN STYLE

Large country houses called villas were built for important Roman officials or for local British rulers who remained loyal to Rome. They were surrounded by large farm estates. Over the years, villas became more and more luxurious, with under-floor central heating, baths and dining rooms where visitors from Rome would be entertained with lavish banquets.

Roofs
Roofs were wooden framed and covered with tiles of baked clay.

← *The most impressive Roman villas were built in the AD 200s and 300s.*

Roman dining
Guests ate lying down on couches around a low central table.

In the kitchen
Cooks prepared dishes with food from the villa farm. Hunting in the forests provided wild game. Roman food was highly spiced.

Serving the master
The villa was kept running by a large team of slaves and servants.

Gardens
Walkways with columns and statues passed through gardens of shrubs, herbs and fruit trees.

Temples and Shrines

The Romans believed in many gods and goddesses. There was all-powerful Jupiter, Venus the goddess of love, Mercury the messenger of the gods, Diana the goddess of hunting and Saturn the god of farming. Every Roman knew old stories about the gods. In these, the gods behaved very much like humans, quarrelling and falling in love.

SHRINES TO THE GODS

Some Roman temples were built in stone, often with splendid pillars and painted walls. At the centre was a sanctuary or shrine. People might make offerings or give thanks to the gods, but there was no public worship.

← *A statue of Jupiter, king of the Roman gods. Images of the gods were placed in temples and public places.*

70   700 BC–AD 446

C.AD 300
Chedworth Villa, Gloucestershire, rebuilt with great luxury.

C.AD 300
A fine villa is built at Brading on the Isle of Wight (Insula Vectis).

FOREIGN RELIGIONS

All sorts of foreign religions became popular in Britannia over the years. Isis was an ancient Egyptian goddess who gained many followers. Mithras, the Persian god of light, was very popular with the troops. Many temples were built to honour Mithras, including one in London.

▶ *Mithras, the Persian god of light, was often shown slaying a bull.*

EMPEROR GODS

Some Roman emperors were officially worshipped as gods. It helped them keep control over the people, if they could claim to be super-human. A great temple to the emperor Claudius was built at Colchester. He was a lame, stammering man, who was very clever. He must have smiled to himself at the thought of being honoured as a god.

◀ *The great temple of Claudius at Colchester was one of the first in Britannia. It was built to impress the Britons, but was destroyed by Boudicca. It had to be rebuilt after her rebellion was crushed.*

TEMPLES AND SHRINES

71

Roman Towns

The Romans built towns, often on the sites of the former tribal capitals of the Britons. Smaller towns and villages grew up around crossroads, along rivers and by the sea. The Romans who moved into these towns were officials, lawyers, traders or craftworkers. They were soon joined by those Britons who could afford to take up the Roman way of life.

LONDINIUM (LONDON)

Sited on the banks of the river Thames, London was ideally sited for trade with the rest of the empire. A long, wooden bridge was built across the river. London became a great centre of trade and was the biggest city in the province. At its peak it had a population of about 45,000. An army fort was built, a huge town hall, or basilica, a market place, or forum, and temples.

↑ The biggest towns in Britannia, such as Londinium, served as military bases.

The Fall of Rome

The mighty empire of Rome began to look less powerful after AD 200. There were bitter civil wars and struggles for power. In AD 286 the empire was divided into an eastern and western part. Britain was in the west, and so was still ruled from Rome. However in AD 287 Carausius, commander of the Roman fleet in Britain, declared himself ruler of Britain. He was murdered by a fellow rebel, Allectus, in AD 293. Rome regained control in AD 297, but not for long. Frontier defences were now being breached all around the empire.

A beacon blazes on top of a lighthouse as Roman ships patrol the English Channel.

A Germanic people, the Saxons, sailed across the North Sea to attack Roman Britain and test its defences.

THE TROUBLED EMPIRE

The entire Roman empire was increasingly in crisis. Germanic tribes were under attack from Asiatic invaders in the east and were soon being pushed into western Europe. Germanic warriors poured into Roman territories in Gaul (modern France), Spain, southeastern Europe and Italy itself. As Roman troops were deployed to meet these threats, Britain itself lay open to attack on all sides.

INVADERS CHALLENGE ROME

Roman Britain now came under attack from all sides. In the far north the Picts overran Hadrian's Wall and advanced south. Western shores and shipping were under attack from the Gaels, the unconquered Celts of Ireland. The English Channel was plagued by pirates. Southern England and East Anglia were attacked by a people from Germany, the Saxons. From about AD 280 Romans built a chain of massive stone forts to defend southeastern coasts, which became known as the Saxon Shore.

THE FALL OF ROME

THE MILDENHALL TREASURE

In 1946 it was officially reported that four years earlier a Roman treasure hoard had been ploughed up at Mildenhall in Suffolk, England. The pieces discovered were made of solid silver and dated from about AD 350. They may have originally been imported from Roman North Africa. They included spoons, splendid dishes, plates and wine goblets – 34 pieces in all. In the days before banks and safes, people stored their wealth as precious metals. In times of war they would bury them at a secret spot, to prevent them falling into enemy hands. Hoards like this one suggest that by the 300s, Roman Britain was no longer a peaceful or secure place to live.

▲ *This splendid dish from the Mildenhall treasure hoard is now in the British Museum, in London.*

MAGNUS MAXIMUS

Magnus Maximus was a Spanish-born commander of the Roman troops in Britain. He made treaties with Celtic peoples such as the Votadini and Dumnonii to take on defending Britain against the Picts and Gaels. In AD 383 he marched with his troops to Rome and seized the throne. He was killed five years later. His memory survives in the folklore of Wales, where he is known as Macsen.

➡ *In AD 410 Alaric, leader of a Germanic people called the Western Goths, sacked the city of Rome itself.*

THE EMPIRE FALLS

Between AD 401 and 410, Roman troops were withdrawn from Britain as Germanic tribes crossed the River Rhine and poured into Gaul. Within the empire there were revolts and uprisings, and more attempts to seize local power. The economy collapsed. In AD 410, Rome itself was sacked by northern invaders called Goths. The emperor Honorius declared that from now on, the Britons would have to defend themselves. In AD 446 British leaders made one last appeal to Rome, but it was hopeless. It took just 30 more years for the Roman empire in Western Europe to come to an end. Rome had ruled Britain for nearly 400 years. It had changed the history of the island forever, with its language, its law, its towns and roads, its technology and its religion. Rome was never forgotten.

Anderitum (modern Pevensey, in Sussex) was the site of a stone fort built by the Romans to defend Britain from attacks by Saxons. It probably dates from about AD 343 and was re-fortified in the Middle Ages. Other forts already built on the 'Saxon shore' included Brancaster, Burgh Castle, Walton Castle, Bradwell, Reculver, Richborough, Dover, Lympne and Portchester.

Raiders and Settlers

AD 446–1066

THE WORLD AT A GLANCE

ELSEWHERE IN EUROPE

AD 476
End of the Roman empire in western Europe.

c.AD 500
Migrations of Slavs begin, to east, west and south of their homeland in eastern Europe.

AD 529
Justinian, emperor of East Rome, or Byzantium (now Istanbul), draws up laws.

AD 711
Muslim Moors (Arabs and Berbers) invade Spain from North Africa.

AD 732
Charles Martel, ruler of the Franks, drives Arab invaders from France.

AD 800
Charlemagne, ruler of the Franks, is crowned emperor in Rome.

AD 912
The Viking warlord Rollo becomes Duke of Normandy in France.

AD 962
King Otto I of Germany becomes Holy Roman Emperor.

ASIA

AD 531
The Sassanid empire expands in Persia (Iran) under Chrosroes I.

AD 535
Collapse of the Gupta empire in India.

AD 552
The Buddhist faith reaches Japan from China.

AD 570
Muhammad the Prophet, founder of Islam, is born in Mecca, Arabia.

AD 610
A Grand Canal links China's two greatest rivers, the Huang He and the Chang Jiang.

AD 618
China is ruled by the Tang emperors, a golden age of arts and science.

AD 786
Harun al-Rashid is Caliph (ruler) of Baghdad and head of a vast empire.

AD 802
The Angkor kingdom is founded by Khmer rulers in Cambodia.

AFRICA

AD 500
Bantu-speaking migrants arrive in southern Africa.

AD 531
A Christian Church is founded in Ethiopia, North Africa.

AD 600
Rise of the powerful gold-producing kingdom of Ghana, in West Africa.

AD 641
Arabs invade Egypt, beginning their conquest of North Africa.

AD 750
Trade across the Sahara Desert between North and West Africa.

AD 900
Rise of Swahili culture on the coast of East Africa.

AD 969
Foundation of the city of Cairo, on the River Nile in Egypt.

c.1000
First settlement at Great Zimbabwe.

"*Monks take refuge as bands of warriors invade the island.*"

NORTH AMERICA

AD 500
Teotihuacán city in central Mexico has a population of about 200,000.

AD 700
Temple mounds built in the valley of the Mississippi river.

AD 700
Cahokia, the first town in the region now taken up by the United States.

AD 700
Hohokam, Anasazi and Mogollon peoples in the southwest.

AD 800
The 'Dorset' culture amongst Inuit hunters of Canada and Greenland.

AD 950
The Toltecs found the city of Tula in central Mexico.

1000
Vikings try to found settlements in Labrador and Newfoundland.

1050
The Anasazi build defensive settlements in the southwest.

SOUTH AMERICA

AD 500
Tiwanaku city, near Lake Titicaca, has a population of 40–100,000.

AD 600
The great Gateway of the Sun is raised at Tiwanaku.

AD 700
The Andean city state of Wari becomes very powerful.

AD 700
The decline of the Moche culture in northern Peru.

AD 750
The Nazca civilisation of southern Peru comes to an end.

AD 800
The Chimú city of Chan Chan, northern Peru, covers an area of 15 sq km.

AD 900
The Chimú empire at the height of its power in northern Peru.

1000
The city of Wari is abandoned.

OCEANIA

c.500
Polynesians settle in the southern Cook Islands.

c.AD 700
Easter islanders raise platforms of large stone blocks.

c.AD 800
Earliest evidence for Polynesian hand clubs made of wood and whalebone.

c.AD 850
The Maoris, a Polynesian people, settle New Zealand coasts.

c.AD 850
Maoris begin to hunt large flightless birds such as the moa.

c.AD 900
Aborigines mining rock for axes, Mount Isa, bartering routes across Australia.

c.1000
Last phase of Pacific settlement by Polynesian seafarers.

c.1000
Easter Islanders begin to raise huge heads of carved stone.

Sign of the Cross

One of the new eastern religions that appeared in Britain towards the end of the Roman period was Christianity. Its founder, Jesus Christ, had been put to death by the Roman rulers of Jerusalem in about AD 30. Christians believed that there was just one God, and that Jesus was his son. They taught people that they should love their enemies.

CHRISTIANITY SPREADS

At first the Romans punished the Christians for believing that their God was more powerful than the emperor. Even so, the new faith spread quickly, among both Romans and Britons, rich and poor alike.

Jesus Christ was pictured in this floor mosaic found at a Roman villa in Hinton St Mary, Dorset, England. It dates from the early years of Christianity in Britain. The symbols in the background are the Greek letters Chi and Rho, the first two letters of the name 'Christ'.

C.AD 313
Christians given full rights of worship in Roman empire.

C.AD 390
St Ninian (Nynia) founds church in southern Scotland.

CHRISTIANS AND PAGANS

In Britain, a Christian legionary called Albanus (St Alban) was executed in about AD 300. However the emperor Constantine made Christianity legal in AD 313 and himself became a Christian. The new faith spread among both Romans and Britons. As the ages passed, the old Celtic beliefs only survived as country customs. The word 'pagan', meaning non-believer, originally came from the Latin word for 'countryside'.

Christian burial grounds and chapels date from the fourth century AD. Finds have included silver chalices, the cups used during Christian worship. Lead tanks have been discovered, too, which held the water in which new Christians were baptised.

Silver chalice

 Constantine, son of emperor Constantius, addressing troops in York. In AD 306 the legions serving in York proclaimed their backing for Constantine, who had been a successful soldier. He succeeded his father as emperor and became known as Constantine the Great. Constantine made Christianity legal, and in AD 324 it became the official religion of the empire.

SIGN OF THE CROSS **81**

THE CELTIC CHURCH

After the Romans left Britain, raids by non-Christian Saxons increased in southern and eastern Britain. Christianity spread most rapidly in the west, in Wales and Cornwall. Many place names in these areas today begin with 'Llan-' or 'Lan-'. A 'llan' was a religious enclosure, where monks would teach people about the life of Christ, farm the land and care for the sick. A type of Christianity grew in Celtic lands that was rather different from that of Rome. It was influenced by the teachings of a British monk called Pelagius. He believed that people were basically good, that they were not born sinful. He also attacked wealth and privilege. It was AD 664 before the Celtic and Roman Churches finally came together.

← *Jesus Christ, like many condemned to death by the Romans, had been crucified – left to die on a wooden cross. The cross eventually became the most common symbol of Christianity. Early and medieval Celtic crosses were beautifully carved in stone and often formed a 'wheel' design, which became popular once more in modern times. This cross is at Iona, in Scotland, a Christian site since AD 563.*

AD 574
Rome orders conversion of Anglo-Saxons.
Mission postponed to AD 597.

AD 601
Death of St David (Dewi Sant) South Wales.

THE AGE OF SAINTS

St Patrick (*c.*AD 385–460) was born in western Britain. Kidnapped by pirates, he escaped to Ireland and later studied in Gaul. In about AD 432 he went back to Ireland, probably to Armagh, to spread the Christian message.

St Ninian or Nynia (*c.*AD 390) was a Briton born near the Solway Firth. He studied in Rome, became a bishop and founded a church in what is now Wigtownshire, Scotland. He converted the southern Picts to Christianity.

St David or Dewi Sant (*c.*AD 520–601) was born in southwest Wales. He founded religious centres in South Wales and the West of England and became Bishop at Menevia (St David's).

⬆ *St Patrick was made a bishop at the age of 45. He was probably sent back to Ireland by Pope Celestine I.*

➡ *Monks of the early Celtic Church lived in beehive-shaped cells called clocháns. This style of building has been adapted to a rectangular stone chapel on the Dingle peninsula in Ireland. The Gallarus Oratory (chapel of prayer) may be 1400 years old.*

AD 430
Possible date for rule of Ambrosius (Emrys) over Britons.

AD 448
Vortigern asks Hengist and Horsa to help him fight the Picts.

The Age of Arthur

The thousand years between the fall of Rome and the start of modern European history are known as the Middle Ages. After Rome withdrew from Britain, the country was divided between local rulers. Many of them still tried to follow the Roman – and Christian – way of life. However trade was disrupted by war and grass grew through cracked pavements as Roman towns and villas fell into disrepair.

AD 455
Hengist and Horsa attack Vortigern. Horsa is killed.

AD 456
Hengist and his son Aesc defeat Britons in Kent.

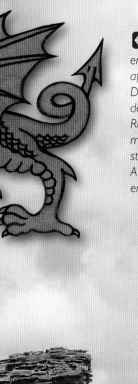

← *Dragons were used as emblems (left) by the Britons after the Roman withdrawal. Dragons, originally an Asian design, were used on some Roman cavalry standards and may have appeared on the standard of Magnus Maximus. A red dragon remains the emblem of Wales today.*

← *Legend has it that Arthur was born at Tintagel, on the northern coast of Cornwall. This cliff-top site was inhabited in Roman times and by AD 500 had a Christian monastery. It also has the ruins of a castle from 500 years later.*

WHO WAS ARTHUR?

It cannot be proved that Arthur or Artorius, one of the most famous names in British history, existed at all. However many clues suggest that he was indeed a historical figure. If so, he was probably of noble birth, a British Celt and a Christian who followed the Roman way of life.

Arthur would have been a war leader or general rather than a king. He would have led a band of armoured, mounted warriors that could assist local defence groups, moving at speed to meet invading Saxons or Picts. He is linked with a great victory at somewhere called Mount Badon in about AD 516 and is said to have been killed at the battle of Camlan in AD 537.

During the later Middle Ages, tales about Arthur spread far and wide. Many of them mixed him up with ancient Celtic gods and heroes. He became a king in shining armour, famous for his bravery. Stories about Arthur and his companions were told in France, Germany and Italy.

AD 495
Saxons under Cerdic invade Wessex
(central Southern England).

AD 516
Possible date for Battle of Mount Badon.
Britons halt West Saxon advance.

The British probably used small bands of cavalry to pursue the Saxon armies. They did slow down the Saxon advance, but they could not stop it.

NORTH SEA INVADERS

In eastern Britain there had been small settlements of retired auxiliaries from Germany since Roman times. Now roving Germanic warrior bands arrived across the North Sea. They were Angles, Saxons, Frisians and Jutes. They raided southern and eastern England and then seized the land. Their conflict with the Britons would last hundreds of years.

AD 539
Supposed date for battle of Camlan and death of Arthur.

AD 547
Ida founds the Saxon kingdom of Bernicia at Bamburgh, Northumberland.

Saxon settler

BATTLING FOR BRITAIN

We know little of the kings and armies who defended Britain against the new invaders. Emrys or Ambrosius seems to have been a very powerful ruler in about AD 430, possibly later. In AD 449 another king called Vortigern invited two Jutes called Hengist and Horsa to help him fight the Picts, in return for land. By AD 455 they had turned against Vortigern and were waging war on the Britons.

← → *The Saxons from Germany were just some of the people who tried to invade Britannia as Roman power declined.*

Saxon war chief

ANCIENT TALES

The first mention of Arthur in literature comes in a series of fantastic tales, which were written down in Wales later in the Middle Ages. They had been passed down over the ages by word of mouth. Some are tales of ancient Celtic gods and the underworld, of severed heads and magical animals. Others refer to Magnus Maximus (Macsen), the age of Arthur and the Christian period. Today this group of tales is known as the *Mabinogion*.

THE AGE OF ARTHUR 87

Saxon Swords

The early Middle Ages were troubled times in Western Europe. Historians used to call this period the 'Dark Ages', because it seemed that the light of Roman civilisation had been put out forever. This name was never really fair, for the period also saw beautiful arts and crafts, great poetry and scholarship in the new monasteries. However this was often a violent age. Invasions by Slavs and Huns in eastern and central Europe were pushing the Germanic peoples ever westwards, where they carved out new kingdoms for themselves in the ruins of the Roman empire.

→ *Anglo-Saxon warriors of the AD 400s and 500s might be armed with a battle axe, a long sword, a spear, or a long knife called a sax. They wore woollen tunics over trousers and carried round shields. Chieftains wore helmets and shirts of mail.*

GERMANIC INVASIONS

The invaders came from the lands now occupied by Germany, Denmark and the Netherlands. They crossed the North Sea and English Channel in wooden boats and fought their way westwards.

◄— Frisians and Jutes

◄— Angles and Saxons

◄— Franks

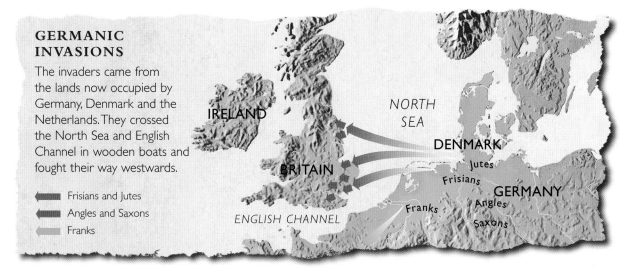

IRELAND

NORTH SEA

DENMARK

Jutes

Frisians

GERMANY

Angles

Franks

Saxons

BRITAIN

ENGLISH CHANNEL

THE DAY OF WODEN

The newcomers brought with them worship of the ancient Germanic gods. These survive in English names for days of the week. Tuesday is named after Tiw, god of war. Wednesday is the day of Woden, the chief god. Thursday is the day of Thor, god of thunder. Friday is from Frigg, goddess of love.

BRITONS AND SAXONS

The Anglo–Saxon invaders killed and enslaved many native Britons. Some fled westwards into Wales and Cornwall, or escaped to lands across the Channel that the Britons had already settled, a region known as Brittany. The Britons believed that the Angles and Saxons were savages. These peoples had never experienced Roman civilisation, nor were they Christians. In reality the two peoples shared similar European origins. They both lived in small kingdoms and depended on farming and fishing. They used similar technology and both were fine craftworkers.

Woden, also known as Wotan or Odin, rode an eight-legged horse.

SAXON SWORDS   **89**

AD 625
Probable date of the Sutton Hoo burial in East Anglia.

AD 625
First Anglo-Saxon coins to be minted in England.

ANGLO-SAXON LANDS

Modern names for counties and regions of England recall the first advances of the Anglo-Saxons. Essex comes from East Seaxe, land of the East Saxons. Sussex come from Suth Seaxe, land of the South Saxons. East Anglia was East Engle, the eastern territory of the Angles. By AD 550 the Anglo-Saxons controlled large areas of eastern and southern Britain. The Britons still ruled in the west and much of the north.

THATCH AND TIMBER

The Anglo-Saxons built small, compact farming villages in the lands they conquered. Many Anglo-Saxon place names are found on the map of England today, containing elements such as '-stead', '-ham', '-ing', '-ford', –ton', '-stow', '-wich' or –'wick'. Houses were rectangular, with walls of timber planks and pitched roofs covered in a heavy thatch. These were surrounded by a fenced yard. In some areas, huts seem to have been raised over sunken pits. which may have been boarded over.

➡ *An Anglo-Saxon farmstead was surrounded by a few large fields cleared from the forest. Within these, farmers worked their own strips for cultivation and harvest.*

AD 642
Penda of Mercia kills Oswald of
Northumbria at Maserfeld.

AD 655
Penda of Mercia killed by Oswiu of Northumbria
at Battle of the Winwaed.

A ROYAL SHIP BURIAL

In 1939 a grave was discovered at Sutton Hoo, near Woodbridge in Suffolk, England. It was a royal burial, probably that of Raedwald, a ruler of East Anglia who died in about AD 625. He was buried in a ship beneath a mound of earth. His ship was 27 metres long and was rowed by 40 oars. Inside a wooden chamber in the boat was a rich treasure hoard. There were buckles and fasteners of shining gold, a jewel-covered purse containing 37 gold coins. There was a musical instrument called a lyre. There was a sword, a shield and the remains of a splendid helmet made of iron and bronze.

← *The ornate Sutton Hoo helmet shows the influence of Roman styles on European design 200 years after the collapse of the Roman empire.*

c. AD 500
The founding of the kingdom of Dál Riada by Fergus Mór.

AD 574
Colmcille crowns Aedán MacGabráin High King of Dál Riada.

The Making of Scotland

Scotland takes its name from a people whom the Romans called Scoti. These 'Scots' were Gaels who sailed from northern Ireland to raid Britain's western coasts and islands as the Roman empire collapsed. By AD 500 they had founded a kingdom called Dál Riada on the Scottish mainland. For many years the Scots battled with the Picts, who still controlled the lands of the northeast, around Aberdeen.

⬇ For hundreds of years after the Picts first built brochs, they used these round towers for shelter when attacked by enemies. This is Don Carloway Broch on the Isle of Lewis.

AD 604
Strathclyde and Dál Riada defeated by Angles
at Degsástan.

AD 642
Owain of Strathclyde defeats Dál Riada
at Strathcarron.

Columba arrived on the
Scottish island of Iona with a
handful of companions. He
converted many people to the
Christian faith.

IONA AND COLMCILLE

Colmcille, or Columba, was born in
AD 521, into a noble Irish family. In the
old days he would probably have been
a druid, but instead he was an
enthusiastic Christian. In AD 563 he set
up a monastery and centre of learning
on the island of Iona, in the Hebrides.
He and his monks travelled through
Scotland, founding churches and
preaching Christianity to the northern
Picts. It was another monk from
Iona, Aidan, who set up a monastery
at Lindisfarne, in Northumbria, in
about AD 635.

C.AD 650
Dál Riada loses its territories in
northern Ireland.

AD 685
Picts stop northern advance of Angles at
Nechtansmere.

DÁL RIADA

The new kingdom of Dál Riada
included part of northern Ireland, islands
such as Iona, and the Argyll region of
the Scottish mainland. By about AD 650
the Scots had lost their lands back in
Ireland. Cut off from their homeland,
the dialect of Irish that they spoke
gradually developed into the Gaelic
language still spoken today in the
islands and highlands of Scotland.

⬆ *This beautiful wooden box, the Monymusk Reliquary,
is decorated with gilt and silver. It was made in the 600s
or 700s and is said to have contained the remains of
Colmcille (Columba).*

BATTLE FOR THE LOWLANDS

The Angles who had founded Bernicia
(later part of Northumbria) soon
pushed further northwards, into the
Scottish Lowlands. The Britons living
in the Lowlands were under pressure
from all sides. They made an alliance
with the Scots to fight the Angles, but
were defeated at the battle of Degsástan
(perhaps near Jedburgh) in AD 603. The
Angles now controlled the Lothian
region – eastern Scotland below the
Firth of Forth. This left the Britons of
the Lowlands isolated in their kingdom
of Strathclyde. Their lands to the south
were also being overrun by Angles and
they were soon cut off from their
fellow Britons in Wales.

← *Picts were
one of four
groups of people
living in Scotland
at this time.*

THE KINGDOM OF ALBA

In AD 685 the Picts halted the northward advance of the Angles with a desperate battle at Nechtansmere, Dunnichen. But it was not until AD 843 that northern Scotland finally became united. That was when a ruler of the Scots called Kenneth MacAlpin ('mac' meaning 'son of') joined his kingdom with that of the Picts. The centre of the Christian Church in Scotland now moved eastwards from Iona to Dunkeld, in Perthshire. The new kingdom was called Alba and it linked most of the region lying to the north of the Firth of Forth and the River Clyde. It was one of the most important kingdoms in the Celtic world and formed the chief building block of the future kingdom of Scotland. Alba rarely knew peace, for it was under constant attack by Anglo-Saxons from the south and by Scandinavians around its coasts.

THE STONE OF DESTINY

A ceremonial slab of sandstone was brought by the Scots from Ireland to Iona. From there it was taken to Dunstaffinage and later to Scone, near Perth. This 'Stone of Destiny' was used at the coronation of the kings of Alba and of united Scotland. In 1297 the English King Edward I stole the stone and took it south to London. There it stayed until 1950, when it was reclaimed by four Scottish students. The stone was recovered in Arbroath and returned to England. However in 1996 it was officially installed in Edinburgh Castle.

⬆ *Kenneth I succeeded his father Alpin as King of the Scots in AD 841. Two years later he united the lands of the Scots and the Picts. He died in AD 858.*

c. AD 540
The voyages of Brendan around North Atlantic coasts.

c. AD 550
Start of the age of the monasteries in Ireland.

Across the Irish Sea

As Roman power declined and finally vanished, Irish ships raided the western coasts of Britain. Irish settlements were founded in West Wales and in Scotland. Whilst Angles and Saxons were streaming into eastern Britain, trade prospered in the west, around the Irish Sea. Merchants and monks sailed between Ireland, Scotland, Wales, Cornwall, Brittany and southwestern Europe. Ireland was entering one of the greatest ages in its history.

⬇ *An Irish raiding party clambers ashore on the west coast of Britain, looking for cattle, slaves and plunder.*

AD 561
Brendan founds Clonfert monastery, Galway.

c.AD 600
Ogham script now replaced by the Roman alphabet.

THE VOYAGE OF BRENDAN

Brendan, or Brandan, was born in Tralee, in County Kerry, in AD 484. A Christian saint, he is said to have founded Clonfert monastery in Galway in AD 561. Tales about him were written down later in the Middle Ages, describing his sea voyages. Brendan seems to have been a navigator who sailed the North Atlantic Ocean and knew its eastern coasts. A description of the 'mouth of hell' suggests that he may have seen volcanic eruptions off the coast of Iceland.

CHILDREN OF NIALL

The greatest ruler of the Gaels at the end of the Roman era was Níall Naoi-Ghiallach (Níall of the Nine Hostages). He became High King of Ireland at the end of the fourth century AD and was renowned for carrying out raids on Britain and Gaul. He was the founder of the O'Neill dynasty, which remained a powerful force in Ireland throughout the Middle Ages and beyond.

c.AD 650
The Book of Durrow, start of the golden age of Celtic Christian art.

AD 697
Synod of Birr discusses Christian treatment of women and children.

▼ *The Tara brooch is made of gilded bronze and silver and is decorated with glass and amber. It probably dates from about AD 700.*

OGHAM SCRIPT

A kind of alphabet made up of criss-cross lines was carved on Irish stones from about AD 300. It is called ogham. Ogham fell out of use as Christian monks in the 600s and 700s introduced the letters of the Roman alphabet.

▼ *The Book of Kells may have been produced on the Island of Iona, but finished in Ireland.*

ART OF THE MONKS

Christian monasteries in Ireland became great centres of learning. They also held great political influence. Important monasteries grew up at Clonmacnois in County Offaly and Clonard in County Meath. Derry, Durrow and Kells were linked with the church at Iona. Armagh was another great Christian centre. The Irish monasteries inspired beautiful works of art and craft. In the Book of Kells, produced before AD 800, religious texts are decorated with elaborate patterns, animal designs and pictures.

c.AD 700
Fine metal working, such as the Tara brooch and Ardagh chalice.

c.AD 800
The Book of Kells, the masterpiece of Celtic Christian art.

KINGS, LORDS AND PEASANTS

Irish society was divided into three classes. At the bottom were the commoners. These included some slaves, serfs (labourers who were not allowed to leave the land) and freemen who owned their farms. Life for poor people was very hard. They lived largely on a diet of porridge and oatcakes. Hunger and disease were common. Labourers toiled on the land. Commoners had to declare their loyalty to the lords and the lords to the kings. There were many minor kings, but real power lay with the regional kings of Ulster, Meath, Munster, Leinster and Connaught. A High King was based at the ancient royal site of Tara, but rarely ruled all Ireland because of the endless wars between Ireland's royal families.

↑ *This chalice, a cup used during Christian worship, was dug up at Ardagh, in County Limerick, in 1868. It is one of the finest pieces of metal working produced in Europe during the early Middle Ages. It is made of silver and gilt bronze, with a central stud of rock crystal. It dates from about AD 700.*

AD 577
West Britons defeated by Wessex at the Battle
of Dyrham.

AD 600
Earliest known Welsh poetry, the *Gododdin*.

The Making of Wales

The advancing Angles and Saxons gradually conquered the lands of the Britons. After the Battle of Dyrham in AD 577 the Britons of Devon and Cornwall were cut off from the Britons to the north. However independent kingdoms survived in the far west. The Saxons called these Britons 'Welsh', meaning 'foreign'. The western Britons began to call themselves 'Cymry', meaning 'compatriots'.

WELSH RULERS

Houses of Gwynedd, Powys and Dyfed

✤ Rhodri Mawr ('the Great')	AD 844–878
✤ Anarawd	AD 878–916
✤ Hywel Dda ('the Good')	AD 915–950
✤ Iago ab Idwal	AD 950–979
✤ Hywel ab Ieuaf	AD 979–985
✤ Cadwallon II	AD 985–986
✤ Maredudd ap Owain	AD 986–999
✤ Cynan ap Hywel	AD 999–1008
✤ Llywelyn ap Seisyll	1018–1023
✤ Iago ap Idwal ap Meurig	1023–1039

⬆ *At the courts of the Welsh kings, harpists praised rulers for their wisdom and bravery, or lamented their defeat by the Anglo-Saxons.*

AD 607
The battle of Chester. Aefelfrith of Northumbria defeats the Britons.

AD 635
The West Britons start to call themselves *Cymry* – the Welsh.

THE OLD NORTH

In Welsh history, the lands of the northern Britons are known as the Old North. This region was divided into several kingdoms. They included Elmet (around the hills of the Pennines), Rheged (Cumbria), Manaw Gododdin (around Edinburgh) and the kingdom of Strathclyde. All but the last were invaded by the Angles. An Anglo-Saxon victory at Chester, in AD 615, drove a wedge between Wales and the Old North. Links between the two were finally broken after AD 654.

⬇ *This tombstone records the death of King Cadfan of Gwynedd in AD 625. The words are written in Latin and his name is made Roman (Catamanus). The words mean 'King Cadfan, wisest and most renowned of all kings'.*

"MEN WENT TO CATRAETH…"

Welsh poetry has a very long history. Some of the earliest and finest verse was written down later in the Middle Ages. The story of the *Gododdin* comes from the Old North and is dated to about AD 600. It describes a British war band that sets out, perhaps from Edinburgh, to attack the Angles at Catraeth (today's Catterick, in Yorkshire). The war band suffers a terrible defeat.

AD 784
Offa's Dyke marks the eastern border of Wales.

AD 844
Rhodri Mawr becomes king of Gwynedd and extends its power.

KING OFFA

In AD 784, Saxon King Offa ordered that a great dyke be built between his kingdom of Mercia in the English midlands and Wales. The dyke acted as a defence against Welsh attacks.

▲ *This penny coin, made from silver, is decorated with King Offa's portrait and his name.*

WELSH KINGDOMS

Even when Wales was cut off by the Anglo-Saxons, its merchants and monks could still sail to Ireland, Cornwall, Brittany and beyond. Wales was made up of rival kingdoms. Gwynedd was in North Wales. This kingdom became the most powerful under the rule of Rhodri Mawr ('the Great'), who died in AD 877. In southwest Wales, an area settled by Irish invaders, was the kingdom of Dyfed. It later joined with Ceredigion to make a kingdom called Deheubarth. The royal house of Powys in mid-Wales was said to have been founded by Vortigern. Gwent and other small kingdoms of southeast Wales joined together to form Morgannwg (Glamorgan).

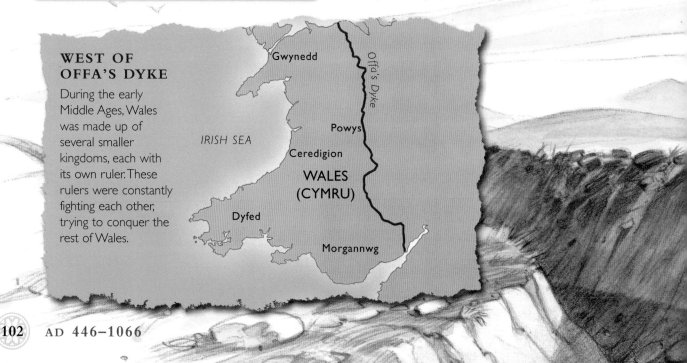

WEST OF OFFA'S DYKE

During the early Middle Ages, Wales was made up of several smaller kingdoms, each with its own ruler. These rulers were constantly fighting each other, trying to conquer the rest of Wales.

Gwynedd

Offa's Dyke

Powys

Ceredigion

IRISH SEA

WALES (CYMRU)

Dyfed

Morgannwg

THE LAWS OF HYWEL

Hywel ap ('son of') Cadell was a grandson of Rhodri Mawr. He came to rule most of Wales and made peace with the Anglo-Saxons. In AD 928 he went on a pilgrimage to Rome. Hywel is famed as a law-maker, for it was in his reign that the ancient laws of Wales were written down. The laws deal with property, murder, theft and the rights of women. They describe compensation for crimes, oath-taking and the part played by witnesses. Welsh law was carried out by trained judges and remained in use for over 500 years. Hywel died in AD 950 and is remembered as Hywel Dda ('the Good').

Welsh warriors patrolled the lands to the west of Offa's Dyke. They sometimes raided parts of England for cattle and slaves.

AD 597
Augustine becomes first Archbishop of Canterbury.

AD 634
Oswald becomes king of Northumbria, introduces Celtic Christianity.

The Making of England

Anglo-saxon kings such as Offa of Mercia held great power. They constantly attacked neighbouring kingdoms in their search for wealth and more land. Kings demanded personal loyalty and support from their lords, who were called thanes. Many of the peasants were conquered Britons. They included free men called ceorls, as well as serfs and thralls (slaves). Anglo-Saxon merchants traded across the English Channel, the North Sea and the Baltic.

→ *Most Anglo-Saxons lived by farming. They laboured on the land of the thane, ploughing, harvesting, and raising sheep and pigs. They cleared the oak forest for new land.*

AD 664
Synod of Whitby unites Roman and Celtic Churches in England.

AD 698
The *Lindisfarne Gospels* produced by monks in Northumbria.

ANGLO-SAXON KINGDOMS

Kent, Sussex and Essex ruled the southeast. Wessex, in the southwest, grew more and more powerful. Mercia, occupying the English Midlands, was the biggest kingdom. The kingdoms of Deira and Bernicia united as Northumbria, taking in all northern England and Lothian.

CELTS

Northumbria

NORTH SEA

ANGLO-SAXONS

Mercia

East Anglia

CELTS

Essex

Wessex

Sussex

Kent

CELTS

ENGLISH CHANNEL

AD 700
The Old English poem of *Beowulf* is written down.

AD 731
Bede writes his history of the English Church.

BEOWULF AND THE MONSTER

In about AD 700 an exciting tale was told and retold in the halls of the Anglo-Saxon kings. It was written down in the Old English language of the Anglo-Saxons. It took the form of a long poem about a monster called Grendel, which terrorises the Danes until they are saved by a hero called Beowulf. The verse is alliterative, which means that it plays on repeated sounds.

CHRISTIAN ENGLAND

In AD 597 St Augustine and 40 of his monks arrived from Rome with a mission – to convert the Anglo-Saxons to Christianity. King Ethelbert of Kent, who had a Christian wife, became a Christian too. England's first cathedral was built at Canterbury. In Northumbria, however, the Roman teachings clashed with the Celtic version of Christianity, as preached by the monks of Lindisfarne. In AD 664, a meeting, or synod, was held at Whitby. Here the Celtic Church agreed to recognise the Roman Church.

AD 735
York becomes an archbishopric.

AD 757
Offa makes Mercia the most powerful
Anglo-Saxon kingdom.

BEDE'S HISTORY

Bede or Baeda was born in about AD 673 at Monkwearmouth,
in Tyne and Wear. He became a monk at Jarrow in AD 703
and studied Latin, Greek, Hebrew, medicine and astronomy.
In AD 731 he wrote *The Ecclesiastical History of the English
People* in Latin. It was translated into Anglo-Saxon and still
serves as a very useful guide to early English history. Bede
was buried at Jarrow in AD 735 and his remains were later
moved to Durham.

As Christians, the Anglo-Saxons
built many fine churches of timber
and stone. This example, dating
from AD 960, is St Mary's Church at
Breamore, in Hampshire. It is a
large church built largely of round
flints, but originally these would
have been plastered over.

Viking Raids

In AD 793 the monastery of Lindisfarne was ransacked and burnt down. A few years later the island of Iona came under attack and its monks were slaughtered. The raiders were known as Northmen or Danes. They are often called Vikings, from an Old Norse word meaning 'sea raiders'. Vikings came from the lands of Scandinavia – Denmark, Norway and Sweden. No sight in Europe was feared more than the sails of their ships coming over the horizon.

GREENLAND
ICELAND
NORWAY
SWEDEN
CANADA
IRELAND
RUSSIA
BRITAIN
DENMARK
NORMANDY
GERMANY
NEWFOUNDLAND
FRANCE
ITALY
SPAIN
BYZANTINE
EMPIRE

■ Viking homeland
□ Viking settlements
— Viking routes

THE VIKING WORLD

The Vikings were Germanic peoples who originated from the lands we call Scandinavia. They were fearless seafarers, warriors, pirates, farmers, merchants and explorers, who formed settlements over a vast area of the world, from North America to Russia.

LANDS IN PERIL

Soon no region of the British Isles was safe from the Vikings. They raided along all English Channel and North Sea coasts. They attacked villages and towns in Wales, Scotland, Ireland and the Isle of Man. They sailed along the coasts of Germany, the Netherlands, France and Spain. Vikings travelled east into Russia and down to the Middle East. They sailed west, settling Iceland and Greenland. They even reached North America.

↑ *Viking longships were sleek, wooden vessels about 18 metres long. They had a single sail and could speed through the waves. The oars were manned by a crew of 30 or more.*

AD 838
Vikings ally with Britons in Cornwall, defeated by
Egbert of Wessex.

AD 839
Vikings kill the king of the Picts.

BERSERK!

Viking warriors believed that a heroic death
in battle would bring them glory and a
place in Valholl, the heavenly hall of the
Germanic gods whom they still
worshipped. They despised the Christian
monks. Vikings were masters of the
surprise attack and raiding from beach
or river. When cornered in a pitched
battle, they would form a wall of
shields and fight to the bitter end.
Leading warriors would work
themselves up into a frenzied rage
before battle. They were called
berserkir, or 'bearskin shirts',
after their dress.

*◀ Swords were double-edged in steel.
Many were given pet names by their owner. The
battle-axe was another favourite weapon and
every ship carried bundles of spears and arrows.*

*▲ Many Vikings spent most
of the year farming and fishing
before joining a war band for
the sea voyage. Some hired
themselves out as mercenaries –
soldiers who fight for a wage.*

Battle dress
Most Viking warriors wore simple
tunics, trousers and cloaks. The
wealthier ones wore mail shirts.

⬆ *A ship in full sail is shown on this carved stone from Gotland in Sweden. Above it the god Odin rides his horse to Valholl.*

SEA WOLVES

Whalers and seal hunters from Norway had already settled many of the bleak islands to the north and west of Scotland. Norse Vikings came seeking more southerly lands too. Their homeland had barren mountains, forests and cold, dark winters. The milder climate and more fertile lands of the British Isles offered rich prizes. Danish Vikings attacked eastern and southern Britain in search of wealth and adventure. They kidnapped slaves from coastal villages and stole jewellery, silver and gold. They looted the precious chalices, plates and even the bells from churches and monasteries.

⬇ *The violence of the Viking raids shocked Europe. Records of the attacks were written down by Christian monks, who were often targeted by the raiders as they plundered religious communities.*

Jorvik to Dublin

During the 800s, many areas of the British Isles were permanently settled by Vikings. They included the isles of the Shetlands, Orkneys, and Hebrides and the northern and western coasts of the Scottish mainland. The Vikings invaded the Isle of Man and occupied the northern Irish coast. After the 830s the Vikings founded settlements at Dublin and other places in southern Ireland, too. Dublin Vikings later married into the royal family of Gwynedd, in North Wales. In England, Vikings captured York, which they called Jorvik, in AD 867. Three years later they invaded East Anglia and killed King Edmund. Their next prize was the Midland kingdom of Mercia.

Vikings settled from Scotland in the north of Europe to Sicily in the south. Everywhere they went they founded new villages and towns. Sometimes they fought for land from local peoples, and sometimes they lived peacefully alongside them.

IN A VIKING TOWN

A typical Viking settlement in the British Isles was built around quays on a coast or river bank. Moored at the jetties there might be a *knarr*, a broad-beamed merchant ship. A small four-oared *færing* might be seen rowing in from a day's fishing, followed by squawking gulls. Buildings were rectangular and normally made of wattle and daub or oak planks. In the northern islands, stone and turf were common building materials.

AD 850
Viking settlements on Isle of Man.

AD 850
Viking raiders over-winter in England for the first time.

BLACKSMITHS AND WOODCARVERS

Viking settlements included smithies, where sparks flew as the blacksmith forged swords and spears on the anvil and repaired iron tools for the farm. Metalworkers and jewellers produced finer craft, working with gold, silver, pewter (an alloy of lead and tin), with black jet and yellow amber. The Vikings carved wood, stone and whale bone, often using intricate designs of animals. Vikings often formed a business fellowship called a *felag*, which was rather like a company. The members, who might be craft workers, merchants or mercenaries, put up money and shared the risks and the profits of the enterprise.

Hair
Viking men wore their hair long or tied back.

Plaits and scarves
Women's hair was worn long. It was tidied with a comb made of horn or bone before being plaited or covered by a scarf.

Dress
Viking women wore a shift of linen or wool covered by a long woollen tunic with shoulder straps fastened by brooches.

Tunic
Men wore a knee-length long-sleeved tunic over trousers. Cloaks would be worn against the cold.

➡ *Fragments of Viking clothing have been discovered by archaeologists at York, including boots, shoes and socks.*

AD 851
Norwegian and Danish Vikings battle for control
of Dublin.

AD 867
The Vikings take York (Jorvik), which becomes their
chief settlement in England.

THE VIKING LONGHOUSE

Viking farmers often settled on remote shores, far from towns such as Jorvik and Dublin. In places such as the Orkney Islands they built longhouses, from timber or stone. When these materials were in short supply, turf was used to cover the roof. The growing grass kept the warmth in and the rain out. The longhouse was built around a central hearth and provided sleeping and living quarters, storage for food, tools and weapons, and stabling for livestock.

Walls made
of logs

Animals were kept
in the longhouse

Loom for weaving cloth

Meat was smoked
to preserve it

AD 914
New wave of Viking attacks on Ireland.

AD 950
Death of Erik Bloodaxe, last Viking king of
Jorvik (York).

⬇ *Longhouses were usually built on sloping ground so that waste from the animals ran downhill, away from human living rooms.*

Turf (earth with growing grass) roof

Wooden rafters

THE TYNWALD

Vikings passed laws and settled disputes at a public assembly called a *Thing*. The Isle of Man assembly met at a grassy mound called the Tynwald. This is still the name of the Manx parliament today. It claims to be the world's oldest legislative (law-making) assembly with an uninterrupted history. Viking assemblies were attended by all free men, but not by women or slaves.

▲ *A Viking chieftain rides to the assembly. Here there would be discussion about new laws and judgements to be passed.*

Outside lavatory

AD 829
Egbert of Wessex becomes overlord of the
Anglo-Saxon kingdoms.

AD 866
The Grand Army of 'Danes' arrives in England.

Alfred and the Danes

The Scandinavian conquest of East Anglia, Mercia and Northumbria was not carried out by a Grand Army of Danes. This was an alliance of warriors recruited in AD 866 from many different Viking settlements. Their chief enemy was Wessex, in southern England, for in AD 829 King Egbert of Wessex had become overlord of all the other Anglo-Saxon kingdoms. In AD 871, Egbert's grandson, Alfred, came to the throne. If the Danes conquered Wessex, all England would be in their grasp.

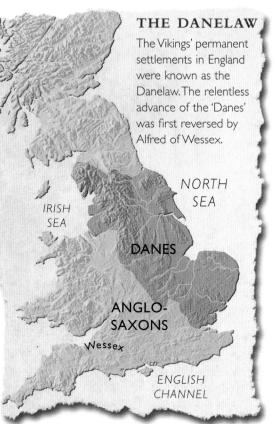

THE DANELAW
The Vikings' permanent settlements in England were known as the Danelaw. The relentless advance of the 'Danes' was first reversed by Alfred of Wessex.

NORTH SEA

IRISH SEA

DANES

ANGLO-SAXONS

Wessex

ENGLISH CHANNEL

⬇ A statue of Alfred stands in Winchester, Hampshire.

ALFRED FIGHTS BACK
A great army of Danes descended on Wessex again in the winter of AD 876. Alfred took refuge at Athelney, in the marshes of Somerset. He then fought back and defeated the Danes in AD 878. They gave up the lands of southern Mercia and their leader Guthrum agreed to become a Christian – but Alfred had to recognise the rule of Danelaw to the north.

D 871
Alfred becomes the king of Wessex.

AD 879
Treaty of Wedmore. Alfred recognizes the Danelaw.

DANEGELD

Shortly after Alfred became king of Wessex, his army was defeated by the Danes. Alfred could think of only one solution – bribery. He paid the Danes money to leave Wessex alone. They did – but only for four years. A later king adopted the same policy. Ethelred II, who came to the throne in AD 978, brought in a tax called Danegeld ('Dane money') to keep the Danes out of the south. Needless to say, they kept coming back for more. The name Ethelred means 'wise counsel' or 'good advice'. He of course became known as 'Redeless' – meaning 'ill-advised'.

◄ In the 700 and 800s, the Anglo-Saxons began to produce large numbers of silver pennies and other coins. Many of these found their way back to Scandinavia. Viking settlements minted their own coinage as well.

◄ King Alfred is named on this jewelled ornament found at Athelney.

◄ After the Vikings invaded England, King Alfred and his soldiers hid in the Athelney Marshes, Somerset. In AD 886 the Vikings agreed to a peace treaty, which meant that southwest England was ruled by the Anglo-Saxons.

ALFRED AND THE DANES

AD 926
Athelstan brings the Britons of Cornwall under
Anglo-Saxon rule.

AD 991
Danes win Battle of Maldon. Payment of Danegeld
by Ethelred.

➡ *Alfred learned many lessons from the
Vikings. One was the importance of ships in
warfare. He was the first English ruler to
build a fleet. He also reorganised the fyrd,
the Anglo-Saxon peasant army.*

ALFRED'S LEGACY

Alfred proved to be a wise ruler.
He encouraged learning and wrote
down the laws of England. In the
890s he planned a new type of
stronghold called a *burh* and built
many of these to hold back the
Danes. His lands grew wealthy
from trade. Alfred's daughter,
Ethelflæd of Mercia, fought the
Danes in battle and Alfred's good
work was continued by his sucessors
Edward the Elder, Athelstan and
Edgar. However peace broke down
after AD 979 and Ethelred II
provoked a major Danish invasion by
the Danish king Svein 'Forkbeard'.

1016
Battle of Ashingdon. England under Danish rule.

1042
Witan appoints Edward the Confessor as English king.

⬇ *Cnut I reigned from 1016–1035. He was a Christian king, and once, to display his piety, stood on a beach and attempted to turn back the tide. Of course he could not – he was simply trying to demonstrate that his power was insignificant compared to God's.*

ENGLAND UNITES

After many battles and treaties, in 1016 England came under the rule of Svein's son, Cnut I (Knut or Canute). He married Ethelred II's widow, Emma, and went on to reign over Denmark and parts of Sweden and Norway as well. The appointment of Anglo-Saxon kings had to be approved by a council of nobles, called the Witan. In 1042 the Witan chose Edward, the son of Cnut I and Emma. The ruler of a united England, he was a devout Christian and is remembered in history as 'the Confessor'. He founded Westminster Abbey near the growing city of London.

RULERS OF WESSEX AND ENGLAND
Houses of Cerdic and Denmark

✤ Egbert	AD 802–839	✤ Eadwig	AD 955–959
✤ Ethelwulf	AD 839–855	✤ Edgar	AD 959–975
✤ Ethelbald	AD 855–860	✤ Edward 'the Martyr'	AD 975–978
✤ Ethelbert	AD 860–866	✤ Ethelred II 'the Redeless'	AD 978–1016
✤ Ethelred I	AD 866–871	✤ Edmund 'Ironside'	AD 1016
✤ Alfred	AD 871–899	✤ Cnut I	1016–1035
✤ Edward 'the Elder'	AD 900–924	✤ Harold I 'Harefoot'	1037–1040
✤ Athelstan	AD 924–939	✤ Cnut II 'Harthacnut'	1040–1042
✤ Edmund I	AD 939–946	✤ Edward 'the Confessor'	1042–1066
✤ Eadred	AD 946–955	✤ Harold II	1066

ALFRED AND THE DANES **119**

AD 866
High King Áed Finlliath drives Vikings from
northern coast.

AD 919
Vikings defeat the Irish at the Battle of Dublin.

Bloodshed at Clontarf

The Viking attacks on Ireland came in several waves. At first, in the 800s, the Scandinavians – mostly from Norway – came to plunder. Later they built permanent camps and then settlements and towns. The Vikings met fierce resistance from the Irish kings and often from the monks, too. After AD 914 there was another great wave of Viking invasions, and in AD 919 King Niall Glúundúb, along with many lords of Ireland's most powerful family, the O'Neills, were killed at the Battle of Dublin.

VIKING TOWNS IN IRELAND

The Vikings' chief town was Dublin, but there were also settlements at Strangford, Carlingford, Limerick, Waterford, Wexford, Cork and Youghal. The Irish Vikings were known as Ostmen ('men from the east').

VIKING IRELAND

The Viking hold on Ireland was less complete than that of the Engish 'Danelaw', being made up of scattered settlements and coastal and river ports.

OSTMEN AND IRISH

In these times of trouble, tall, round towers were built at many Irish monasteries, such as Glendalough in the Wicklow mountains. They served as lookouts and shelters against Viking raiders. Sometimes, however, the invaders joined forces with one Irish king to fight another. The Vikings had a great effect on Irish life. They influenced Irish arts and crafts and encouraged long-distance trade. They also taught the Irish their boat-building and sailing skills.

➡ *Brian Boru, born in AD 926, was a ruthless fighter who spent as much time battling with other Irish kings as with the Ostmen.*

HIGH KINGS OF IRELAND
House of Níall of the Nine Hostages (Tara)

✤ Máel Sechnaill I   AD 842–862
✤ Áed Findliath   AD 862–879
✤ Flann Sinna   AD 879–916
✤ Níall Glúundub   AD 916–919
✤ Donnchad Donn   AD 919–944
✤ Congalach Cnogba   AD 944–956
✤ Domnall ua Néill   AD 956–980
✤ Máel Sechnaill II   AD 980–1002
✤ Brian Boru   1002–1014
✤ Máel Sechnaill II   1014–1022

BRIAN BORU, HIGH KING

During the 900s, the royal family of Munster, the Eóganacht, lost pride of place to a dynasty from North Munster, called the Dál Cais. Their king, Cennétig, died in AD 951. One of his sons was called Brian Bóruma, or Boru ('Brian of the Tribute'). By AD 976 Brian had gained control of Munster. By AD 984 he was king of Leinster and by 1002 he ruled all Ireland as High King, going on to conquer the Vikings' settlements.

AD 999
Leinster-Viking alliance defeated at battle of
Glenn Máma.

1002
Brian Boru rules all Ireland as High King.

THE BATTLE OF CLONTARF

The people of Leinster had never been happy with the rule of Brian Boru, and he soon faced revolt on many sides. Brian's son was sent to subdue Leinster in 1013. Leinster allied with the Dublin Vikings and in the spring of 1014 there was a fierce battle at Clontarf, to the northeast of Dublin. The ageing High King's forces won the day, but he was murdered after the battle. Clontarf marked the end of Viking power in Ireland. The *Ostmen* who remained gradually took on Irish ways and language.

The battle of Clontarf was brutal and bloody, even by the standards of the day.

1014
Death of Brian Boru. Máel Sechnaill II regains
High Kingship.

1022
Power of the Irish High Kings fragments.

IRELAND FRAGMENTS

With the death of Brian Boru, the office of High King passed back to Máel Sechnaill II of the Uí Néill, who had been High King before Brian rose to power. He died in 1022. After that, real power passed back to the kings of the provinces. It was they who laid down the law and taxed the people heavily in order to fight the endless wars they waged upon their rivals.

This beautiful crozier or staff belonged to the abbot of Clonmacnois in the 1100s. In the century after Clontarf, the powerful Irish Church was reformed by Rome.

THE RAVEN STANDARD

A key figure at the Battle of Clontarf was Sigurd Hlodvirsson, the Earl of Orkney. He had a flag with a picture of a raven on it. Sigurd believed that whoever carried this flag was sure of victory for his army – but would die himself. In 1014 Sigurd carried his flag at the Battle of Clontarf. He died – and his army lost the battle.

After Sigurd Hlodvirsson lost the Battle of Clontarf, Viking power in Ireland began to decline.

BLOODSHED AT CLONTARF 123

1018
Battle of Carham. Malcom II defeats Northumbrians.

1034
Duncan I becomes king of all Scotland.

Macbeth's Scotland

In 1018 Macolm II, King of Alba, marched southwards across the River Tweed and defeated the Northumbrians at the battle of Carham. Lothian was now in Scottish hands. In 1034 another piece of the jigsaw puzzle fell into place when King Duncan of Strathclyde, (the kingdom of the Britons in the southwest) inherited the throne of Alba. The kingdom of Scotland had now been created and within it were Scots, Britons and Angles. However Norwegian Vikings still held on to the northern and western fringes of the kingdom, and the southern border would be fought over for hundreds of years.

STRUGGLES FOR POWER

The lands of Scotland may have been united under the rule of Duncan I, but all around the throne there were old scores to settle and quarrels betwen rival groups or factions. One faction was led by Macbeth, the Mórmaer (chief) of Moray who married Gruoch, granddaughter of Kenneth III. He defeated and killed Duncan in 1040 and banished Duncan's sons, Malcolm and Donald Bán, from the kingdom.

Duncan's son Malcolm avenged his father's murder, killing Macbeth at Lumphanan in 1057.

1039
Duncan I launches attack on the English city of Durham.

1040
Macbeth kills Duncan I and seizes throne.

↓ *The island of Skye is part of Gaelic Scotland, but the strong Norse presence there is confirmed by many place names and by hoards of coins.*

MACBETH'S SCOTLAND

Scotland was fashioned out of four smaller kingdoms – Dál Riada, Pictland, Stratchclyde and Lothian. Its southern borders were constantly shifting.

NORSE LANDS

Dál Riada

Pictland

ALBA (SCOTLAND)

NORTH SEA

Strathclyde

Lothian

IRISH SEA

ENGLAND

NORSE AND GAELIC

In the Hebrides, the old Gaelic way of life was now mixed with the Norse. A group of independent chieftains arose, part Scots and part Norwegian. They sailed in longships and answered to no king. It was not until the 1100s, when Somerled, ancestor of the Macdonald clan, gained control of the islands, that the Viking way of life finally began to disappear. But even then, the islanders were a law to themselves.

1045
Duncan's father, Crínán, fails in revolt against Macbeth.

1057
Malcolm Canmore kills Macbeth.

RULERS OF ALBA AND SCOTLAND
House of MacAlpin

♣ Kenneth I MacAlpin	AD 843–858
♣ Donald I	AD 858–862
♣ Constantine I	AD 862–877
♣ Aed	AD 877–878
♣ Eochaid and Giric	AD 878–889
♣ Donald II	AD 889–900
♣ Constantine II	AD 900–943
♣ Malcom I	AD 943–954
♣ Indulf	AD 954–962
♣ Dubh	AD 963–966
♣ Culen	AD 966–971
♣ Kenneth II	AD 971–995
♣ Constantine III	AD 995–997
♣ Kenneth III	AD 997–1005
♣ Malcolm II	1005–1034
♣ Duncan I	1034–1040
♣ Macbeth	1040–1057
♣ Lulach	1057–1058
♣ Malcolm III 'Canmore'	1058–1093

MALCOLM CANMORE

Malcolm III came to the Scottish throne in the following year. He was nicknamed Canmore, from the Gaelic *Ceann Mor*, which could mean either 'big head' or 'great chief'! He built a new palace at Dunfermline, which was now the Scottish capital. Malcolm's long reign was marked by endless wars south of the border, with Cnut I and the kings of England that followed him. He was killed at Alnwick in 1093.

DEATH AND REVENGE

The famous play *Macbeth* was written in England by William Shakespeare hundreds of years after the real Macbeth ruled Scotland. In the play, Macbeth is a murderous villain, driven by personal ambition. In reality, Macbeth may have been no more villainous than many other kings of his day. His motives for killing Duncan were probably part of a family feud. Macbeth went on a Christian pilgrimage to Rome and Scotland prospered under his rule. However Duncan's son, Malcolm, supported by his uncle Earl Siward of Northumbria, returned to kill Macbeth in 1057.

MARGARET, QUEEN AND SAINT

Malcolm Canmore's first wife was Ingiborg, the widow of a powerful Norse leader called Thorfinn, Earl of Orkney (the son of Sigurd Hlodvirsson who died at Clontarf). She died and in about 1070 there was another royal wedding, at Dunfermline. The bride was 24 year-old Margaret, daughter of an exiled claimant to the English throne, called Edward the Ætheling. Born in Hungary, Margaret brought the customs of mainland Europe to the Scottish court. Her palace shone with gold and silver, but she was a careful manager of finances. She founded many monasteries and was later made a saint.

▶ *Under Margaret's influence, Roman forms of Christian worship replaced traditions of the Celtic Church that had survived in Scotland.*

⬇ *Dunfermline Abbey was built by King David I in 1072, in honour of his mother Margaret.*

MACBETH'S SCOTLAND **127**

Castles and Knights

1066–1509

ELSEWHERE IN EUROPE

1220
King Frederick II of Sicily and Germany becomes Holy Roman Emperor.

1226
Louis IX (St Louis) comes to the throne in France.

1237
Mongol armies invade East and Central Europe (to 1241).

1378
A split in the Roman Church, with one Pope in Rome and another in Avignon, France.

1453
Turks capture Constantinople (Istanbul). End of the Byzantine empire.

1462
Lorenzo de Medici rules over splendid court at Florence, Italy.

1480
Ivan the Great, first Tsar of Russia, expels the Mongols and unites his country.

1492
Christians finally reconquer all of Muslim Spain, rule of Ferdinand and Isabella.

ASIA

1096
European Crusaders attack Muslims in the Near East and found Christian kingdoms.

1170
The Hindu Srivijaya kingdom rules Java, Southeast Asia.

1190
Temujin (Genghis Khan) starts to create the Mongol empire.

1192
Yoritomo Minamoto becomes first Shogun (military dictator) in Japan.

1206
The Islamic Sultanate rules in Delhi, India.

1271
Mongol ruler Kublai Khan becomes the emperor of China.

1368
Ming emperors rule China, capital at Nanjing.

1405
Death of Timur the Lame (or Tamberlaine), Tatar ruler of a vast Asian empire.

AFRICA

1200
The rise of the state of Mali in West Africa.

1200
Rise of Hausa city-states in northern Nigeria and Kanem-Bornu in Lake Chad region.

1250
Rise of the Benin empire in southern Nigerian forests.

1250
High stone enclosures built at Great Zimbabwe, in southeast Africa.

1300
Founding of the Kongo kingdom in southern Central Africa.

1400
Chinese, Arab and Indian traders along East Africa's Swahili Coast.

1400
Fine heads made from bronze in the Benin empire.

1450
Height of Songhai power in southern Sahara, university at Timbuktu.

> *"The peasant toils,
> the king rules – and
> God is in His heaven…"*

NORTH AMERICA

1100
Thule culture of the American Arctic, based on whaling.

1150
The Anasazi people settle Mesa Verde in the southwest.

1170
Collapse of Toltec rule in Mexico, period of wars and strife.

1300
The Maya people return to power in Mexico, with capital at Mayapán.

1345
Aztecs build the great city of Teotihuacan on the modern site of Mexico City.

1428
The Aztec empire expands and becomes very powerful.

1492
Christopher Columbus, in the service of Spain, lands in the Caribbean.

1493
The Spanish settle on the Caribbean island of Hispaniola.

SOUTH AMERICA

1100
The city of Cuzco, Peru, is founded by the first Inca emperor.

1370
The Chimú empire expands in northern Peru.

1450
The founding of the Inca town of Machu Picchu, high in the Andes.

1470
The Incas conquer the Chimú empire.

1492
The Incas conquer northern Chile.

1493
The Treaty of Tordesillas. Spain and Portugal divide up the Americas.

1498
The Inca empire is at its greatest extent under ruler Wayna Qapaq.

1500
The Portuguese claim Brazil.

OCEANIA

1100
Increased farming and irrigation begins on the Hawaiian islands.

1200
Powerful chiefdoms grow up in Polynesia.

1200
The Tu'i Tonga dynasty rules the Tongan Islands and part of Samoa.

1200
Large numbers of stone platforms and houses built in the Society Islands.

1250
Funeral of the Melanesian ruler Roy Mata on the island of Retoka.

1300
Giant moa is hunted to extinction in New Zealand, increase in agriculture.

1350
Classic Maori period begins on New Zealand, large fortresses.

1400s
Malay fishermen camp on shores of northern Australia.

1064
Harold swears to support William of Normandy.

1066
Harold II chosen as King of England. King Harald III of Norway defeated at Stamford Bridge.

Hastings 1066

In the summer of 1066 a large fleet assembled along the French coast. Its commander was William, Duke of Normandy. Ships wallowed at anchor in choppy seas, waiting for the northerly wind to turn. Norman lords galloped to and fro on horseback. Carts trundled along the beach loaded with spears, swords, arrows and axes, iron helmets, shields and coats of mail. This would be the last major invasion of England in the Middle Ages.

CLAIMS FOR THE THRONE

Harold of Wessex was the son of a powerful Anglo-Saxon earl called Godwin. In January 1066 the Witan named Harold as King of England, but their decision was challenged at once. Edward the Ætheling, nephew of Edward the Confessor, claimed the throne. So did Harold's own brother, Tostig. A third claimant was King Harald III of Norway, known as 'Hardraade the Ruthless'. The fourth was William of Normandy. William swore that in 1064 Harold had made a solemn vow to support the Norman claim.

1066

Norman invasion. Harold II defeated at Battle of Hastings.

1067

William I starts to build the Tower of London.

Anglo-Saxon England was defeated at the Battle of Hastings, in Sussex, in 1066. The battle began in King Harold's favour. However he was killed by a stray arrow and the day was won by the Norman invaders.

WHO WERE THE NORMANS?

The Anglo-Saxon kings were not the only ones who attempted buy off the Vikings. In AD 911 Charles 'the Simple', King of France, offered a Viking warlord called Rollo part of northern France in a desperate bid to win peace. It became called Normandy ('land of the Northmen'). Rollo became a duke and married Giselle, a French princess. Like their Viking ancestors, Norman warlords stormed their way around Europe. They invaded the Italian island of Sicily in 1060.

ONE BATTLE TOO MANY

Harold II's troops were waiting for the Normans when word came that Harald III of Norway had joined forces with Tostig. Harold marched northwards at speed. He defeated and killed them both at Stamford Bridge, near York. Just three days later, Norman troops landed in Sussex. Harold had to march his exhausted army south again. On 14 October 1066, the two great armies clashed at Senlac Hill, near Hastings. All day, wave after wave of Normans broke against the Anglo-Saxon shields. Harold's men stood firm but, scenting victory, they broke rank too soon. The victory belonged to William – 'the Conqueror'.

This tapestry of wool on a linen backing has a 70-metre long 'strip' format, which tells the story of the Noman invasion of England. It can still be seen today in Bayeux, Normandy.

The Tower of London was added to over the ages. It played a central role in English history, with many famous prisoners being locked up in its dungeons.

1070
Rebellion in East Anglia by Hereward 'the Wake'.

1087
War with France, William I dies after he falls from horse.

THE CONQUEST

On Christmas Day 1066, William I was crowned king in Westminster Abbey. Within months of his coronation, William ordered the building of a new fortification by the River Thames, in London. Its great keep, or stronghold, was the White Tower. This became the centre of the Tower of London.

Within two years most of England was under his control. Revolts led by Edward the Ætheling and an Anglo-Saxon lord called Hereward the Wake ('the Watchful') were crushed.

THE DOMESDAY BOOK

Exactly 19 years after his coronation, William I announced that all the lands in England south of the rivers Ribble and Tees (and excluding the cities of London and Winchester) were to be registered in a great book. From 1086 onwards, royal officials travelled from one estate to another. They wrote down the details of buildings, land and resources, so that they could be taxed.

RULERS OF ENGLAND

House of Normandy

⚜ William I 'the Conqueror'	1066–1087
⚜ William II 'Rufus'	1087–1100
⚜ Henry I 'Beauclerk'	1100–1135
⚜ Stephen	1135–1154

1066
The Norman Channel Islands come under the English crown.

1072
William I of England leads army into Scotland.

The Mailed Fist

The Norman kings of England and their successors wanted to be recognised as overlords of all the British Isles. Their fleets sailed north and their armies were soon battling with the Scots. Norman warlords were given territories on the Welsh borders (the 'Marches'), and stormed into North and South Wales. Within 100 years, their great castles of stone could be seen in Ireland, too.

Braided hair
Norman ladies often wore their hair in plaits. Heads were sometimes covered with a short veil, secured by a circlet of silver or gold.

Cloak
A long woollen cloak was worn for warmth, fastened across the front by a cord.

Girdle
A cord or jewelled belt was worn around the waist.

Flowing dress
A long-sleeved shift was covered by a long tunic called a bliaut, which was laced at the side.

Supplies
Weapons and equipment had to be carried with the troops. Food and grain could be seized by force along the way.

Norman lady

THE NORMANS IN SCOTLAND

After repeated Scottish invasions of his new kingdom, William I marched into Lothian at the head of a large army in 1071, but he made peace with Malcolm Canmore at Abernethy. In 1092 the Normans took Cumbria from the Scots, but a full-scale invasion of Scotland never occurred. Norman settlers did arrive, bringing their ways to the Lowlands and to the Scottish court. Later Scottish kings, including Robert Bruce and the Stewarts, were of Norman descent.

1092
Normans build castle at Pembroke in South Wales.

1094
'Marcher' Lordships established in the Welsh borders.
Norman invasion of North Wales.

STRONGBOW'S IRELAND

In Ireland, warring between provincial kings gave a chance for Norman descendants to invade. In 1166 Dermot MacMurrough, King of Leinster, appealed to Henry II of England for help. He had lost his lands in the wars between Ireland's provincial kings. Henry authorised Norman lords to carry on this fight independently. In 1169, Richard fitz Gilbert de Clare, Earl of Pembroke, agreed to help Dermot in return for land. De Clare, half Norman and half Welsh, was known as 'Strongbow'. His invasion of Ireland was successful – too much so for Henry II, who was jealous of Strongbow's new-found power. The English king and his army arrived in Ireland in 1171.

➡️ *Dermot, the Irish ruler of Leinster, needed the support of Strongbow (right). In return he offered him the hand of his daughter, Aoife, and succession to the throne of Leinster.*

Metal in motion
The mounted knight was the key to Norman success.

Horse power
The Normans used highly mobile forces to control their conquests.

⬅️ *The Norman invasion did not stop at the borders of England.*

1097
Normans defeat Donald III of Scotland.

1100
William II of England is killed, possibly murdered, in the New Forest.

WALES AND THE MARCHES

The Norman kings did not intend to rule Wales directly, but they wished to control it. As early as 1067, William I gave land on the borders to William Fitzosbern, Roger Montgomery and Hugh d'Avranches. These 'Marcher Lords' were a law to themselves. They launched savage raids into North Wales in the 1080s. By the 1090s Norman warlords were gaining control of large areas of South and West Wales. They met fierce resistance, but this was a period when the Welsh kingdoms were at war with each other. The Normans were defeated in 1096 at Gelli Carnant, Gwent, but they kept their foothold in Wales.

Wooden watchtower

Motte
The motte was an area of raised earth.

Henry I of England defeats and imprisons his brother Robert in Normandy.

Dermot MacMurrough of Leinster invites Normans into Ireland.

GWENLLIAN GOES TO WAR

Gwenllian was the daughter of Gruffudd ap Cynan, ruler of Gwynedd in North Wales. She married another Grufudd, son of Rhys ap Tewdwr, ruler of Deheubarth. In 1136 her husband went to meet her father, to plan a rising against the Normans in South Wales. While he was away, Gwenllian led a warrior band to storm Kidwelly Castle. They were beaten back and defeated by Maurice de Londres. Gwenllian was captured and executed.

Palisade

A wooden palisade surrounded the bailey, which was the enclosure where people and livestock lived.

At first the Normans built simple 'motte and bailey' castles. Each had a wooden tower, standing on a tall earth mound called a 'motte', surrounded by a strong wooden fence called a 'bailey'.

Ditch

A ditch was dug around the motte for extra defence. Sometimes this was filled with water to become a moat.

1086
Population of two million in area surveyed by the Domesday Book.

1191
First record of windmills being used for grinding wheat.

The Feudal System

The division of society into classes of serfs, free men, nobles and rulers had started earlier in the Middle Ages. The Normans were the first to enforce this 'feudal' system rigidly. The king was at the top, ruling by the will of God. He parcelled out land to his lords in return for their support. The land was worked by free men and serfs (or 'villeins'), who provided the nobles with food and served in their armies. In return, the poor were, in theory at least, protected by their lord.

⬇ *The feudal economy was based on land and services rather than money. It only worked if people stayed on the land. Villeins were not allowed to leave their village and were forced to work on their lord's estates.*

Field use
One field might be for oats and another for wheat. The third might lie 'fallow' (uncultivated) and be grazed by cattle. Field use changed from year to year so that the goodness in the soil was not all used up.

1200s
Rapid growth of towns and cities.

1300s
Feudal system begins to be replaced by a money-based economy.

OATHS OF LOYALTY

The feudal system was a series of two-way contracts, reinforced by oaths of loyalty. The loyalty was not to a nation, but to a noble or royal family. A lord could even insist that 'his' people take up arms against their own countrymen. The feudal system crossed national borders. Europe's ruling classes were allied with each other, rather than with the peasants who worked for them. If a king from one royal family married the princess of another, the lands they ruled might be joined together, regardless of public opinion or geography.

⬆ *Kings of the Middle Ages held extreme power over their subjects. Every royal document was marked with a personal badge called a seal, pressed into soft wax. This one belonged to Henry III of England.*

Windmill

Windmills, originally an Asian invention, were first built in Britain during the 1190s. They were mounted on an upright post, and could be turned so that the sails caught the wind. They were used for grinding grain into flour.

Harrow

A harrow was a spiked frame used for preparing the soil ready for the seeds to be scattered by the sower.

1300s
Rise of a middle class made up of merchants and craft producers.

1300s
Cloth production moves out of towns, water power needed for fulling. Spinning wheels introduced.

WOMEN IN THE MIDDLE AGES

In the medieval (Middle Ages) period, most women in Europe had few rights. Strict vows bound together man and wife, just as society was bound by oaths of feudal loyalty. It was the men who held real power and wealth. Despite this, many women were strong characters and became widely respected in their own right. There were powerful queens and noblewomen, abbesses and nuns, scholars and poets, and able working women in every village. In the later Middle Ages, poets began to sing the praises of women, but in a very idealised way.

▲ Women may have been honoured in medieval poetry but in reality had hard lives. Many died in childbirth.

RICH AND POOR

The Norman lords who had supported William I during the invasion of England profited hugely. They were rather like the lottery winners of today, only their new-found wealth was based on land rather than money. This created problems for kings that followed, for there were now many very powerful lords who could challenge their rule. At the other end of the scale were the villeins. They had to labour on the lord's land for, say, three days a week. They also had to pay taxes and supply farm produce to the lord. The Church too demanded one-tenth (a 'tithe') of their harvested crops.

← *A knight and his squire ride through the busy streets of a medieval town. The feudal system ensured that the upper classes had great powers within their own domain.*

1100
Death of William II of England, called 'Rufus'.

1135
Stephen is crowned English king. Start of civil war.

Is Might Right?

In the days of William the Conqueror, life was short and violent. The road to kingship was not through election or consent. It was often through murder and battle. Even the laws reflected the belief that 'might is right'. A legal dispute might be settled by an official fight – 'trial by combat' – or by making the accused grasp a red hot bar of iron – 'trial by ordeal'. God, it was believed, would punish the guilty and protect the innocent.

A KING'S NIGHTMARES

In 1100, William II of England was killed in a hunting accident in the New Forest. Or was it murder? Nobody knew for sure. Six years later his successor, Henry I, imprisoned his own brother for 28 years. A series of pictures drawn in the 1140s shows Henry I haunted by royal nightmares. Haughty bishops, armed knights and angry peasants all protest by his bedside.

THE FIGHTING EMPRESS

When Henry I's son was drowned at sea in 1120, he named his daughter Matilda as his heir. She lived in Germany at that time, for she had been betrothed (engaged to be married) at the age of just seven to the Emperor Henry V. She had married him in 1114, aged twelve. Widowed in 1125, Matilda soon remarried another very powerful but younger man, Geoffrey of Anjou. She fought desperately for the English throne until 1148.

▼ Matilda flees from Oxford. She was unpopular with the English people. At one time she captured Stephen, but was never crowned queen.

A TIME OF TERROR

Henry I did manage to keep order in the land, but after his death in 1135, there was chaos. Before his chosen heir, Matilda, arrived back in England, the throne was seized by Stephen, a grandson of William I. There followed 13 years of war between the two. It was a terrible period for the common people, as lord fought lord and armies looted the land.

THE CHURCH IN CONTROL

The Roman Church was very powerful. Popes believed that as God's representatives they had the right to control European politics. Quarrels between kings and the Church became common. In 1170 supporters of Henry II of England murdered Thomas Becket, the Archbishop of Canterbury.

⬆ *Armed might invades the peace of Canterbury Cathedral in 1170. Four knights have burst in to murder English archbishop Thomas Becket while he prays.*

TRIAL BY JURY

A fairer legal system was brought in by Henry II of England during the 1100s. Punishments for crimes were still often brutal, but now courts were held around the country in the king's name. Juries were called to decide guilt or innocence. In those days, juries were not independent members of the public but people who may have known the accused or witnessed the crime.

RISE OF THE BARONS

In 1215, English barons forced King John to agree to recognise their legal rights. The agreement was known as Magna Carta ('the great charter'). The barons did not need protection, but at least the law was now recognised as more important than the word of kings and queens.

King John was a weak ruler. In 1215, at Runnymede, near the River Thames, he caved in to the demands of his rebel barons and signed the Magna Carta.

Magna Carta

A SUMMONS TO PARLIAMENT

Magna Carta may have been one of the first moves towards social justice, but its immediate effect was to make the warring barons even more powerful. When Henry III of England came to the throne in 1216, he was only a child. In 1258 he was forced to hand over power to the barons. Their leader was Simon de Montfort, Earl of Leicester and brother-in-law of the king. He imprisoned Henry III at Lewes, Sussex, in 1264. The next year de Montfort called a great council, or 'parliament'. Each county sent a knight and each town sent a burgess (leading citizen). De Montfort was killed in 1265, but parliaments were again summoned by later kings. By 1352 parliament had two sections or 'chambers'. The House of Lords was for the nobles and the bishops, while the House of Commons was for knights and burgesses.

The Angevin Empire

Although Matilda failed to win the throne of England, her son was crowned King Henry II in 1154. His royal line is sometimes called Plantagenet, named after the sprig of broom (in Old French, *plante genêt*) that his father Geoffrey wore in his cap. Henry II ruled over a huge area of western Europe called the Angevin (Anjou) empire.

THE ANGEVIN EMPIRE

The patchwork of territories claimed by Henry II made England a major European power.

Acquisitions by marriage with Eleanor

- under direct rule
- owing allegiance
- other acquisitions 1169–72
- control by marriage of Geoffrey with Constance of Brittany
- unsuccessfully claimed
- Kingdom of France
- inherited through Henry's father
- under direct rule
- owing allegiance

SCOTLAND

NORTH SEA

IRELAND

WALES

ENGLAND

London

ENGLISH CHANNEL

Normandy

Paris

FRANCE

Brittany Anjou

Poitou

Bourges

Aquitaine

Bordeaux

Gascony Toulouse

Béarne

The lute, a musical instrument of Arab origin, was widely played in western Europe in the Middle Ages. Musicians performed at court and poets and singers travelled from one castle to another.

1154
Henry II is crowned first Plantagenet king of England.

c.1167
Students start to study at Oxford.

ROYAL LANDS

Henry II's lands stretched from the sunny vineyards of Bordeaux in southwest France, to the rainy Scottish borders. He had inherited Anjou from his father and gained Poitou, Aquitaine and Gascony on marrying Eleanor of Aquitaine. Henry also claimed to be overlord of Brittany, Wales, Scotland and Ireland.

ELEANOR OF AQUITAINE

Eleanor of Aquitaine was one of the most remarkable women in medieval Europe. She was born in about 1122. She became Duchess of Aquitaine in 1135, when she married the heir to the French throne. He was crowned Louis VII two years later. Eleanor was unconventional and beautiful. She and a troop of women, dressed as classical warriors, joined the Second Crusade (one of the wars between Christians and Muslims in the Near East). After her marriage was annulled (cancelled) in 1152, Eleanor married young Henry of Anjou, who became King Henry II of England. Their love soon turned sour and when Henry was unfaithful she supported his sons in rebellion against him. She was imprisoned from 1174 until the death of Henry in 1189. She died in 1204.

➡️ *Eleanor's court in Poitou attracted poets, musicians and scholars from all over Europe.*

1198
Richard I 'Cœur de Lion' dies from a crossbow wound.

1205
England loses Normandy to France.

THE EMPIRE UNRAVELS

Henry II of England was energetic and fiery-tempered. He was a very able ruler, but he quarrelled bitterly with his wife and with his sons. They rebelled against him and the great empire began to break up. Royal power lessened under Stephen and John, but the struggle to control France would continue for hundreds of years.

WHICH LANGUAGE?

The English spoken today began to take shape in medieval England. It grew out of several languages. The court used French, while scholars and the Church used Latin. Most ordinary people spoke dialects of English. Other languages spoken in the British Isles at this time included Cornish, Welsh, Scots Gaelic, Irish and Norse.

➡ *Henry III's beautiful tomb still survives and is admired by visitors at Westminster Abbey today.*

RULERS OF ENGLAND

House of Anjou (Plantagenet)

✤ Henry II 'Curtmantle'	1154–1189
✤ Richard I 'Cœur de Lion'	1189–1199
✤ John 'Lackland'	1199–1216
✤ Henry III of Winchester	1216–1272
✤ Edward I 'Longshanks'	1272–1307
✤ Edward II	1307–1327
✤ Edward III 'of Windsor'	1327–1377
✤ Richard II	1377–1399

A LONG REIGN

Henry III was the son of King John. After coming to the throne as a child in 1216, he ruled England for 56 years. The country prospered, but he was not popular. Despite raising taxes to pay for wars against France, his armies won few victories.

SCHOLARS AND INVENTORS

Under Plantagenet rule in England, few people could read or write. Some children were taught in church schools or were tutored by monks or nuns. University students may have been studying at Oxford as early as 1167, and Cambridge University was founded in 1215. One scholar who studied at Oxford and Paris was Roger Bacon (c.1214–1292). He was a scientist who predicted the use of flying machines and telescopes. At this time all sorts of exciting new inventions were arriving in Britain from abroad, including gunpowder, clocks and spectacles.

Boar's head

MEDIEVAL FOOD

The common people of Britain ate coarse bread of rye or barley, cheese and buttermilk, 'pottages' (thick soups or stews of vegetables), pickled herrings and bacon. In the great halls of the feudal lords, splendid banquets would be served, sometimes made up of 20 or more courses. These included fine wheaten bread, roast boar, venison, mutton, geese, swan or peacock. All sorts of pies and custards and dishes were served, sometimes dyed in brilliant colours or served with precious spices imported from Asia.

← *From the 13th century onwards, Cambridge University became one of the great centres of European scholarship. This is St John's College, Cambridge, founded in 1511.*

The Crusades

In 1075 the city of Jerusalem was captured from its Christian rulers by Turkish Muslims. Twenty years later, Pope Urban II appealed to all Christian knights to launch a holy war, or Crusade. Its aim was to recapture Jerusalem and the 'Holy Land'. The First Crusade began in 1096 and Jerusalem was taken after three long years.

➡ *The crusaders built huge castles to defend their lands against the much larger Muslim armies. The biggest castles could house up to 2000 soldiers as well as servants and horses. In the port of Acre the crusaders had constructed a vast underground fortress.*

The First Crusade leaves Europe for the Holy Land.

Crusaders capture Jerusalem, massacre 10,000 Jews and Muslims. Christian kingdom founded at Jerusalem.

JEWS, CHRISTIANS AND MUSLIMS

By now, most of Europe was Christian. The Moors (Muslims Berbers and Arabs) had conquered much of Spain, but were under constant attack by Christian armies from the north. There were communities of Jews in many parts of Europe, too. Their ancestors had been expelled from Jerusalem by the Romans in AD 70. In Moorish Spain, Muslims, Christians and Jews lived peaceably together. However in most of Christendom, religious hatred against Muslims and Jews ran rife. Jews were persecuted terribly in England and in 1290 they were expelled by Edward I.

RELIGIOUS WARS

There were several further Crusades between 1096 and 1270. These shameful wars poisoned relations between Christianity and Islam into modern times. Religious motives soon gave way to looting and land-grabbing. Muslims were not the only enemy. In 1204, Crusaders turned aside to sack the Christian city of Constantinople. In 1208 a Crusade was launched against Christians in southern France, who differed from Rome in their beliefs. German Crusaders invaded Poland and the Baltic lands in the 1200s.

1148
The Second Crusade fails to capture Damascus in Syria.

1189
The Third Crusade is launched, Richard I pledges support.

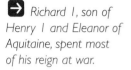
Richard I, son of Henry I and Eleanor of Aquitaine, spent most of his reign at war.

RICHARD THE LION HEART

One of the most famous English kings, Richard I spent only 10 months of his reign in England and probably spoke only French. In 1189 he became King of England. In the following year he joined the Third Crusade, at first with King Philippe Auguste of France. In 1191 he captured the city of Acre. Richard's exploits brought him fame and the nickname Cœur de Lion ('Lion Heart'). Journeying home, Richard was shipwrecked and forced to cross the lands of his enemy, Duke Leopold of Austria. He was captured and handed over to Emperor Henry VI. A huge sum ('a ransom') had to be paid for his release and it was the English people who had to find the money. Richard was killed fighting against France in 1199.

The Crusader

Crusaders were armed with swords, lances, axes and maces. Their armour varied over the years. Chain mail gave way to solid plate armour.

Saracen armour

Muslim troops either wore tunics that were padded or sewn with metal plates, or coats of mail.

CRUSADERS AND SARACENS

Crusaders came from all over Europe, including the British Isles. Some joined international 'orders', such as the Knights of St John (founded in 1099), or the Knights Templar (1119). The Muslim soldiers of the 'Holy Land' were called Saracens and included Arabs, Turks and Kurds. Their most famous leader was Salah-ed-din Yussuf ('Saladin', 1137–1193). He earned the respect of many Crusaders. Contact with Arab civilisation opened the eyes of many Europeans to the wider world.

Saracen weapons

The Saracens had swords of the finest steel, spears and round shields. Archers fired arrows from small bows while riding.

← Fighting in the dry heat and dust of the Near East, when weighed down with armour and weapons, was often an ordeal. Although the Crusades were meant to be 'holy' wars, the citizens of besieged towns were often slaughtered without mercy. The Crusades left a bitterness between Christianity and Islam that still affects the politics of southwest Asia today.

THE CRUSADES   153

Knights in Armour

I n the 700s, a simple invention had reached Europe from Asia – stirrups. They supported the legs of a horseback rider and made it possible for mounted soldiers to charge the enemy really hard, without falling. By Norman times, horse soldiers called knights had become the most important part of most armies. Even lords and kings had to learn how to be good knights. In the 1100s and 1200s, almost every battlefield shook to the thundering hooves of great war-horses leading a cavalry charge.

THE AGE OF CHIVALRY

In the high Middle Ages, knights developed a code of behaviour, called 'chivalry'. It was based on Christian virtues. A knight vowed to protect the weak, honour women, keep his word and respect his enemies. These ideas were admired by many later generations, but they were only ever an ideal. Battles may have had strict rules, but they were still brutal affairs. Respect was certainly not extended to peasants or to enemy foot soldiers, who were slaughtered without mercy.

1200s
Horses protected with padded or mail coats called trappers.

1292
Statute of Arms lays down rules for English tournaments.

⬇ *Knights would also engage in foot combat wearing full plate armour. Skill and speed were more important than strength.*

HERALDRY

In a tournament or a battle, it was hard to tell one armoured knight from another. Knights began to use personal badges or emblems, which were displayed on surcoats (tunics worn over armour), on shields and standards. These emblems were passed down from one generation of a family to another. They became known as coats-of-arms and can still be seen carved on castle stones or coloured in the stained glass of old churches. The rules for drawing up coats-of-arms are known as heraldry.

▲ *Heraldic design and colouring followed strict rules. It used various geometric patterns as well as emblems such as the fleur-de-lys ('lily flower', above right).*

1300s
'Coat of plates' – armoured plates stitched to tunics.

1330s
Solid breastplate encases the upper part of the body.

SPLENDID TOURNAMENTS

More than 800 years ago, knights turned their military training into a sport. They fought mock battles called mêlées and later fought one-to-one, galloping at each other with lances raised. This was called jousting. It was a very violent sport and deaths were common. Grand competitions called tournaments were held, at which young knights sought fame and fortune. Before they took part, they dedicated their fight to a lady of the court.

A joust gave a knight the chance to prove himself in front of the woman he loved. Jousts were social events watched by ladies of the court as well as ordinary people.

Edward I of England was a keen supporter of tournaments and jousts. He banned spectators from carrying weapons themselves because this caused too much trouble among the watching crowds. Knights could show off their skills and bravery to impress the spectators.

1334
Edward III of England founds knightly Order of the Garter.

1400s
Full plate armour covers whole body.

➡ *By the 1400s, plate armour encased the knight's whole body.*

Helmets now protected the whole face as well as the skull

Gorgets were plates that prevented the throat being stabbed

Pauldrons shielded the shoulders from heavy blows

Breastplates covered the ribs

Cowters covered the elbows

Skirts (plate strips) protected the waist

Gauntlets were jointed, armoured gloves

Poleyns protected the kneecaps

Cuisses protected the thighs

Greaves protected the shins and lower leg

Sabatons were pointed, armoured shoes

BECOMING A KNIGHT

Young boys started to learn how to be a knight at about the age of seven, when they were sent to serve as a page in a castle. They were taught to fight, ride and use weapons. At about 14 they became an esquire, or assistant to a knight, and could go into battle. At about 21, or earlier if they showed great courage, esquires would be made full knights.

⬇ *Weapons used in hand-to-hand fighting included clubs (called 'maces') and all kinds of swords and daggers.*

Sword
A double-edged blade like this was used in the 1300s.

Mace
Knights used clubs like this one after about 1250.

c.AD 950
Motte-and-bailey castles built in France.

1066
Normans bring castle building to the British Isles.

The Age of Castles

Fortresses had been built in Britain in Roman times. After the Normans invaded England in 1066, powerful kings and lords began to build new kinds of fortresses, called castles. Castles served as homes, as well as military bases and centres of government. They were used to control conquered lands and show off the power of their owner. Kings and lords sometimes owned several castles and moved from one to the other during the year.

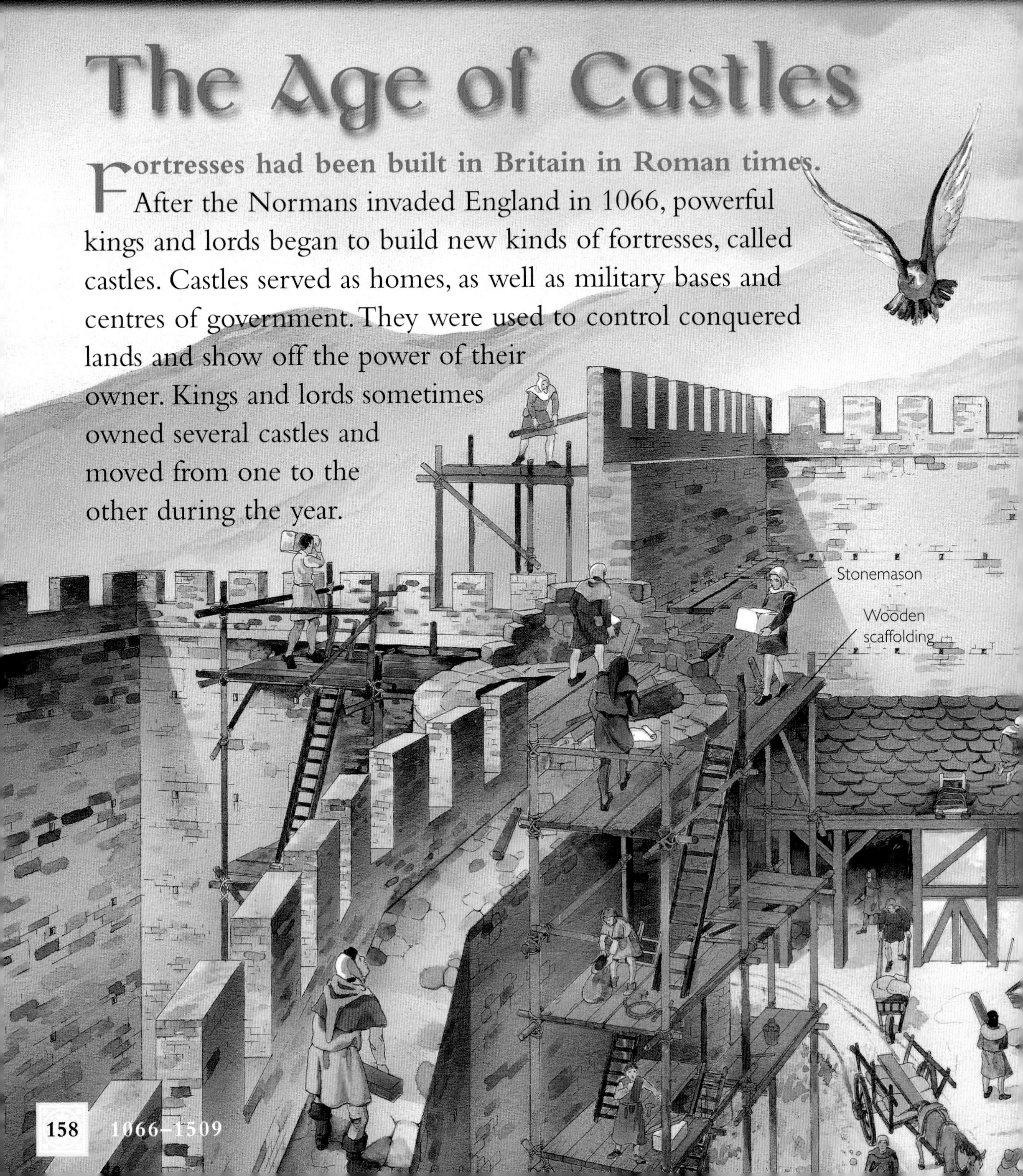

Stonemason
Wooden scaffolding

1100s
Castle defences centred on massive stone towers called keeps.

1180s
Castles built with square wall towers.

The best place to build a castle was on top of a hill. A hilltop position gave good views over the surrounding countryside, and made it harder for an enemy to launch a surprise attack. Sometimes a castle was built on the banks of a river or lake, and its waters were used to create a moat.

Wheel for haulage

Architect

THE AGE OF CASTLES   159

1220s
Castles built with round wall towers.

1224
Bedford Castle in England is captured. Its garrison is hanged.

LIFE IN A CASTLE

The centre of activity in the castle was the Great Hall. This was where banquets and important meetings were held. In the kitchens, meat sizzled on spits in front of the fire. The bedrooms and the main living room (called a 'solar') were often cold and draughty. Fresh reeds were strewn on the stone floors, as there were no carpets. There were rooms for the servants, guard rooms and stables.

→ *Castles were built with rings of defences and were hard to attack. They were garrisoned by footsoldiers, archers and men-at-arms.*

KING OF THE CASTLES

Beaumaris Castle is on the Isle of Anglesey, in Wales. Work on it began in April 1295 and cost a fortune. It employed no fewer than 2000 labourers, 200 stonemasons and 400 quarrymen. Beaumaris was the last in a powerful chain of castles built by King Edward I of England to secure his conquest of North Wales. He was the greatest castle builder of his day.

◄ *Stonemasons and carpenters were recruited from all over the kingdom of England.*

Arrow loops
Archers could shoot arrows through loops – narrow slits in the castle walls.

Outer walls
Thick stone walls were fireproof and hard to knock down.

Battlements

The walls were topped by battlements. These walk-ways were defended by stone blocks called merlons and firing gaps called crenels.

Machicolations

Chutes overhung the outer walls, for dropping missiles on the enemy.

Gatehouse

A strong gate called a portcullis could be dropped to seal off the entrance to the castle.

1320s
The age of gunpowder begins, new threat to castles.

1350s
Bricks begin to be used in building some castles.

UNDER ATTACK

When an army attacked a castle it often tried to surround it and cut off its supplies, so that the defenders starved. This was called a siege. Blazing arrows were shot into roof timbers. The walls were pounded with boulders from giant catapults, or undermined with tunnels dug beneath the foundations. More sieges ended by treaty or agreement than by the fall of the castle.

Siege tower
This wooden tower was wheeled up to castle walls so that attacking solders could reach the battlements.

Arbalest
This siege engine was like a gigantic crossbow that could launch missiles with great force.

Trebuchet

This had a long wooden arm with a heavy weight at one end and a sling at the other. A heavy stone was placed inside the sling. As the weight dropped, the stone was hurled towards the castle walls, sometimes travelling as far as 300 metres.

A siege could last for many months, if the defenders had sufficient water and food. Defenders had to wait for supporters to come to their rescue, launch a counter-attack – or surrender the castle.

Battering ram

A massive beam shod with iron would be wheeled up to gates or weak points in the walls. It was then swung into the stone or timber with a mighty crash.

To the Glory of God

In later medieval Europe, the Christian faith was part of everday life. It was expressed in the great stone cathedrals and abbeys that were raised all over the British Isles in the Middle Ages. Building styles changed over the years. Some cathedrals had massive, awe-inspiring towers. Others were graceful, with tall spires pointing to heaven. Inside, gold glittered in candle light and coloured ('stained') glass windows glowed like precious gems.

➡ *Durham Cathedral, towering above the River Wear in the northeast of England, was started by the Normans in 1093. It contains the tombs of St Cuthbert and Bede. During the Middle Ages the bishops of Durham were as warlike as any barons and had great political power.*

In the Middle Ages, the language of the Roman Church was Latin, which few ordinary people could understand. Most were unable to read either. Stained glass windows were an ideal way of telling worshippers stories from the Bible or the lives of the saints.

LETTERS OF GOLD

Before the days of printing, books had to be copied out by hand. The work was often done in monasteries. The pages were made of vellum (animal skin) and decorated with elaborate letter designs and small pictures, called 'illuminations'. Books were such rare and precious objects that they were often chained to the shelf.

▶ Illuminated letters were decorated with coloured paint and gold leaf. They were works of art in themselves.

➡️ *Monks and nuns lived in monasteries and convents. Some cared for the sick or taught young people. Some travelled from one town to another, living on charity. Religious orders such as the Franciscans ('Grey Friars') or the Dominicans ('Black Friars') were founded in the 1200s.*

MONKS AND NUNS

By about 1215 the Roman Church was at the height of its power and wealth. It was at that time that an Italian monk called Francis of Assisi called for Christians to give up riches and help the poor and the sick. By the 1220s his ideas were being spread through the British Isles by wandering monks, or friars. However many church officials remained greedy and corrupt. They were condemned by an English priest called John Wycliffe, who gained many followers in the 1300s.

CANTERBURY PILGRIMS

Many people went on pilgrimage to holy sites, such as the tomb of Thomas Becket in Canterbury. They prayed for healing or forgiveness of sins. Between 1387 and 1400, a poet called Geoffrey Chaucer wrote about these pilgrims and of the stories they told to pass the time. The *Canterbury Tales* was one of the first and greatest works of English literature.

➡️ *Amongst Chaucer's pilgrims were a knight, a nun, monks, a miller, a lawyer, a merchant and a doctor – a cross-section of medieval society.*

MYSTERIES AND MIRACLES

Many people believed in miracles or in the healing power of relics such as saints' bones (which were often fakes). Some Christians became hermits, living alone to meditate. A woman called Julian of Norwich wrote about the meaning of religious visions she had in 1373. At that time a poem called *Piers Plowman* was also written, which celebrated

⬆ *A modern adaptation of Noah. The play is one of the 32 Wakefield Mystery Plays, composed between the mid-14th and 15th centuries, which tell the biblical story of the Creation.*

the simple faith of ordinary people. The Bible was not translated into English until the 1380s. One way people could learn about the scriptures was through acting. Religious ('mystery') plays, featuring angels and devils, were performed outside many cathedrals.

1063
Death of Gruffudd ap Llywelyn, having briefly
united Wales.

1164
Founding of Strata Florida abbey (Ystrad Fflur).

The Welsh Princes

Wales in the 1100s and 1200s was a rural land, with few large towns. People farmed and hunted, travelling by narrow tracks through the mountain passes, which were guarded by castles built by the Welsh rulers. They also endowed (funded) great monasteries such as Strata Florida (Ystrad Fflur) in the Teifi valley and Llanfaes, on Anglesey. There was a rich tradition of music, and a great gathering of poets (an *eisteddfod*) was held at Cardigan in 1176.

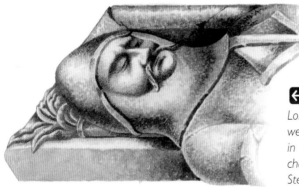

← *Rhys ap Gruffudd ('the Lord Rhys' of Deheubarth) weakened Norman power in South Wales during the chaotic reign of King Stephen in England.*

WHO HOLDS POWER?

Under rulers such as Rhys ap Gruffudd in the south and Owain Gwynedd in the north, Norman power in Wales declined. The Marcher Lords still held the borders, however, and the English kings regarded themselves as overlords of the Welsh. The division of Wales into separate kingdoms played into the hands of the English. In 1157 Madog ap Maredudd of Powys helped King Henry II of England invade Wales, in order to weaken his rivals in Gwynedd.

THE GREAT LLYWELYN

In 1170 three sons of Owain Gwynedd fought each other at Pentraeth, on Anglesey, for the throne of Gwynedd. Hywel was defeated by Rhodri and Dafydd and the kingdom was divided. By 1194 all Gwynedd had come under the rule of Llywelyn ap Iorwerth, 'the Great'. Llywelyn married Joan or Siwan, daughter of King John of England, but the two rulers later became enemies. Llywelyn was the most powerful ruler in medieval Wales, a strong supporter of the Church and the law.

⬆ *Llywelyn the Great fought against rival princes and forced them to swear loyalty to him and his son.*

THE LAST PRINCE

Llywelyn was succeeded by his younger son, Dafydd, but he died in the sixth year of his reign. He was to be followed by his nephews Llywelyn and Owain, but the former seized the throne for himself and gained control of all Wales. Llywelyn II ap Gruffudd was recognised as Prince of Wales by the English in 1267. However he would be the last Welsh prince. He quarrelled with King Edward I and after long wars, was killed in a skirmish with English troops near Cilmeri. His severed head was displayed in London.

⬅ *Llywelyn II's death near Cilmeri in 1282 marked the end of Welsh independence. He is remembered in Wales as 'The Last Prince'.*

RULERS IN WALES

- ❖ Gruffudd ap Llywelyn — 1039–1063
- ❖ Bleddyn ap Cynfyn — 1063–1075
- ❖ Trahaearn ap Caradog — 1075–1081
- ❖ Gruffudd ap Cynan — 1081–1137
- ❖ Owain Gwynedd — 1137–1170
- ❖ Dafydd ap Owain Gwynedd — 1170–1194
- ❖ Llywelyn 'Fawr' ('the Great') — 1194–1240
- ❖ Dafydd ap Llywelyn — 1240–1246
- ❖ Llywelyn ap Gruffudd — 1246–1282

GERALD OF WALES

Gerald de Barri was born in about 1146. His ancestry was part Norman, part Welsh. Gerald became a talented writer in Latin and a great churchman. In 1188 he travelled through Wales with Archbishop Baldwin, and his *Journey Through Wales* and *Description of Wales* give us lively and good-humoured pictures of Wales in the high Middle Ages. He died in 1223 and has gone down in history as Giraldus Cambriensis, or Gerald of Wales.

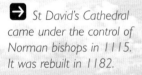

➡ *St David's Cathedral came under the control of Norman bishops in 1115. It was rebuilt in 1182.*

THE CONQUEST

King Edward I of England was now the undisputed ruler of Wales. His castles ringed the land. English criminal laws replaced Welsh ones and the Statute of Rhuddlan (1284) divided Wales into counties, along English lines. In 1301 Edward I's son (the later Edward II) was declared Prince of Wales, and ever since then the title has been held by the eldest son of the English monarch.

Edward I's Welsh castles were designed with strong 'curtain' walls and tall look-out towers. Many were also surrounded by deep moats filled with water. Conwy Castle is one of the great fortresses of medieval Europe.

1174
William I of Scotland forced to recognise English king as overlord.

1264
Norwegian invasion defeated at Largs.

Scottish Freedom

In the 1100s, Scotland saw great changes. Norman families gained Scottish lands. Three sons of Queen Margaret ruled the country in turn – Edgar, Alexander I and the great David I. Many fine churches and abbeys were built during their reigns, and around them developed prosperous 'burghs' (large towns). Peasants lived in small farming villages called 'touns'.

RULERS OF SCOTLAND

❖ Donald III Bán	1093–1097
❖ Duncan II	1094
❖ Edgar	1097–1107
❖ Alexander I 'the Fierce'	1107–1124
❖ David I 'the Saint'	1124–1153
❖ Malcolm IV 'the Maiden'	1153–1165
❖ William I 'the Lion'	1165–1214
❖ Alexander II	1214–1229
❖ Alexander III	1249–1286
❖ Margaret 'Maid of Norway'	1286–1290
❖ Throne disputed	1290–1292
❖ John (Balliol)	1292–1296
❖ Edward I of England	1296–1306

House of Bruce

❖ Robert I Bruce	1306–1329
❖ David II	1329–1371
❖ Edward Balliol	1306 & 1333–1336

SCOTLAND STANDS FIRM

In 1174, William I of Scotland was captured by English troops and forced to recognise Henry II as his overlord. It was an act never forgotten by the English – or the Scots. Alexander III, who came to the throne as a boy, had another old enemy to deal with – Norway. The Norwegians invaded in 1263, but were forced to withdraw and finally lost their mainland and island territories.

SCOTLAND FALLS

Tragedy now struck the Scots. In 1286 Alexander III fell from his horse and was killed. Four years later his successor, the young girl Margaret of Norway, also died. Who should reign next, was unclear. The Scots turned to Edward I of England for advice.

His candidate was John Balliol, a distant descendant of David I. Edward I thought he could control his chosen man, but instead Balliol turned and made an historic alliance with France. Edward I stormed into Scotland in 1296 and defeated Balliol at Dunbar.

WAR OF INDEPENDENCE

Resistance to English rule was fierce. Its champion was William Wallace, who defeated an English army at Stirling Bridge, but was himself defeated at Falkirk in 1298. Captured in 1305, Wallace was horribly executed in London. Parts of his body were sent to Newcastle, Berwick, Stirling and Perth.

← *William Wallace blocked the northern advance of English forces at Stirling Bridge in 1297 and became Edward I's most hated foe.*

SCOTTISH FREEDOM **173**

Legend has it that Robert Bruce was inspired to keep fighting the English by watching a spider try time after time to rebuild its web. At last it succeeded. Bannockburn was the turning point, although the war continued for another 14 years.

ROBERT BRUCE

The fight was taken up by Robert Bruce (who had stabbed his chief rival, John Comyn, to death). Robert was crowned king by the Scots in 1306. Edward I died in the following year and at Bannockburn, on 24 June 1314, Bruce turned the tide and defeated 20,000 troops of Edward II. The English finally recognised Scotland's independence in 1328.

LORDS OF THE ISLES

In the Highlands and Western Isles, the old Gaelic way of life continued. Here, first loyalty was to the chief of the clan (a group sharing descent from a common ancestor). The lands of Clans Dugall, Donald and Ruairi became known as the Lordship of the Isles. The first Lord of the Isles was John of Islay of Clan Donald, who died in 1387. The Lordship was in constant conflict with the Scottish kingdom and was brought to an end in 1493.

◀ *The Mull of Oa, Islay.*

→ *Arbroath Abbey was founded in 1178. Its abbot, Bernard de Linton, drafted the Declaration for Robert Bruce.*

1175
Treaty of Windsor. Rory O'Connor recognises
Henry II as overlord.

1210
Irish kings submit to King John of England.

The Pale and Beyond

The word 'pale' means fence or enclosure. In medieval Ireland it came to mean the area of the country that was directly controlled by the kings of England. It lay in the east of the country, around Dublin. Within the Pale, English language, laws, fashions, architecture and customs became normal. The Pale was settled not just by English royal officials, but by merchants and labourers too, from across the Irish Sea.

THE STATUTES OF KILKENNY

From the early days of English rule in Ireland, the official policy was one of separation and apartness. In 1366 the English, under Prince Lionel of Clarence, called a parliament at Kilkenny and passed a wide range of statutes (laws). According to these, English colonists were not allowed to marry into Irish families, or to adopt Irish dress or customs. They were not to speak Irish or use the ancient Irish legal system, known as Brehon Law.

THE ENGLISH PALE IN IRELAND

The area of the Pale varied greatly during the later Middle Ages. By 1464 it included the counties of Dublin, Kildare, Louth and Meath.

ULSTER

CONNAUGHT

Louth

Meath

THE PALE

IRISH SEA

Kildare

Dublin

Limerick

LEINSTER

MUNSTER

Waterford

Wexford

Cork

➡️ *The Breac Maedhóc is a bronze shrine from Drumlane, County Kavan. Its figures show the Gaels of Ireland in the 1100s. The men have long hair and beards and wear long cloaks. The women wear their hair in ringlets.*

THREE WORLDS, ONE LAND

Beyond the Pale, lay the lands of two other groups – the Irish-speaking Gaels and the powerful, independent Norman families who had seized Irish land. Over the years, many of the latter adopted Irish ways. The English kings, however, firmly believed that civilisation ended 'beyond the Pale'. This phrase is still sometimes used today to describe unacceptable or uncouth behaviour. From time to time the English attempted to expand their rule by founding colonies beyond the Pale. These were English settlements protected by soldiers.

➡️ *The Abbey of the Holy Cross at Thurles. Founded by Donald O'Brien, King of Thomond, in 1169, it was rebuilt by the wife of King John of England, Isabella of Angouléme, around 1233.*

➡ *These stone carved tombs represent two of Ireland's most powerful families at the close of the Middle Ages. They may be seen in St Canice's Cathedral, Kilkenny. They belong to Piers Butler, Earl of Ossory and Ormond, and his wife Lady Margaret Fitzgerald.*

BARLEY FOR THE TAKING

When Henry II of England landed in Ireland in 1171, his chief aim had been to make sure that 'Strongbow' and his adventurers did not set up a Norman kingdom in Ireland to rival his own. As the years went by, the English found another reason for staying in Ireland. The lush, green pastures and fields of ripe barley were a valuable economic resource. Grain from Irish estates could be exported to England or mainland Europe for rich rewards.

⬇ *The Rock of Cashel is crowned by splendid buildings from the Middle Ages. Cormac's Chapel dates from 1127–34, while the great cathedral was built about 100 years later.*

⬆ Kilcrea Friary, in County Cork, was founded by Cormac Laidir MacCarthaigh, Lord of Muskerry, in about 1465.

KERN AND GALLOGLASS

Ireland saw wave after wave of English invasion. John came in 1185 as prince and again in 1210 as king. Richard II arrived in 1394–1395 and again in 1399. There were long battles between the old Norman families and amongst the Irish kings. By recognising the English kings, some Irish royal families managed to survive and even thrive in this changing world. The poor peasants experienced endless warfare. All sides used roving bands of troops who would fight for anyone who paid and fed them. These mercenaries included Norman men-at-arms, Irish footsoldiers called kerns and Scottish adventurers called galloglass, meaning 'foreign (ie Scottish) Gaels'.

A Medieval Town

Towns were now beginning to grow quickly. They were noisy, rowdy places and often foul-smelling, too, for there was no proper drainage. Water had to be carried to each house from wells. Carts brought vegetables to market and cattle were herded though the muddy streets. Women tied wooden platforms called pattens to their shoes, to walk through the puddles. Travellers slept huddled together on straw mattresses, in flea-infested inns.

Timber houses
In the Middle Ages, most houses were still built with timber frames and walls of wattle-and-daub. Some of these may still be seen in Britain today.

➡ *In the early Middle Ages, towns were often little more than places of refuge, protected by the lord of the local castle. By the 1250s, many towns had purchased their independence and appointed mayors. They had become thriving centres of craft manufacture and trade.*

WALLS AND CHIMNEYS

Medieval cities were surrounded by walls and at night the gates were locked and barred. Tall wooden-framed houses were crowded together. House fires were common and straw thatch was often banned in favour of slates and tiles, which could not blaze.

All cooking fires had to be covered each night – the time of 'curfew' (from the Old French *cuevre-feu*). At first smoke came out through holes in the wall. It was not until the 1400s that chimney pots topped the roofs.

Shop signs
When most people couldn't read, shop signs had to be visual. A boot might hang above a cobbler's shop, or a horse-shoe above a smithy. A green bush was the sign of an inn. Many English public houses are still called The Bush.

Animals to market
Even large cities echoed to the sound of cattle, sheep and geese being driven through the streets to market.

Open sewers
Waste was thrown into the street and streams were used as open sewers. Birds and dogs scavenged rubbish tips.

MONEY AND MERCHANTS

Merchants became wealthy. In London there were great warehouses owned by the Hanseatic League, a powerful organisation that traded right across Germany to the Baltic Sea. Bankers lent money in return for payment of interest. Even kings borrowed from them to pay for their wars. When bankers became richer than kings, it was clear that the old feudal system was breaking down. Craft workers formed trading guilds that controlled the marketing of their wares. Young lads came to stay in the house of the master of their trade and learned how to be a weaver, a tailor or a goldsmith. They were called apprentices.

FOOTBALL HOOLIGANS

Apprentices were an unruly lot and often tried to avoid work. They formed gangs on the streets. One of their favourite sports was football. A blown-up pig's bladder served as a ball. There were no rules and the game was played on the street. It was very rough. In 1314 the sport was banned by King Edward II of England.

GROWING CITIES

Although nine out of ten English people still lived in the countryside during the Middle Ages, most lived within reach of a market town. Outside the capital city of London, cities such as Lincoln, York, Norwich and Bristol prospered and expanded. About 800 years ago new towns sprang up – Hull, Liverpool, Leeds, Portsmouth, Newcastle upon Tyne. Salisbury replaced the older settlement of Sarum.

⬅ *The wealth of merchants began to compete with that of the nobles and the Church.*

TROUBLED TIMES

The communities of medieval England were not just of Anglo-Saxon and Norman descent. Many 'Flemings' came from the Low Countries as a result of the trade in wool, and there were thriving Jewish communities. Roma, or Gypsies, a people of Indian origin, arrived towards the end of the Middle Ages. All incomers were subjected to sporadic outbreaks of racial violence, even murder. Edward I, a violent anti-Semite, expelled the Jews from England in 1290.

⬆ *Rich merchants began to build with stone. The Jew's House (above) in Lincoln is over 800 years old and has a hall on the first floor.*

OLD LONDON BRIDGE

The first versions of London Bridge were made of wood, and they really did keep falling down, just as it says in the old nursery rhyme. However a 19-arch stone bridge, built between 1176 and 1209, lasted until 1831. On this bridge there were rows of houses and even a chapel. Sometimes the bridge was used for jousting. Traitors' heads were often displayed on the bridge after they had been chopped off.

The Hard Life

On 14 April 1360 the weather was so foul and bitter that many horseback riders were reported to have died of cold, frozen to death in their saddles. There were few comforts in the Middle Ages. Castles were draughty and stank of sewage from the cesspit or the moat. People rarely bathed and disease was common. Many women never survived childbirth and children often died when young.

"OUR DAILY BREAD"

While the nobles ate fine wheaten bread, the poor ate crusts of coarse rye. Rye crops were sometimes spoiled by a fungus disease called ergot. People who ate flour made from mouldy rye became sick and saw strange visions. Country people preserved their own food, salting fish and smoking bacon. They ate eggs and caught hares and waterfowl. If the harvests failed and prices rose, then people starved.

Dairy produce

Rye bread

Hare

▲ Food supply was seasonal and depended on good harvests. Famine was common.

THE BLACK DEATH

In August 1348 a new disease appeared at the port of Weymouth, in the southwest of England. It was known as the Pestilence, later as the Black Death. This terrible plague, spread by rats and their fleas, had already devastated Central Asia and Europe. Soon it was raging across England, Wales, Scotland and Ireland. The Black Death took various forms. One poisoned the bloodstream and caused horrid swellings and boils on the body. Another affected the lungs and could be passed on by coughing and sneezing.

The sick were sometimes cared for by nuns. The Black Death killed many carers as well as the patients. Soon, plague victims were being buried in mass graves and there were no priests left to pray for their souls.

MEDIEVAL MEDICINE

Medical knowledge had grown little since the days of the Romans. Surgeons could mend bones and monks grew herbs to make medicines. Some of these cures worked, but many didn't. One common treatment was bleeding – taking blood from the patient.

Leprosy was an infectious disease. Lepers had to carry a wooden clapper, to warn people that they were coming along the road.

SINNERS AND LEPERS

Natural disasters and illnesses were often believed to be punishments sent by God, because of human sinfulness. One of the most feared diseases was leprosy, which causes lumps, discoloured patches and ulcers to form on the body. Fingers and toes would sometimes become numb and fall off. Sufferers (lepers) were banned from public places and were only allowed to watch church services through a slit in the wall.

THE FEAR OF DEATH

The worst plague years were 1348–49. However, the dreadful 'pestilence' returned in 1361, 1369 and 1390. No doctors understood the cause of the disease or how it was passed on. They blamed bad smells  or warm air rather than rats and fleas. Many people believed that the disease was God's punishment for sinful behaviour. Some predicted the end of the world. In many European countries people called 'flagellants' paraded through the streets carrying holy images and whipping themselves, in order to atone for their sins.

↑ *Many Europeans responded to the widespread deaths by becoming more religious. Flagellants (people who deliberately whipped themselves) marched through many towns.*

A LABOUR SHORTAGE

In the years 1347 to 1351, the plague may have killed 75 million people in Asia and Europe. Many villages in the British Isles lost half to two-thirds of their population. In some there were no survivors at all. There was a great shortage of labour, so workers now found that they could demand high wages. In 1349 and 1351 the English government passed harsh laws in a desperate bid to keep wages at the same level.

↑ *Edward III tried to address the the labour shortage by passing the Statute of Labourers law in 1351, which tried to fix peasants' wages at their pre-plague level. But eventually the labour force rebelled against opressive measure.*

THE PEASANTS' REVOLT

Taxes on all citizens, regardless of their income, were introduced after 1377. These 'poll taxes' made life wretched for the poor. In 1381, 20,000 peasants from Kent and Essex, led by Wat Tyler and a priest called John Ball, stormed London. They burned the palace of John of Gaunt, Duke of Lancaster. They killed the Archbishop, captured the Tower of London and freed the prisoners. The rising was savagely suppressed.

King Richard II, aged only 14, rode out to make peace. However the rebels were betrayed, attacked and killed.

1337
Edward III of England declares himself King of France.

1340
Naval battle off Sluys won by England.

The Hundred Years War

The period we know as the Hundred Years War was a long drawn out, bloody struggle between England and France. It took place across the muddy battlefields of northern France and Flanders (in what is now Belgium). It was never really one war, but a series of raids, battles, campaigns and treaties. Nor did it last 100 years, but from 1337 until 1453.

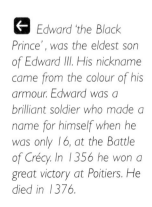

← *Edward 'the Black Prince', was the eldest son of Edward III. His nickname came from the colour of his armour. Edward was a brilliant soldier who made a name for himself when he was only 16, at the Battle of Crécy. In 1356 he won a great victory at Poitiers. He died in 1376.*

WHO RULES FRANCE?

King Edward III of England was related to the French royal family and in 1337 he claimed the throne of France as his own. England had fought for its lands in France ever since the days of the Normans and the Angevin empire. What was more, France was now a close ally of Scotland, England's enemy. The result was a war that cost Edward III's subjects dearly. They had to pay for it with taxes, loss of trade – and their lives.

In October 1415, Henry V found his route blocked by a huge French army (foreground) at the village of Agincourt. His 6000 troops were sick with dysentery and greatly outnumbered, but he won a great victory. The French knights became bogged down in mud, while flight after flight of arrows whistled through the air.

THE GAME OF CHESS

The English were not alone in their attacks on the French kings. At times they were allied with the Bretons of the northwest, at times with powerful barons from Burgundy, in the east. At first the English achieved some great victories. At Poitiers in 1356 the French king, Jean II ('the Good'), was captured. Three years later, the Treaty of Brétigny offered Edward III one-third of France if he gave up his claims to the throne.

WEAPONS AND TACTICS

For campaign after campaign, the English raided and plundered northern France. Long columns of battle-weary knights, waggons, footsoldiers and archers trailed across the countryside. Some carried new-fangled handguns, others hauled early cannon. When it came to pitched battles, England's great strength lay in its use of archers, armed with deadly longbows. They could fire up to 12 arrows a minute.

◀ The crossbow was more accurate than the longbow, but slower to reload.

THE TABLES ARE TURNED

Peace did not last. When Henry V came to the throne of England, he led his army back across the Channel and was victorious. In 1420 the Treaty of Troyes made him heir to the French throne – but within two years he was dead. French fortunes now began to turn. Their knights were inspired by a peasant girl called Joan of Arc. She claimed that voices of the saints had called her to free her homeland. The English accused her of witchcraft and burned her alive in 1431. However by 1453 France had regained most of the English-occupied lands.

French fortunes improved in 1429. Joan of Arc (or Jeanne d'Arc) rode out with the French army to break the siege of the city of Orleans, and succeeded in nine days.

"DEAR KATE"

In Shakespeare's play *Henry V*, she is called 'dear Kate'. 'Kate' was Catherine de Valois, daughter of Charles VI of France. In 1420 she married Henry V of England, at the height of his success, but her husband became sick while away at the wars and died in 1422. Nine years later, Catherine secretly married a handsome young Welsh courtier. His name was Owain Tudur or Tudor, and it was their grandson, Henry VII, who founded the most famous dynasty in English history.

◄ Catherine de Valois married Henry V at Troyes. She was crowned Queen of England and gave birth to a son, the future Henry VI, in 1421. Her eldest son by Owain Tudor was Edmund, Earl of Richmond, and he was father to Henry VII, the first Tudor monarch.

One of the major battles of the Hundred Years War was fought at Crécy in 1346. English soldiers defeated a much larger French army, killing almost half the French soldiers. During the battle, the English army used gunpowder and cannons for possibly the first time.

Deadly weapons called caltrops were used in the Hundred Years War. A caltrop was a star-shaped piece of metal. These were scattered along the ground in front of an attacking army. They stopped both horses and footsoldiers in their tracks.

The Welsh Rise Up

Wales was changing under English rule. Towns had already been developing in the days of the Welsh princes. Now, new shire or county towns controlled all local trade, and they prospered. In the Welsh heartlands, the new towns took the form of colonies, settled by incomers from England, France or Flanders. Welsh citizens were sometimes forcibly removed to other settlements.

⬆ Harlech Castle, completed by King Edward I of England in 1289, was besieged and captured by Owain Glyndŵr's rebels in the spring of 1404. It remained in Welsh hands until 1409.

POET OF LOVE AND NATURE

Dafydd ap Gwilym is believed by many to be the greatest writer in the Welsh language. He was born in the parish of Llanbadarn Fawr, near Aberystwyth, and wrote his masterpieces between 1320 and 1370. He broke with traditional Welsh verse forms and was influenced by French literature. Dafydd wrote light-hearted and joyful poems, many of them about his sweethearts, Morfudd and Dyddgu. He wrote about nature, too, describing the grace of a seagull's flight in a way that still seems very modern today.

▲ Love and life in 14th century Wales is described in the poems of Dafydd ap Gwilym.

TROUBLED TIMES

Many Welsh people protested against the taxes and laws brought in by the English. An uprising began in 1294, led by Madog ap Llywelyn, but it was put down in 1295. In 1317 there was a revolt in South Wales, led by Llywelyn Bren. Perhaps the greatest danger to English rule came from Owain Lawgoch, grandson of Llywelyn Fawr. He fought as a mercenary for the French, who called him Yvain de Galles. He planned to reconquer Wales with French help, but was murdered by a secret agent in 1378.

A SPARK CATCHES FIRE

In 1400, Lord Grey of Ruthin, a personal friend of the English king, Henry IV, siezed some land from his neighbour in the Marches of northeast Wales. Owain Glyndŵr was a middle-aged Welsh nobleman of royal descent. He appealed to the English parliament for justice, but they reacted with contempt, declaring the Welsh to be 'barefoot rascals'. A simple land dispute became a full-scale national uprising. Owain was supported by all ranks of Welsh society, including monks and bishops. Welsh labourers and students returned from England to join him.

➡ *Owain Glyndŵr had studied law in London and fought with the English army, but he now became leader of a Welsh uprising. He summoned Welsh parliaments at Machynlleth and Dolgellau.*

MASTERS OF THE LONGBOW

Welsh archers are said to have been the first to develop the longbow. Unlike the shorter Norman bow, it was the full height of a man. It was normally made of yew and had a pull of about 40 kilograms. Arrows were about 78 centimetres long, made of ash with long metal tips. Goose-feather flights made them spin as they flew through the air. They could even pierce armour. The English used companies of Welsh archers to devastating effect during the Hundred Years War with France.

THE LONG FIGHT

Owain Glyndŵr was acclaimed the true Prince of Wales and by 1401 most of his country had joined the uprising. Castles were captured from the English and towns were sacked. Owain planned to join forces with rebel English barons Henry Percy ('Hotspur') and Edmund Mortimer, but they were defeated at Shrewsbury in 1403. In 1404 Owain was at the height of his power, having taken Harlech, Aberystwyth and Cardiff. In that year he held a parliament at Machynlleth.

← *The longbow was a deadly weapon in the hands of Welsh archers.*

A FINAL MYSTERY

In 1405 the French sailed to the support of the Welsh, but were defeated. The war became a guerrilla campaign and resistance continued until 1413. Glyndŵr however had vanished. Had he gone into hiding? Was he already dead? Many Welsh people believed the myth that he was sleeping in the hills, and would return to lead them one day.

➡️ *Castles remained the focus of warfare in the 1400s. By 1408 the English were regaining control over Wales. The countryside lay ravaged by their armies and many castles were recaptured.*

1399
Henry IV, son of John of Gaunt, is first Lancastrian king.

1453
Henry VI suffers from mental illness.

Wars of the Roses

As battle-hardened soldiers returned from the French wars, many entered the service of powerful English lords. Their job was to bully peasants for payment of taxes, or to fight in private armies. There was no shortage of work for them. For 30 years, from 1455 until 1485, there were civil wars as rival branches of the royal family fought for the throne of England.

LANCASTER AND YORK

The Houses of Lancaster and York were both descended from Edward III. Their rivalry came to a head when a Lancastrian king, Henry VI, became too mentally ill to rule. In 1454, Richard, Duke of York, was appointed Protector. When Henry VI got better, Richard would not give up his new-found power, and went to war. Henry VI was defeated at St Albans in 1455, but then Richard was killed at Wakefield in 1460.

Lancaster

York

↑ *A red rose stood for the House of Lancaster. A white rose was the badge of the House of York. When Henry VII came to the throne, he combined both designs in a red-and-white 'Tudor rose'.*

ENGLISH KINGS		
House of Lancaster	**House of York**	**House of Tudor**
✤ Henry IV 1399–1413	✤ Edward IV 1461–1470 &	✤ Henry VII 1485–1509
✤ Henry V 1413–1422	1471–1483	
✤ Henry VI 1422–1461 &	✤ Edward V 1483	
1470–1471	✤ Richard III 1483–1485	

WARWICK 'THE KINGMAKER'

The most powerful man in England at this time was not the weak king, but Richard Neville, Earl of Warwick. It was he who had Richard's son proclaimed Edward IV in 1461, the first Yorkist king. Henry VI was imprisoned and exiled. Later, Warwick fell out with Edward and brought Henry VI back to the throne. No wonder he was remembered in history as the 'kingmaker'. Edward returned to seek revenge. Warwick was killed in battle and Henry was murdered in the Tower of London in 1471.

A NEW POWERFUL KING

Edward IV was a brave fighter, a clever army commander and a good politician. He became king in 1461. Edward liked food, drink and pretty women. He was also ruthless in his search for power and he gave orders for Henry VI to be murdered. When he suspected his brother of plotting against him, he ordered him to be drowned. Edward died in 1483.

➡ *Edward IV won his first battle in 1416 when he was 18. Nobles fighting with him against Henry VI agreed he should be the next king.*

Printing press

THE AGE OF PRINTING

In 1471 an Englishman called William Caxton travelled to the German city of Cologne. There he learned about a new technology that had been invented in China and developed in Germany and the Netherlands. It was called printing, and it would change the world. Caxton set up his own printing press at Westminster in 1476 and produced about 100 titles.

◀ *Famous books published by Caxton at Westminster include* Le Morte d'Arthur *and Geoffrey Chaucer's* Canterbury Tales.

THE MARCH TO BOSWORTH

Edward IV died in 1483. His heir, Edward V, was too young to rule for himself, so he and his young brother were left in the care of their uncle, Richard of Gloucester. They went to live in the Tower of London, but mysteriously, were never seen again. Gloucester was crowned Richard III in the same year, at the request of parliament. He did not rule for long. In 1485 the Earl of Richmond, a Lancastrian, landed in Wales. His name was Henry Tudor and he defeated and killed Richard III at the battle of Bosworth, near Leicester.

WHO MURDERED THE PRINCES?

Did Richard III murder the princes in the Tower? He had every reason to. Skeletons were found in the Tower in 1674 and buried in Westminster Abbey. However some historians believe that Richard III was not such a villain as he is often made out to be. Might Henry VII have been the true murderer?

Henry VII married Elizabeth of York and united the houses of Lancaster and York. The Wars of the Roses had ended.

Richard III was killed at the battle of Bosworth in 1485. This brought about the end of the Wars of the Roses.

A NEW DYNASTY BEGINS

Henry VII founded a new ruling family. Henry Tudor was the son of a Welsh lord, Edmund Tudor, and an English noblewoman, Lady Margaret Beaufort. He had a weak claim to be king but he brought peace to England, and an end to the Wars of the Roses. When he died in 1509, England was richer and calmer than it had been for hundreds of years.

palaces and players

1509–1714

ELSEWHERE IN EUROPE	ASIA	AFRICA
1512 Michelangelo completes painting of the Sistine Chapel, in Rome.	**1526** Babar defeats Delhi and founds the Moghul empire in northern India.	**1546** Songhai destroys the empire of Mali in West Africa.
1517 German monk Martin Luther starts the Protestant Reformation.	**1566** The Ottoman (Turkish) empire is at its greatest extent.	**1517** Egypt is conquered by the Turks and becomes part of the Ottoman empire.
1571 Naval Battle of Lepanto, Christian fleet led by Venice defeats the Turks.	**1581** The Russians begin their conquest of Siberia (northeast Asia).	**1575** Portuguese found Luanda and settle the coast of Angola.
1618 Religious strife in the Holy Roman Empire leads to the Thirty Years War.	**1587** Abbas I 'the Great' rules Persia, a golden age of arts and crafts.	**1578** Moroccans defeat Portuguese in North Africa.
1643 Louis XIV the 'Sun King' becomes ruler of France.	**1603** Tokugawa Ieyasu becomes Shogun, brings all Japan under his rule.	**1600** The Oyo state is at the height of its power in Nigeria.
1648 Spain recognises independence of the Netherlands, art and trade flourish.	**1619** The Dutch found colonial empire in the East Indies, based at Djakarta.	**1632** Emperor Fasilidas closes Ethiopia to foreigners.
1701 Frederick I becomes first King of Prussia, in east Germany.	**1644** Manchurian emperors now rule China: the Qing dynasty.	**1662** Portuguese defeat the kingdom of Kongo, southern Central Africa.
1703 Peter the Great, Tsar of Russia, builds new capital at St Petersburg.	**1707** The death of Emperor Aurangzeb, decline of Moghuls, power in India.	**1700** Rise of Ashanti power in Ghana, West Africa.

"New faiths, new nations and faraway lands..."

NORTH AMERICA

1510
First African slaves begin to arrive in North America.

1519
Spanish begin conquest of Aztec empire in Mexico.

1570
Northeast Native Americans form an alliance, the Iroquois Confederacy.

1607
English found a permanent settlement at Jamestown, Virginia.

1608
French colonists found a settlement at Québec, in Canada.

1625
Dutch settle New Amsterdam (later New York City).

1684
French explore the Mississippi region and claim Louisiana.

1692
Port Royal, Jamaica, a notorious pirate haven, is destroyed by an earthquake.

SOUTH AMERICA

1519
Portuguese Ferdinand Magellan explores the Strait named after him.

1532
The Spanish invade and defeat the Inca empire of Peru.

1536
The first Spanish settlement at Buenos Aires, Argentina.

1541
The Spanish found a settlement at Santiago, in Chile.

1545
Spanish develop silver mining in the Andes mountains.

1560
The Portuguese lay out sugarcane plantations in Brazil.

1620
Dutch West India Company settles Guyana, northern South America.

1667
Dutch colonists take Suriname, in northern South America.

OCEANIA

1519
Portuguese explorer Ferdinand Magellan enters the Pacific Ocean.

1526
Portuguese explorer Jorge de Menezes visits New Guinea.

1600
Decline of Easter Island culture due to over-population and warfare.

1600
Tu'i Kanokupolu dynasty comes to power in Hawaiian islands.

1606
Dutch explorer Willem Jansz sights Cape York Peninsula, Australia.

1616
Dutch crew under Dirck Hartog lands in Western Australia.

1642
Dutch explorer Abel Tasman reaches Tasmania and New Zealand.

1643
Tasman sails to the Pacific islands of Tonga and Fiji.

1509
Henry VIII marries Catherine of Aragon (Spain).

1512
Henry VIII claims French throne. War with France.

King Harry's Days

Young Henry VIII, crowned King of England in 1509, loved to fight tournaments in gleaming armour. In 1520 he met François I of France at the Field of the Cloth of Gold, near Calais. Both sides wore the most splendid clothes imaginable. Standards fluttered in front of luxurious tents. However although royal courts still dreamed of chivalry, the period we call the Middle Ages had already slipped away.

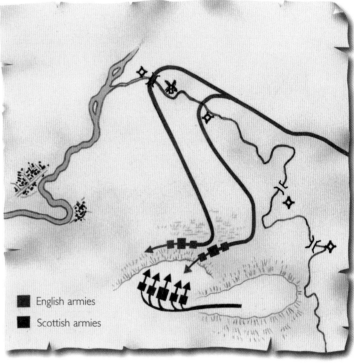

■ English armies
■ Scottish armies

FLODDEN FIELD 1513

In 1513, while Henry VIII was away fighting in France, the Scots invaded England. They were defeated at Flodden. Ten thousand were killed, including James IV, who was married to Henry's sister Margaret.

THE EARLY TUDORS

Henry VII had been a skilful ruler, who survived false claims to the throne and rebellions over his harsh taxation. His sickly eldest son, Arthur, died young. However his second son, who became Henry VIII, was strong and energetic.

In the new Europe, nations were constantly competing for power and trade. Henry was also a cunning statesman, as was his Lord Chancellor, a bullying, arrogant churchman called Thomas Wolsey.

1520
English-French meeting at Field of the Cloth of Gold.

1530
Wolsey falls from power over divorce crisis.

⬆ Henry VIII's personal life led to an historic break with the Church of Rome.

THE KING WITH SIX WIVES

The young Henry VIII cut a fine figure, but by the time of his death in 1547 he had become bloated, overweight and diseased. He married no fewer than six times. His marriages were marked by passion, political intrigue, jealousy, rage and selfishness. Henry's love for a beautiful courtier called Anne Boleyn led him to demand a divorce from Catherine of Aragon. The Pope refused and this led to a crisis that changed the direction of English history.

▲ Catherine of Aragon was the widow of Prince Arthur. Henry demanded a divorce.

▲ Henry married Anne Boleyn in 1533, but they quarrelled and she was executed in 1536.

▲ Henry married Jane Seymour the day after Anne was executed. She died in childbirth.

▲ The fourth marriage was for political reasons and Henry found Anne of Cleves too unattractive.

▲ After another divorce, Henry married Catherine Howard, but executed her too, for being unfaithful.

▲ Henry's sixth wife, Catherine Parr, was a wise queen, who survived Henry's death.

1536
Anne is executed. Henry VIII marries Jane Seymour.

1540
Henry VIII marries Anne of Cleves and Catherine Howard.

MONEY, LAND AND SHEEP

While Henry VIII spent lavishly on court life and on wars, ordinary people suffered extreme hardship. The Spanish were now mining gold and silver in the Americas, and this upset the economy of other European countries. Prices began to rise and rents with them. For many years common land that had always been used by the public for farming and grazing, was seized by greedy landlords. Many poor people were forced off the land, to become beggars and outlaws. In July 1549 Robert Kett, from Wymondham in Norfolk, led a rebellion against the enclosure of common land for sheep pasture. Kett attracted 16,000 supporters to his cause and they killed 20,000 sheep as a protest. They occupied the city of Norwich, but Kett was captured and hanged.

▲ *The Guildhall at Lavenham in Norfolk was built in 1529. Lavenham was the centre of the wool trade, and wool was the mainstay of the English economy.*

↑ *Henry VIII's royal court was a place of pleasure, but also one of political intrigue.*

DIVORCE AND REBELLION

When Henry VIII demanded something, he usually got it. Thomas Wolsey was unable to persuade Pope Clement VII to agree to Henry's divorce with Catherine of Aragon, so he was thrown out of office. In 1534 a law was passed making Henry VIII head of the Church in England, so that he could decide his own fate. The arrogance of the king and his officials led to many uprisings. In 1536–37 there was a major rebellion in Yorkshire and Lincolnshire, called the Pilgrimage of Grace.

A ROYAL NAVY

Henry VIII was the first king to realise that England, an island, needed a proper navy. He commissioned the building of 20 new ships, all specially designed for war, and employed full-time captains to command them. The most famous ship was the splendid *Mary Rose*, which sank in an accident after leaving harbour in Portsmouth in 1545, drowning most of the soldiers and sailors on board. An archaeological project started in 1979 recovered the ship's timbers as well as guns, bows, tools and navigational equipment.

RULERS OF ENGLAND	
House of Tudor (continued)	
✤ Henry VIII	1509–1547
✤ Edward VI	1547–1553
✤ Mary I	1553–1558
✤ Elizabeth I	1558–1603

⬇ The Mary Rose *was unstable and keeled over, allowing water to pour in through her open gun-ports (the holes through which cannon were fired).*

1517
Martin Luther starts Protestant movement in Germany.

1521
Henry VIII is made Defender of the Faith by the Pope.

Clashes of Faith

In 1521, Pope Leo X had honoured Henry VIII of England with the title 'Defender of the Faith', because of his support for the Roman Church. Within 13 years, however, Henry had broken with Rome and made himself head of the Church in England. This marked the start of centuries of religious conflict in the British Isles.

← The conflict between Henry VIII and the Roman Catholic Church eventually led to the seizure of Church properties by the state. These are the ruins of Glastonbury Abbey, in Somerset. The last abbot, Robert Whiting, was executed in 1539. Many people profited personally from the religious turmoil. It has been suggested that one of these was Whiting's steward, Thomas Horner, and that he is commemorated in the well-known nursery rhyme 'Little Jack Horner'.

1531
English priests recognise Henry VIII as head of the Church in England.

1534
Henry VIII breaks ties with the Church of Rome.

THE PROTESTANTS

New ideas were entering the British Isles from mainland Europe during the reign of Henry VIII. They came from people who were known as Protestants, because they were protesting against the Roman 'Catholic' (meaning 'universal') Church, its teachings and its customs. Leading Protestant campaigners included a German called Martin Luther and a Frenchman called John Calvin. Their demands for reform led to this period of European history being called the Reformation.

➡ The early Tudor period produced some beautiful church architecture. The roof of King's College Chapel, Cambridge, fans out into a delicate tracery of stone. It was completed in 1515.

THOMAS MORE'S UTOPIA

Sir Thomas More was appointed Lord Chancellor of England in 1529. He did not want the job, but he carried it out dutifully. Although More wished to see many changes in the Roman Church, he refused to accept Henry VIII as head of the English Church. More was beheaded for treason in 1535. In 1516 More wrote a book in Latin, which compared the social problems of his day with an imagined island where there was an ideal society. The name of the book was *Utopia* – from the Greek words for 'nowhere'.

◀ Thomas More's perfect land of Utopia was far removed from the realities of Henry VIII's England.

AN ENGLISH CHURCH

Henry VIII broke with Rome for political reasons, rather than because of his religious beliefs. He had little sympathy for the English supporters of Martin Luther and intended the English Church to follow basic Catholic teachings. During the reign of Henry's successor, Edward VI, the Church in England did adopt Protestant policies.

DISSOLUTION OF THE MONASTERIES

The year 1535 saw Henry VIII order the closing down of Roman Catholic abbeys, monasteries and convents across England, Wales and Ireland. This act became known as the Dissolution or Suppression of the Monasteries. The properties were mostly sold off to nobles who supported the king. This raised huge amounts of money for the state. The operation was organised by Thomas Cromwell, who became Henry VIII's chief minister and was made Earl of Essex. However by 1540 Cromwell too had fallen from royal favour, and his head was chopped off at the Tower of London.

▲ *Knox had a very strong character and was an influential campaigner. In an age of powerful queens, he claimed that it was against the will of God for women to be rulers.*

THE SCOTTISH REFORMER

John Knox was born at Haddington, Lothian, in about 1513. He became a Catholic priest in 1540, but soon fell under the influence of the Lutheran George Wishart. Wishart was burnt for his beliefs in 1547, and Knox became a Protestant minister. He spent some time in England in the service of Edward VI and then went to Switzerland, where he studied the teachings of John Calvin. Knox returned to Scotland in 1559. Despite the efforts of the Scottish Catholics, a Protestant Church of Scotland was recognised in 1560.

The Roman Catholic monasteries were stripped of their valuables and their precious libraries were often destroyed. The loss of the charitable services provided by monks and nuns led to hardship amongst the poor.

A Tudor Palace

In Tudor times, the River Thames was the lifeline of the growing city of London. Rowing boats called wherries carried passengers across to the south bank and sometimes a splendid royal barge could be seen, its oars dipping in the water. It would leave the royal landing stage by Whitehall Palace and beat upstream to the royal palaces at Richmond or Hampton Court, or downstream to the grand palace of Greenwich.

The Tudors moved from one palace to another during the year. Hampton Court was their favourite.

1526
German artist Hans Holbein makes portraits of the Tudor court.

1533
Anne Boleyn gives birth to Elizabeth at Greenwich palace.

The court of Henry VIII followed French fashions, with rich velvets, satins and brocades for both men and women.

LIVING IN LUXURY

Nobles no longer lived in draughty castles. They built fine country houses, often of brick, surrounded by beautiful gardens. These were laid out in complicated patterns, their gravel paths and sunny flower beds being hedged with lavender or box shrubs. The most impressive buildings of all were the royal palaces, built near the capital. They were decorated by the finest craftsmen in Europe. Hampton Court, in Surrey, was built by Thomas Wolsey. He offered it to Henry VIII as a present, when it looked as though he might be falling from favour.

OAK AND PLASTER

In Tudor country houses and palaces, there were wooden panels and great carved staircases. Furniture included cupboards and heavy chests of oak. Ceilings were often decorated with raised plaster patterns, which were sometimes picked out in bold colours. Rich tapestries on the walls might show scenes of hunting or woodland views. Fireplaces were enormous, leading to high, ornate chimney pots.

▶ Feather beds were enclosed by a carved four-poster frame, hung with heavy curtains.

A TUDOR PALACE   **211**

COURT AND CULTURE

In the 1500s there was a renewal of interest in learning, in the civilisations of ancient Greece and Rome, in painting and sculpture and in invention. This period, called the Renaissance or 'rebirth', began in Italy, but its influence was also felt in northern Europe. The Tudor rulers were well educated and intelligent. Artists such as the great German painter Hans Holbein the Younger came to the English court. Henry VIII and his courtiers loved music, dancing and playing royal or 'real' tennis, a version of the game that was played in an indoor court. They also loved to hunt deer in the royal parks and forests.

← *Dances at the royal courts in Tudor times included the pavane, a sequence of stately steps around the floor, and the galliard, an energetic dance that involved leaping.*

1540
The astronomical clock is installed at Hampton Court palace.

1572
A royal firework display is staged at Warwick Castle.

TIME, SUN AND EARTH

The ingenious clock at Hampton Court was made for Henry VIII by Nicholas Oursian, in 1540. It not only tells the time, but shows the month, the number of days since the year began, high tides, phases of the Moon and signs of the zodiac. It also shows the Sun moving around the Earth. A book by the Polish astronomer Nicolaus Copernicus, explaining that actually it is the Earth that moves around the Sun, was not published until 1543.

▶ *The clock at Hampton Court was installed before the discoveries of Galileo and Copernicus.*

MUSIC OF THE TUDORS

Henry VIII was a keen and knowledgable musician, both as a patron and a performer. Popular musical instruments at the time of the Tudors included recorders, flutes, lutes, harps, trumpets, trombones, bagpipes and drums. The virginal was a keyboard instrument, an early version of the harpsichord. As the Roman Catholic Church fell from power, more and more songs were composed in the English language instead of Latin.

 Henry VIII himself had studied music as a boy and later composed both religious music and popular songs.

1523
Poets gather at Caerwys for an *eisteddfod.*

1536
The first Act of Union. Wales is annexed by England.

Wales Under the Tudors

Wales during the reign of the Tudors was still mostly a land of farms and villages, of windmills and water wheels. Women spun and wove their own cloth. Few towns had more than 2000 inhabitants. There was little industry, although coal was already being mined in South Wales during the reign of Elizabeth I. Ships traded with Ireland, with other parts of Great Britain, France and Spain.

NO RIVALS FOR POWER

As a member of the Tudor family, Henry VII was of Welsh descent. However he and his successors reinforced the centralised power of the monarchy and ruled Wales harshly in order to suppress any ideas of another uprising. On the borders, the powers of the Marcher Lords were removed, and in South Wales even Rhys ap Gruffudd, whose grandfather Rhys ap Thomas had helped put Henry VII on the throne, was executed on trumped up charges of treason in 1531 by Henry VIII, who wanted his rich estates.

⬆ *On the modern flag of Wales, the white and green derive from the family colours of the Tudors, while the red dragon is a much older emblem of the Welsh. The use of the dragon had been revived by the future Henry VII, who featured it on his battle standard at Bosworth in in 1485.*

THE ACTS OF UNION

By the Acts of Union, passed in 1536 and 1542, Wales and the Marcher lordships were annexed, or taken over, by England. In doing this, Henry VIII took the first step towards creating a United Kingdom. Welsh law and Welsh customs were to be abolished. No Welsh person could hold public office unless they could speak English, a ruling that excluded 95 percent of the population. Otherwise, Welsh citizens did now have equal rights with English citizens before the law, and were represented in the English parliament.

⬇ *This fine map of Wales was published in 1573, during the reign of Elizabeth I. It was made by the cartographer Humphrey Llwyd who was born in Denbigh, North Wales, in about 1527. He was educated at Oxford University and died in 1568. The place names are shown in three languages – Latin, English and Welsh.*

⬆ *A stained glass window in the church at Penmynydd in North Wales recalls that this was the ancestral home of the Tudor family. The window is decorated with the Tudor rose emblem and symbols of royal power.*

WALES UNDER THE TUDORS   **215**

SCHOLARS AND BISHOPS

In 1571 Hugh Price, an expert in Church law from Brecon, founded Jesus College, in Oxford, England, for Welsh students. Over the ages it kept its special links with Wales. After 1588, students would have been able to read the Bible for the first time in the Welsh language. The brilliant translation was by William Morgan, who in 1595 became Bishop of Llandaff. Morgan's masterpiece helped to shape the Welsh language and keep it alive into modern times.

▲ William Morgan, born in 1545, was the first to translate the whole of the Bible into Welsh. He was a scholar who understood Latin, Greek and Hebrew. He died at St Asaph, North Wales, in 1604.

➡ One of the finest Tudor town houses in Britain survives at Plas Mawr, in Conwy, North Wales. It was built in 1577 for a wealthy local gentleman named Robert Wynn. Robert Wynn had fought for the Tudors at the Siege of Boulogne in 1544 and also in Scotland. He owned lands at Dolwyddelan and married into the powerful Griffith family of Penrhyn.

Servants' bedrooms
Servants slept in male and female dormitories in the attic.

The cellars
Barrels of ale and wine were stored in the basement. Robert Wynn was an importer of French wines into the port of Conwy.

1584
Roman Catholic campaigner Richard Gwyn is hanged.

1588
Translation of the Bible into Welsh by William Morgan.

Roofs and gables
The roof was supported by massive wooden beams and tiled with slate. The stepped design of the gable ends was copied from Flanders. Robert Wynn had travelled widely in Europe, in the service of a courtier named Sir Philip Hoby.

ELIZABETHAN WALES
In the second half of the 16th century, Wales was controlled by a few powerful families who found favour with the Tudors. Some were nobles at the royal court, others were lower in the social scale – squires, landowners and wealthy businessmen who built large country houses. A fair number of Welsh people formed a community in London, including merchants, lawyers, doctors, cattle drovers and servants. English became more widely spoken in Wales, but the attempt to eradicate the Welsh language by the Acts of Union failed. By 1563 Elizabeth I had signalled the intention that churches in Wales should have prayerbooks and Bibles in Welsh as well as in English.

The great chamber
The chief reception room had decorated plasterwork, showing Tudor roses and coats of arms.

Preparing food
On the ground floor was the kitchen, the pantry and the brewhouse.

WALES UNDER THE TUDORS   **217**

1547
Somerset becomes Protector as Edward VI is still a boy.

1549
First Book of Common Prayer is printed in English.

Protestant or Catholic?

Henry VIII died in 1547. Would England become Protestant or Roman Catholic? Living through the years that followed was like riding a see-saw, as rulers swung from the one faith to the other. There were fierce struggles between powerful nobles. Many common people suffered economic hardship.

THE BOY KING

Edward VI was just 10 when he came to the throne. The son of Henry VIII and Jane Seymour, he was raised as a strict Protestant. He was very clever and learned Greek, Latin and French. His uncle Edward Seymour, Duke of Somerset, governed as Lord Protector in his place. However Somerset was overthrown and executed in 1552, to be replaced by John Dudley, Duke of Northumberland. Edward VI died from tuberculosis in 1553.

Edward VI was a sickly boy who died young.

THE GRAMMAR SCHOOLS

Now that there were no more monks to teach, schools became more important. Many new schools were named after the Tudors, others after the rich merchants who funded them. It was mostly boys who received formal schooling. The school day lasted from six in the morning until five in the afternoon. Pupils learned to write using slates. They learned to read and did sums and were beaten if they made mistakes. A lot of the time was spent learning Latin grammar, so these were known as 'grammar schools'.

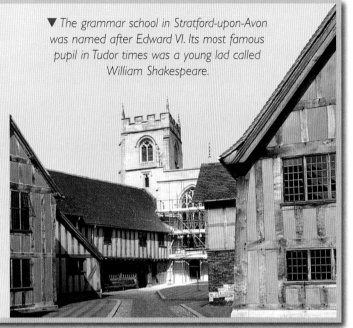

▼ The grammar school in Stratford-upon-Avon was named after Edward VI. Its most famous pupil in Tudor times was a young lad called William Shakespeare.

⬇ Jane was a quiet, intelligent girl, a Protestant and a great grand-daughter of Henry VII. Against her will, she became a pawn in a deadly game of power politics.

QUEEN FOR NINE DAYS

The Duke of Northumberland had persuaded the young king to make his daughter-in-law, Lady Jane Grey, heir to the throne of England. She was crowned queen in 1553, but within just nine days had been forced from the throne by the supporters of the rightful heir, Mary Tudor. Jane was imprisoned. After Sir Thomas Wyatt the Younger started a rebellion in her name, she was beheaded at the Tower of London in 1554, at the age of 16.

1553
Edward VI dies. Lady Jane Grey declared queen.

1553
Jane Grey is imprisoned. Mary I becomes queen.

 Protestant churchmen who went to their death in the years 1555–1556 included Hugh Latimer, Nicholas Ridley and Archbishop Thomas Cranmer.

BLOODY MARY

Mary Tudor was the daughter of Henry VIII and Catherine of Aragon. Her father had forced her to sign a document stating that his marriage to her mother had been illegal. Mary remained a very unhappy woman for most of her life. She was a Roman Catholic and in 1554 married King Philip II of Spain. He spent little more than a year in England and the marriage was very unpopular. Mary began to bring back the Catholic faith. During the last three years of her reign, 300 leading Protestants were burned alive. This earned her the nickname of 'Bloody Mary'.

PRINCESS ELIZABETH

Mary I had a young half-sister, the daughter of Henry VIII and Anne Boleyn. Princess Elizabeth loved learning as well as playing music, dancing and riding. She was raised as a Protestant and this aroused the suspicion of Mary, who imprisoned her for a time. Elizabeth had to tread very, very carefully. However when Mary died without a child, in 1558, it was Elizabeth who became the next Queen of England.

MARY AND PHILIP

Mary Tudor was determined to marry a Roman Catholic and to exclude her half-sister Elizabeth from the throne. After all, Elizabeth was the daughter of Anne Boleyn, who had replaced Mary's own mother as queen. Mary was advised to marry Prince Philip of Spain, who became king as Philip II. It was a bad decision. Although she found him attractive, he felt nothing for this older woman other than a certain admiration.

▲ *Mary I of England*

The English people wanted her to marry an Englishman, while the politicians feared that England would fall under the control of Spain. The couple had no children and Mary died in 1558.

◄ *Philip II of Spain and King Consort of England*

← *Princess Elizabeth's troubled childhood made her a wise and cautious ruler when she grew up.*

The Red Queen

Elizabeth, pale-skinned with flaming red hair, was crowned Queen of England in January 1559, dressed in heavy robes of gold and ermine fur. She was 25 years old. The new queen was warmly welcomed by the people, for they longed for an end to the religious strife and struggles for power.

STATESMEN AND SPIES

During the reign of Mary I, Elizabeth had learned how to survive in a world of plots and intrigue. As a queen, she possessed all the diplomatic and political skills that Mary had lacked. She surrounded herself with cunning statesmen such as William Cecil (who became Lord Burleigh) and set up a secret service under Sir Francis Walsingham. Elizabeth, like her father, enjoyed power and would let nobody stand in her way.

→ *Every ruler feared plots against them. Elizabeth I's trusted minister, Francis Walsingham, created Europe's first modern spy service. His well-educated agents worked to uncover traitors to the queen.*

THE VIRGIN QUEEN

Who would the new queen marry? The throne of England was a rich prize. Elizabeth kept everyone guessing, playing off one suitor against another in order to gain political advantage. In the end, she married no one. She said that she was already married – to the English people. Elizabeth I left no heir to the throne and so became known as the Virgin Queen. The newly formed North American colony of Virginia was named in her honour. The queen was probably reluctant to marry a foreign prince or king in view of the unpopularity of Mary I's marriage to Philip II of Spain. Even though Elizabeth I remained unwed, she openly favoured certain men at the royal court. These included Robert Dudley, Earl of Leicester, Christopher Hatton, and, until they quarrelled, Robert Devereux, Earl of Essex.

← *Large areas of land were set aside as royal parks and forests. The queen and her courtiers would attend stag hunts, breaking off to enjoy open-air picnics and entertainments.*

AT HOME AND ABROAD

The court moved around the country, making royal 'progresses'. Elizabeth's hosts had to spend a fortune on her entertainment and food. These journeys helped Elizabeth find out what was going on in her kingdom and made her aware of any local problems or needs. It also showed off her power and authority. Elizabeth I could speak Latin, French and Italian fluently, and she also knew ancient Greek and some Spanish. She spoke to foreign ambassadors directly – and often very forcibly – in protection of English trading interests.

GLORIANA

Elizabeth I ruled over a glittering court. It was like a continuous dramatic performance, in which all eyes were drawn to her. She is said to have owned over 1000 dresses. Courtiers competed for her approval and greatly feared falling from favour. Elizabeth I inspired a great poetical work by Edmund Spenser, called *The Faerie Queene*. Characters in the book, which was written between 1590 and 1596, were meant to represent virtues and vices. Elizabeth is called Gloriana, the ideal queen.

▼ *Elizabeth's signature was scrawled across the page in ink, with a quill pen. The R stands for regina, which is Latin for 'queen'. The loops are intended to prevent anyone else adding an extra message to the bottom of the document.*

1601
Last parliament summoned by Elizabeth I. Poor Laws, to support the poorest in society.

1603
Elizabeth I dies of pneumonia at Richmond Palace.

A PROTESTANT RULER

Elizabeth I steered England and Wales away from the Roman Catholic faith that had been restored by her sister. However this direction was not at all popular in Ireland. The English prayer book was restored by the Act of Uniformity in 1559. Elizabeth I was declared the Supreme Governor of the English Church, and public figures had to endorse this appointment under the Act of Supremacy passed in the same year. Elizabeth made her peace with France, but found a potentially dangerous enemy in Catholic Spain.

➡ *Elizabeth I was much-loved, and knew how to win public approval. However when she was crossed, she showed a fierce temper.*

1560s
Plays are acted in the yards of London inns.

1572
A law is passed classing actors as rogues and beggars.

Shakespeare's Genius

Let us imagine the scene as an Elizabethan drama gets under way, to a fanfare of tumpets. Elizabeth I loved the theatre, and she and her courtiers set up their own companies of players (actors). The first players had performed in the yards of inns and been generally regarded as rogues. Some private theatres were set up, but soon the first commercial theatres were also being built in London. These were rowdy, exciting places.

WELCOME TO THE GLOBE

An actor groans as he brandishes his sword, while cannonballs (rolled across wooden boards) make the sound of thunder. The actress is really a boy wearing a wig, for an actor's life is said to be too disreputable for a woman. In front of the stage, the audience is packed into an open-air yard, entrance fee one penny. They laugh, roar and shout out during the play. The better-off members of the audience watch from the covered galleries that ring the yard.

Several theatres were built in Elizabethan London, including the Swan, the Rose and the Hope. The most famous was the Globe theatre, built in 1599 on the south bank of the River Thames, in the Southwark area. It burned down during a performance in 1613, but reopened and was finally demolished in 1644.

Play in progress
A flag was flown to show if a play was about to begin.

Tiring house
This was where the actors changed their costumes and prepared for the show.

Galleries
Covered galleries ringed the yard. Plays were performed in daylight, normally during the afternoon.

▲ *The reconstructed Globe theatre, in modern London.*

THE GLOBE TODAY
The foundations of the original Globe theatre were discovered under the streets of London in 1989. A recreation was constructed, and 'Shakespeare's Globe Theatre' opened in 1997, very close to the original site beside the River Thames. The open-air, half-timbered, thatch-roofed building looks most unusual in the modern city, but it has proved to be more than just another tourist attraction. It has staged excellent plays, proving that the basic design of the Elizabethan theatre was just as effective four centuries later.

The pit
The area in front of the stage was called the pit or the yard. Here, the poorer members of the public packed in to watch the play. These 'groundlings' paid one penny for admission and munched on nuts and oranges during the performance.

c.1587
William Shakespeare arrives in London.

1593
Christopher Marlowe stabbed to death in a tavern brawl.

WILLIAM SHAKESPEARE

Out of the taverns, theatres and royal courts of the Elizabethan age came some of the finest plays ever written. The master playwright and most brilliant poet was William Shakespeare. Born at Stratford-upon-Avon, Warwickshire, in 1564, he came to London in about 1587. In 1594 he bought a shareholding in a new company of players called the 'Lord Chamberlain's Men', whose leading actor was Richard Burbage. Shakespeare wrote witty comedies and heartbreaking tragedies, many of them based on British history.

↑ *William Shakespeare lived until 1616. His great plays still speak directly to us today, wherever we live in the world.*

↓ *William Shakespeare was probably born in this house in Stratford-upon-Avon in 1564.*

1599
The Globe theatre is built by the Burbage brothers.

1616
William Shakespeare dies in Stratford-upon Avon.

William Shakespeare had a complete understanding of the theatre and was himself an experienced actor.

COMPANIES OF ACTORS

Actors formed theatrical companies, and the Globe theatre was home to the 'Lord Chamberlain's Men'. After 1603 they were renamed the 'King's Men'. The Globe's most famous shareholders were Richard Burbage and William Shakespeare.

POETRY, MUSIC AND ART

The late 1500s and early 1600s were a rich period for the arts in England. Several of Elizabeth I's courtiers, such as Sir Philip Sidney and Sir Walter Raleigh, were poets. The playwright Ben Jonson worked with Shakespeare in the 1590s and John Webster wrote the first of his tragedies, *The White Devil*, in 1612. The artist Nicholas Hilliard was making exquisite miniature paintings at the royal court, while Thomas Tallis and William Byrd were composing music for church and palace.

KIT MARLOWE

Christopher ('Kit') Marlowe was born in 1564, the son of a shoemaker. He went to King's School, Canterbury, and studied at Cambridge. He was very intelligent but also loved drinking and brawling. He was rumoured to be an atheist, someone who does not believe in God. Marlowe wrote poetry and several great plays, including *Tamburlaine, The Tragical History of Dr Faustus, The Jew of Malta* and *Edward II*. He may have worked as a secret agent and was killed in a fight in a tavern ('pub') in 1593.

◀ Christopher Marlowe led life to the full, but died in a drunken brawl.

Ireland Rebels

During the early Tudor period, the most powerful people in Ireland belonged to an old Norman family, the Fitzgeralds. As Earls of Kildare, Gerald Mór (1478–1513) and Gerald Óg (1513–1534) came to control most of the country. England was happy for the Fitzgeralds to look after the royal interests in Ireland – but only so long as they did not challenge English rule.

RELIGIOUS DIVISIONS

The political divisions of Ireland were further complicated when Henry VIII broke with the Roman Church. The Irish-speaking Gaels remained faithful to Rome. Of the rest, some remained loyal to the king, but could not accept him as head of the Church. Others accepted the new order, and did well for themselves, as they profited from wealth seized from the Church. In 1534 the Fitzgeralds declared themselves for the Pope. One of them – Thomas, Lord Offaly – rose up against Henry VIII but was defeated by an English army.

← *In the Gaelic west, long-haired mercenary soldiers, the 'kern', were armed with long swords and daggers. Their home villages were made up of simple thatched houses, often grouped around a fortified tower.*

1593
Hugh O'Neill leads rebellion in Ulster.

1607
Flight of the Earls. Irish nobles flee to mainland Europe.

THE PIRATE QUEEN

During the 1560s, shipping off the west coast of Ireland came under attack from a fleet of pirate ships. These were based in Clew Bay, where they could hide out amongst a maze of small islands. The fleet was commanded by an Irish noble woman called Gráinne ní Mháille, or Grace O'Malley. In 1593 she negotiated a pardon from Elizabeth I, in person.

◀ *Grace O'Malley's pirate galleys attacked English and Irish ships. In 1557 she repelled an English attack on her stronghold.*

REBELLION AND FLIGHT

The most serious Irish rebellion broke out in Ulster, in 1595. It was led by Hugh O'Neill, Earl of Tyrone. In 1598 he led a victory over the English at the battle of the Yellow Ford, but was himself defeated by 1601. By the Treaty of Mellifont, signed in 1603, vast areas of land were seized from the Irish. By 1607 the Irish nobles were in despair. Many cut their losses and fled to mainland Europe – the 'Flight of the Earls'.

UNWELCOME SETTLERS

Mary I may have been a Roman Catholic, but she supported an English policy of colonization or 'plantation' in Ireland. English settlers were 'planted' in Laois and Offaly, which were now to be known as Queen's County and King's County. Under Elizabeth I, Irish colonization became a religious drive, with Protestant nobles eager to grab land from the Catholic Irish. Elizabeth I 'planted' Ulster, in the north. Most early plantation attempts failed, but they started a process that proved to be disastrous for Ireland.

⬆ *In 1607 Hugh O'Neill fled to the Netherlands, which were at that time ruled by Spain. He died in Rome in 1616.*

IRELAND REBELS **231**

Stuart Scotland

The Stewart (later, Stuart) family ruled Scotland for nearly 340 years. Many of their early kings came to the throne in their childhood, and this allowed powerful Lowlands families, highland chieftains and Lords of the Isles to grasp power for themselves. There were court plots, royal murders and endless wars with the English. Scotland's closest links were with France, which kept to the 'auld alliance'.

⬇ *James IV and many leading Scottish nobles were killed by the English army at Branxton, near Flodden in Northumbria, in 1513. The battle was fought not only with pikes, swords and longbows, but also with cannon.*

1513
James IV killed by English at the battle of Flodden.

1538
James V marries Mary of Guise, a French Catholic.

THE STEWART COURT

The greatest of the Stewart kings was James IV, who became king in 1488. He married Margaret Tudor, sister of Henry VIII. His court attracted poets and musical composers such William Dunbar and Robert Carver. James IV built new palaces and a fleet of warships. Tragically, he was killed at the Battle of Flodden in 1513. He was the last Scottish king to speak the Gaelic language.

⬆ *King James IV was an energetic, wise and intelligent ruler. He was devoted to education and also licensed the first printing press in Scotland. However, his military strategy was flawed and his death at Flodden was a tragedy for Scotland.*

THE MASSACRE AT FLODDEN

When James IV marched into England with an army of 35,000 men, it was because Henry VIII of England was attacking France. James was duty bound under the terms of the Scottish-French alliance to support his ally. The battle of Flodden was disastrous for the Scots. It did not serve its purpose of diverting English troops from France, yet it killed the king and devastated the Scottish nobility.

STUART SCOTLAND   **233**

SCOTLAND UNDER JAMES V

James V, son of James IV, was born in 1512. He was still a baby when his father was killed at Flodden. His mother was Margaret Tudor. While James V was a child, Scotland was ruled by regents who were hungry for power. The young king finally won power in his own right in 1528. He brought Scotland under his control and strengthened the alliance with France.

➡ *James V of Scotland was asked by his uncle, Henry VIII of England, to follow him in breaking with the Roman Catholic Church James did not play Henry's game, and the two countries again went to war. The Scots were defeated at Solway Moss in 1542. James V was ill with a fever, and died two weeks later.*

MARY, QUEEN OF SCOTS

James V's widow, Mary of Guise, ruled as regent, for her daughter Mary was still a baby. A French Catholic, she soon clashed with the Protestants. The young queen was sent to the French court and raised as a Catholic. In 1558 she married the heir to the French throne, but her husband – and her mother – both died in 1560. Mary Stuart (as the family name was now spelt) returned to Scotland. In 1565 Mary married her cousin, Henry Darnley. It was a disastrous mistake.

➡ *Edinburgh's castle towers over the Scottish capital. Visitors can still see the rooms of Mary of Guise and Mary, Queen of Scots, as well as the room in which James VI was born.*

HOLYROODHOUSE

James IV and James V built a royal palace called Holyroodhouse in Edinburgh. It was here, in Queen Mary's apartments, that secretary David Rizzio was horribly murdered in 1566. His killers included William Ruthven and James Douglas, Earl of Morton.

▼ Holyroodhouse was built on the site of a medieval abbey founded by David I. The palace was repeatedly destroyed by the English. Much of it was rebuilt after the 1650s.

IMPRISONED IN ENGLAND

Darnley became involved in a plot to murder Mary's Italian secretary, and was then murdered himself. Mary then married the suspected murderer, the Earl of Bothwell. Mary was forced off the throne and imprisoned. Her baby son, James VI, became king. Mary escaped and fled to her cousin, Elizabeth I. In England, however, she was held prisoner for 19 years. Elizabeth feared that Catholics would plot to put Mary on the English throne.

➡ The life of Mary, Queen of Scots ended tragically. The English secret service uncovered a Catholic plot and claimed that Mary was involved. She was beheaded at Fotheringay Castle in February 1587.

The Spanish Armada

In May 1588 a massive invasion fleet or 'Armada' sailed from the port of Lisbon. It was made up of 130 ships fitted with 2500 guns. They carried 30,000 soldiers and sailors. The ships included large warships called galleons, armed merchant ships, galleys (which used oars as well as sails) and supply vessels. This great war fleet was bound for the English Channel.

WHY DID THE ARMADA SAIL?

Spain had become the richest and most powerful country in Europe. It was still ruled by King Philip II, former husband of Mary I of England. From 1580 he was also king of Portugal. The Netherlands too were under Spanish rule, as were vast, newly discovered regions of the Americas. When Dutch Protestants rose up against rule by Catholic Spain, English armies were sent to help them. And across the Atlantic Ocean, the English were fiercely competing with the Spanish to grab the riches of the Americas.

⬆ *When the English sea captain Francis Drake carried out illegal raids on Spanish shipping in the Americas, Elizabeth I ignored complaints from Spain. In 1587 Drake set fire to the Spanish port of Cadiz. The raid was described as 'singeing the King of Spain's beard'.*

DRAKE'S DRUM

This drum was beaten during the Armada crisis, when Sir Francis Drake called his crew to action on the deck of the *Revenge*.

1586
English and Dutch defeat Spanish at battle of Zutphen.

1587
Francis Drake raids Spanish port of Cadiz.

SEA DOGS FROM DEVON

Most of the great Elizabethan seafarers spoke English with strong west-country accents. Francis Drake, John Hawkyns, Humphrey Gilbert, Walter Raleigh and Richard Grenville were all from Devon, in the southwest of England. Francis Drake was a hero to the English and was knighted by Elizabeth I. To the Spanish, who called him *El Draco*, he was a common pirate.

The smaller, faster English ships defeated the mighty Spanish fleet, or Armada.

IN PLYMOUTH AND TILBURY

As the Armada approached Cornwall, naval squadrons were stationed along the Channel coast, under the command of Lord Howard of Effingham. Drake's ships lay in Plymouth harbour. An army of 20,000 men was drawn up at Tilbury, on the River Thames, as a Spanish army from the Netherlands was expected to invade the southeast. Elizabeth I rode out to speak to the troops and steady nerves.

SCATTERED BY STORMS

The English ships sailed out to meet the Armada. They had long-range guns and chased the big galleons as they wallowed in high seas, driven by westerly winds. Fighting off Portland Bill and the Isle of Wight was followed by an eight-hour sea battle off Gravelines. The Armada was badly damaged. It was now driven northwards and scattered by roaring gales.

BUILDING A FLEET

Elizabeth I's new navy was built at the royal dockyards in Chatham, Kent. The navy was still small, having only 34 ships – although merchant vessels could also be used in warfare. The old ships of the Middle Ages, which were really floating troop carriers, were replaced by new ships of oak. These were faster and less clumsy than the big Spanish galleons – sleeker and lower in the water.

▼ *The English sea captain John Hawkyns was responsible for the navy's new ship designs.*

1589
Francis Drake fails to capture port of Lisbon.

1591
Battle of Flores off the Azores. Richard Grenville is killed.

← The Spanish fleet was devastated by fireships – small boats that were packed with timber, pitch and explosives. It was then the victim of storms. Spanish ships were wrecked off Norway, blown around Scotland and driven ashore in Ireland. Only 70 battered ships returned to Spain.

1562
John Hawkyns ships slaves from Africa to the New World.

1576
Martin Frobisher seeks 'Northwest Passage' round Canada to Asia.

New Worlds

Curopean seafarers had begun to discover the world beyond their own shores in the 1400s, as they searched for new trading routes. Portugal and Spain led the way, exploring the coasts of Africa, Asia and the 'New World' of the Americas. English exploration began in the reign of Henry VII, who sent Italian-born navigator John Cabot to find a northwestern route to Asia. In 1497 Cabot sailed as far as Nova Scotia, Canada, and discovered rich fishing grounds off Newfoundland.

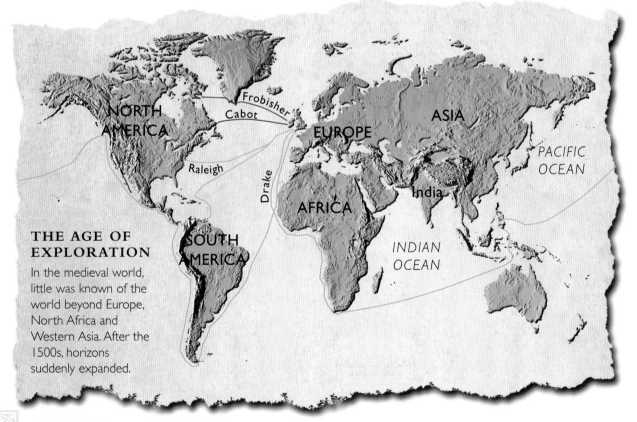

THE AGE OF EXPLORATION

In the medieval world, little was known of the world beyond Europe, North Africa and Western Asia. After the 1500s, horizons suddenly expanded.

⬆ *Drake's ship, the* Golden Hind, *became the first English vessel to sail round the world. In 1581 he was knighted on board the* Golden Hind *by Elizabeth I.*

EXPLORERS AND COMPANIES

Many more English seafarers sailed off into the unknown. Martin Frobisher reached Labrador, Canada, in 1577. Francis Drake completed his voyage around the world in 1580. In 1595 Walter Raleigh explored the coasts of Trinidad and sailed up the River Orinoco, in South America. Following the explorers, came the merchants. Companies were set up to control foreign trade. The British East India Company opened its first trading post in India at Surat in 1612.

ALL-AMERICAN CROPS

It is easy for us to forget that many of the foods we take for granted today were unknown in Europe before the 1500s and 1600s. New food plants from the Americas included maize, tomatoes, pineapples and potatoes. Spain was probably the first European country to grow potatoes. Legend has it that it was Sir Walter Raleigh who first introduced them into the British Isles, in 1585.

Potato   Pineapple   Tomato

COLONIES IN THE AMERICAS

The Spanish controlled most of Central and South America, but Britain did gain Caribbean islands such as St Kitts (1623), Barbados (1625) and Jamaica (1665), as well as the mainland territory now called Belize (1638). Scottish merchants tried to found a colony in Darién, Panama, in the 1690s, but it failed. Britain's most successful settlements were on the Atlantic coast of North America. The first of these was Jamestown, Virginia (1607). Plymouth Colony was founded in Massachussetts in 1620, by a group of religious exiles from England, known as the 'Pilgrims'.

⬆ *Sir Walter Raleigh was a favourite courtier of Elizabeth I. In 1585 he sent settlers to Roanoke Island, off North Carolina. Their colony failed, as did his first attempts to colonize Virginia.*

THE STORY OF POCAHONTAS

Matoaka, or Pocahontas, was born in 1595, the daughter of a native American chief called Powhatan. She became a Christian and married a Virginian settler called John Rolfe. In 1616 she went with him to England and was received at the royal court. Sadly, she died of smallpox in 1617, at Gravesend. Her ship had been preparing to sail down the River Thames for the return voyage to America.

▶ *Pocahontas kept the peace between her people and the settlers.*

THE SLAVE TRADE

The first Europeans came to Africa's Guinea Coast in search of ivory and gold dust, but they soon were dealing in another commodity – human misery. The first Englishman to trade in slaves was John Hawkyns, in 1562. Slave-traders took on board West African men, women and children, who had been captured and put in chains. The slaves were then shipped to the Caribbean and North American colonies and sold into a wretched life of toil on the plantations.

⬆ *West African slaves were packed below decks, like animals. Many of them perished during the sea voyage, and their bodies were thrown overboard.*

Treason and Gunpowder

In her old age Elizabeth I was still riding, dancing and hunting, but her face was drawn and haggard. She died of pneumonia, at Richmond palace, in 1603. The throne now passed to James VI of Scotland, the protestant son of Mary, Queen of Scots, and descendant of Margaret Tudor. He was crowned James I of England.

⬆ *This silver coin, minted in 1603–1604, was called a 'crown'. It shows James I on horseback and gives his name in Latin – Jacobus.*

AT THE COURT OF KING JAMES

The thrones of Scotland and England were now united, but in 1607 the English parliament rejected a full union of the two countries. James remained absent from Scotland for 14 years. He brought in harsh anti-Catholic laws, but they were never enough to satisfy the growing number of extreme protestants, or Puritans. People also resented the favours he gave his personal friends at court, such as Robert Carr, Earl of Somerset, and George Villiers, Duke of Buckingham.

⬅ *The first version of the Union Flag was flown from 1606 until 1801. It combined the English flag (a St George's cross, red on a white field) with the Scottish flag of St Andrew (a saltire or diagonal cross, white on a blue field).*

➡️ *King James failed in his bid to stop people smoking tobacco.*

ANTI-SMOKING CAMPAIGN

The Spanish were the first Europeans to bring back tobacco from the Americas. In 1586 Francis Drake and Ralph Lane (the first governor of Virginia) presented Walter Raleigh with tobacco and a pipe. Soon it became the fashion to puff on a long pipe made of clay – much to the disgust of King James, who campaigned against this new tobacco habit.

A WITCH HUNT

Laws against witchcraft were passed in 1563 and 1604. There was public hysteria about so-called pacts with the devil and many poor, innocent women were accused of being witches. They were thrown into ponds, tortured and hanged. In 1645 a lawyer called Matthew Hopkins turned 'witchfinder', prowling East Anglia in search of people he could send to the gallows.

▼ *Lancashire had major witch trials in 1612 and 1633.*

RULERS OF GREAT BRITAIN AND IRELAND

House of Stuart

✤ James I of England
(VI of Scotland)   1603–1625
✤ Charles I   1625–1649

Commonwealth and Protectorate

✤ Council of State   1649–1653
✤ Oliver Cromwell   1653–1658
✤ Richard Cromwell   1658–1659

House of Stuart

✤ Charles II   1660–1685
✤ James II of England
(VII of Scotland)   1685–1688
✤ William III of Orange 1689–1702
✤ Mary II   1689–1694
✤ Anne   1702–1714

THE GUNPOWDER PLOT

On the night of 4 November 1605, a search party was sent to Parliament buildings in London. A suspicious letter had been discovered. Was there a Catholic plot to blow up King James there, the following day? In the cellars, lantern light revealed barrels of gunpowder and one of the conspirators, Guy Fawkes. He was arrested, tortured and executed for treason along with seven others. His death is still celebrated each year on 5 November, with dummy 'guys' being burnt on bonfires. However some historians argue that the conspirators were set up – in order to discredit the Catholics.

 Guy (or Guido) Fawkes (centre) was just one of the people accused of the murder plot. The leader was said to be Robert Catesby.

1622
Inigo Jones builds the Banqueting Hall,
City of London.

1624
A submarine is tried out in the River Thames.

IN A COUNTRY COTTAGE

Life for working people in the
countryside had improved since the
Middle Ages. Even so, it was far from
easy. Most cottages now had some
furniture and some pots and pans.
Bedsteads had sheets of coarse hemp,
occasionally of linen. Fuel was hard
to come by, as woodland was fast
disappearing. Poor people often
burnt peat or bracken in the hearth,
for only the rich could afford coal.

➡️ *Parishes were supposed to help the poor, but times
were often hard and many families suffered. Many
country people moved to the rapidly growing towns.*

Cavaliers and Roundheads

On 22 August 1642, King Charles I raised his standard at Nottingham. His enemy was not a foreign power, but forces loyal to the parliament of his own country. This was a Civil War, which would rage across England, Wales, Scotland and Ireland, dividing communities and even families.

⬆ *Charles I reigned for 24 years. He married Princess Henrietta Maria of France and had six children. However his failure to come to terms with Parliament put the future of the monarchy at risk and cost him his life.*

Royalist musketeer

Soldier of Parliament's New Model Army

⬅ *Both sides in the Civil War fought with swords, muskets, pikes, and pistols. Soldiers wore long hair and broad-brimmed hats. Royalist commanders (often referred to as Cavaliers meaning 'knights') sometimes wore costly, elaborate clothes, whilst the Puritans amongst the Parliamentary troops preferred to dress plainly. A new highly disciplined force was founded by Parliament in 1644. It was called the New Model Army. With their cropped hair and helmets, these soldiers became known as Roundheads.*

1634
Charles I brings in a tax called ship money to fund the navy.

1637
Attempt to force Scots to use English form of worship.

COVENANTERS IN SCOTLAND

Charles I had little understanding of Scotland. The Scottish Church was Presbyterian – it was against having bishops. Charles I tried to force the Scots to follow English forms of worship. In 1638 the Scots drew up a petition, the National Covenant, rejecting his demands. Charles I went to war with the Covenanters in 1639 and 1640, but was forced to make peace. He had made enemies which, in the end, would cost him dearly.

CHANGING TIMES

King James I of England (VI of Scotland) died in 1625. His son, Charles I, came to the throne of a country that was going through many changes. The power of the extreme Protestants, or Puritans, was growing and they were suspicious of his marriage with a Roman Catholic. The middle and lower classes of society were beginning to have more economic power. The country squires and landowners who were members of the House of Commons were demanding more say in running the country. Charles I treated them with disdain.

ROADS AND COACHES

The roads tramped by Civil War armies were still muddy and potholed, but attempts were now being made to map them, improve them and carry out repairs. Road works were the responsibility of each parish. Major roads became the route for postal services, with riders called post boys blowing their horns as they galloped between towns and cities with their satchels of mail.

◀ The first stage coach service began in 1640.

1638
The Covenant is signed in Scotland.

1642
Charles I fails in bid to arrest 5 Members of Parliament.

A GROWING CRISIS

From 1629 to 1640, Charles I summoned no parliaments at all. He brought in unpopular taxes, which caused protests and unrest. In 1641 Parliament demanded that the king replace his ministers and bring in religious reforms. In 1642, Charles I forced his way into the House of Commons and attempted to arrest five Members of Parliament. He failed, and so went to war.

THE FIRST CIVIL WAR

The first battle took place at Edgehill in 1642. Both sides claimed to have won. In 1643 Parliament allied with the Scottish Covenanters and defeated the Royalists at Marston Moor in the following year. They were crushed again at Naseby, near Leicester, in 1645. In 1646, Charles I surrendered to the Scots.

1642
Start of the first phase of the Civil War.

1648
A second phase of Civil War. Charles I is seized by the army.

↓ *Weapons are brandished and horses whinny as a battle of the Civil War is re-enacted. The commander of the New Model Army was Oliver Cromwell. His well-drilled troops numbered about 22,000 and included large forces of cavalry and dragoons.*

THE SECOND CIVIL WAR

Charles I now tried to come to an agreement with the English Parliament, but failed. In 1647 he fled to the Isle of Wight. He made a secret deal with his former enemies in Scotland, promising them the reforms they desired. The Scots marched on England and there were Royalist risings in Wales, too. However all were defeated and by 1649 Charles was imprisoned.

Commonwealth

On 30 January 1649, Charles I was marched from St James's Palace to Whitehall. It was a bitterly cold day in London, with flurries of snow. At one o'clock the king stepped to the scaffold, or execution platform. When the axe had fallen, his head was shown to the ranks of soldiers and the crowd.

THE KING IS DEAD

It was reported that although Charles I had been an unpopular king, a groan passed through the London crowd when he died. Ever since the Middle Ages, people had believed that kings ruled by the will of God. Charles I himself believed in this 'divine right' of kings. He kept silent throughout his trial. News of the king's death spread like wildfire through the British Isles and mainland Europe. To many people, it was simply unbelievable.

➲ *Charles I died bravely, within sight of the Parliament he despised.*

A LORD PROTECTOR

The nation was now a republic, or 'Commonwealth'. Parliament ruled the land instead of a king or queen. It governed through a Council of State, made up of 40 members. However as far as the army was concerned, Parliament was much too cautious in its reforms. In 1653 power was handed over to one man, Oliver Cromwell, who was appointed Lord Protector. His rule was harsh but effective. He attempted to bring in military rule, and in 1556 he was even offered the crown.

⬆ Oliver Cromwell was a squire from the Huntingdon countryside. He made sure that no ruler could ever again afford to ignore the wishes of Parliament.

NO MORE FUN

▲ Playing cards were believed to be the work of the Devil.

Many of Cromwell's supporters were Puritans. The only joy that they could accept was through religious worship. Dancing and theatre were banned. Meat or ale could not be consumed on a Sunday, and even Christmas Day was no longer to be celebrated with plum puddings and merry-making.

THE QUAKERS

In 1646 a Puritan called George Fox preached a new kind of faith. He called upon his followers to 'quake at the word of the Lord'. They became known as 'Quakers', or the Society of Friends. The Friends worshipped God in silence, with no priests or prayers or churches. Many of them were imprisoned for their beliefs or forced to flee the country.

1651
Scots crown Charles II king, but are defeated at Worcester.

1653
Oliver Cromwell becomes Lord Protector.

WHAT KIND OF REVOLUTION?

The English revolution was controlled by landowners and wealthy merchants, but its footsoldiers were poor people, craftworkers, small farmers and tradesmen. Some of these formed a political movement called the Levellers. They demanded true democracy (rule by the people), but were quickly crushed by Cromwell in 1649. In 1650 an even more radical group was broken up. These True Levellers or 'Diggers' demanded equality for all and the common ownership of land.

TUMBLEDOWN DICK

Warfare did not come to an end with the Commonwealth. In 1651 Charles I's son was crowned Charles II in Scotland. The Scots marched south, but were defeated and Charles II fled abroad. From 1652–1654, Britain fought the Netherlands (now a free and increasingly wealthy nation) over trade. Oliver Cromwell died on a stormy night in 1658. His son Richard (known as 'Tumbledown Dick') was made Lord Protector, but had little taste for power. The revolution was over.

◄ *Oliver Cromwell, who became Lord Protector in 1653, raises a Bible as he makes a rousing speech to Parliament troops. Religion played a major role in the Civil War, with both sides believing that God would deliver victory to them.*

COMMONWEALTH   255

The Road to Drogheda

Thomas Wentworth, Earl of Strafford, was recalled from Ireland by Charles I to organise the wars against the Scottish Presbyterians. Following an English defeat, he was executed in London in 1641.

More and more lands belonging to Irish Catholics were seized and given over to Protestant English and Scottish settlers. This continuing policy of 'plantation' was supported by the Dublin parliament. In 1628 Charles I decided to allow Roman Catholic worship to continue alongside the Protestant Church, but this infuriated Ireland's Protestants.

THE IRISH ECONOMY

Thomas Wentworth was an arrogant man, who had little respect for he Irish people. However he was a capable administrator and built up the Irish economy. He set up new trading links with Spain, stamped out piracy around the Irish coast and developed the linen industry.

▶ Linen is made from the flax plant.

WENTWORTH AND ULSTER

In 1633 Charles I appointed a new man to govern Ireland. He was Thomas Wentworth, who later became Earl of Strafford. Wentworth's only aim was to increase royal power in Ireland. He managed to earn the hatred of Catholics and Protestants alike. He drew up plans for further plantation. As a result, violence broke out in Ulster in 1641 and soon spread far and wide. Perhaps 2000 Protestants were killed and many more were stripped and chased naked from their homes.

FROM WAR TO WAR

The tragic fate of the Protestant settlers in Ulster was used to whip up extreme anti-Catholic feelings in Britain. In 1642 an army of Scottish Covenanters arrived in Ulster to defend the Scottish Protestants who had settled there. A Catholic army was formed too by Owen Roe (Eoghan Ruagh) O'Neill. An alliance was made between Old English royalists and Irish Catholics, but there were bitter divisions.

The royalist alliance was called the Catholic Confederation. Its general assembly met in Kilkenny Castle (above).

A ROMAN LIFELINE

Irish Catholics were supported by the Church in Rome, which trained priests for work in Ireland. Political support also came from Roman Catholic countries in Europe. When Oliver Cromwell came to Ireland, he blamed Catholic priests for all the country's problems. Many of them were murdered by his troops.

▶ Luke Wadding was a monk who founded St Isidore's College in Rome in 1625. He worked tirelessly to keep the Roman Catholic faith alive in Ireland.

CROMWELL INVADES

Events were overtaken by the Civil War in Britain. Oliver Cromwell invaded Ireland in August 1649, with a battle-hardened army of Puritan troops. They hated all Roman Catholics and wanted revenge for the events of 1641. Cromwell besieged and sacked Drogheda, ordering the defenders to be slain with no mercy. Another massacre at Wexford also claimed many lives. Some have claimed that as many as a quarter of all Irish Catholics were killed during this savage campaign. Cromwell followed it up in 1652 by seizing Catholic lands and granting them to his soldiers and followers. Cromwell's campaign would be remembered with bitterness into modern times.

↑ The River Shannon became a new frontier after Oliver Cromwell's invasion. Irish Catholic landowners were told that they had until 1 May 1654 to resettle west of the Shannon.

← Oliver Cromwell sacked Drogheda in September 1649. Some of the defenders were burnt alive in a church he set on fire. Cromwell's official report called the massacre 'a righteous judgement of God upon these barbarous wretches'.

ROAD TO DROGHEDA   **259**

1660
The monarchy is restored. Charles II returns.

1661
The Church of England is established.

The Restoration

Great Britain and Ireland had a king again, Charles II. In 1660 Parliament had finally asked him to return from exile and be crowned. In return, Charles had to agree to recognise Parliament and the limits of his power. There was great rejoicing as he entered London on his 30th birthday. Oliver Cromwell's remains were seized from his tomb in Westminster Abbey and publicly hanged from the gallows at Tyburn.

THE WORLD OF POLITICS

During the reign of Charles II, the way in which the British political system was organised became rather more like the one in use today. From 1667–1673, Charles II began to consult with a group of ministers instead of just one. These were rather like the Cabinet in modern times. They were known as the 'Cabal', because of their initials (Clifford, Ashley, Buckingham, Arlington, Lauderdale). The world 'cabal' is still used to describe a small, powerful group of people. The first political parties were formed in the 1680s. They were known as Tories and Whigs.

◄ *Charles II is chiefly remembered as a pleasure-loving king, the 'merry monarch'. He married a Portuguese Catholic, Catherine of Braganza, but was never faithful to her.*

THE DIARY OF SAMUEL PEPYS

In January 1660, a Londoner called Samuel Pepys began to write a diary. It was written in a secret code. Pepys offers us a lively look at how people lived in the 1660s. He knew many famous people and was mixed up in all sorts intrigues at the court. He describes the news stories of his day, as when Dutch warships sailed up the River Thames.

◀ Nell Gwyn began her career as an orange-seller. She became a famous actress, much admired by Samuel Pepys, and was a lover of the king himself.

▼ Samuel Pepys wrote freely about his private life and everyday pastimes.

RELIGIOUS FREEDOM?

In 1662 the Church of England was recognised as the official Church. In the following year Charles II declared that both Catholics and Puritans would be free to worship in their own way. However, he was forced to end this offer in 1673, when Parliament ruled that Catholics could not hold public office.

⬇ During Stuart times, the climate was colder than today. Often, the River Thames froze solid. 'Frost Fairs' were held on the ice and people practised ice-skating – a sport recently brought in from the Netherlands.

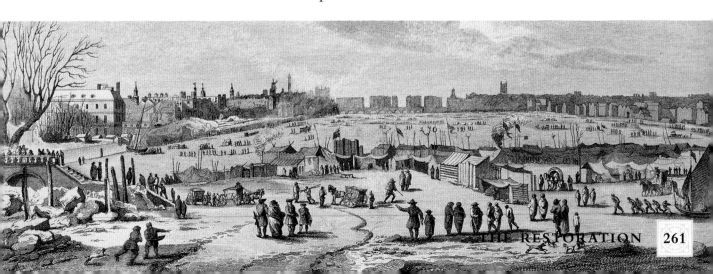

THE RESTORATION 261

1672
The Third Anglo-Dutch War (until 1674).

1678
John Bunyan writes first part of *Pilgrim's Progress*.

1678
A ' Popish Plot' is faked by Titus Oates.
Catholics executed.

1685
Charles II has a fit and dies, aged 55.

A MERRY DANCE

After the Restoration, the English begin to enjoy life again. Theatres re-opened in 1660. Female parts in plays were now taken by actresses, who became as popular as film stars would be 300 years later. Dancing was never more popular, from the royal court to the village maypole. Women wore make-up and fancy dresses. Fashionable men wore long, curled wigs. There were river trips, fireworks, processions and fairs. In the 1660s and 1670s it became fashionable to drink new beverages – coffee and tea.

THE PLOT THAT NEVER WAS

There was growing anti-Catholic hysteria in England. In 1678 an English spy called Titus Oates claimed that Catholics were plotting to kill the king. He had actually made the whole story up, but 35 Catholics were executed because of this 'Popish Plot'.

◄ *After the strict rules of the Puritans, people welcomed the more relaxed rule of Charles II.*

THE RESTORATION   **263**

Great Minds

The **1600s was an age of exploration and discovery.** The old ways were challenged and knocked down. This exciting new world was reflected in literature, the arts, in philosophy and especially in science. In 1660 the Royal Society of London was founded to encourage learning. Leading members included Robert Boyle, Samuel Pepys and Isaac Newton.

METAPHYSICAL POETS

In the 1600s many English poets broke away from the forms of poetry that had been popular in Elizabethan times. These 'metaphysical' poets included John Donne, George Herbert, Richard Crashaw and Andrew Marvell. They used unusual and sometimes complicated images, some of them taken from new discoveries in science and geography.

→ The English scientist Robert Hooke used the newly invented microscope to study the structure of plants and chemicals. His Micrographia was published in 1665.

← Paradise Lost, one of the greatest works of English literature, was published by the English poet John Milton in 1667. During the Civil War, Milton was a keen supporter of Parliament. He became blind in middle age.

GRAVITY AND LIGHT

Isaac Newton was born in Lincolnshire in 1642 and studied at Cambridge University. He was a brilliant mathematician and became one of the world's greatest scientists. Newton studied the nature of light and gravity. He improved the design of the reflecting telescope. He worked out the Laws of Motion and was elected president of the Royal Society in 1703.

➡ *In September 1665, an apple falling from a tree in a garden is said to have inspired Isaac Newton to think about gravity. Could the same process that pulled the apple downwards be applied to moons and planets? Newton worked out that gravity kept the Moon in orbit around the Earth.*

COURT MUSICIANS AND PAINTERS

In the 1630s the great Flemish painters Peter Paul Rubens and Anthony van Dyck came to the court of Charles I, as did the Dutch painter Peter Lely in the 1640s. The English musical composer Henry Purcell wrote the first English opera in 1689 and music for the coronations of James II of England (VII of Scotland).

THE PHILOSOPHERS

Thomas Hobbes (1588–1679) was a keen royalist. He wrote about politics and the human mind. John Locke (1632–1704) argued that governments ruled only with the agreement of the people. If they broke faith, they deserved to be overthrown.

BREAKTHROUGHS IN MEDICINE, ASTRONOMY...

The new science was based on careful observation and experiments. In 1628 an English doctor called William Harvey became the first person to describe how the heart pumps blood around the body through arteries and veins. An English mathematician called Edmond Halley became a great astronomer. The most famous comet is named after him, for in 1680 he accurately predicted that it would return to the Earth's skies every 76 years.

↑ *In 1654 the Irish scientist Robert Boyle came to Oxford University to study gases, vacuums and the burning process.*

↓ *William Harvey was doctor to Charles I. His theories on blood circulation were ridiculed by many scientists of his day.*

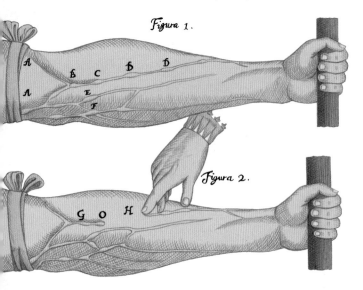

... AND CHEMISTRY

Robert Boyle (1627–1691) developed ideas and experiments that became the basis of modern chemistry. Boyle wrote *The Sceptical Chymist*, which introduced the idea of chemical elements and compounds for the first time, and insisted that ideas should be proven with chemical experiments. Boyle is also remembered for an important physics law – Boyle's law. This shows how the volume of a gas changes if the pressure is changed.

1680
Musical composer Henry Purcell's *Dido and Aeneas*.

1686–87
Isaac Newton's publishes *Principia Mathematica* (Mathematical Principles).

GREENWICH OBSERVATORY

In 1675 King Charles II founded a Royal Observatory at Greenwich, overlooking the River Thames. It was built by Christopher Wren and its first director was an astronomer from Derbyshire, called John Flamsteed. Its purpose was to observe the Sun, Moon, stars and planets, in order to help ships navigate across the oceans.

⬇ *Today, the Royal Greenwich Observatory is a museum. However its work continues at Herstmonceux, Sussex, and at Cambridge.*

Out of the Ashes

London, by now a city of about half a million people, was hot and stifling on 6 June 1665. That was the day on which an outbreak of plague was reported in the city. It caused little fuss at the time. Since the Black Death of the Middle Ages, the plague had returned time after time.

THE GREAT PLAGUE

This time, though, it was different. The bubonic plague, marked by foul swellings on the body, claimed 70,000 lives in just the first few months. As Londoners fled to the country, they brought the dreaded disease to villages and market towns. Survivors clutched bunches of sweet-smelling flowers to ward off the stench. The air itself seemed poisoned. An old nursery rhyme recalls plagues past: *Ring-a-ring o' roses, A pocket full of posies, Atishoo! Atishoo! We all fall down.*

↑ *Children today still sing the nursery rhyme 'Ring-a-ring o'roses'. The 'roses' refer to the bleeding spots of plague victims. The 'posies' of flowers were believed to ward off the disease. 'Falling down' refers to dying.*

← *The cobbled streets and alleys of London had changed little since medieval times. They still swarmed with rats and their deadly fleas. The plague was first brought to England by black rats that infested almost every ship.*

↑ *Crosses were painted on the doors of houses stricken by plague. Carts rumbled down the streets, collecting corpses.*

1669
Christopher Wren is appointed Surveyor-General.

1675
Work starts on the rebuilding of St Paul's Cathedral, London.

Many people took to the river to escape the heat and flames. After the fire, the old city with all its familiar landmarks was gone forever.

1677
The Monument is completed in memory of the Great Fire.

1710
The new St Paul's Cathedral is completed.

LONDON BURNS

After more than a year of plague, another disaster struck London. In the early hours of 2 September 1666, a fire started at a baker's in Pudding Lane. The flames were soon blazing over a wide area and continued to do so for five whole days, driven by the wind. Timber houses had to be blown up to stop the fire spreading. By the time it was over, the Great Fire had burnt down 13,200 houses, the old city gates, the Guildhall, 89 churches and the great cathedral of the City of London, St Paul's.

ASYLUM SEEKERS

The British Isles were not the only part of Europe to experience religious conflict in the 1500s and 1600s. In France there were wars between Roman Catholics and the Protestant followers of John Calvin, known as Huguenots. After 1598, Protestant rights were protected by the Edict of Nantes, but during the reign of Louis XIV many Huguenots were persecuted or forced to become Catholics. In 1685 the Edict of Nantes was cancelled, and 400,000 Huguenots fled the country. Many sought refuge in London. France's loss was England's gain, for many were skilled workers.

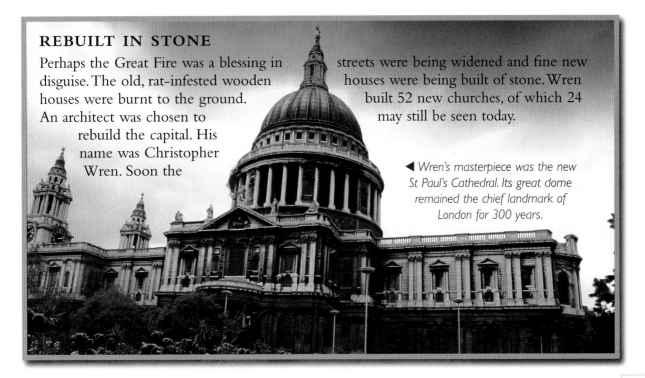

REBUILT IN STONE

Perhaps the Great Fire was a blessing in disguise. The old, rat-infested wooden houses were burnt to the ground. An architect was chosen to rebuild the capital. His name was Christopher Wren. Soon the streets were being widened and fine new houses were being built of stone. Wren built 52 new churches, of which 24 may still be seen today.

◀ *Wren's masterpiece was the new St Paul's Cathedral. Its great dome remained the chief landmark of London for 300 years.*

James, William and Mary

Charles II died in February 1685. He was followed as king by his brother, who became James VII of Scotland and II of England. James was a Roman Catholic and this dismayed the Protestants. Many belonged to the more radical political party, the Whigs. They had had enough of Stuart kings who showed little regard for the people's wishes.

← *Rebel fighters gathered at Sedgemore, Somerset, in support of Monmouth's rebellion. They were defeated by forces loyal to King James.*

LILLIBOLERO

The dramatic events of the Glorious Revolution of 1688 were played out to a popular political song of the day. It was called *Lillibolero*. The music was a march by Henry Purcell while the words, written by Thomas Wharton in 1686, mocked King James and the Catholics of Ireland. The song was sung as violent anti-Catholic mobs celebrated James's downfall in London.

BLOODY ASSIZES

In June 1685 the Protestant James, Duke of Monmouth, a son of Charles II born outside marriage, landed in Lyme Regis, in southern England. He claimed the throne, but was defeated in July at Sedgemoor and executed. His followers were dealt with savagely by a judge called George Jeffreys, in a series of trials called the Bloody Assizes. A death sentence was passed on 320 people and 840 more were sold into slavery. It was a bitter start to the reign.

THE GLORIOUS REVOLUTION

By 1688 leading politicans had decided on a drastic plan. They invited the Dutch ruler, William of Orange, to become king. He was a Protestant and married to Mary, the king's daughter. William landed at Torbay in Devon and gained rapid support. James fled to France and it was agreed that William III and Mary II would rule jointly. This change of power became known as the Glorious Revolution.

➡ *In 1688, Mary II and her husband William were called back to Britain from the Netherlands to become king and queen.*

REIGNING TOGETHER

Both Mary II and William III ruled together, as joint monarchs with equal rights. It was the only time this had happened in English or Scottish history. This reign confirmed that the state would be Protestant rather than Roman Catholic, and brought to an end the long years of strife between the kings and parliament. After the death of Mary, from smallpox in 1694, William ruled the country on his own.

At the battle of Boyne in 1690, the Protestant William III finally defeated the Catholic James II, an event still celebrated by the protestants of Northern Ireland.

ENGINEERS AND BUILDERS

Engineering works began to change the face of many parts of Britain in the 1600s and early 1700s. The wetlands of East Anglia were drained and channelled by experts from the Netherlands. Harbours were rebuilt and new lighthouses guarded rocky shores. Gates called turnpikes were set up along the highways to collect money from travellers for repairs and road-building.

▶ The first Eddystone lighthouse was built off Cornwall between 1695 and 1699, but was destroyed by severe autumn gales in 1703.

1689 May
Highland Scots rebel in support of James.

1690
Battle of the Boyne in Ireland. James is defeated.

SCOTLAND AND IRELAND

William and Mary did not enjoy an easy reign. The Highland Scots rose up in support of James. Their leader was John Graham of Claverhouse, Viscount Dundee, a persecutor of the Covenanters. They won the battle of Killiecrankie in May 1689, but Dundee was killed and the rising failed. James now landed with French troops in Ireland, trying to regain the throne. William too led an army into Ireland, reinforced with Ulster Protestants. They met at the battle of the Boyne in 1690 and James was defeated.

A BILL OF RIGHTS

The most important outcome of the Glorious Revolution was a Bill of Rights, passed in December 1689. This made it very clear that Parliament was now the chief governing body in the land, and that the power of kings and queens was strictly limited.

MASSACRE AT GLENCOE

At this bleak spot, Glencoe in Stratchclyde, 37 members of the MacDonald clan were massacred in 1692. William III demanded that all the clans in the Scottish Highlands swear an oath of loyalty. They obeyed, but MacIain MacDonoald of Glencoe signed late, due to a misunderstanding. Troops sealed off the ends of the glen, while others, billeted in MacDonald homes, carried out a brutal attack. They were commanded by Campbells, old enemies of the Macdonalds.

▼ *Glencoe in Stratchclyde*

1668
Henry Morgan leads buccaneer army on Spanish Main.

1671
Irish adventurer Thomas Blood tries to steal Crown Jewels.

A Rogues' Gallery

Gallows were a familiar sight to travellers through the British Isles in the 1600s and 1700s. The corpses of those who had been hanged were left to rot, swinging in the wind. Their eyes were pecked out by crows. Gallows often stood at crossroads, as a warning to highway robbers or sheep-stealers. They were erected at Tilbury docks, in London, too, as a grim reminder to would-be pirates as they sailed down the River Thames and out to sea.

➡ *One of the best ways to slow a ship was to fire at the sails and rigging.*

1684
Highwayman John Nevison hanged in York.

1695
Pirate Henry Avery captures flagship of the Moghul emperor.

SMUGGLERS ON THE COAST

People who lived in fishing villages around the coasts of the British Isles had always raided shipwrecks for cargoes and timber. About 300 years ago they found a new source of income – smuggling. In order to pay for foreign wars being fought at that time, the government greatly increased the taxes on imported goods. Smugglers would meet up with merchant ships out at sea and run untaxed cargoes ashore in small boats, hiding them in caves or cellars. The illegal brandy, tobacco or silk was often sold on to the local squire – or even to the parson – at a handsome profit.

↑ *This iron cage was used to display the bodies of executed pirates. It acted as a deterrent, warning people that this could happen to them too.*

1700s
Increase in taxes leads to smuggling around coasts of British Isles.

1701
Captain William Kidd hanged in London for piracy.

WOMEN PIRATES

Mary Read was an English girl who dressed herself up as a young man in order to join the English army. She married a Flemish soldier. When he died, she sailed off to the Caribbean, where she was captured by pirates. She joined forces with them, only to find an Irish woman, Anne Bonny, was already serving in the crew. The two fought fiercely under the command of Captain 'Calico' Jack Rackham, sailing out of the Bahamas. In 1720 Rackham and his crew were captured and hanged in Jamaica. The women were expecting babies and so they escaped the gallows, but Mary Read soon died anyway, of a fever.

ON THE HIGH SEAS

Piracy increased between the 1630s and the 1720s. As European nations grabbed land and plunder around the world, independent adventurers, escaped slaves, mutineers and murderers were washed up on foreign shores. At first, the British were happy to leave the Caribbean pirates alone – as long as they attacked the their enemies' ships. In 1668 a Welsh adventurer called Henry Morgan was commissioned to lead a buccaneer army against the Spanish. He ended up as deputy governor of a British colony, Jamaica. Bristol-born Edward Teach, the dreaded 'Blackbeard', had the governor of another British colony, North Carolina, in his pay. Once pirates began to prey upon British trade, many were hunted down and executed. Blackbeard was shot and beheaded in 1718.

← *Black Bart Roberts was a Welsh pirate. He raided West Africa's Guinea coast in 1719.*

1719
Howell Davis and Bart Roberts raid West African coast.

1729
Dick Turpin takes up highway robbery.

▲ While Anne Bonny and Mary Read fought for their lives, Calico Jack hid below decks.

⬆ Stage coach guards carried heavy firearms called blunderbusses to protect their passengers.

⬇ Highwaymen lurked in woods and on lonely heaths such as Hounslow, to the west of London.

GENTLEMEN OF THE ROAD

Highwaymen held up stage coaches and robbed the travellers. A former soldier called John Nevison (known as 'Swift Nicks') only robbed the rich. He was sent to the gallows in York in 1684. The most famous highway robber of all was Dick Turpin, also hanged in York in 1739. He was a burglar, murderer, smuggler and horse-thief. The public loved to watch hangings and read the popular ballads written about the dreadful crimes that had been committed.

1701
Act of Settlement decides the royal succession.

1702
William III falls from horse and dies. Anne becomes queen.

Queen Anne

Queen Anne came to the throne in 1702, after William III died in a fall from his horse. She was a Protestant, the daughter of James VII of Scotland (II of England) and the sister of Mary II. It was during her reign, in 1707, that the Scottish and English parliaments united. Great Britain, for the first time, was a single political unit rather than a union of kingdoms.

Queen Anne married Prince George of Denmark in 1683, but all their 17 children died, mostly in infancy.

LAST OF THE STUARTS

Anne was the last Stuart monarch. In 1701 she had agreed that on her death, the throne would pass to the royal house of Hanover, in Germany. Anne was easily influenced by her circle of friends. Her closest companion was Sarah, wife of a brilliant soldier called John Churchill. Anne made him Duke of Marlborough in 1702. After 1710 Anne quarrelled with the Churchills and fell under the spell of Sarah's cousin, Abigail Masham.

WAR OF SPANISH SUCCESSION

In 1701 a wrangle broke out between the great powers of Europe. Who would inherit the throne of Spain? On one side was Louis XIV's France, the south German kingdom of Bavaria and Spain. On the other was the Grand Alliance – Britain, Austria, the Netherlands, Denmark and Portugal. The Duke of Marlborough commanded the Dutch and English armies and won spectacular victories at Blenheim in Bavaria, and Ramillies and Oudenaarde in what is now Belgium. Peace was made at the treaties of Utrecht (1713) and Rastatt (1714). The war was a success for Britain and its allies and signalled the decline of Spain as a great power. Britain gained from Spain the territory of Gibraltar, the great rock that guards the entrance to the Mediterranean Sea. It was a small patch of land, but one of great strategic importance as a naval base.

⬇ *British troops commanded by John Churchill, the first Duke of Marlborough, took part in the struggles between European powers in the 1700s. Casualties were very high on all sides.*

⬇ Blenheim Palace was named after the Duke of Marlborough's most famous victory. It was largely paid for by public funds, as a reward for the Duke's military successes in Europe. It was decorated by the finest craftsmen of the day, such as the woodcarver Grinling Gibbons, and it was surrounded by lakes and gardens. It was here that Winston Churchill, a descendant of the first duke, was born in 1874.

WHIGS AND TORIES

In the days of Queen Anne, society was rigidly divided between the two political parties of the day. The Whigs were supporters of the Bill of Rights and of the Hanoverian succession. Many of them were merchants and business men with radical Protestant views. The Tories were conservative and royalist, and included many churchmen. Queen Anne disliked the Whigs and was determined to use all her personal powers to control British politics.

'QUEEN ANNE' FURNITURE

Furniture made by craftsmen in the reign of Queen Anne is still much admired today. It is simpler than the furniture of the Restoration period, and is much more practical. It includes bureaus, card-tables, chests of drawers, mirrors and dressing tables. The most popular wood was English walnut.

◄ The finest pieces of the period are chairs that are comfortable and solid. By the end of Anne's reign, more ornamental styles were coming back into fashion.

BAROQUE PALACES

A new European style of architecture became fashionable in Britain during the reign of Queen Anne. The 'baroque' style was exuberant and ornamental, packed with artistic detail and designed to impress. There were grand staircases and ornate mirrors. Two of the finest examples are palaces. Castle Howard, to the north of York, was built from 1699 to 1712 for the Earl of Carlisle. Blenheim Palace, in Oxfordshire, was built between 1705 and 1722 for the Duke of Marlborough. Both were designed by the architect Sir John Vanburgh, who was also a playwright, a theatre manager, a soldier, and a political activist who supported the Whigs.

A World Power

1714–1901

THE WORLD AT A GLANCE

ELSEWHERE IN EUROPE

1720
Russia defeats Sweden in the Great Northern War, gains Estonia.

1740
Frederick II becomes King of Prussia, Maria Theresa becomes Empress of Austria.

1789
Outbreak of the French Revolution in Paris. King Louis XVI is executed in 1793.

1804
Napoleon Bonaparte is crowned Emperor of France. Draws up new code of laws.

1815
The Congress of Vienna redraws the map of Europe. Poland is united with Russia.

1821
Greeks rise against Turkish rule. Greece is recognised as independent in 1832.

1871
Germany unites as a single empire under the rule of Wilhelm I, King of Prussia.

1871
Rome becomes capital of a united Italy for the first time since the Roman empire.

ASIA

1739
Persia (Iran) invades India and captures the city of Delhi.

1750
The French gain control of southern India.

1819
British empire-builder Stamford Raffles founds modern port at Singapore.

1858
Rule of India passes from the East India Company to the British government.

1867
The Meiji Restoration: Japan modernises under the rule of Emperor Mutsuhito.

1883
One of the world's worst ever volcanic eruptions destroys island of Krakatoa.

1891
Work begins on the Trans-Siberian Railway (from Moscow to the Pacific).

1900
Defeat of nationalists ('Boxers') rebelling against foreign influence in China.

AFRICA

1720
Sultan of Zanzibar takes control of the East African coast.

1730
Revival of the Bornu empire, south of the Sahara Desert.

1806
Britain gains control of Cape Colony, South Africa, from the Dutch.

1818
Shaka founds the Zulu kingdom in South Africa.

1822
Liberia is founded in West Africa, as a colony for liberated slaves.

1869
Suez Canal opens, European powers have growing influence in Egypt.

1896
Emperor Menelik II of Ethiopia defeats an Italian army at Adowa.

1899
Boer War begins between British and Afrikaners in South Africa.

"A British empire is founded on cotton, coal and toil…"

NORTH AMERICA

1718
French found the port of New Orleans, Louisiana.

1759
Britain defeats France to capture the Canadian city of Quebec.

1776
American colonists declare their independence from Britain.

1823
Mexico becomes an independent republic.

1838
Slavery ended in Jamaica and other British Caribbean colonies.

1861
Civil war in the United States (until 1865, abolition of slavery).

1867
Canada becomes a self-governing Dominion within British empire.

1876
Native Americans defeat US Cavalry at the Battle of Little Bighorn.

SOUTH AMERICA

1763
Rio de Janeiro becomes capital of Spanish Brazil.

1780
Uprising of indigenous peoples in Peru under Tupac Amaru II.

1816
Argentina declares its independence from Spain.

1818
Chile becomes independent from Spain, under Bernardo O'Higgins.

1819
New Granada (Colombia, Venezuela, Ecuador) independent under Simon Bolívar.

1822
Brazil proclaims its independence from Spain under Pedro I.

1826
Peru gains its independence from Spain.

1888
Slavery is finally abolished in Brazil.

OCEANIA

1768
British navigator James Cook visits Tahiti, New Zealand and Australia (to 1771).

1788
British convicts and settlers arrive at Botany Bay, southeast Australia.

1840
Treaty of Waitangi: Maori chiefs cede New Zealand to British.

1843
First Maori War, start of many conflicts with the British colonists (into the 1860s).

1850
Self-government granted to Britain's Australian colonies (New Zealand 1856).

1851
A Gold Rush begins in Australia.

1884
Northeastern New Guinea taken over by Germany. Britain claims the southeast.

1901
Australian colonies unite within a federal Commonwealth.

1714
Start of rule by the House of Hanover.

1739
Trade dispute with Spain, the War of Jenkins's Ear.

The House of Hanover

George I, ruler of Hanover in Germany, came to the throne as a distant descendant of James VI of Scotland (I of England). He was 54 years old, a dull and uninspiring man. His kept his divorced wife, Sophia Dorothea, imprisoned in a German castle from 1694 until her death in 1726. George I cared little for life in Britain and never learned to speak English.

↑ *This medal was made in memory of the coronation of George I, the first Hanoverian ruler of Britain, in October 1714.*

THE NEW DYNASTY

George I was unpopular, but he was supported by the Whigs simply because he offered the best chance of stopping a return to Stuart rule. In return, he supported the Whigs against the Tories. His son came to the throne in 1727. In 1743 George II became the last British king ever to lead his troops onto the field of battle – at Dettingen, in Bavaria, against a French army. Under his rule, the British began to build up a large overseas empire.

→ *George II's reign saw war and rebellion, bitter quarrels within the royal family, and the growing power of politicians.*

RULERS OF GREAT BRITAIN AND IRELAND
House of Hanover

* George I Elector
  of Hanover   1714–1727
* George II   1727–1760
* George III   1760–1820
* George IV   1820–1830
* William IV   1830–1837
* Victoria   1837–1901

A MAN OF MUSIC

George Friedrich Händel was from Saxony, in Germany. In 1710 he was appointed court musician to the Elector of Hanover, but irritated his employer by spending more and more time in London. When that ruler was crowned King George I in England, Händel made his peace by composing his *Water Music*, for a royal procession on the River Thames. Händel wrote 46 operas, but his best-loved piece of music was *The Messiah*, first performed in Dublin in 1742. He died and was buried in Westminster Abbey in 1759.

▲ Händel liked to write music for public festivities. His Music for the Royal Fireworks *was first performed in Green Park, London, on 27 April 1749.*

1752
Public protests when the calendar is revised by removing 11 days.

1756
Seven Years War: European powers fight over their empires.

THE MADNESS OF GEORGE III

George III, grandson of George II, came to the throne in 1760 and ruled for 60 years. He was an energetic but obstinate ruler, often clashing with the politicians of his day. His reign saw Britain lose its colonies in North America. In 1810 George became mentally ill, probably as a result of a body disorder called porphyria.

← *George III, whose long reign saw rebellions in America and Ireland, and a war in France.*

THE EAR THAT STARTED A WAR

The great powers of Europe were almost continuously at war in a pattern of shifting alliances. Wars were caused by disputes over trade and territory and rival claims to thrones. In 1739, a British sea captain claimed that his ear had been cut off by Spanish customs officials, so Britain went to war with Spain in the 'War of Jenkins's Ear'. This was followed by the War of the Austrian Succession (1740–48) in which Britain supported Austria against France. That was followed in turn by the Seven Years War (1756–63), in which Britain was allied with the growing military power of Prussia against France. This war spread far beyond Europe to North America and India. As European colonies were established around the globe, warfare increasingly took on a global dimension.

FROM ORCHARD TO PALACE

In 1762, George III bought a large residence near St James's Park, in London. It was called Buckingham House, because it had originally been built for the Duke of Buckingham, a friend of Queen Anne's, in 1703. A century before that, the land had been used as a mulberry garden by King James I. George III gave the house to his wife, Charlotte, and it became known as Queen's House. It played an important part in the life of the royal family, and was much enlarged over the years. The building took on its modern appearance in the 1820s and in 1837 it became the official chief residence of the British monarch. Since then it has been known to the public as Buckingham Palace.

HOW PEOPLE DRESSED

The fashions of the 1700s were similar to those of the 1600s, only rather more practical. The long, full wigs worn by important men (giving them the nickname 'bigwigs') were replaced by smaller wigs. Women wore gowns based upon the latest Paris fashions. The first fashion plates appeared in *The Lady's Magazine* in the 1770s. Children's clothes were scaled-down versions of adult clothes, with the boys in knee breeches and the girls in full-skirted dresses.

⬆ *Men wore a coat and waistcoat, breeches, stockings and buckled shoes. Wigs were still worn, but it became the fashion to tie them at the neck. Hats were three-cornered and made of felt.*

➡ *Women wore dresses with full skirts, often made of cotton or silk. Court dresses were stretched out over wooden hoops and decorated with frills. Women too now wore high, powdered white wigs.*

1708
The Old Pretender lands in Scotland, but rising fails.

1715
The Old Pretender joins Jacobite rising, which again fails.

Bonnie Prince Charlie

Support for the exiled **Stuarts did not suddenly disappear.** People who wished them to return to rule Britain and Ireland were called Jacobites (from Jacobus, the Latin for 'James'). They presented a serious threat to the House of Hanover, for they had supporters all over the British Isles. However their most loyal supporters were to be found in the Highlands of Scotland.

 James Francis Edward Stuart (1688–1766) was raised in exile in France. His refusal to give up the Roman Catholic faith barred him from the throne, and he failed to raise enough popular support to win it back by force during campaigns in 1708 and 1715. He died in Rome.

THE OLD PRETENDER

Someone who claims to be king or queen is called a 'pretender' to the throne. James Francis Edward Stuart became known as the Old Pretender. A Roman Catholic, he was the son of James VII/II and had been taken away to France as a baby. He landed in Scotland in 1708, but the French fleet sent in his support was defeated. In 1715 the Earl of Mar launched a Jacobite rising and James landed once more at Peterhead.

THE '15 RISING FAILS

The rising, known as the '15, came to grief at Preston and Sherrifmuir. James fled to exile in Rome and his followers were executed. The Jacobite cause had many supporters in Catholic Europe, and in 1719 Spanish troops invaded Scotland, but were defeated at Glenshiel. The Old Pretender married a Polish princess, Clementina Sobieski, and died in 1766.

> ### THE OUTLAW ROB ROY
> Robert MacGregor, known as Rob 'Roy' (meaning the 'red-headed') was born at Buchanan in Stirlingshire in 1671. He raised a private army that supported the Jacobites. In 1712 his lands were seized by the Duke of Montrose and he became an outlaw. A raider and rustler, he became famous for his daring exploits and his help for the poor and needy. He died in 1734.

BONNIE PRINCE CHARLIE

The Young Pretender was James's son, Charles Edward Stuart. He landed at Eriskay in the Hebrides in 1745 and raised his father's standard at Glenfinnan. The '45 rising very nearly succeeded. 'Bonnie Prince Charlie' won a victory at Prestonpans, captured Carlisle and reached Derby. London was in a state of panic, and Jacobites were planning to rise in Wales. Then, Charles's support began to falter and he turned back to Scotland.

← *The rebellion of Bonnie Prince Charlie (1720–1788) was more successful than that of his father, but it was doomed once the Jacobite sympathisers in England and Wales failed to rally to his cause.*

1744
Charles Edward Stuart plans invasion.
French fleet is scattered.

1745 July
Charles raises battle standard in Glenfinnan.

LIFE OF EXILE

Flora Macdonald disguised Bonnie Prince Charlie as her maid and spirited him out out of Scotland. A ship carried him from the island of Benbecula into a life of exile.

1745
Battle of Prestonpans: Jacobite victory.

1746
Battle of Culloden. Jacobites defeated by Duke of Cumberland.

CULLODEN AND AFTER

In 1746 Charles won another battle at Falkirk, but his Jacobites soon received a crushing defeat on Culloden moor, Inverness, at the hands of William, Duke of Cumberland – 'the Butcher'. In England a flower was named 'sweet william' in honour of Cumberland, but Scottish Jacobites called it 'stinking billy'. Highland clansmen were ruthlessly hunted down. The carrying of weapons, even the wearing of the kilt and the playing of bagpipes were banned. Scotland's future now lay in the growing towns of Lowlands, where manufacturers and merchants were becoming wealthy.

◄ Burns died in 1796, but his birthday is still honoured around the world each 25 January.

AULD LANG SYNE

Scotland's greatest poet was born in 1759 in Alloway, near Ayr. Robert Burns created simple, bold verse in the language of the Lowlands Scots. He wrote about country life, nature and love. His most popular poems include *A Red, Red Rose*; *Scots, Wha Hae*; *John Anderson, my Jo*; *Tam O'Shanter* and *Auld Lang Syne*.

← *Jacobite forces at Culloden included massed ranks of clansmen from the Scottish Highlands. They were gunned down and bayoneted without mercy. Charles became a fugitive with a price in his head.*

Money and Politics

The gap between rich and poor people in the British Isles was growing ever wider. London society in the 1730s and 40s is shown up in the paintings and engravings of William Hogarth. Poor families brawl, desperate young mothers drink cheap gin on the street until they fall into a stupor. Adventurers are on the make, climbing their way up the all too corrupt social scale, only to fall back down and end their days in a debtors' prison.

⬇ *Dealers in shares, or stockjobbers, drove up the trading price far beyond the real value.*

THE SOUTH SEA BUBBLE

Trading shares in the hope of making a profit is called speculation. It is a form of gambling, and can lead to reward or ruin. Britain's first great financial crash happened in 1720. Shares in the South Sea Company, founded in 1711 to trade with South America, rose to a ridiculous value, driven up by feverish speculation and crooked government dealings. When this South Sea 'bubble' burst, thousands of people were ruined. Many committed suicide.

BANKS AND MONEY

Paper bank notes were first issued in Britain in 1695. There was a growing view of wealth as an abstract idea, of deals made on paper rather than as chests full of gold coins. New companies, many of them founded in order to make money in distant colonies overseas, issued shares. At first these were bought and sold in coffee shops. A Stock Exchange was founded in the City of London in 1773.

1773
Founding of the London Stock Exchange.

1776
Adam Smith argues that government should not interfere in trade.

PRIME MINISTERS AT NO 10

Because George I spoke no English and was often away in Hanover, government affairs began to be dealt with by his chief ('prime') minister, who chose a working committee of ministers (the 'cabinet'). From 1721 the first – unofficial – Prime Minister was a formidable Whig politician, Sir Robert Walpole. The use of Number 10 Downing Street as the London residence of British Prime Ministers dates back to 1731.

➡️ *Robert Walpole entered politics in the reign of Queen Anne and was made Chancellor of the Exchequer by George I, in 1715. He died in 1745.*

⬆️ *The few men who were allowed to vote did so in public. There was opportunity for bullying and corruption. Drunken crowds, in the pay of one party or another, often rioted at election time.*

PRIME MINISTERS OF GREAT BRITAIN

✤ Sir Robert Walpole (Whig)	1721–1742
✤ Earl of Wilmington (Whig)	1742–1743
✤ Henry Pelham (Whig)	1743–1754
✤ Duke of Newcastle (Whig)	1754–1756
✤ Duke of Devonshire (Whig)	1756–1757
✤ Duke of Newcastle (Whig)	1757–1762
✤ Earl of Bute (Tory)	1762–1763
✤ George Grenville (Whig)	1763–1765
✤ Marquess of Rockingham (Whig)	1782
✤ Earl of Shelburne (Whig)	1782–1783
✤ Duke of Portland (coalition)	1783
✤ William Pitt the Younger (Tory)	1783–1801

THE GREAT DEBATERS

Powerful debaters could be heard in the House of Commons. William Pitt the Elder entered politics in 1735, part of a group within the Whigs who were opposed to Walpole. He was a great supporter of Britain's overseas wars. His popular son, William Pitt the Younger, served over 17 years as Prime Minister. His great opponent was Charles Fox, who became a Member of Parliament at the age of just 19.

Faraway Lands

By the 1740s, Europe's most powerful countries were warring with each other around the world. The stakes were extremely high – rich trade and new lands. The first overseas colonies were often founded by commercial companies, which had their own armies and fleets of ships. Local people were powerless in the face of heavily armed European troops.

Ramrod
Each new charge had to be rammed down the muzzle. The iron ramrod could be fitted under the barrel.

Long barrel
The great length of the musket's barrel was meant to help it fire straight, but it was not very efficient. Later gun barrels were 'rifled', having spiral grooves that made the bullet spin.

Bayonet
A long dagger could be fitted to the barrel for hand-to-hand fighting.

'BROWN BESS'

To fire a musket, the cock first had to be set at the safety position. The metal pan was opened, filled with a small amount of gunpowder and closed. The main charge of gunpowder and a ball were then rammed down the muzzle. When the trigger was pressed, it released a hammer containing a flint. This struck against the raised pan cover, dropping sparks into the gunpowder. When this ignited, the shot was fired.

The flintlock
The flintlock mechanism was slow to use and unreliable. Gunpowder had to be kept dry.

◄ *British troops carried a type of flintlock musket known as 'Brown Bess'.*

THE EAST INDIA COMPANY

As India's mighty Moghul empire fell into decline in the 1740s and 50s, the British East India Company seized land from local rulers. It ended up controlling much of the country, fighting its French rivals every step of the way. British success was largely due to a brilliant general called Robert Clive. By fair means or foul, Company officials became hugely rich. When they returned to Britain, they found themselves not only envied but mocked for their new-found wealth. They were nicknamed 'nabobs' (from the Hindi word *nawab*, 'governor').

In 1757 the British defeated the 43,000-strong army of Siraj-ud-Dawlah at Plassey, to the north of Calcutta. Clive's victory brought the whole of Bengal under British control.

1763
Treaty of Paris. Britain gains Canada and
Caribbean islands.

1768
James Cook explores the Pacific Ocean (to 1771).

ACROSS THE ATLANTIC

In Canada, the story was similar. The French had a colony
on the St Lawrence River, while the British Hudson's
Bay Company controlled land to the north. In 1759
British troops captured Quebec. By the Treaty of
Paris, which ended the Seven Years War in 1763,
Britain gained Canada and also some of France's
Caribbean islands – Tobago, St Vincent, Grenada
and Dominica.

AUSTRALIA AND THE PACIFIC

In 1761, a naval captain called James
Cook sailed to explore the Pacific
Ocean. He mapped the coast of New
Zealand and landed in Australia,
claiming New South Wales for
Britain. On later voyages, Cook
explored the coasts of Antarctica and
discovered many Pacific islands. He
also sailed along the North America's
west coast as far as the Bering Strait.
He was killed in Hawaii in 1779.

FROM AFRICA TO ENGLAND

In about 1760, a 10 year-old Nigerian boy
called Olaudah Equiano was kidnapped from
his West African home and sold to slave
traders. He was transported to the Caribbean,
but ended up buying his freedom from his
master. He became a sailor and took ship to
London, where he campaigned against slavery
until his death in 1797. He wrote about his
experiences in a book published in 1789.

1770
James Cook claims New South Wales, Australia for Britain.

1789
Crew of *HMS Bounty* mutiny on Pacific voyage.

⬇ *James Cook was a Yorkshireman, the son of a farm worker. He captained British ships to the far ends of the Earth. A brilliant navigator, he was well-liked by his crews.*

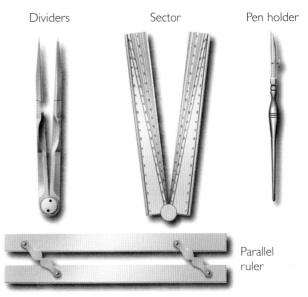

Dividers   Sector   Pen holder

Parallel ruler

⬆ *Precise measuring instruments and advances in the making of chronometers (accurate time-keepers) improved seafarers' ability to navigate and draw up charts.*

DISTANT DISCOVERIES

Explorers such as Captain James Cook (1728–1779) opened up the world to the Europeans. Navigators charted unknown coasts and discovered new lands. They made geographical, botanical and other scientific discoveries that brought about a new understanding of the world. However the explorers were followed by settlers and colonisers and soldiers. The peoples who already lived in these lands now often suffered from war, exploitation and the destruction of their traditional ways of life. This happened across North and South America, Africa, Asia, Australia, New Zealand and the Pacific.

1732
Colony of Georgia is founded, named after George II.

1763
Treaty of Paris gives Britain territory west to the Mississippi.

The Loss of America

By 1763, Britain had gained control of North America from the Atlantic shore to the Mississippi River. Their lands were divided into 13 colonies. The colonists were independently minded. Many of them were descended from people who had come to America to escape injustice – Puritans, Quakers, political rebels. They resented the British government's strict controls on shipping and trade across the Atlantic Ocean. They were furious when the British demanded that they pay for the wars against the French – through taxation.

→ This statue commemorates Paul Revere, a famous American rebel against British rule. He kept a secret watch on British troop movements and on the night of 18 April 1775 he made a ride from Boston to Lexington and Lincoln, to warn the people that the regular troops were on their way. The colonies were now at war with their masters.

← Native American warriors were used by the British in their colonial wars with the French.

→ A colonist militia, the Green Mountain Boys were formed in Vermont as early as 1770.

← In 1776 Britain recruited about 29,000 Hessian troops (German mercenaries) to fight for them in North America.

↑ *In 1773, colonists disguised themselves as Native Americans and boarded British ships anchored in Boston harbour. They threw the cargoes of tea into the sea. This protest against taxation was jokingly called the 'Boston Tea Party'.*

THE RIGHTS OF MAN

Thomas Paine was an English political thinker. He went to live in Philadelphia in 1774 and became a keen supporter of American independence. In England in 1791, he started to write *The Rights of Man*, supporting the French Revolution and calling for an end to monarchy in Britain. Accused of treason, Paine fled to France. His last years were spent in America, but his refusal to believe in God made him few friends in his old age.

TAXES – BUT NO VOTES

Britain first attempted to tax its American colonies in 1765. A costly tax was placed on all legal documents. This was soon withdrawn, but it was replaced by other taxes. Customs duties had to be paid on European goods. The colonists declared that it was unfair for them to pay taxes to a government in which they were not represented. Britain responded by sending in troops and in 1770 they massacred protestors in Boston.

AN AMERICAN REVOLUTION

The American War of Independence broke out in April 1775 when George Washington defeated the British at Lexington. In 1776 the American colonists declared their independence from Britain. One of them, a Scot called John Paul Jones, sailed across the Atlantic to attack British shipping. In 1778 both France and the Netherlands joined the American side against Britain. The fighting continued until 1781, when the British surrendered at Yorktown, in Virginia. Britain had lost its richest prize.

BATTLES IN THE AMERICAN WAR OF INDEPENDENCE

- Bunker Hill *British victory*   1775
- Lexington *American victory*   1775
- Saratoga Springs *American victory* 1777
- Brandywine Creek *British victory* 1777
- Yorktown *American victory*   1781

The 'Redcoats' fought the rebel colonists for six long years. Britain's defeat led to the creation of a new federal republic, the United States of America.

1728
First performance of *The Beggars' Opera* by John Gay.

1732
Vauxhall pleasure gardens are developed and improved.

Town and Country

In the 1700s, a new kind of story became popular with **English readers.** It was called the **novel.** Famous novelists included Daniel Defoe and Henry Fielding. Some novels told tales of the rich and the poor, of adventures in foreign lands or of young men who came from the country to seek their fortune in the city. Witty plays were popular, too. Those by the Irish writer Richard Brinsley Sheridan mocked the world of high fashion.

← → *The architecture of the Hanoverian period is known as 'Georgian', being named after the dynasty's four King Georges. Georgian buildings in red brick or stone are noted for their beautiful proportions and symmetry, whether town houses (left) or elegant mansions (right). Fine examples still stand throughout Britain and Ireland, notably in the cities of London, Bath and Dublin.*

TASTE AND FASHION

Lords and ladies liked to put their wealth and good taste on display. Inside their houses were cabinets in the Chinese-style by Thomas Chippendale or elegant chairs designed by George Hepplewhite. On the walls, paintings by Joshua Reynolds or Thomas Gainsborough flattered the beauty of the lady of the house or showed off the family's estates. Outside, formal gardens were now being replaced by more natural looking landscapes, often planned by the great gardener Lancelot 'Capability' Brown.

↑ *Pleasure gardens were laid out at Vauxhall on the south bank of the River Thames. Fashionable Londoners would parade and dance by the light of lanterns, or listen to music.*

1753
The British Museum is started in London.

1768
Joshua Reynolds is the Royal Academy's first president.

COUNTRY SQUIRES

In country districts, the most important person was the squire, who lived in the manor house. He would keep a watchful eye on the parson and the teacher, on land improvement and law and order. Many squires enjoyed shooting or fox-hunting with horse and hounds. A few had enquiring minds, following politics or reading the latest work of scientists, geographers and the French and English philosophers. In Wales, squires took over from the old nobility as patrons of poets and musicians.

⬇ *Along stage coach routes, inns provided stables for horses as well as accommodation. A coach journey from London to Holyhead, the seaport for Ireland, took about 48 hours. Mail was carried by horseback riders called Post Boys until 1785, when coaches began to carry mail as well as passengers.*

1779
School for Scandal, a play by Richard Brinsley Sheridan.

1780
The 'Derby' horse race is first run at Epsom, Surrey.

CHAPELS AND PREACHERS

Country labourers, craft workers and many city dwellers too preferred a more direct kind of Christianity than that offered by the Church of England. They were called Nonconformists, because they did not conform to standard worship. Preachers toured the country and gained huge support in Wales, Cornwall and northern England. They addressed vast crowds at open-air sites such as Gwennap Pit, which can still be seen near Redruth, in Cornwall. Nonconformist chapels were built in many villages and towns. John Wesley, who founded the Methodist movement in 1738, preached over 40,000 sermons in his lifetime. His brother Charles wrote many famous hymns.

SERVANTS AND LABOURERS

Big country estates and town houses employed many servants and cooks. The men wore a uniform, called livery. Maids ran up and down the stairs, carrying boiling water for the bath tub or long-handled warming pans for the beds. Servants slept in attic bedrooms. At least they escaped the misery of living in city slums or run-down country cottages. Housing for farm workers may have looked pretty, but it was mostly damp and draughty. Poor living conditions brought on all kinds of medical problems.

➡ *In the inns of Fleet Street, in London, groups of friends met to discuss literature, language, art and politics. Their leader was Dr Samuel Johnson, who in 1747 started to write his* Dictionary of the English Language. *Johnson is especially remembered for his sharp, robust and often witty sayings, many of them recorded by his friend James Boswell during travels in Scotland. Other members of Dr Johnson's social circle included the painter Joshua Reynolds, the politician Edmund Burke, the actor David Garrick and the playwright Oliver Goldsmith.*

1709
Abraham Darby uses coke instead of charcoal to smelt iron.

1712
Thomas Newcomen's piston-operated steam engine.

New Technologies

Britain was rich in coal and its overseas empire could provide valuable raw materials such as cotton or jute. These new lands also offered a huge market for manufactured goods such as textiles. Clever inventions made it possible to produce goods more quickly and cheaply than ever before. A new system of canals made it much easier to move goods from cities to ports. An 'industrial revolution' had begun.

← *Tin and copper had been mined in Cornwall since ancient times. By 1800 this industry was being transformed, with steam engines pumping out the mines, and with new roads and foundries being constructed. Soon the Cornish mines were employing 50,000 workers.*

1730
Charles Townshend's theories on the rotation of crops.

1733
John Kay's flying shuttle for the weaving industry.

STEAM AND COAL

Steam power was developed in 1712 by two Devonshire engineers, Thomas Savery and Thomas Newcomen, to pump out water from mines. In the 1770s the steam engine was perfected by a Scottish engineering genius called James Watt. His successful steam pumps allowed deep mine shafts to be bored into the Northumberland and Durham coalfields.

MILLS AND MINES

Britain became the world's first industrial country. By 1757 glowing furnaces rose from the heads of the South Wales valleys. The great ironworks at Carron brought industry to the Scottish Lowlands in 1759. The world's first iron bridge spanned the River Severn in Shropshire, England, by 1779. Factories and mills spread through Yorkshire, Lancashire and the English Midlands. Tin was mined in Cornwall, lead in Derbyshire, copper in Wales. The poet William Blake wrote of 'dark, satanic mills' appearing in a 'green and pleasant land'.

⬆ *Massive, hissing steam engines provided the power for Britain's industrial revolution.*

THE POTTERIES

Staffordshire, in the northwest of England, became the centre of pottery manufacture. The leading producer was Josiah Wedgwood, who set up the famous Etruria works in 1769. He produced black-and-cream-coloured wares, but his most famous design was of an unglazed blue decorated with a raised white pattern.

▲ *Wedgwood was inspired by classical designs. He made a copy of the Portland Vase, a fine piece of Roman glassware.*

SCIENCE AND TURNIPS

Science and technology were beginning to change farming as well as manufacture. In 1701 Jethro Tull invented a drill that dropped seeds in rows instead of scattering them across the field. In 1730 a retired politician called Charles Townshend (nicknamed 'Turnip') developed a new system of improving the soil by switching ('rotating') crops, using wheat, grass and turnips.

⬇ *From the 1760s, a network of canals was dug by gangs of labourers called navigators, or 'navvies'. Pottery and other manufactured goods were transported in horse-drawn boats. Seed drills allowed crops to be planted in straight rows, which made hoeing easier during the growing season.*

➡ *The spinning-jenny of 1768 was a machine that operated several spindles at once. It was developed in Lancashire, England, by James Hargreaves and mechanic Thomas Higgs, who named it after his daughter.*

A TEXTILE REVOLUTION

Few industries changed so much in the 1750s and 60s as spinning and weaving. Output soared as new spinning frames and shuttles were invented by pioneers such as Richard Arkwright, James Hargreaves and Samuel Crompton. Work once carried out in the home was transferred to big textile mills powered by water or, later, by steam. By the 1800s, the industrial revolution was gaining speed. It would change the world forever.

NEW TECHNOLOGIES **311**

Irish Rebellion and Union

In the 50 years after the Battle of the Boyne, the Irish economy improved. Trade passed along rivers, canals and much improved roads to the the seaports of the east and south. Farms prospered on the more fertile lands, although the Irish-speaking peasant farmers of the west struggled along on the verge of famine. The Protestant ruling class built splendid country homes. From the 1750s onwards, Dublin was laid out with broad streets of fine brick town houses and bridges over the River Liffey. The population of Ireland rose to about five million.

▲ *Swift uses the experiences of Gulliver to point out human follies.*

GULLIVER'S TRAVELS

Jonathan Swift was born in Dublin, of English parents. He became known for his poetry. He was appointed Dean of St Patrick's Cathedral, in Dublin, and campaigned against British restrictions on Irish trade. In 1726 Swift wrote *Gulliver's Travels*, in which the hero describes his visits to various fantastic worlds. The result is a bitter but humorous look at the foolishness of mankind.

DUBLIN AND LONDON

At the beginning of the 1700s, Catholics made up 90 percent of the Irish population, but owned only 14 percent of the land. The British attitude to Ireland was that of a colonial power. When Irish exports in woollen cloth and cattle were so successful that they threatened trade in England, they were simply banned. Catholics were not allowed to worship freely or even to vote. Ireland still had its own parliament in Dublin, but real power lay in London.

The tidal reaches of the River Liffey pass through the heart of Dublin, the Irish capital. The domed Four Courts building was the centre of Ireland's judicial system under British rule. It was constructed between 1796 and 1802.

1795
Foundation of the Orange Order by Irish Protestants.

1798
Uprising in Wexford. French land in Killala.

→ *Politician Henry Grattan speaks to the Irish Parliament in 1780. He campaigned tirelessly for Ireland to be allowed to make its own laws.*

WHO HOLDS POWER?

More and more people in Ireland, Protestant as well as Catholic, wanted to see political reform. One leader of opinion was a member of the Irish Parliament called Henry Grattan. Many of his supporters were inspired by the American War of Independence and the calls for freedom grew louder. When the French Revolution took place in 1789, the British decided it might be best if they went along with Grattan's demands.

↑ *The production of linen cloth from flax was a major industry among the Protestants of Ulster. Much of the work was home-based.*

UNITED IRISHMEN

After 1791 a Protestant from Kildare called Theobald Wolfe Tone recruited many Irish people to a society called the United Irishmen. It called for equal religious rights and Irish independence. At first it had support both from Protestant militias called the Volunteers and from Irish Catholics. It soon became linked with more radical groups and sought help from the revolutionary government in France. In 1796 a French revolutionary fleet appeared off Bantry Bay in the south, but was scattered by storms.

1801
Act of Union between Great Britain and Ireland.

1803
Robert Emmet's rising Union Flag includes red saltire (cross) of St Patrick.

DEFEAT OF THE REBELS

In May 1798 the Irish rebellion began in Wexford, and in August the French landed troops in support. It was too late. Both were defeated and many Irish rebels were hanged. Grattan's reforms were thrown out. A new Act of Union, in force from 1 January 1801, abolished the Irish parliament. Ireland was now a part of the United Kingdom, and the red saltire (diagonal cross) of St Patrick was added to the Union flag. The United Kingdom had reached its greatest extent, an arrangement that lasted over 100 years.

A TROUBLED UNION

The new political order was in trouble from the start. A United Irishman called Robert Emmet organised another uprising. He manufactured guns and explosives, and attempted to seize Dublin Castle in 1803. The Lord Chief Justice was killed in the street. However the rebellion was suppressed and Emmet was executed. Although he had failed, Emmet's fame spread far and wide and he became widely seen as a martyr, as a symbol of the Irish nationalism that would grow throughout the coming century.

The 1798 rebellion came to an end at Vinegar Hill, near Wexford, on 21 June. That September, Wolfe Tone was captured. He committed suicide in prison.

The Napoleonic Wars

George III's Britain and the revolutionary government in France were bitter enemies. They hated each other's politics and they were rivals for power. They went to war in 1791. Two remarkable characters made their name in the 11 years that followed. One was a popular British naval commander called Horatio Nelson. He defeated the French fleet at Aboukir Bay, Egypt, in 1798. The other was a brilliant French soldier called Napoleon Bonaparte. Napoleon had political ambitions.

↑ Admiral Horatio Nelson was killed in battle at Trafalgar, on the deck of HMS Victory.

← Napoleon was a military genius, great law-maker and a ruthless politician.

A NEW EMPEROR IN EUROPE

A peace made between Britain and France in 1802 did not last. By 1804 the two countries were at war again – only by now Napoleon Bonaparte had crowned himself emperor of France and was planning to invade Britain. Round forts called 'Martello towers' were built to defend the Channel coast. The English anxiously peered through telescopes across the Straits of Dover. Mothers threatened naughty children that 'Boney' would come for them in the night if they did not behave – but the bogeyman did not invade.

1803
Start of Napoleonic Wars with France.

1805
British defeat French and Spanish at Trafalgar. Nelson is killed.

LAND AND SEA

In 1805 a French-Spanish fleet was defeated by Nelson off Cape Trafalgar, in Spain. Britain's navy ruled the seas. On land, however, Napoleon won stunning victories against the great powers of the day – Austria, Prussia, Russia. His empire soon stretched across Europe. In 1812 Napoleon invaded Russia, but his troops were caught in the winter snows and many perished. By 1814 France's enemies were in Paris. Napoleon was forced from power and exiled to the Mediterranean island of Elba.

⬇ Nelson's defeat of the French and Spanish fleet at Trafalgar was a major blow to Napoleon's plans to control Europe.

↑ Sailors rest in their hammocks, exhausted afer a long session of hard work. Conditions below deck were cramped and dark.

BELOW DECKS

A sailor's life was tough during the 1700s and 1800s. Naval discipline was severe and punishment included floggings. Voyages were long, with hammocks slung between the decks for sleeping. Hard biscuits and salted-down meat were eaten, and a ration of rum was allowed. Battle conditions were terrifying, as cannon balls splintered masts and brought down rigging. In 1797 there were major mutinies by British sailors at Spithead and the Nore. Admiral Horatio Nelson, however, was popular with all ranks under his command and inspired loyalty.

THE PENINSULAR WAR

In 1808 Napoleon invaded the Iberian peninsula (Portugal and Spain). He made his brother Joseph King of Spain. The British sent a force under Sir Arthur Wellesley (the later Duke of Wellington) to help Spanish and Portuguese resistance fighters. The British suffered setbacks during the campaign, with a desperate retreat to La Coruña in 1809. They won a great victory at Salamanca (1812) and also at Vittoria (1814).

▶ Arthur Wellesley, 1st Duke of Wellngton, was born in Dublin in 1769. He was a brilliant soldier, cautious but thorough in his organisation.

1814
End of war in Spain. Napoleon exiled to island of Elba.

1815
Napoleon escapes. Defeated by British and Prussians at Waterloo.

WATERLOO

Napoleon slipped away from Elba and on 1 March 1815 he landed in France. Loyal troops rallied to him as he marched through the land. On 18 June they reached Waterloo, near Brussels, for a final and terrible battle. They were defeated by Prussian, Dutch and British troops under the command of the Duke of Wellington. The victors met in Vienna in 1815 to re-draw the map of Europe. Napoleon was sent to the remote Atlantic island of St Helena, where he died in 1821.

Waterloo was one of the most famous battles in British history. The British infantry formed squares, with the men facing outwards and firing in turn. The French cavalry could not break their ranks. The French suffered 25,000 dead and wounded, the British 15,000 and the Prussians about 7000.

THE 'IRON DUKE'

After Waterloo, the Duke of Wellington took up a career in politics. He became Prime Minister for the Tories in 1828. Wellington supported Catholic rights in Ireland, but his past fear of French revolutionary ideas and his rigid military discipline made him extremely conservative and he was against more people getting the vote. He became very unpopular and rioters attacked his house in London. Wellington fell from power in 1830 and retired from politics in 1846. He died in 1852 and was buried in St Paul's Cathedral – next to Lord Nelson.

1805
The artist JMW Turner paints *The Shipwreck*.

1812
The waltz becomes the most popular dance in Britain.

The Regency

George III was getting old and increasingly insane. His son George was eager for power and in 1811 he was made Prince Regent, to rule in his father's place. The years until his father's death in 1820 are known as the Regency period. For noble ladies and gentlemen, this was a time of high fashion and society scandals. Horse-drawn carriages bowled through newly laid out green parks. Elegant, candle-lit balls were held at Bath or at the Prince's new palace beside the sea at Brighton, Sussex.

↑ The Royal Crescent, Bath. This city in Somerset became a centre of fashion, theatre – and gossip.

THE DANDIES

Some Regency fashions for men were extreme. 'Dandies' squeezed into corsets and wore wide trousers and frock coats that flared from the hips. Extraordinary hair styles peeked out from top hats. They were a source of amusement to many. Leader of the dandies and self-appointed judge of all that was fashionable was George 'Beau' Brummell. He fell out with 'Prinny' (the Prince Regent) in 1813. Ruined by his gambling debts, he fled to France, where he died in the madhouse in 1840.

◄ Standard dress for a Regency gentleman included trousers rather than breeches, a frock coat and a waistcoat.

1820
Prince Regent becomes George IV on the death of his father.

1820
The artist John Constable paints *Flatford Mill*.

HEAD *and* BRAINS!!

CARTOONS – AND CAROLINE

The Prince Regent was a well-meaning, intelligent and witty man, a lover of art, literature and fine architecture. However, he was savagely mocked by the cartoonists of his day. He was despised for his lavish, extravagant way of life. Dinner guests at his Brighton Pavilion could be offered a choice of 116 dishes, at a time when large sections of society were desperately poor and hungry. When George tried to divorce his second wife, Caroline of Brunswick, his treatment of her outraged the public.

← *Public opinion turns against George in favour of Caroline, as shown in this satirical cartoon of the day.*

PEN TO PAPER

The 1800s was an exciting time for writers. Jane Austen's novels tell us just what it was like to live in Regency England, describing courtship, marriage and money. The Romantic poets were fired by imagination and emotion. William Wordsworth and John Keats praised the power of nature. The poets George Byron and Percy Bysshe Shelley led wild lives. Lord Byron went to fight in the Greek war of independence, but died of fever in 1824.

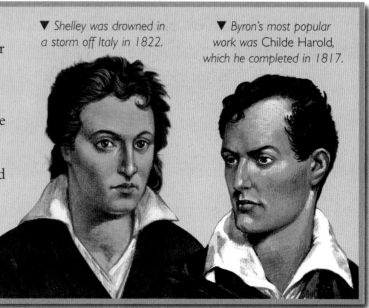

▼ *Shelley was drowned in a storm off Italy in 1822.*

▼ *Byron's most popular work was Childe Harold, which he completed in 1817.*

1826
Royal Zoological Society founded in London.

1830
George IV dies. His brother becomes William IV.

A TIME OF CHANGE

The Prince Regent escaped an assassination attempt in 1817 and was crowned George IV in 1821. He had always been pro-Whig, but as ruler he gave his support to the Tories, who opposed political reform. When his brother William came to the throne nine years later, he opposed the Reform Act of 1832. However democratic reform could not be held back for long. All over Europe old empires were breaking up. New nations were being created and their citizens were calling for freedom.

➡️ *By 1822 the Prince's Pavilion beside the sea at Brighton, in Sussex, had been transformed by the architect John Nash into a splendid palace in the Asian style. Here was a lavish banqueting room, a magnificent music room, galleries and saloons. The rooms were filled with mirrors and chandeliers, and all sorts of ornament in the Chinese style that was fashionable at the time.*

PRIME MINISTERS
OF THE UNITED KINGDOM

- Henry Addington (Tory) — 1801–1804
- William Pitt the Younger (Tory) — 1804–1808
- Lord Grenville (coalition) — 1806–1807
- Duke of Portland (Tory) — 1807–1809
- Spencer Perceval (Tory) — 1809–1812
- Earl of Liverpool (Tory) — 1812–1827
- George Canning (coalition) — 1827
- Viscount Goderich (Tory) — 1827–1828
- Duke of Wellington (Tory) — 1828–1830
- Earl Grey (Tory) — 1830–1834

Puffing Billies

The countryside of Britain and Ireland had been quiet and unspoiled throughout its history. In the 1800s, that peace was shattered. First came railway engineers, laying track, digging cuttings and building bridges. Then came clanking, steam-powered locomotives, huffing and puffing through the fields. Horses bolted in fright.

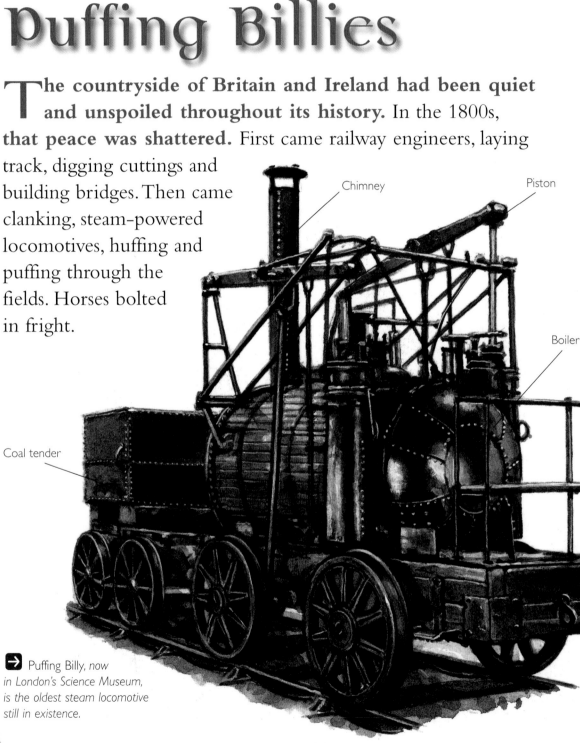

Chimney

Piston

Boiler

Coal tender

→ Puffing Billy, *now in London's Science Museum, is the oldest steam locomotive still in existence.*

THE RAINHILL TRIALS

In October 1829 the Manchester to Liverpool railway company offered a prize for the most reliable steam locomotive. Huge crowds gathered to see the locomotives battle it out on a length of track near Liverpool. *Perseverance* was much too slow. *Novelty* could travel at 48 kilometres an hour, but kept breaking down. *Sans Pareil* burned too much coal. The winner was the *Rocket*, built by George and Robert Stephenson.

▼ The Stephensons' *Rocket* could average a speed of 24 kilometres an hour and it did not break down once.

↓ Trevithick's second locomotive was called Catch Me Who Can. *He demonstrated it in 1808 on a circular track in London. It travelled at 16 kilometres an hour.*

BIRTH OF THE RAILWAYS

The railway age began in 1804. A Cornish engineer called Richard Trevithick was working at Penydarren, near Merthyr Tydfil in South Wales. He mounted a steam engine on a wagon and created the world's first locomotive. He proved it could haul a heavy industrial load – and passengers too. By 1813 William Hedley's famous *Puffing Billy* was steaming away at Wylam Colliery, near Newcastle. Wylam was the birthplace of engineering genius George Stephenson. He greatly improved the design of locomotives and rails and between 1821 and 1825 he built the Stockton and Darlington Railway. His son Robert was also an engineer, and in the 1840s and 50s he constructed magnificent railway bridges across the Menai Strait and the Conwy, Tyne and Tweed rivers.

1830
Passenger service opens, Liverpool to Manchester railway.

1833
IK Brunel appointed chief engineer of the Great Western Railway.

⬆ *Brunel's magnificent railway bridge across the River Tamar, between Plymouth and Saltash, opened in 1859.*

ISAMBARD KINGDOM BRUNEL

The son of an engineer, IK Brunel (right) was born in Portsmouth, England in 1806. He was a great builder of bridges, tunnels and docks and in 1833 became chief engineer of the Great Western Railway.

He also designed great steamships for the Atlantic crossing. *Great Britain* (1845) was driven by propeller screws, and *Great Eastern* (1858) held the record of the world's biggest ever vessel for over 40 years.

SS *Great Eastern*

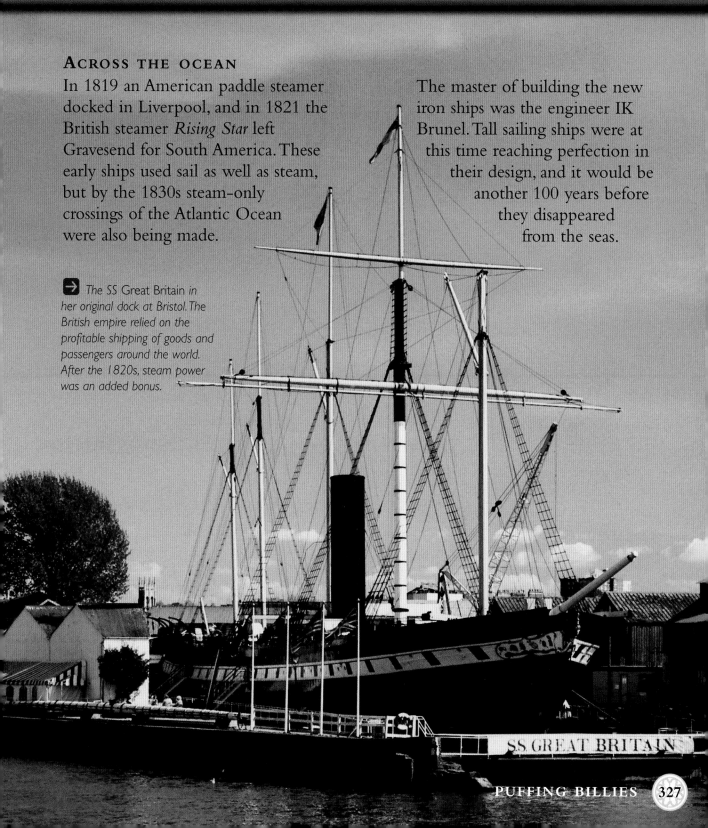

ACROSS THE OCEAN

In 1819 an American paddle steamer docked in Liverpool, and in 1821 the British steamer *Rising Star* left Gravesend for South America. These early ships used sail as well as steam, but by the 1830s steam-only crossings of the Atlantic Ocean were also being made.

The master of building the new iron ships was the engineer IK Brunel. Tall sailing ships were at this time reaching perfection in their design, and it would be another 100 years before they disappeared from the seas.

→ *The SS Great Britain in her original dock at Bristol. The British empire relied on the profitable shipping of goods and passengers around the world. After the 1820s, steam power was an added bonus.*

SS GREAT BRITAIN

Long May She Reign

In June 1837 Princess Victoria, niece of William IV, was woken to be told she was queen. She was only 18 years old. Victoria ruled the United Kingdom at a time when it was the world's most powerful nation, with a vast overseas empire. In 1840, Victoria married a German prince, Albert of Saxe-Coburg and Gotha. They had four sons and five daughters, who married into many of Europe's royal families.

➡ *Prince Albert and Queen Victoria. The Queen ruled for 63 years, becoming the United Kingdom's longest-reigning monarch.*

VICTORIAN MORALITY

In 1861 Albert died of typhoid fever. Victoria was grief-stricken and disappeared from public view for many years. People began to grumble about this, but towards the end of her reign she did regain her popularity. Victoria was not known for her sense of humour or fun. She believed in strict religious morality and in duty to one's country. These values were shared by many of her subjects. The Victorian upper and middle classes preached of progress, of doing good and improving society. Improvements were certainly needed. Living conditions for the poor in both cities and countryside were very harsh.

THE PEELERS

The first uniformed police went on parade in London in 1829. The force was founded by Sir Robert Peel and so the constables became known as 'Peelers' or 'Bobbies'. They wore blue-frock coats and top hats reinforced with metal. Helmets and tunics were worn as from 1864.

▶ The Peelers worked 12 hours a day, seven days a week. At first they were treated with little respect by the public.

◀ From about 1855, women wore a dress called a crinoline, whose bell-shaped skirt stretched out over hoops of whalebone and steel. Hair was worn in ringlets. By 1875 dresses were narrower, with a bottom pad called a bustle. Underwear included tightly-laced corsets.

LONG MAY SHE REIGN **329**

1852
Balmoral Castle becomes Victoria's
Scottish residence.

1861
Prince Albert dies of typhoid. Victoria retires
to Windsor.

THE QUEEN AND POLITICS

In the 1830s the old political parties changed their names. The Tories became known as the Conservatives and the Whigs as the Liberals. Queen Victoria took a great interest in politics. Viscount Melbourne, the first Prime Minister of her reign, was her personal friend and advisor. She did not take so well to Sir Robert Peel or Viscount Palmerston. Later in her reign, Victoria clearly preferred the charming, conservative Benjamin Disraeli to William Gladstone, his more radical rival.

The Great Exhibition of 1851 was planned by Prince Albert. It was staged in Hyde Park, London, in a huge building made of iron and glass, designed by Joseph Paxton. This was nicknamed the 'Crystal Palace'. The exhibitions showed off produce and craft work from all over the world. They attracted over 6 million visitors. In 1854 the Crystal Palace was moved to South London, where it was destroyed in a fire in 1936.

THE PENNY POST

A modern postal service using stamps paid for by the sender was introduced by Rowland Hill, the Postmaster General, in 1840. The first stamps were called 'Penny Blacks' and 'Twopence Blues'.

Ribs and pillars

The glass panels were supported by 4064 tonnes of prefabricated iron ribs and pillars.

PRIME MINISTERS OF THE UNITED KINGDOM

✤ Viscount Melbourne (Whig)	1834
✤ Sir Robert Peel (Conservative)	1834–1835
✤ Viscount Melbourne (Whig)	1835–1841
✤ Sir Robert Peel (Conservative)	1841–1846
✤ Lord Russell (Liberal)	1846–1852
✤ Earl of Derby (Conservative)	1852
✤ Lord Aberdeen (Peelite)	1852–1855
✤ Viscount Palmerston (Liberal)	1855–1858
✤ Earl of Derby (Conservative)	1858–1859
✤ Viscount Palmerston (Liberal)	1859–1865
✤ Lord Russell (Liberal)	1865–1866
✤ Earl of Derby (Conservative)	1866–1868

Enclosure

The exhibition building covered 8 hectares of parkland, enclosing fully grown elm trees.

LONG MAY SHE REIGN **331**

The Factory Age

Families were leaving the countryside to seek work in the new factories and mines. They left a hard life for an even harder one. They toiled in the cotton mills of Manchester, in the steel mills of Sheffield, on the docksides of Liverpool, Glasgow and Newcastle-upon-Tyne. Industry depended on steam and steam depended on coal. The number of miners in Britain's coalfields doubled between 1851 and 1881.

⬇ *Children worked underground in the mines, hauling coal waggons with chains or opening trap doors in the tunnels.*

▶ *The Davy lamp was first tested in 1816, at Hebburn Colliery.*

THE DAVY LAMP

Mining disasters killed hundreds of people in Victorian times. Deep underground, just one spark amongst the coal dust could set off an explosion, causing fires to rage or shafts to collapse. One invention that saved the lives of many miners was a safety lamp, developed by Cornish scientist Humphry Davy in 1815.

1842
It becomes illegal for women and children to work down mines.

1848
Health of Towns Act, to improve water supply and drainage.

WORKING CONDITIONS

Many factory owners put profit above the health and safety of their workers. Children and young women were employed in wretched conditions in textile mills and mines. Small boys worked as sweeps, being made to crawl up tall, narrow chimneys in houses and factories until they bled. Furnaces were operated without proper safety checks. Workers in factories and mills were deafened by steam hammers and machinery. Hours were long and there were no holidays.

↑ *A cotton mill in about 1830 uses a new type of 'spinning mule' invented by Richard Roberts. It produced good quality yarn and kept its place in the textile industry until the 1950s. In the 19th century a young boy (top right) would be employed to crawl underneath and sweep up.*

1851
Over half the British population now lives in towns.

1864
New law stops children being used as chimney sweeps.

THE GROWING CITIES

New cities were eating their way into the surrounding countryside. Terraces of red-brick houses sprawled back-to-back, as far as the eye could see. In big cities, families were packed into slums and children ran barefoot in the streets. There would be a pump in the yard and an outdoor toilet, both serving many families. Many toilets were still not flushed by water. Deadly diseases such as typhoid and cholera spread quickly in these unhealthy conditions. Gradually, drainage was improved and new sewers were built under the cities.

SOOT AND SMOKE

In London, the Thames had become a foul-smelling, polluted river, deserted by its fish. In northern English cities the air was filled with smuts from factory chimneys. Buildings were covered in black soot. In winter, smoke and fog made it hard to find one's way. Gas lamps, which first appeared on streets during the Regency period, became common in the Victorian period.

➡ *During this 'Industrial Revolution' there was a growing divide betweeen rich and poor.*

VICTORIAN SCHOOLING

Children from poor homes received little education at all. 'Ragged schools' were set up to teach children from the factories and slums in the 1820s and 30s. From 1870 onwards, all children were sent to state-run primary schools. For the first time in the nation's history, poor people were receiving an education.

1799
Socialist pioneer Robert Owen purchases New
Lanark Mills, Scotland.

1811
'Luddites' destroy industrial machinery in north
of England.

Changing Society

The industrial age, which was now spreading rapidly
through Europe and North America, completely
changed society. However old methods of government stayed
in place. Some people campaigned against injustice and tried to
reform society. Many called for greater democracy. Some
revolutionaries wanted the workers to seize power for themselves.

FIGHTERS AGAINST INJUSTICE

William Wilberforce, Member of Parliament for Hull, led
a long campaign against the slave trade in the colonies.
In 1807 British ships were banned from carrying slaves
and in 1833, one month after Wilberforce died, slavery
was finally abolished throughout the British empire.
Another great reformer was a Quaker called Elizabeth
Fry, who from 1813 campaigned against terrible
conditions in the prisons. Changes were made to the
system, but Victorian prisons remained grim.

⬇ *Prisoners are exercised
in the yard. Political protest
and petty crimes were met
with harsh sentences. Many
convicts were transported to
prison colonies in Australia.*

↑ *As new machinery was brought into farming, labourers began to fear for their jobs.*

VIOLENT PROTEST

New machines meant fewer jobs. In 1811, laid-off Nottingham workers began to smash machinery. In the five years that followed, protests spread across northern England. The protestors claimed their leader was a 'General Ludd', so they were called 'Luddites'. Many were hanged or transported to Australia. New machines were replacing labourers on farms, too. In 1830, farm workers in south England destroyed threshing machines and set fire to haystacks. Their leader was commonly known as 'Captain Swing'.

THE COMMUNIST MANIFESTO

Karl Marx was a German writer on economics who moved to London. Friedrich Engels, another German, came to Manchester to work for his family's textile business. In 1848 Marx and Engels wrote the *Communist Manifesto*. They described how economic systems had developed through history and the conflict between social classes. They called upon workers all over the world to overthrow capitalism and create a society in which classes would exist no more.

▶ *The writings of Marx (right) and Engels had a great influence on world history.*

1834
'Tolpuddle Martyrs' – farm workers arrested for joining trade union.

1839
First National Convention of the Chartist Movement.

A PEOPLE'S CHARTER

The Reform Act of 1832 gave the vote to more people and representation to the new cities. Between 1838 and 1848, working people campaigned for further reforms. They were called Chartists, because they presented a 'People's Charter' to Parliament. This demanded that all adult men should have the vote, that ballots should be secret and that anyone could become a Member of Parliament (MP).

Parliament rejected the Charter, in 1840 and 1842. Mass protests and armed risings followed, but were put down by troops. However laws passed in 1867 and 1884 did bring in many democratic reforms.

⬇ *In 1819, reformists meeting in St Peter's Fields, Manchester, were charged by mounted troops and volunteers. Eleven of the crowd were killed and 500 injured. Just four years after the Battle of Waterloo, the event became known as the Peterloo Massacre.*

1844
Cooperative movement set up in Rochdale for mutual help in trade and housing.

1846
Corn Laws, which kept the price of bread high, abolished by Robert Peel.

▼ *The poverty, violence, humour and humanity of Victorian London was recorded by Charles Dickens.*

DICKENSIAN LONDON

Charles Dickens, born in 1812, had a hard childhood. His father was imprisoned for debt and he had to work in a factory making boot blacking. In 1828 he became a journalist and from the 1830s onwards began to write popular novels, many of them serialised in magazines. They tell us how the Victorians lived. *Oliver Twist* (finished in 1839) shows us life in the workhouse and the beggars and thieves of the London slums. Such tales shocked many people and encouraged social reform. Dickens died in 1870.

TRADE UNIONS AND SOCIALISTS

Many working people organised trade unions, to fight for better conditions. Six Dorsetshire farm workers did this in 1834. Transported to Australia for this 'crime', they became known as the 'Tolpuddle Martyrs'. The richest people in Victorian society did not work. They used their money ('capital') to speculate, buying and selling shares. Socialists believed that the profits made by capitalists belonged rightfully to the workers who actually produced the goods.

➡ *The glittering world of the rich and fashionable depended on the hard work of countless poor labourers, servants and maids.*

Nature, Science and Technology

The Victorians were fascinated by the natural world and how it worked. There were breakthroughs in the understanding of physics, chemistry, botany, zoology and geology. Science was now studied at universities, and introduced to the public in splendid new museums, botanical gardens and zoos.

⬆ *From 1831–1836 the crew of HMS Beagle carried out a scientific survey of South American waters. The chief scientist was a naturalist called Charles Darwin. He collected and studied fossils, animals and plants.*

THE FOSSIL COLLECTOR

Mary Anning was born in Lyme Regis, Dorset in 1799. She was already a first-rate fossil collector as a child, discovering the first fossil skeleton of an ichthyosaur in 1810. In 1821 she found the first fossilized plesiosaur and in 1828 the first *pteranadon*.

▼ *By studying Mary Anning's fossil ichthyosaur, scientists could work out how such creatures lived in prehistoric times.*

LIFE ON EARTH

Many people were becoming interested in the fossils of animals and plants. The scientists Alfred Russel Wallace and Charles Darwin both travelled the world, studying wildlife. They came to believe that life forms on Earth had evolved, or gradually developed, over many millions of years. Their ideas were opposed by many Christians, who believed that the world was only a few thousand years old and that all existing life had been created by God in its present form.

HISTORY OF THE BICYCLE

The first bicycle to be powered by pedals was made by Scottish blacksmith Kirkpatrick Macmillan in 1840. Pneumatic (air-filled) tyres were first tried out in 1887 by John Boyd Dunlop.

Hobby 1818

Velocipede (Boneshaker) 1861

Penny Farthing early 1870s

NEW TECHNOLOGIES

Scientific discoveries were soon applied to technology. New inventions in Western Europe and North America transformed industry, transport, medicine, commerce and home life. Inventions in Great Britain and Ireland included waterproofing of cloth (Charles Macintosh,1832) and cellulose (a form of plastic patented by Alexander Parkes in 1855).

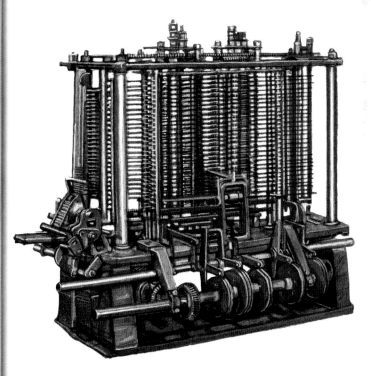

↑ *A calculating machine. This mechanical calculator was one of several designed by Charles Babbage from the 1820s to 1840s. It may be seen as an early attempt at making a computer.*

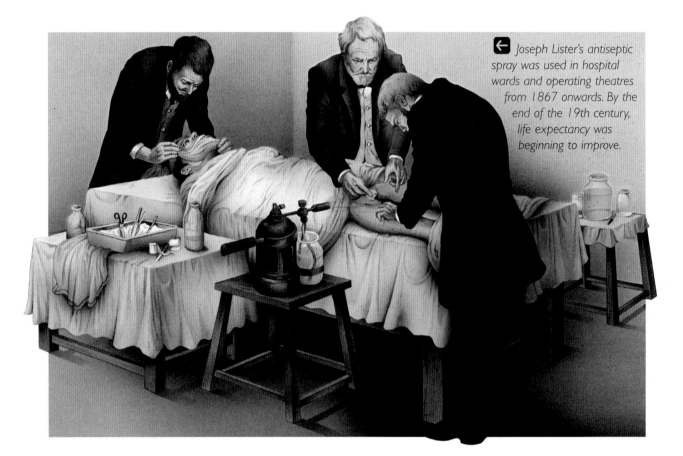

Joseph Lister's antiseptic spray was used in hospital wards and operating theatres from 1867 onwards. By the end of the 19th century, life expectancy was beginning to improve.

MEDICAL RESEARCH

Great medical advances were made in Western Europe in the 1800s. An English doctor called Edward Jenner had carried out the first successful vaccination against smallpox in 1796. Vaccination against disease became widely accepted in Victorian hospitals, as did the antiseptic treatment of surgical instruments to kill germs. This change, brought in by the surgeon Joseph Lister in the 1860s, saved countless lives.

SCIENCE AND ELECTRICITY

Michael Faraday's discoveries about electricity and magnetism in the 1830s changed the way in which people lived. In 1878 Joseph Swan demonstrated an electric light bulb in Newcastle upon Tyne. The first electric telegraph was developed by WF Cooke and Charles Wheatstone in the 1830s. The telephone was first demonstrated in the USA in 1876, by Scottish-born inventor Alexander Graham Bell. The 'wireless telegraph' or radio was invented by Italian scientist Guglielmo Marconi. He sent the first trans-Atlantic radio signal, from Cornwall to Newfoundland, in 1901.

⬇ *The Royal Botanical Gardens at Kew, to the west of London, became a world centre of research into plants and seeds. A fine palm house, built of glass and iron, was completed there in 1848.*

⬆ *Alexander Graham Bell experimented with different machines for transmitting sound, especially speech, while working as a teacher of deaf people.*

1839
The Rebecca Riots in West Wales (until 1844).

1855
The first coal mine is opened in the Rhondda valley, South Wales.

Victorian Wales

Wales had known peace since the Civil War, apart from a brief landing by French revolutionary troops at Fishguard in 1797. However the 1800s were less peaceful. There were no more wars or foreign invasions, but there was a period of violent social unrest brought about by rapid economic change.

↑ *The demand for social reform and voting rights led to violent clashes with the authorities in the 1830s.*

THE MERTHYR RISING

In 1829 there was widespread unemployment in South Wales and wages were cut. The troubles came to a climax in 1831. Prisoners were broken out of jail and a series of marches and riots turned into a full-scale uprising. In Merthyr Tydfil, troops were brought in to face a crowd of some 10,000 people. The soldiers opened fire, killing about 24 and wounding many more. A young miner called Richard Lewis, nicknamed 'Dic Penderyn' was later hanged for wounding a soldier, despite his innocence. The Merthyr rising was followed by ten years of bitter political protest.

CHANGING TIMES

The economy of 19th century Wales still depended on agriculture, but also on fishing, shipbuilding, and in North Wales copper mining and the quarrying of limestone and slate. In the south, coal was exported through the growing port of Cardiff. For 130 years from 1855, coal would rule the Welsh economy. Religious differences emerged too, as more and more people turned away from the Church of England to follow 'non-conformist' forms of worship in the chapels. The Wesh language, often forbidden in the schools, was kept alive by the chapels' Sunday schools.

OLD AND NEW

The ancient poetry festivals called *eisteddfodau* were reinvented in the 1790s. After the 1850s, these annual meetings became a focus for Welsh cultural – and often political – life. Young Wales (*Cymru Fydd*), a movement for Welsh self-government, was started in 1886. It was soon eclipsed by support for a rising star in the world of politics, a young Liberal called David Lloyd George. He became MP for Caernarfon in 1890. By 1916 he would be Prime Minister.

WALES IN PATAGONIA

In 1865 a group of Welsh settlers sailed to Argentina, in South America. They founded a colony in the Chubut valley, in the remote region of Patagonia. Another colony was later founded at Cwm Hyfryd, at the foot of the Andes mountains. The settlements prospered and the colonists built their own farms, chapels and law-courts. During the 1900s they became outnumbered by new Spanish and Italian settlers, but the Welsh language can still be heard in Patagonia to this day.

↓ *The Menai Suspension Bridge, an engineering marvel of its age, was built by Thomas Telford and opened in 1826. It lay on a new road built from London to Holyhead, the port for Ireland.*

Victorian Scotland

Queen Victoria liked to visit Scotland. Her family would hunt the moors and fish for salmon. They made popular a romantic view of Scotland that was quite at odds with the harsh reality. In the Highlands, poor people were being forced from their cottages. In the industrial Lowlands, fortunes were being made while children starved in the sprawling slums of Glasgow.

ROMANTIC TALES

Two great writers of adventure tales lived in 19th-century Scotland. Sir Walter Scott wrote thrilling historical novels such as *Ivanhoe* (1819). Robert Louis Stevenson, wrote *Kidnapped* (1886) and that unforgettable story of buccaneers and gold, *Treasure Island* (1883).

▶ *Robert Louis Stevenson (1850–1894).*

HIGHLAND CLEARANCES

Between the 1750s and the 1860s, landowners in the Scottish Highlands reorganised their estates along more commercial lines. They brought in sheep, which were more profitable than cattle. In the Victorian age, they encouraged deer hunting and fishing. A large workforce was no longer needed and tenants simply stood in the way of the landowners' profits. Families were evicted by force and their cottages were destroyed. By the 1860s, the Highlands had become largely depopulated and the Gaelic language spoken there was under threat. It was the 1880s before the rights of remaining tenants were protected by law.

1848
Scotland linked with England by rail.

1850s
Number of homeless people in Scotland reaches 200,000.

LEAVING THE OLD COUNTRY

Many of the evicted Highlanders sought work in the Lowland cities. Others gave up and sailed off to foreign lands. Many emigrated to the coastal regions and cities of eastern Canada, to the United States and Australia.

 The 'clearance' of the Highlands caused great hardship. In the 1830s and 40s things were made even worse by food shortages and starvation.

1884
The Highland Land League is founded.

1886
The Crofters' Act protects the rights of
Highland tenants.

SCOTTISH CLOTH

The tartan cloth of the Scottish
Highlands, which had been banned
after the Jacobite rebellion of 1745,
was made fashionable once more
by the novels of Sir Walter Scott
and by the royal family.

THE DISRUPTION

In 1843 there was a major crisis in the
Church of Scotland. In this Disruption',
large numbers of people left the established
Church. They were unhappy with the way
in which it was influenced by the state, so
they set up their own Free Church. In an
age when
Churches were
deeply involved
in education
and social
welfare, this had
a great effect on
everyday life.

RADICAL POLITICS

The economic changes in Scotland encouraged calls
for political change. In the early 1800s a Welsh
socialist called Robert Owen set up the New Lanark
Mills, with the aim of benefiting the workers. In
1819–1820 there was widespread rioting and three
Scottish radicals, James Wilson, Andrew Hardie and
John Baird were hanged. Scotland remained a centre
of Chartist and Liberal politics and in 1893 a former
Scottish miner called Keir Hardie founded the
Independent Labour Party, the forerunner of the
modern Labour Party.

→ *Keir Hardie became an MP in 1900. His new Labour Party transformed
British politics and led to the decline of the Liberal Party. Hardie also
campaigned for women's rights and self-government for India.*

SCOTLAND AT WORK

The eastern ports of Scotland were home to large fleets of sailing ships, which trawled the North Sea for herring. Women worked on shore gutting and cleaning the fish. Textiles and iron were the major industries around Lanark and Glasgow, and the River Clyde became a great centre for shipbuilding and shipping. Dundee grew wealthy processing jute imported from the lands of the British empire. By the time of Queen Victoria's death in 1901, one in three Scots lived in the cities – in Edinburgh, Glasgow, Dundee or Aberdeen.

⬇ *A new railway bridge over the Firth of Forth was opened in 1890. It was the world's first big steel bridge, with spans of 521 metres, and it immediately became one of the best-known sights in Scotland. It restored confidence in engineering that had been set back by a disaster on the Tay Bridge, destroyed by a storm in 1879.*

Famine in Ireland

In Ireland, industry chiefly developed in the north. Belfast soon grew to be larger than the Irish capital, Dublin. Belfast's economy depended upon linen textiles, engineering and shipbuilding. At the same time, much of rural Ireland was suffering from poverty and hunger. Ireland may now have been part of the United Kingdom, but its citizens did not seem to be treated equally. The Union was challenged time after time.

THE BOYCOTT

A new word entered the English language in 1880: 'to boycott'. It meant 'refusing to deal with someone'. The name came from Charles Boycott, the land agent for Lord Erne, who had an estate in County Mayo. When Boycott would not lower the rents, the tenants protested by refusing to speak or deal with him in any way.

O'CONNELL AND 'YOUNG IRELAND'

The fight for Irish Catholics to be able to vote was taken up by Daniel O'Connell, a popular lawyer known as 'the Liberator'. His campaign succeeded in 1829, but most Catholics did not own enough property to qualify for the vote. O'Connell went on to campaign against the Union with Great Britain. At first he was allied with a nationalist movement called 'Young Ireland', but its members soon disagreed with his policy of non-violence. They organised an armed uprising in 1848, but it was too small to succeed.

← *Daniel O'Connell, lawyer, politician and veteran campaigner for Irish rights, died in 1847, heartbroken by the tragedy of the famine.*

THE IRISH FAMINE

Tenant farmers of rural Ireland lived a wretched life. The rents they had to pay to landlords meant that they had to sell all the grain they could grow. For their own food, they relied on potatoes and little else. In 1845 the potato crop was struck by a blight, or mould. People starved and began to die of fever and dysentery. The landlords never went hungry and crops that could have saved lives were exported to England. The blight continued and the famine lasted three years.

↓ *In 1841 the population of Ireland was about 8 million. Perhaps 800,000 to a million people died during the years of famine.*

LANDLORDS AND FENIANS

The famine left lasting bitterness. It was felt that the government had done very little to prevent the tragedy and that landlords had neglected their tenants. New campaigns were now launched to protect tenants, in a long 'land war'. The Irish Republican Brotherhood grew up in the late 1850s. Its members, known as Fenians ('warriors') organised unsuccessful risings in 1865 and 1867 and campaigns of violence in England. Their aim was an independent Ireland.

IRISH AMERICANS

Many Fenians did not live in Ireland, but in the large Irish communities that were growing up overseas. The Irish who had settled in the eastern United States kept the campaign for Irish independence alive.

← *The State of Liberty was presented to the United States of America by France in 1886. It was erected at the entrance to the harbour in New York City, and so became a symbol of freedom and hope to the many poor people fleeing Europe at that time. These included generation after generation of Irish emigrants.*

EMIGRATION

During the famine and the years that followed, some 1½ million Irish people left their homeland to seek a better life overseas. Many ended up in Glasgow, Liverpool or London. Others sailed to seek a new life in the United States, Canada and Australia. They left behind deserted villages – and large areas where the Irish language was no longer heard.

HOME RULE FOR IRELAND?

In the 1870s the campaign for Irish tenants' rights was taken up by a Protestant politician called Charles Stewart Parnell. He won the support of many Fenians, but was cleared of involvement in acts of terror such as the murder of two English officials in Phoenix Park, Dublin, in 1882. Parnell's constant demands for 'home rule' by an Irish parliament were at last supported in London by the Liberal leader, William Gladstone. New laws were brought in to protect tenant's rights in the 1880s, but when Parnell died in 1891, Parliament still had not agreed to Irish home rule.

➡ *Charles Stewart Parnell (1846–91) was known as the 'uncrowned king of Ireland'. He became a Member of Parliament for Meath in 1875, standing for the Home Rule League. His tireless campaigning on the Irish question made it one of the leading issues of the day.*

SEXTON, M.P.   J.W. SULLIVAN, M.P.   PATRICK EGAN. T
CHARLES STUART PARNELL, M.P.
PRESIDENT OF THE IRISH LAND LEAGUE - ADDRESSING A MEETING.

THE GAELIC ATHLETIC ASSOCIATION

A Gaelic Athletic Association (*Cumann Lúthcleas Gael*) was founded in 1884 at Thurles, in County Tipperary. Its aim was to revive interest in traditional Irish sports and to give them formal rules. Chief amongst them were hurling, a fast stick and ball game, and Gaelic football, a variety of the sport in which the ball is punched as well as kicked. The Association was a success and became a cultural focus of the Irish nationalist movement, promoting the Irish language. With its headquarters at Croke Park in Dublin, the Association still plays an important part in Irish life today.

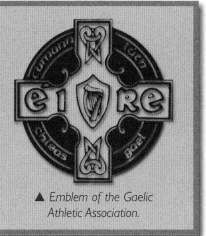

▲ *Emblem of the Gaelic Athletic Association.*

FAMINE IN IRELAND   353

1819
Highland Games held in Perthshire, Scotland.

1829
Oxford wins the first University Boat Race on the River Thames.

Sports and Entertainment

Many of today's sports were first given proper rules in the 19th century. Some were developed at famous public schools. In the later Victorian period, improved working conditions gave middle-class and working-class families more leisure time and holidays, making sports such as association football massively popular. The oldest football club, Sheffield, was founded in 1857.

↓ *Rugby was invented when a pupil at Rugby School, in England, picked up a football and ran with it. His name was William Webb Ellis and the year was 1823. The Rugby Football Union was founded in 1871.*

TEAM SPORTS

Some popular sports were updated versions of old favourites such as golf or cricket. The most successful Victorian cricketer was a bearded doctor called WG Grace, with whom few umpires dared to argue. Each year huge crowds would gather to watch the University Boat Race between Oxford and Cambridge, first rowed on the River Thames in 1829.

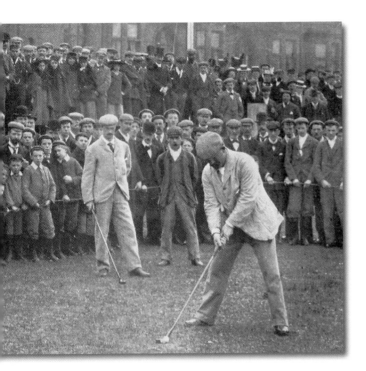

 A golf match takes place in about 1873 at St Andrew's, in Scotland, the ancient home of this sport.

THE GREAT OUTDOORS

Tourists now began to visit areas once considered as wilderness, climbing the Welsh and Scottish mountains. Cyclists left the towns for the country, some wobbling on high 'penny-farthing' machines that had one large wheel and one little one. Active lives made standards of dressing more free and easy. For leisure pursuits, men would wear blazers and round straw hats called 'boaters'. Some women cyclists caused outrage by wearing baggy breeches instead of long dresses.

A VICTORIAN CHRISTMAS

In 1832 young Princess Victoria was very excited by a Christmas tree put up at Kensington Palace, in London. The royal family had adopted this German custom as early as 1800, but it was not until the 1840s that Christmas trees became more commonly seen. It was then that the first Christmas crackers were made, too.

▼ *Christmas cards were first printed in London in 1843 and soon became highly popular.*

A Bright and Happy Christmas.

↓ *In an age when most people still travelled on horseback, rocking horses were popular toys in many nurseries.*

TOYS AND GAMES

Victorian children played with lead soldiers, cheap tin toys and trumpets, wooden bricks, jack-in-the-boxes and Noah's arks full of model animals. Children flew kites and bowled hoops in the street. Board games, card games and jigsaw puzzles were popular, too. Teddy bears did not appear in the shops until 1903.

TREADING THE BOARDS

Popular Victorian entertainments included over-acted plays with sentimental story lines or plots based on dreadful murders. From the 1880s onwards, rowdy crowds packed into 'music halls' to watch comedians, singers and dancers. For more polite audiences, light operas were written in the 1870s and 80s by Sir WS Gilbert and Sir Arthur Sullivan. These were witty and light-hearted, poking fun at Victorian society.

→ *Marie Lloyd started playing the music halls in 1885. She was a comedian and singer, and is still remembered for her hit songs 'Oh, Mr Porter' and 'My Old Man Said Follow the Van'.*

1872
A lawn tennis club is founded at Leamington, England.

1886
Founding of the Hockey Association in England.

A DAY AT THE SEASIDE

The Victorians loved trips to the seaside. Cheap rail travel meant that seaside resorts such as Blackpool in the north of England and Brighton on the south coast became popular holiday spots. Many people, including the royal family, enjoyed sea bathing, the wealthy often in bathing machines. These were horse-drawn huts that were wheeled into the sea, from where you could be lowered into the water by servants.

Brighton beach 1859. Rich and poor flocked to seaside towns. It was thought that the sea air helped to improve health.

The Great Powers

Russia had grown into a huge empire, stretching from Central Europe into Asia. In 1853 it invaded the region now known as Romania. At that time, this was ruled by the powerful Ottoman empire of the Turks. Turkey went to war with Russia. Because the United Kingdom and France wanted to stop Russia gaining control of the Balkan region, they joined forces with the Turks.

THE CRIMEAN WAR

In 1854 France and Britain sent troops to the Black Sea, even though the Austrians had already forced the Russians out of Romania. The allies landed on the Crimean peninsula, part of the Russian empire, and laid siege to the Russian naval base of Sebastopol. They won victories on the River Alma, at Balaclava and Inkerman, but the war is chiefly remembered for a disastrous charge by the British cavalry. Ordered in error to launch a direct attack on Russian guns at Balaclava, the Light Brigade galloped to certain death. The war was won in 1855, when a French force finally burst through the defences of Sebastopol.

➡ *The charge of the 600-strong Light Brigade at Balaclava in 1854 was commemorated by the great Victorian poet Alfred, Lord Tennyson. He described them riding 'Into the jaws of Death, Into the mouth of Hell'.*

REPORTS FROM THE BATTLEFIED

Magazines such as the *Illustrated London News*, with its drawings of current events, were very popular with the Victorians. However reports of the Crimean War, published by *The Times* newspaper, shocked the public. They were sent directly from the war zone by an Irish journalist called William Howard Russell. It was during the Crimean War that the first war photographs were taken, too. For the first time in history people could read about distant battles and see the reality of warfare for themselves.

▲ *This van was used to process photographs taken during the Crimean War.*

THE LADY WITH THE LAMP

The blunder at Balaclava showed that the British army was run by ageing aristocrats who had little understanding of modern warfare. The troops were poorly dressed and equipped and died in their thousands from cholera and frostbite. One person did care for the wounded and dying. In 1854 an English woman called Florence Nightingale arrived at Scutari (Üsküdar) with 38 nurses. With her strict concern for hygiene, she saved countless lives. On return to England, Florence Nightingale started the training of professional nurses.

PRIME MINISTERS OF THE UNITED KINGDOM	
✤ Benjamin Disraeli (Conservative)	1860
✤ William Gladstone (Liberal)	1868–1874
✤ Benjamin Disraeli (Conservative)	1874–1880
✤ William Gladstone (Liberal)	1880–1885
✤ Marquess of Salisbury (Conservative)	1885–1886
✤ William Gladstone (Liberal)	1886
✤ Marquess of Salisbury (Conservative)	1886–1892
✤ William Gladstone (Liberal)	1892–1894
✤ Earl of Rosebery (Liberal)	1894–1895
✤ Marquess of Salisbury (Conservative)	1895–1902

↑ *Florence Nightingale visited the sick and wounded by night, with a lantern. She became known as the 'lady with the lamp'.*

AT THE FRONT LINE

Another British nursing hero was Jamaican-born Mary Seacole. She came to London to volunteer as a nurse, but was turned down. She therefore travelled by herself to the Crimea in 1855, opened a hotel there and treated wounded soldiers on the battlefield, often when under fire. She helped British, French and Russian soldiers alike. Left in poverty after the war, a public fund was raised to help her, in recognition of her work.

1856
Introduction of the Victoria Cross, the highest military award for bravery.

1856
Florence Nightingale starts training nurses in England.

RIVAL NATIONS AND EMPIRES

New nation states were being founded across Europe. Italy united as a single kingdom in 1861. In 1867 the twin nation of Austria-Hungary was created. In 1871 Germany became a single country for the first time. Its *Kaiser* (emperor) was Wilhelm I. He was followed onto the throne in 1888 by Wilhelm II, a grandson of Queen Victoria. This was an age of petty nationalism, or 'jingoism', in which each nation tried to outdo the others.

By 1914, this would lead to the bloodiest war in history. In the meantime, European nations were building up vast empires overseas. The British empire now stretched around the world.

Italian nationalist Giuseppe Garibaldi and his 'Redshirt' volunteers reunited Italy in a series of daring military campaigns. Garibaldi became hugely popular in Britain and received a hero's welcome when he visited London in 1864. Many were inspired by his political ideals.

Jewels in the Crown

By 1869, ships could sail directly to Asia through the new Suez Canal. Passengers included troops and merchants, who were rapidly turning Asia's ancient empires into colonies from which they could reap rich rewards. Britain's Asian empire grew to take in the countries and ports now known as Aden, Pakistan, India, Bangladesh, Sri Lanka, Myanmar (Burma), Malaysia, Singapore, Brunei and Hong Kong.

← Indian brokers examine bales of cotton in Bombay. British cotton mills obtained about 20 percent of their cotton from India. However this changed when the civil war in the United States (1861–65) interrupted supplies from America. The result was a boom in Indian cotton.

BRITISH INDIA

British rule had a great influence on India, and India impressed the empire-builders in return. Generations of them came to know India's hot, dusty plains better than the distant islands of 'home'. They fought the Afghans along the Northwest Frontier, built railways, planted tea or played polo. Many of them were racists, who believed themselves to be superior to the Indians. Others worked hard for the country and its people, but British rule did not bring an end to poverty or starvation.

THE CHINA TRADE

One crop grown in India was the opium poppy. It was made into a very addictive drug. Britain exported Indian opium to China. When the Chinese government tried to ban this deadly trade in 1839, Britain declared war. Britain won this shameful conflict and as a result gained the Chinese port of Hong Kong as a colony. The rest of China remained an independent empire, but was forced to grant more and more trading rights to Western nations. British and French troops sacked Beijing, the Chinese capital, in 1860.

➜ One of China's chief exports was tea. Fast merchant ships called clippers raced back to Britain with their cargo. Clippers were the finest sailing vessels ever built. One of them, the Cutty Sark, can still be seen beside the River Thames at Greenwich, London.

1841
James Brooke becomes Rajah of Sarawak.

1842
Britain gains South China port of Hong Kong as colony.

THE JUNGLE BOOKS

Rudyard Kipling was an English writer born at Bombay, India in 1865. He was fascinated by India and wrote short stories and poems about common soldiers, officers and Indian life. For children he wrote the two classic *Jungle Books*. Although Kipling was inspired by the empire, he often criticized imperialism and realised that it must pass.

THE INDIAN MUTINY

In 1857 Indian soldiers (or 'sepoys') serving Britain's East India Company rose up against their commanders in northern India. In some regions this mutiny turned into a general uprising. The rebels captured Delhi and laid siege to Kanpur and Lucknow. They were defeated in 1858. From now on, however, India would be ruled not by the Company but by the British government itself. In 1877 Queen Victoria was declared Empress of India.

↓ *During the Indian Mutiny, the city of Delhi was held by the rebels for three months. British troops under the command of Sir Colin Campbell stormed its defences in September 1857.*

⬇ British government rule in India
(the 'Raj') lasted from 1858 to 1948.

IN SOUTHEAST ASIA

The British, French and Dutch all sought to control the rich Southeast Asian trade in spices, rubber, timber and minerals. An Englishman called Stamford Raffles founded Singapore in 1819, and in 1826 it joined Penang and Malacca as the Straits Settlements. In 1841 another Englishman, James Brooke, helped to defeat a rebellion against the Sultan of Brunei, on the island of Borneo. As a reward he was made the ruler, or Rajah, of Sarawak.

WORDS FROM THE EMPIRE

As the British empire spread, the English language reached new areas of the world. It is still widely spoken today in many parts of Asia and Africa. Sometimes English became mixed up with local languages and formed new dialects or simplified forms to create 'creole' or 'pidgin' speech. At the same time, English picked up many foreign words in return. From India alone came the words 'pyjamas', 'bungalow', 'curry', 'shampoo', 'bangle', 'cot', 'punch' (the drink), 'thug', 'chintz', 'loot' and 'jungle'.

To the Ends of the Earth

Britain's empire grew to take in the vast, unknown land of Australia, as well as New Zealand and many South Pacific islands. At first, the British only used Australia as a place to send prisoners. Many convicts died on the outward voyage and life in the prison colonies was harsh. Some escaped and sailed to New Zealand.

← *Aborigines were masters of survival in a harsh environment. They had lived in Australia for over 50,000 years, but the settlers claimed that they had no right to their own land.*

BRITAIN'S AUSTRALIAN COLONIES

By 1793 the first free settlers had arrived in New South Wales, but it was 1868 before all transportation of convicts to Australia came to an end. Settlers gradually opened up the dry lands of the interior. New or breakaway colonies were founded – Van Diemen's Land (Tasmania) in 1804, Western Australia in 1829, South Australia in 1836, Victoria in 1851, Queensland in 1859. While farmers and itinerant workers struggled to tame the dry and dusty lands of the 'outback', new cities sprang up around the coast. Railways and roads and seaports were built, and more and more colonists arrived to seek a new life 'down under'. The Aborigines, the first Austalians, suffered greatly. Some were employed as police scouts or as hands on the farms, but many were chased off their own land, moved to reserves or murdered.

1845
Start of First Maori War, New Zealand
(Second War 1860).

1851
Start of the gold rush in Australia.

GOLD NUGGETS, WOOLLY SHEEP

In 1851 gold was discovered in New South Wales.
Settlers poured into Australia in search of a fortune.
The miners had few legal rights and a major
revolt took place at Eureka, near Ballarat
in Victoria, in 1854. Thirty miners were
killed by mounted police. Another great
source of wealth was sheep farming. By
1890 there were 100 million
sheep in Australia.

*In 1860, Robert O'Hara Burke and
William John Wills set out on an expedition
across the unknown interior of Australia.
The explorers travelled with camels, horses
and wagons. However seven of the
explorers died, including the two leaders,
on the return journey in 1861.*

NED KELLY THE OUTLAW

Ned Kelly, the son of an Irish convict, was born in Victoria in 1855. He became an outlaw, or 'bushranger', whose gang robbed banks and stole cattle. After a train was held up at Glenrowan, three of the gang were killed. Ned Kelly was captured and hanged in 1880.

▶ When Ned Kelly was finally captured he was dressed in home-made armour.

NEW ZEALAND AND THE MAORIS

New Zealand was inhabited by the Maoris, a Polynesian people, and by a small number of mostly British settlers. In 1840 the British signed a treaty with Maori chiefs at Waitangi and New Zealand became a British colony. The settlers failed to honour the treaty and Maoris fought them from 1845 to 1847 and again from 1860 to 1872. From 1856, the settlers had their own Parliament. Many gold miners and farmers now arrived in New Zealand. From the 1880s, advances in refrigeration meant that lamb could be shipped back to Britain.

WHOSE AUSTRALIA?

Between 1823 and 1855, the Australian colonists gained increasing rights to govern their own affairs, and by 1901 the various colonies had come together to form a federation, the Commonwealth of Australia. There was a new Parliament – but the true Australians, the Aborigines, were denied the vote until 1967.

⬇ This war canoe was made by Solomon Islanders. Britain gained control of these Pacific islands between 1893 and 1900.

1901
Australian colonies unite as a federal Commonwealth.

1907
New Zealand becomes a Dominion of the British empire.

ACROSS THE PACIFIC

European seafarers, planters and Christian missionaries were now spreading out through the islands of the South Pacific. Many islanders fell victim to kidnappers called 'blackbirds', and were shipped off illegally to forced labour in Australia. Fiji became British in 1874 and Britain claimed southeastern New Guinea (Papua) in 1884. By the end of the century, most Pacific islands were under foreign rule.

HMS CHALLENGER

In 1872, a ship set out to explore a new world – the bottom of the sea. But the *HMS Challenger* wasn't a submarine. It measured the seabed, using ropes to find out the depth of the ocean. On its round-the-world voyage, *Challenger*'s crew also found many new species of sea creatures.

▼ *HMS Challenger*

TO THE ENDS OF THE EARTH 369

Into Africa

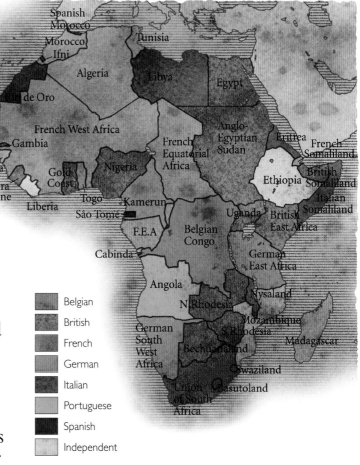

Spanish Morocco
Morocco
Ifni
Tunisia
Algeria
Libya
Egypt
Rio de Oro
French West Africa
Gambia
Anglo-Egyptian Sudan
Eritrea
French Somaliland
Port Guinea
Gold Coast
Nigeria
French Equatorial Africa
Ethiopia
British Somaliland
Sierra Leone
Togo
Kamerun
Italian Somaliland
Liberia
São Tomé
Uganda
British East Africa
F.E.A
Belgian Congo
Cabinda
German East Africa
Angola
Nyasaland
N. Rhodesia
Mozambique
German South West Africa
S. Rhodesia
Madagascar
Bechuanaland
Swaziland
Union of South Africa
Basutoland

Belgian
British
French
German
Italian
Portuguese
Spanish
Independent

⬆ *European powers competed with each other to control Africa. There were wars of resistance all over Africa, but people were helpless against troops armed with modern firearms. This map shows who ruled Africa in 1890.*

T he British may have ended their part in the slave trade, but it remained a curse in many parts of Africa. European explorers and Christian missionaries were now braving lions, spears and tropical fevers as they led expeditions into Africa. They were followed by traders, prospectors, colonists, hunters – and soldiers. By the end of Victoria's reign, most of Africa was under European rule.

SHARING THE SPOILS

Africans were used as a labour force, but were little better off than slaves. Their job was to extract the riches of the continent for colonial rulers. In southern and eastern Africa the best farmland was seized by white settlers.

At the Conference of Berlin in 1884–1885, regions of Africa were shared between European powers. They knew little about the peoples living there and did not care about their needs.

STANLEY AND LIVINGSTONE

In 1869, Livingstone went missing. He had gone exploring in East Africa and no one had heard from him. Everone thought he had died. An American writer, Henry Stanley, went to look for Livingstone. He found him in the town of Ujiji, in Tanzania. He greeted him with the words: "Dr Livingstone, I presume?"

▶ It took Henry Stanley eight months to find Dr Livingstone in Africa.

SCOTTISH EXPLORER

Dr David Livingstone was one of the most famous explorers of Africa. He went there in 1840 as a missionary, to try to teach African people to be Christians. He trekked right across the dusty Kalahari Desert with his wife and young children and discovered Lake Ngami. Livingstone became the first European to travel all the way across Africa. On the way, he discovered a huge, beautiful waterfall on the Zambezi River. The locals called it *Mosi Oa Tunya*, meaning 'the smoke that thunders'. Livingstone renamed it Victoria Falls, after Britain's Queen Victoria.

EAST AFRICAN LANDS

In 1887 the British East African Company leased the Kenya coast from its ruler, the Sultan of Zanzibar. Eight years later, Britain claimed the interior, eventually creating a colony called Kenya. British rule extended into neighbouring Uganda and (after 1918) into Tanganyika (now the mainland of Tanzania). Railways were built by labourers brought in from India, while farmers seized the highlands and planted coffee.

SUEZ TO SUDAN

In 1875 Britain became chief shareholder in the new, French-built Suez Canal, which cut through Egypt. Britain soon became more powerful in Egypt than the government itself. It also took control of Sudan, to the south. In 1877 British General Charles Gordon became governor of Sudan. He was killed at Khartoum in 1885, after an uprising led by the fiery religious leader Muhammad Ahmed, known as the *Mahdi* ('saviour'). In 1898 the British avenged Gordon's death at Omdurman, killing 11,000 Sudanese warriors.

➡ *A Zulu impi (armed unit). In South Africa, the British clashed with the highly disciplined armies of the Zulu nation. These inflicted a crushing defeat on British troops at Isandlhwana in 1879. The Zulu warriors fought with stabbing spears, clubs called knobkerries, and long shields.*

Ostrich plumes

Headband of fur

Fringes made from cows' tails

Spear

SOUTHERN AFRICA

In 1806 the British gained control of Cape Colony, South Africa. The Dutch had settled the area since the 1650s and resented British rule. In 1837 these 'Afrikaners' or 'Boers' ('farmers') left the Cape. They headed for the interior, where they founded independent republics. When reserves of diamonds and gold were found there, British businessman Cecil Rhodes saw this as a opportunity. His miners poured into the area, but Afrikaner president, Paul Kruger would not give them rights. In 1899 a war broke out between the British and the Boers. Peace was made in 1902 and the Union of South Africa was formed in 1910. Away from the battlefield, a British force at Rorke's Drift fought off Zulu attacks. British rule spread from South Africa into the countries we now call Lesotho, Botswana, Swaziland, Malawi, Zambia and Zimbabwe.

Knobkerrie

Shield made from cow hide

INTO AFRICA 373

North and South Atlantic

Queen Victoria's empire took in remote Atlantic outposts such as St Helena, Tristan da Cunha and the Falkland Islands. It governed Bermuda and many Caribbean islands. On the American mainland, the lands now known as Guyana and Belize were all part of her empire, as well as Canada's vast forests and prairies.

↑ *The Inuit or Eskimo people lived in scattered settlements in the Canadian Arctic.*

CANADA BECOMES A DOMINION

In 1791 Canada had been divided along the Ottawa River. Lower Canada was the French-speaking area, while Upper Canada was English-speaking. These two were united in 1840, taking in the provinces of Ontario, Quebec, Nova Scotia and New Brunswick. A parliament was set up in 1849 and in 1858 Ottawa became the Canadian capital, the personal choice of Queen Victoria. In 1867 Canada was made a self-governing Dominion of the British empire. This was set up along federal lines, with each province keeping its own elected assembly.

PRAIRIES AND FORESTS

Canada continued to expand into lands occupied by its First Peoples and by the Métis (people of mixed French–Indigenous descent). They rose up in rebellion in 1867, under the leadership of Louis Riel, but were defeated. Manitoba joined Canada (1870), British Columbia (1871), Prince Edward Island (1873), Alberta and Saskatchewan (1905). Poor farmers from all over Europe arrived to settle the Canadian prairies, and prospectors searching for gold arrived in the remote Northwest in 1896. Canada prospered from its timber, oil, mineral wealth and fisheries. The last province to join the Canadian federation was Newfoundland, in 1949.

⬇ The building of railways encouraged settlement of Canada's prairie provinces and the far west. The Canadian Pacific Railway spanned the country coast-to-coast by 1885.

⬇ Prospectors pose at a goldmine in British Columbia in about 1868.

1831
British Guiana (Guyana) becomes a colony.

1834
Slavery ends in Britain's Caribbean islands (to 1838).

THE CARIBBEAN ISLANDS

In the 1830s, slavery was ended in Britain's Caribbean colonies, which were known as the 'West Indies'. Many freed slaves moved off the plantations and lived by farming small plots of land, or fishing. They remained desperately poor and there was an uprising against the British governor on Jamaica in 1865, led by George William Gordon and Paul Bogle. On Trinidad, contracted labourers were brought in from Asia to work on the sugar plantations, but the majority population throughout the Caribbean region was now of African descent.

IN CENTRAL AND SOUTH AMERICA

In 1862 a small region of the Central American coast, occupied by British loggers, was made into a colony called British Honduras (modern Belize). In South America, sugar-producing British Guiana (modern Guyana) had become a colony in 1834. British people played an important part in the development of other South American lands, too, building railways high into the Andes mountains.

CARIBBEAN CARNIVAL

Trinidad and some other Caribbean islands began to celebrate Carnival in the 1800s. This festival had been brought to the region from Catholic Europe. At first, slaves were not allowed to take part, but after they were freed they made it their own, with dancing, singing and drumming to African rhythms. From the Asian community came spectacular costumes and masks.

▶ *Carnival originally marked the beginning of Lent, the Christian period of fasting. It is still celebrated in the Caribbean today.*

BANANAS AND LOGWOOD

Slavery was over, but the people of the Caribbean or 'West Indies' were still poor and working for colonial masters. Sugar, molasses and rum were mainstays of the economy, although internationally sugar was now being made from beet as well as from cane. By the end of the 19th century, other exports were becoming more important, such as bananas, coffee and logwood – a timber used in making dyes.

▶ Bananas have been grown on the Caribbean islands since the beginning of the 16th century.

▼ Slavery had dominated the culture and economy of the Caribbean for 300 years, when it was finally phased out in the 1830s.

The Modern Age

1901–2007

ELSEWHERE IN EUROPE	ASIA	AFRICA
1914 The First World War, fighting across Europe (until 1918).	**1912** The last Chinese emperor, a young boy, is forced to give up the throne.	**1914** First World War: colonial powers fight in Africa, Germany loses empire (1918).
1917 Revolutions in Russia, Bolsheviks (Communists) seize power.	**1931** Japan invades Manchuria (northeastern China).	**1942** Second World War: massive tank battles in North African desert.
1933 The National Socialist (Nazi) party comes to power in Germany.	**1940** Japan starts invasion of Southeast Asia in Second World War.	**1953** Egypt becomes a republic (nationalises Suez Canal 1956).
1936 Civil War between Republicans and Nationalists in Spain (until 1939).	**1945** United States drops atomic bombs on Hiroshima and Nagasaki in Japan.	**1957** The Gold Coast becomes the independent nation of Ghana.
1939 Second World War, Germany overruns Europe (defeated 1945).	**1947** British India divided into two independent states, India and Pakistan.	**1960** Nigeria gains independence from Britain.
1948 Start of 'Cold War'. Europe divided into Communist East and Capitalist West.	**1948** Israel declares an independent state in Palestine, southwest Asia.	**1960** Belgian Congo becomes independent, start of long civil war.
1957 Treaty of Rome: the European Economic Community (later European Union).	**1949** Communists defeat Nationalists in China, found a People's Republic.	**1961** Tanganyika becomes independent (Uganda 1962, Kenya 1963).
1990 Communist governments fall in Eastern Europe, end of the Cold War.	**1979** An Islamist revolution in Iran, the Shah (emperor) is overthrown.	**1994** Democracy introduced in South Africa: Nelson Mandela first black president.

"World science, world wars and the search for world peace…"

NORTH AMERICA

1911
Revolution in Mexico: president overthrown, land reform.

1914
Canada enters the First World War (United States, 1917).

1929
Wall Street 'crash' – US economic problems leads to Great Depression.

1939
Canada enters the Second World War (United States, 1941). War ends 1945.

1959
Revolution in Cuba, Fidel Castro seizes power.

1961
USA becomes involved in Vietnam War, in Southeast Asia (until 1973).

1962
Jamaica and Trinidad gain independence from Britain.

1963
US President John F Kennedy is assassinated in Dallas, Texas.

SOUTH AMERICA

1910
Massive oil reserves discovered in Venezuela.

1946
Juan Perón wins general election in Argentina.

1949
Bitter civil war in Colombia, La Violencia.

1960
Brasília replaces Rio de Janeiro as the capital of Brazil.

1966
Guyana gains independence from Britain.

1973
Chile's elected government is overthrown, Pinochet dictatorship.

1975
Independence for Suriname, mass emigration to Netherlands.

1982
Falklands War between Britain and Argentina in South Atlantic.

OCEANIA

1907
New Zealand becomes a Dominion within the British Empire.

1914
Australia and New Zealand enter First World War (until 1918).

1918
Germany defeated, loses its Pacific island possessions.

1931
Statute of Westminster confirms Australian independence.

1939
Australia and New Zealand enter the Second World War (until 1945).

1941
Japan bombs Pearl Harbor (Hawaii), invades Pacific islands (until 1945).

1967
Aborigines granted citizenship rights in Australia.

1968
Independence for Nauru (Fiji and Tonga 1970, Vanuatu 1980).

The Edwardian Age

Queen Victoria's funeral was held on 2 February 1901. It was attended by rulers from all over Europe, many of them her relatives. The new king was Edward VII. During his 60 years as Prince of Wales, he had led a roguish life of pleasure. How would he fare as a ruler?

↓ Queen Victoria's funeral cortege passes through the High Street, Windsor, on 2 February 1901. After lying in state, the queen was laid to rest at Frogmore Mausoleum on 4 February 1901.

UPSTAIRS, DOWNSTAIRS

The reign of Edward VII is often remembered as a golden age, a brief period of peace before the tide of war broke over Europe. For the aristocracy, it was a time of lavish weekend house parties, of balls, regattas and visits to the theatre. The middle classes in the growing suburbs worked in banks or businesses, played tennis and sang songs around the piano. Even middle class homes could afford servants and cooks. These worked 'below stairs', polishing boots or cleaning the silver. Upstairs were the halls, landings and family rooms, often furnished with umbrella stands, drapes and dark wooden furniture.

> **RULERS OF THE UNITED KINGDOM**
> **House of Saxe-Coburg and Gotha**
> ❧ Edward VII   1901–1910
> **House of Windsor**
> (new name as from 1917)
> ❧ George V   1910–1936
> ❧ Edward VIII (abdicated)   1936
> ❧ George VI   1936–1952
> ❧ Elizabeth II   1952

➡ *Edward VII's reign would only last nine years, but he was an active and effective ruler. His visit to Paris in 1903 helped to prepare the ground for close ties between Britain and France.*

⬇ *Edwardian ladies and gentlemen enjoying the Henley Regatta.*

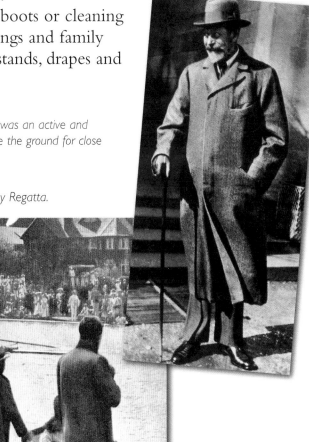

POVERTY AND UNEMPLOYMENT

For the working class, this age was far from golden. By 1904 there were 800,000 people in England and Wales registered for poor relief. In 1913, half a million school children were reported suffering from disease or a poor diet. There were many tragic mining accidents and industrial disasters – and an ever-growing number of strikes, as trade unions campaigned for fairer and safer working conditions. In 1909 the Liberal government brought in the first old age pensions.

⬆ *Many working class women were employed in 'service', as maids in private homes. They wore neat uniforms.*

THE GROWING CRISIS

Europe was arming for war. The German *Kaiser* was building up a naval fleet to challenge British rule of the seas. Britain made alliances with France in 1904 and with Russia in 1907. In 1914, these treaties were put to the test. The heir to the Austrian throne, Archduke Franz Josef, was assassinated in Bosnia by a young Serbian nationalist. Austria, encouraged by Germany, went to war with Serbia. Serbia was in turn supported by Russia. Within just a few weeks, almost the whole of Europe was on the brink of war – including the United Kingdom.

↑ *The German emperor or Kaiser, Wilhelm II, a grandson of Queen Victoria, came to the throne in 1888. He was disabled, a fact that he tried to conceal, and was conservative, rash, militaristic and jealous of British power.*

GOING SHOPPING

In Edwardian shop windows there were elaborate displays of goods or produce, and well-known advertisements for tea or soap. Shop assistants were formally dressed, with starched white aprons and cuffs. Goods could be delivered to the home by bicycle. Department stores, which had first arrived in Britain in the Victorian period, were now popular in cities. Here, clothes and furnishings and other assorted goods were all on sale under the same roof.

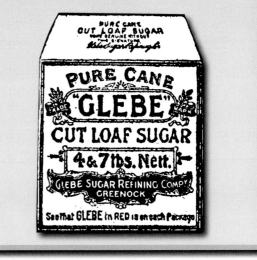

THE EDWARDIAN AGE

An Age of Speed

The new century saw a revolution in transport, even more extreme than the coming of the railways. Motor cars were on the road in ever greater numbers, along with motor omnibuses (buses), charabancs (open coaches), lorries and trams. Huge steamships called 'liners' – after the shipping lines that owned them – were powering their way across the oceans. Most amazingly, the sky itself was conquered, as the first airships and planes took to the air.

Charles Rolls in the racing car that beat the world record for one kilometre at 83 miles per hour. Rolls and Royce would become two of the most famous names in the history of motoring.

ENGINES OF CHANGE

The motoring age gave people more freedom of movement than ever before in history. It seemed as if the distances across the British Isles were shrinking. Motor buses could now reach even remote country districts.

The Wooler 348, a motorbike of the 1920s

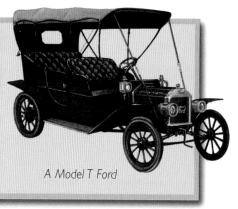

A Model T Ford

⬇ *Steam locomotion had reached its peak by 1938, when Mallard attained the speed of 126 miles per hour (202 kilometres per hour).*

BY LAND...

Steam locomotives were becoming ever more powerful and electric trains were in use in Britain as early as 1904. Some of the first cars were driven by steam too, or by electric batteries. The most successful were petrol-driven. Britain's early manufacturers included Charles Rolls and Frederick Henry Royce, who joined forces in 1904 to produce luxury cars, and WR Morris, who started production of more modest cars in Oxford, in 1913.

⬇ *This bus from the early 1920s was built by adding a coach body to a lorry base.*

John Alcock and Arthur Whitten Brown fly across the Atlantic Ocean.

Britain's first international airline service to Le Bourget, Paris, France.

THE TITANIC

In April 1912 the finest ocean liner ever built, pride of the White Star Line, was making its first voyage, across the North Atlantic. Although the SS *Titanic* weighed 39,380 tonnes, it was said to be unsinkable. However it hit an iceberg at high speed and sank to the sea bed, drowning 1513 passengers and crew in the freezing water. Some 700 escaped in lifeboats.

↑ *The* Titanic *disaster of 1912 became one of the most famous shipwrecks in history.*

BY SEA...

In 1897 an Irish engineer called Charles Parsons built a vessel called *Turbinia* at Heaton, in County Durham. Parsons had perfected the use of steam turbines (vanes rotated at high speed) in order to power ships at speeds of up to 35 knots (64 kilometres per hour).

By 1907 turbines enabled even the huge liner SS *Lusitania* to cross the Atlantic Ocean at an average speed of 23 knots (43 kilometres per hour). Liners were fitted out with luxurious cabins, splendid dining rooms and ballrooms.

1919
British airship R34 flies across the Atlantic from Scotland to New York City.

1930
Amy Johnson flies solo from England to Australia.

→ *Large aeroplanes designed to land on water were popular in the 1930s and 40s. They were called 'flying boats'. The Sunderland (right) saw service with the Royal Air Force.*

... AND AIR

The first flight by an aeroplane took place in 1903, in the United States. Five years later, planes were flying in Britain, too. The first ones were fragile machines, often 'biplanes' (having twin wings). Flight developed rapidly during the First World War (1914–1918) and in the 1920s and 30s air races and flying shows became popular spectator sports. In the 1930s, Imperial Airways were carrying small numbers of passengers to Africa, India and Australia. Airships – large gas-filled, cigar-shaped aircraft powered by engines – competed with aeroplanes until 1937, when a series of accidents made them unpopular.

↓ *Captain John Alcock and Lieutenant Arthur Whitten Brown were the first to fly non-stop across the Atlantic Ocean in 1919.*

First World War

In August 1914 the United Kingdom **and Germany went to war.** Most people believed it would all be over by Christmas, but this terrible conflict dragged on for over four years. It was known as the Great War. Today we call it the First World War, for it was fought in many different lands by armies from many nations.

THE ROAD TO WAR

The world order collapsed like dominoes. Austria-Hungary, backed by Germany, threatened Serbia. Russia, backed by France, supported Serbia. Germany attacked France via neutral Belgium, which was backed by Britain. The result? The worst conflict the world had ever known…

The assassination of the Austrian heir, the Archduke Franz Ferdinand, by a Serbian nationalist triggered the First World War.

Archduke Franz Ferdinand, Sarajevo, 28 June 1914

388   1901–2007

1915
March: British fleet blockades German ports.

1915
April: Australians, New Zealanders and British land at Gallipoli, in Turkey.

THE WAR POETS

Before the First World War, poets used to celebrate victories and write of heroic deeds. Now many wrote of horror and anger at seeing so many young men being killed like cattle. Great poets who served as soldiers included Wilfred Owen (1893–1918) and Siegfried Sassoon (1886–1967).

NATIONS AT WAR

As well as British and Irish soldiers, empire troops included Indians, East Africans, South Africans, Canadians, Australians and New Zealanders. Their allies in the 'Entente' included France and its empire, Japan, Italy (from 1915), Russia (until 1918) and the United States (from 1917). Ranged against them were the 'Central Powers' – Germany, Austria-Hungary, Bulgaria and Turkey.

⬆ *Along the Western Front, the warring armies dug themselves into trenches defended by razor-sharp barbed wire.*

THE PEOPLE'S WAR

In the 1800s, wars had been fought by professional soldiers, far from home. Now, warfare was coming home. Civilians found that they could be bombed in their houses by the new planes and airships, and that passenger liners as well as warships could be attacked by submarines. In 1916 the British government began to conscript members of the public, calling them up to serve in the armed forces.

▲ *The Royal Flying Corps (forerunner of the Royal Air Force) was founded in 1912. During the war, its pilots could expect to live for just two weeks of combat. The most famous British fighter plane was the Sopwith Camel, in production from 1916.*

◄ *Ambulances carried wounded men from the front line. Severe wounds meant a return to 'Blighty' – the British Isles.*

FIRST WORLD WAR **389**

1916
May: Naval battle off Jutland.

1916
July–November: First Battle of the Somme,
1,043,896 killed.

TRENCHES AND MUD

Fighting took place in the snowy forests of eastern Europe, in Turkey and the deserts of Arabia, on the plains of East Africa. There were great naval battles and beneath the waves, submarines stalked Atlantic shipping. The bloodiest fighting was on the Western Front, a long line of defensive trenches that stretched from Belgium, through France, down to the Swiss border. Soldiers on both sides lived and died in wretched conditions. Any who fled were tried for desertion and then shot.

Troops are ordered 'over the top', leaving their trenches for a new assault. Thousands of lives were often sacrificed to gain just a few metres of land. At the battle of Passschendaele, fought in Belgium in 1917, some 270,000 Germans died. Allied losses, from British, Canadian, South African, Australian and New Zealand troops, numbered about 300,000.

ONE SILENT NIGHT

Along one sector of the Western front, on Christmas Eve 1914, the German troops raised Christmas trees from the mud of their trenches and lit candles. They began to sing German carols such as *Stille Nacht*. British troops recognised the tune as *Silent Night* and joined in. The guns fell silent. On Christmas morning troops from both sides left their postions and joined together in 'no-man's-land'. They exchanged rations and played a game of football. The troops were soon ordered back to their lines to resume the slaughter.

German infantryman 1915 nickname: 'Fritz'
The German soldier fought with a Mauser rifle. It was reliable but its magazine held only five bullets, so more time was spent reloading.

CHANGING ALLIANCES

There were changes in the alliances and armies during the course of the war. Italy joined the conflict in 1915, on the side of Britain and its allies. It suffered a dreadful defeat at Caporetto in 1917. The United States too entered the war in 1917, following a 1915 German submarine attack on the *Lusitania*, a liner carrying American passengers as well as munitions destined for Britain. By 1918 American troops (nicknamed 'doughboys') were pouring into Europe. However Russia, one of the original allies, collapsed in revolution during 1917, and many of its troops deserted from the Eastern Front. The new revolutionary government withdrew from the war.

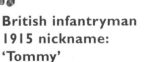

British infantryman 1915 nickname: 'Tommy'
The British soldier fought with a Lee Enfield 0.303 rifle, which could be fitted with a bayonet. Its magazine held 10 bullets, and could be fired at the rate of about 12 shots a minute.

FIRST WORLD WAR   **391**

→ HMS Dreadnought. By 1914 the most modern warships were encased in thick armour and carried large guns mounted in armoured turrets that could turn to face different directions.

◄ A British cavalryman and his horse charge forwards wearing anti-gas masks. The gas attack should have allowed the cavalry to break through the German lines and attack, but this failed to happen.

POISON WARFARE

Terrible new weapons were introduced by both sides during the First World War. The French used tear gas as early as 1914, but the following year the Germans used chlorine gas, a deadly choking poison, against French troops. The Allies soon also adopted gas warfare, and ever more deadly chemicals were developed, such as phosgene and mustard gas. Gas attacks were hard to control, as the chemicals drifted with the wind, and troops had to wear cumbersome gas masks over their faces. Those soldiers who survived gas attacks often suffered terribly from illnesses and mental problems for the rest of their lives.

→ *Equipped with a small gun and carrying only three men this light tank could move quickly to attack enemy infantry, but was highly vulnerable to artillery fire.*

TANK ATTACK

The first tanks were known as 'land ships' and were developed by the British. They terrified the enemy, but they did not work very well and were often stuck in the mud. Conditions for the tank crews were appalling.

• The first use of British tanks was at Delville Wood in 1916. French tanks first appeared in the Aisne offensive of 1917.

• At the Battle of Cambrai in 1917, 474 British machines won the first major tank victory.

• German tanks attacked the British at Villers Bretonneux in 1918, the first battle in which tanks fought against tanks.

A LOST GENERATION

In 1914 the soldiers had marched off to war in a patriotic mood, singing the popular songs of the day. When the guns fell silent in 1918, some 10 million young men had been killed in all the armies. Countless more were left blinded, disabled, or in a state of severe stress called 'shell-shock'. The Allies had won the war, but at a terrible cost.

← *A heavy howitzer with its barrel aimed to hurl shells at a high trajectory. Shells falling steeply onto enemy defences penetrated deep into the soil before exploding. This allowed them to burst under concrete defences and shatter them.*

FIRST WORLD WAR

Easter 1916

The question of Irish home rule had been a burning political issue for 100 years. In 1912 the proposal returned to Parliament in London. In Protestant Ulster, supporters of the union with Britain were prepared to use violence to oppose the bill. Their leader was lawyer Sir Edward Carson. Would Ireland be divided? Would there be civil war? The bill was passed in 1914 but immediately postponed. The First World War had broken out.

THE EASTER RISING

Many Irishmen were soon fighting in the war, but to others there was another priority – fighting against the Union. Sir Roger Casement, a well-known Irish diplomat, sought help from Germany for a rising – but was captured as he landed from a German submarine. It was Easter 1916 and an uprising was taking place in Dublin. The rebels seized the large General Post Office and their leader, Pádraig Pearse, proclaimed a republic. After five days they were shelled into surrender by the British army. At first they had little widespread support, but when 15 of them were executed by the British, Irish public opinion changed. At the general election of 1917, the republican party Sinn Féin ('Ourselves Alone') won an historic victory.

1914
Home Rule is passed, but postponed because of
the war.

1916
The Easter Rising suppressed in Dublin.
Fifteen executed.

↓ *Irish rebels defend ruined
buildings in Dublin against
British troops armed with
machine guns.*

WRITERS AND DREAMERS

The new century was an inspiring time for Irish writers.
George Bernard Shaw (1856–1950) was writing challenging
essays and plays about great social issues. The playwright
JM Synge (1871–1909) was director of Dublin's Abbey
Theatre. The beautiful poems of WB Yeats (1865–1939) took
Ireland as their theme and were inspired by the events of
1916. In 1914 James Joyce published *Dubliners*, short stories
about life in the Irish capital. His later work, in the 1920s
and 30s, shocked the world with a new kind of language that
reflected humans' rambling thoughts, fears and dreams.

IRA AND THE 'BLACK AND TANS'

Sinn Féin, led by Éamon de Valera, did not take up its seats in Parliament. Instead, it set up its own Irish Assembly, or Dáil Éireann. In 1919 a ruthless guerrilla organisation, the Irish Republican Army (IRA), was set up to fight the British. It was countered by special military units sent in from England to help the police. Known from their uniform colours as the 'Black and Tans', their tactics were often brutal. In 1920 Ireland was split in two. In the north, six out of Ulster's nine counties were given their own parliament, while the the rest of Ireland had theirs.

AN IRISH FREE STATE?

In 1921, Sinn Féin sent delegates to London, including Arthur Griffith and Michael Collins. They agreed to the partition of Ireland, with the south becoming a Free State, similar to a self-governing Dominion of the British empire. Back in Ireland their decision was rejected by de Valera, who wanted nothing short of an independent republic. A bitter war broke out within Sinn Féin. Collins was set to be head of the new Irish Free State government when he was murdered by the IRA.

⬇ *A pall of smoke hangs over central Dublin at Easter 1916. The rising by the Irish Volunteers and the Irish Citizen Army resulted in the death of 418 people.*

THE ROAD TO A REPUBLIC

Sinn Féin refused to recognise a Free State government, but in the end de Valera decided that it could be used as a step towards a full republic. In 1926 he founded a new political party, Fianna Fáil ('Soldiers of Destiny'), and in 1933 another party was founded, Fine Gael ('Tribes of the Gaels'). In 1938 the Irish Free State declared independence under the name of Éire. Éire remained neutral in the Second World War (1939–1945) and in 1949 became the fully independent Republic of Ireland.

↑ After 1919, the nationalist cause was fought by the IRA, which opposed the partition of Ireland. In 1969 a breakaway group was formed – the Provisional IRA.

↑ An impression of the Irish landscape by painter Jack B Yeats. The brother of the poet W B Yeats, he also produced portraits of Irish life and designs for theatre.

ARAN ISLANDERS

The Irish nationalists came from many different backgrounds, but they were inspired by the Gaelic culture, language and way of life. Nowhere had this survived in a more traditional form than amongst the fishermen and farmers of the Aran Islands, in Galway Bay. The islanders inspired the writer JM Synge and were the subject of a famous documentary film, *Man of Aran*, in 1934.

Votes for Women

In February 1913, the home of Chancellor David Lloyd **George was destroyed by a bomb.** In May of that year, a bomb was placed in St Paul's Cathedral, London. In June, during the Derby event at the Epsom races, a woman called Emily Davison dashed out and grasped the reins of a racehorse owned by the king. She was trampled beneath the hooves and died the next day.

A STRUGGLE FOR EQUALITY

The 1913 protests were all by women demanding suffrage – the right to vote. They were known as 'suffragettes' or 'suffragists'. Women had never been allowed to take a democratic part in choosing how the country was governed. Most men were shocked by the protests, for in those days women were expected to obey their husbands and raise children rather than take part in political campaigns. In 1889 a campaigner called Emmeline Pankhurst founded the Women's Franchise League and in 1903 she and her daughter Christabel formed the Women's Social and Political Union (WSPU). The suffragists met with public ridicule and abuse, but they argued their case loud and long.

← *Wearing sashes labelled 'votes for women', female suffragists argue their case with labourers carrying out road works.*

THE PANKHURSTS

Emmeline Pankhurst (1857–1928) campaigned for women's rights for 40 years. She and her eldest daughter Christabel were often imprisoned. They stopped campaigning when the First World War broke out in 1914. Emmeline later joined the Conservative Party. Emmeline's other two daughters were also suffragists. Sylvia and Adela (who moved to Australia) actively opposed the war and became socialists.

▼ The Pankhursts all lived to see women gain equal voting rights with men.

▲ Suffragettes protested by breaking windows and chaining themselves to railings. Many were sent to prison.

 A woman bus conductor stands on the platform of a Number 19 double-decker bus. The 20th century saw a revolution in women's role in society.

VOTES FOR WOMEN

1912
Suffragettes smash shop windows and protest at the House of Commons.

1913
WSPU member Emily Davison dies in Derby protest.

↓ *The sight of women brandishing placards and chaining themselves to railings infuriated many men in the Edwardian era.*

PUBLIC PROTEST

The WSPU developed new forms of protest in order to gain publicity for their cause. They committed violent acts against property like smashing shop windows. When they raided the House of Commons, it resulted in 96 arrests. When they were sent to jail, they went on hunger strike, refusing to eat. The prison officers force-fed them through tubes. Under a special law, the authorities could keep releasing women hunger-strikers, only to send them back to prison again once they had recovered.

INTO THE WORKPLACE

During the First World War, men were needed to fight in the armed services and many were killed. Women took over jobs once done by men. They worked on the farms and in munitions factories, making shells and weapons for the front line. By the time the war was over, women had become more accepted as a part of the workforce. Public opinion was changing.

POLITICAL PROGRESS

In 1918, British women at last won the right vote in general elections, but only if they were aged over 30. It was not until 1929 that the voting age for men and women was equalized, at 21. During the 1920s more and more women found work as office secretaries, typists or telephone operators, but still received lower wages than men.

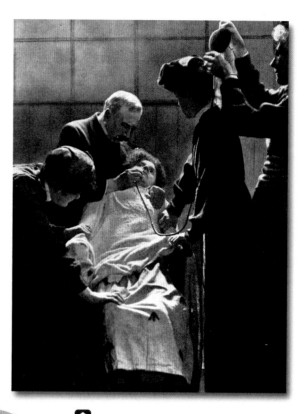

➡ *In 1919 American-born Nancy Astor became the first woman to be elected as a Member of Parliament, winning Plymouth for the Conservatives.*

⬆ *A suffragette prisoner on hunger strike, being force-fed by prison authorities.*

1896
First cinema opens in United Kingdom.

1914
Charlie Chaplin goes to make films in Hollywood, USA.

Dance to the Music

People tried to forget the horrors of the First World War with dancing, popular songs and music, visits to the picture palace (cinema) or summer trips to the seaside. The stuffiness of the Edwardian era disappeared. Women wore shorter dresses. Their hair was now bobbed short, and was often curled into permanent waves ('perms'). They wore lipstick and face powder. They often smoked cigarettes – unaware of the risk to their health.

← Film star 'Charlie' Chaplin (Sir Charles, 1889–1977) became one of the first human beings to be instantly recognisable around the world.

GOING TO THE PICTURES

The first films were silent, in black and white. A pianist played music to fit in with the story. The best-known film star of all was Charlie Chaplin (1889–1977). During a childhood of poverty in south London, he performed on stage in the music halls. After 1914 he made comic films in Hollywood. In many of them he played a tramp. Chaplin hated social injustice and underlying the clowning there was often a serious message about the times he lived in.

← Weekly visits to the cinema offered escape to the magical world of Hollywood stars.

JAZZ – AND JEEVES

The music of the new century was jazz, first played by African Americans in the USA. By 1919 this wild, free-flowing music was being heard in England. Wind-up record-players, or gramophones, now made it possible to play music and dance in the home. The good life of England in the 1920s and 30s was sent up by a witty writer called PG Wodehouse. His world was peopled by flappers, goofy young aristocrats and a butler named Jeeves – who was far wiser than his master.

⬇ *Fashionable, flighty young women were known as flappers. They shocked their parents with 'unladylike' American dances such as the Charleston. They loved parties and driving motorcars. By the 1930s the age of fun was over as economic problems took hold, but after the flapper era, young women were never quite the same again.*

⬇ *One of the most famous jazz musicians was the American Louis Armstrong (1900–1971), a gifted trumpet player from New Orleans – the so-called 'birthplace of jazz'. He first visited England in 1932.*

TUNING IN

The 'wireless' was all the rage. Schoolboys learned how to make very basic radio receivers, called 'crystal sets'. The British Broadcasting Company, established in 1922, was made into a Corporation (the BBC) in 1927. Soon people were listening to plays, music, sport, comedy shows and news, all in their own living room. King George V broadcast to the nation on Empire Day, 23 April 1924.

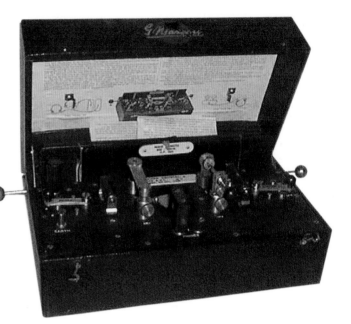

↑ The radio soon became a part of everyday life. News had once taken days to reach every corner of the British Isles. Now it could be broadcast as it happened.

← In 1932, George V became the first monarch to make a Christmas broadcast to the nation.

A ROYAL CRISIS

In 1936 newspaper headlines reported a crisis in the royal family. George V had died and his eldest son Edward was due to follow him as king. However Edward intended to marry an American woman called Wallis Simpson, who was divorced. Divorce was considered to be scandalous in the 1930s. Public opinion forced Edward VIII to abdicate (resign) and his younger brother was crowned George VI in his place.

 The Duke of York (second from right) became king as George VI. He was a shy man who became a popular ruler.

Edward VIII gave up the throne in order to marry Wallis Simpson (below). He became Duke of Windsor instead of king.

The Hunger Years

The glitter of high society in the 1920s and 30s hid desperation and poverty. After 1922, the British economy slowed down and countless men who had fought for their country now found themselves jobless, while their families went hungry. Germany too faced economic chaos after the First World War, made worse by the harsh terms of the 1919 Treaty of Versailles. This dragged down the economy of the rest of Europe.

↑ Life in Glasgow's Gorbals district was tough. It had some of the worst housing in Britain and a wretched record in public health.

→ Armoured cars take to London streets during the General Strike. The government feared a Communist revolution, as had happened in Russia in 1917.

THE JARROW MARCH

During the 1930s, 'hunger marches' were held as workers from Wales, Scotland and the north of England marched on London to protest against unemployment. In 1936, 200 men from Jarrow, on Tyneside, walked all the way to London on what they called a 'Crusade'. They were led by their Member of Parliament, Ellen Wilkinson, and were given food and sleeping places by supporters along the way.

▼ *The dignity and endurance of the Jarrow marchers impressed many people. It brought home to them the desperate poverty in Britain's industrial regions.*

THE GENERAL STRIKE

In 1926 a report on British coal mining called for wages to be lowered, yet the companies were demanding longer working hours. Miners went on strike and called on other workers to join them. Two million did and the country was paralysed. Middle-class volunteers tried to break the strike, driving buses and trains. The Trades Union Congress dropped their support within nine days, but it was another six months before the miners were defeated.

THE GREAT DEPRESSION

The United States now had the most powerful economy in the world. When it began to show signs of weakness in 1929, there was panic as people sold off their shares. The US economy crashed and European economies that depended on US credit came tumbling down too. Within a year, unemployment around the world had doubled. The crisis was so severe that British political parties joined together in a coalition government.

➡ *The dire effects of the US stock market crash in 1929 (right) were soon felt on this side of the Atlantic.*

JOINING THE FIGHT IN SPAIN

During the 1920s and 30s, capitalism seemed to be in a crisis, just as Karl Marx had predicted. Many young people in the British Isles looked to new political ideals such as socialism and communism. From 1936 many of them went as private volunteers to fight in Spain, where a bitter civil war had broken out. It was being fought between the elected Spanish government and their conservative and fascist opponents, led by General Franco. An 'International Brigade' was formed to help fight Franco, but the pro-government forces were defeated.

▼ *The Spanish Civil War was bloody and chaotic. It was described by the British writer George Orwell (real name Eric Blair) in his book* Homage to Catalonia *(1938).*

THE RISE OF FASCISM

A new political system took root amidst Europe's economic chaos. Fascism first developed in Italy in 1921. It aimed to replace 'weak' democracies with thuggery, dicatorship and extreme nationalism. Fascists went under various names. Racist 'National Socialists' (Nazis) seized power in Germany in 1934. In 1936 'Falangists' attacked the democratic government in Spain. Fascist groups were formed in England and Ireland too. London's East Enders came out to stop them marching through the streets.

→ *The Nazi leader Adolf Hitler took power in Germany in 1933. He attacked Jewish citizens, built up the army and prepared for war. The storm clouds were building up yet again over Europe.*

← *Fascism had its sympathisers in Britain. Sir Oswald Mosley founded the British Union of Fascists in 1932. His black-shirted bullies fought with Communists and Jews on the streets of London.*

A Brave New World

In the 20th century, human understanding of life and the universe made rapid advances. New materials were invented, new technologies, new machines. The United Kingdom was often in the forefront of exciting new research and invention. However as science crossed new frontiers, it raised new fears. It could be used to save life and do good – but it could also be used to destroy life on a terrifying scale, in war.

⬇ *Shining new buildings of glass, steel and concrete began to be built around British cities. The Hoover Building, at Perivale, West London, was constructed in 1935.*

TECHNOLOGY IN THE HOME

In the 1920s and 30s many houses began to look less cluttered. Designers, inspired by German ideas, brought efficiency and hygiene to the kitchen. Electricity now powered all sorts of household gadgets, from refrigerators to washing machines. Such goods were still expensive, and it would be the 1950s before they became very common in the British Isles. New everyday materials included plastics – bakelite (1909), cellophane (1912), perspex (plastic glass,1930) and PVC (1943). Artificial fibres were developed too – nylon in 1935 and a British invention, terylene, in 1941.

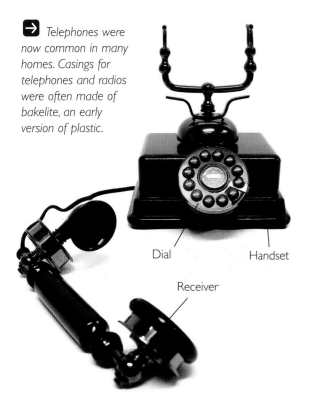

➡ *Telephones were now common in many homes. Casings for telephones and radios were often made of bakelite, an early version of plastic.*

Dial   Handset

Receiver

A TELEVISION PIONEER

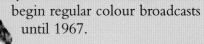

John Logie Baird (1888–1946) was a Scottish electrical engineer. In 1926 he gave the world's first public demonstration of television. The BBC used Baird's systems from 1929 to 1937. It was not until the 1950s that televisions became widely owned in Britain. Baird had experimented with colour television as early as 1928, but the BBC did not begin regular colour broadcasts until 1967.

◀ *John Logie Baird played a very important part in the invention and development of television.*

BIROS AND CATS EYES

Everyday life in Britain and Ireland would be transformed by many other amazing new inventions that were being made around the world at this time, although it often took decades for gadgets to be in common use. Inventions included the aerosol can (1927), frozen food (1930), sticky tape (1930), FM radio (1933), 'cats' eyes' (road reflectors, an English invention of 1934), the ballpoint pen or 'Biro' (1938) and synthetic rubber (1943).

A BRAVE NEW WORLD **411**

THE BOFFINS

In the 1940s and 50s, the slang word for inventors, scientists and engineers was 'boffins'. Frank Whittle was born in Coventry and joined the Royal Air Force. From 1930 onwards, he worked on theories of jet propulsion. The first jet aircraft was produced in Germany, but Whittle's engine was flight-tested by 1941, during the Second World War. Radar (Radio Detecting And Ranging) was also developed in various countries during the 1930s. It is a system that uses radio waves to detect objects such as aircraft. Britain's expert was a Scottish scientist called Robert Watson-Watt, who had an effective radar system up and running by 1935. It would play a crucial part in the coming war. One of the scientists who had been working on radar was Bernard Lovell. He had become interested in cosmic rays and between 1947 and 1957 he developed a site at Jodrell Bank near Manchester, where he used radio telescopes to carry out pioneering space research.

 Frank Whittle's jet engine was the forerunner of those built in the United States and the Soviet Union during the 1940s and 50s.

EARLY COMPUTERS

The most remarkable invention of the 1940s was the electronic computer. Colossus was the first programmable computer in Britain, built in 1943 to crack wartime codes. Manchester University's Mark I computer was built in 1948. The first computers were massive machines compared with today's, weighing many tonnes.

⬆ *Colossus was built in 1943 to decode messages used by the Germans during World War II.*

LIFE AND THE LABORATORY

In 1928 a scientist called Alexander Fleming noticed mould growing on a culture dish in his laboratory. It contained an antibiotic – an organism that could destroy harmful bacteria in the human body. With the help of two Oxford research scientists, Ernst Chain and Howard Florey, it was developed into the drug penicillin. It was in 1953 that one of life's great mysteries was finally solved – the structure of DNA. This is the chemical code that programmes all life, being passed on from one generation to the next. Research was carried out in London and Cambridge by Rosalind Franklin, Maurice Wilkins, Francis Crick and, American, James Watson.

▼ *The structure of DNA turned out to be a double spiral, or helix.*

◄ *Alexander Fleming's discovery saved countless lives.*

A BRAVE NEW WORLD

413

The Second World War

The Nazi dictator of Germany, Adolf Hitler, was building up German military power. In 1938 British Prime Minister Neville Chamberlain made an agreement with Hitler at Munich, promising 'peace in our time'. It was soon broken. German tanks rolled into Czechoslovakia and Poland. By 1939, Britain and Germany were at war. The war spread around the globe like wildfire and claimed the lives of about 55 million troops and civilians, the bloodiest conflict in human history.

⬆ *The trench warfare of the First World War was a thing of the past. The Second World War was highly mobile. The Germans called it* Blitzkrieg *or 'lightning warfare'. Their rapid invasion of Europe was carried out by tanks, like this one, and by fighter aircraft. There were also huge tank battles in North Africa.*

DIVISION OF EUROPE

The map of Europe had been re-drawn by the Treaty of Versailles in 1919. The new borders did not survive for long. Germany annexed Austria, invaded Czechoslovakia, Poland and then France and much of continental Europe. It was 1941 before the Allies were joined by the Russians and the Americans. The Axis powers were joined by Japan in the same year.

KEY

▪ Allies	6 Lithuania	13 Austria
▪ Axis powers	7 East Prussia	14 Hungary
1 Norway	8 Netherlands	15 Albania
2 Denmark	9 Belgium	16 Greece
3 Sweden	10 Luxembourg	17 Bulgaria
4 Estonia	11 Czechoslovakia	18 Republic
5 Latvia	12 Switzerland	of Ireland

1940
Rescue of British troops from Dunkirk. Italy joins the war.

1940
Germans invade the Channel Islands. Battle of Britain fought in the air.

➡️ *Family air-raid shelters were issued in Britain from February 1939. Nearly 2.5 million shelters of this type were erected in gardens during the war. The boy in the picture is trying on a gas mask.*

Outside view

Anderson shelter

WAR BENEATH THE WAVES

Submarines, called U-boats by the Germans, played a major part in the war around the world. The submarines attacked merchant ships, aircraft carriers and warships with torpedoes. The ships responded by dropping underwater explosives, called depth charges. Merchant ships and troop transports steaming between Britain and the United States or the Soviet Union were forced to travel in convoys (large groups defended by heavily armed naval vessels). Submarines could be located with a sound ranging device called Sonar.

⬇️ *The Messerschmitt Me-109 was a German fighter plane, often used for 'reconnaissance' – surveying enemy areas.*

⬇️ *Submarines prowled the Atlantic Ocean in search of their prey. Many sailors and submariners on both sides were drowned during this deadly Battle of the Atlantic.*

THE SECOND WORLD WAR   **415**

1941
Germany invades Soviet Union. Japan attacks USA at Pearl Harbor.

1942
Japan captures Singapore, taking 70,000 Allied prisoners.

BRITAIN STANDS ALONE

In 1940, Germany rapidly invaded Scandinavia, the Netherlands, Belgium and France. Fascist Italy entered the war on Germany's side, and the Balkans and Greece were invaded. Britain was isolated in Europe. In 1941 Germany attacked its former ally, the Soviet Union (as Russia was then called), and Japan declared war on Britain and the United States. Japan had already invaded areas of China and it now advanced through Southeast Asia. Although Britain now had more enemies, it had also gained powerful allies.

⬆ *St Paul's Cathedral rises above a smouldering London. German night-time bombing of Britain's major cities began on 7 September 1940. This 'Blitz' killed about 40,000 civilians and injured many more. Over a million homes were pounded into rubble.*

V FOR VICTORY

In 1940 Winston Spencer Churchill (1874–1965) became British Prime Minister. As a young soldier, he had fought in Sudan and he later served both as a Conservative and a Liberal MP. He was always a controversial politician, but in wartime he inspired people with his gritty personality, his brilliant speeches – delivered in a growling voice – and his shrewd judgement.

▶ *Winston Churchill gestures V – for 'Victory'.*

In the late summer of 1940, the skies of Britain were filled with vapour trails and the sound of fighter aircraft from the Royal Air Force battling in 'dogfights' with the German Luftwaffe. By the end of October, the Germans had lost 1733 planes, and the Allies 915. The 'Battle of Britain' had been won.

RAF fighter pilots relax next to their Spitfires while waiting for the signal to 'scramble' (take off) and battle with the enemy.

↑ *In 1944, British troops were combing the jungles of Burma (Myanmar) in a desperate conflict with Japanese invaders.*

A COMMANDO RAID

From 1940 the British formed small military or naval units known as commandos, which specialised in night-time raids or reconnaissance behind enemy lines. Hitler commanded that all commando prisoners be shot, but most German officers ignored this order.

Helmet
A camouflaged helmet was generally used in action, but commandos also wore dark woollen caps.

Backpacks
Equipment might include explosives, ropes and rations.

Weapon
Commando units might carry sub-machine guns, daggers, sniper rifles and pistols.

WAR IN THE PACIFIC

The Second World War really was a global conflict. Much of the fighting took place in Asia and the Pacific, where the militaristic empire of Japan overran British and Dutch colonies in a bid to control the entire region. Even before the Second World War had begun, Japan had invaded China. Many of the captured troops and civilians now suffered greatly in Japanese prisoner-of-war camps. British troops fought alongside Australian, New Zealand and large numbers of US troops to liberate the region.

↑ *British commando units carried out daring raids in German-occupied Norway and France, in the Middle East and Burma.*

1945
14 August VJ Day (Japanese surrender): End of the war.

1945
November: leading Nazis put on trial in Nuremberg, Germany.

THE TIDE TURNS

By 1943 the tide of the war was turning. The Soviet Red Army was pushing back the Germans in eastern Europe. The Allies had defeated them in North Africa and were advancing through Italy. On 6 June 1944, ('D-Day'), Allied troops landed in occupied France and began to battle their way eastwards. Germany was devastated by Allied bombing raids and surrendered in 1945. After long and bitter fighting in the Pacific, the United States dropped two terrifying weapons of mass destruction on Japan – atomic bombs. Surrender was immediate.

The atomic bombs that were dropped on the Japanese cities of Hiroshima and Nagasaki by the United States in August 1945 brought the Second World War to a terrible end. Tens of thousands of Japanese civilians were killed instantly, while others, sick with radiation, died lingering deaths over many years.

▼ *Slave labourers in Buchenwald camp, April 1945. Cameramen entering the death camps with Allied troops took the first pictures to reveal the full extent of Nazi cruelty.*

HORROR OF THE CAMPS

The Nazis were racists. They blamed all the troubles of Europe on Jews, Slavs and Roma (Gypsies). They built secret 'concentration camps' where these peoples – alongside political opponents, disabled people and homosexuals – were forced into labour, shot, hanged or gassed to death. No fewer than six million Jews were murdered in this 'Holocaust'. As Allied troops invaded Germany and the lands that had been occupied, they were sickened to find starving prisoners and piles of corpses.

Post-war Britain

Soldiers returned to a Britain that was victorious but battered. In the cities there were bomb sites to be cleared. Barbed wire, concrete and mines had to be removed from British coasts. Shortages of food and other goods meant that these had to be strictly rationed – and the birth rate was suddenly rising as families looked forward to a safer, more peaceful world.

GAMES AND FESTIVALS

Post-war life was far from easy, but the British people still had time for celebrations. London staged the first post-war Olympic Games in 1948, and in 1951 a Festival of Britain was held. It looked to the future and was marked by the construction of many very modern-looking public buildings.

▶ The futuristic Skylon was the symbol of the Festival of Britain.

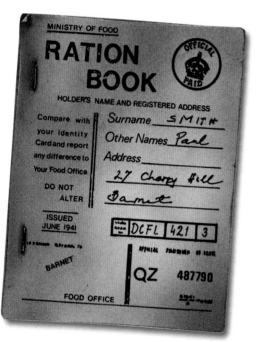

 Ration books, brought in during the shortages of the Second World War, were still necessary in the post-war years. Certain goods could only be purchased with government-issued coupons.

THE WELFARE STATE

The Second World War had convinced many British people of the need for social change. In 1945 the wartime leader Sir Winston Churchill lost the election to the Labour Party under Clement Attlee. By 1950, 650,000 new publicly owned, low-rent 'council houses' had been built across the country. A National Health Service was founded in 1948, with free medicine for all. This 'welfare state', which aimed to provide care for all its citizens, was also supported by Conservative governments, from their re-election in 1951 until 1979.

⬇ *The radical Welsh Labour politician Aneurin ('Nye') Bevan founded the National Health Service. Here, he is at a London health centre site in 1949.*

⬇ *A council estate in Glasgow in 1950. The housing on offer was not always beautiful, but it was cheap to build, affordable to rent, and generally better equipped and healthier than the old slums and tenements.*

↑ *Ploughs were now increasingly hauled by tractors instead of the big shire horses that had been used for centuries.*

COUNTRYSIDE AND TOWN

British farms aimed to increase production. Farms were mechanised, with milking machines being installed and electricity and piped water being brought to many remote country regions. New chemical sprays and fertilisers were used to improve crop yields, but these often proved to have a harmful effect on wildlife and the environment. The Soil Association was founded in 1946 in order to promote organic farming and oppose the new industrial style of agriculture, but it was the 1970s before such campaigns began to have a wider impact. The urban environment was also being tackled. In industrial cities a dense, choking mixture of industrial waste and chimney smoke – 'smog' – was still common in the 1950s. Buildings were black with soot. A Clean Air Act to improve the atmosphere was passed in the UK in 1956.

ON TOP OF THE WORLD

In 1953 the streets of the United Kingdom were decked out in red, white and blue for the coronation of Queen Elizabeth II. Some people watched the ceremony on newly purchased television sets. Crowds lining the streets of London were thrilled by one news report that had just come in. Two members of a British-led expedition had become the first people to climb the world's highest peak, Mount Everest.

▲ *Sir Edmund Hillary and Tenzing Norgay became the first people to climb Mount Everest on 29 May 1953.*

1952
King George VI dies of cancer. Elizabeth II succeeds him.

1954
Food rationing comes to an end in Britain.

SPORTING LEGENDS

The post-war years saw the high point of spectator sports in Britain. Vast crowds gathered in the stands at football matches, and cricket too attracted its largest crowds ever. About 159,000 attended the England–Australia test match in 1948. In 1954, 3000 fans of athletics at Oxford saw Roger Bannister become the first person to run a mile in under 4 minutes (his record time was 3 minutes 95.4 seconds).

◀ *Stanley Matthews was a soccer hero to a generation of schoolboys. He played for Stoke City and Blackpool and was capped for England 54 times. He was named Footballer of the Year in 1948 and was the first footballer to be knighted, as Sir Stanley.*

WHO RUNS INDUSTRY?

The Labour government of 1945 followed socialist policies, nationalising privately owned industries. It believed that public ownership would bring about fairer working conditions and better serve the national interest. Coal mines, railways, road transport and public utilities such as gas, electricity and water were all brought under the control of national or local government. The Bank of England, too, was nationalised. The power of trade unions increased during the 1950s and 60s, and strikes became a common form of protest about pay or working conditions.

TIME TO RELAX

The British theatre had many great actors in the post-war years, including Laurence Olivier and John Gielgud. Stars of the ballet included Margot Fonteyn. Going to the cinema was still a weekly treat for many people. American musicals and 'westerns' were favourites, alongside British-made films about the Second World War or gentle comedies from the Ealing Studios. Radio shows, especially comedies, were hugely popular. Hot days might be spent at an outdoor swimming pool, and summer breaks were offered at cheap and cheerful 'holiday camps' such as Butlins and Pontins.

Winds of Change

SUN SETS ON THE BRITISH RAJ

The campaign for Indian freedom had begun as early as 1885, with the founding of the Indian National Congress. From the 1920s this movement was led by a former lawyer called Mohandas K Gandhi. He used non-violent methods to oppose the British, organising marches and fasts. He was often imprisoned. Amidst bloody riots in 1947, Britain partitioned India into a mainly Hindu India and a mainly Muslim Pakistan. These two nations achieved independence, making the nationalists' dream come true. However Gandhi was dismayed by the religious hatred. He was assassinated by a Hindu fanatic in 1948.

◀ *Gandhi championed the poor and he himself led a very simple lifestyle. He became known as the Mahatma ('great soul').*

In 1960 the Conservative Prime Minister Harold Macmillan spoke in South Africa of a 'wind of change' blowing through the African continent. In reality this wind had been blowing throughout the world for some years. With the Second World War, the age of colonial empires had come to an end. In Africa, Asia and the Caribbean, people were demanding independence from Britain. At the same time, self-governing nations such as Canada, Australia and New Zealand were increasingly breaking ties with 'the mother country' and going their own way.

INDEPENDENCE STRUGGLES

Nationalist movements were founded in many parts of the British empire from the 1920s to the 1950s. Their leaders were often jailed and in some lands the independence campaigns turned violent. In Kenya, there was a bitter uprising from 1952, the Mau-Mau Rebellion. By the end of the 1950s, Britain was forced to realise that it no longer had the power to rule the world. Local political leaders were released from jail and became the leaders of independent nations.

⬇ During Kenya's Mau-Mau Rebellion, about 100 white settlers were killed. Many African Kenyans, mostly Kikuyu people, were also killed and tens of thousands were imprisoned in camps.

⬇ Britain's Princess Margaret reads an address in the name of her sister, Queen Elizabeth, as she open the first meeting of the Jamaican parliament in 1962. Her husband the Earl of Snowdon stands on her left.

A COMMONWEALTH OF NATIONS

In 1931 the lands of the British empire had been formally joined together within a 'British Commonwealth'. After 1947 this became a union of independent nations, most of which had formerly had links with Britain. 'British' was dropped from the title. While some newly independent nations kept the British monarch as their head of state, others became republics. The Commonwealth fostered economic and cultural links between its members.

WINDS OF CHANGE

1960
Nigeria independent.

1961
South Africa leaves the Commonwealth; Tanganyika
becomes independent (Tanzania 1964).

WHITE MINORITIES

In some parts of the former empire, the
ruling Whites were not prepared to allow
democracy or independence. In South Africa,
governments refused to give the vote to
people of African or Asian descent. South
African society was cruelly segregated along
racial lines until democratic government was
introduced in 1994. In 1965 the White
minority government in Rhodesia broke
away from British rule, preventing
independence (as Zimbabwe) until 1980.
Years of bush warfare followed. Black
majority rule also failed to deliver
democracy, with elected president Robert
Mugabe suppressing free opposition.

⬆ *The apartheid system of racial segregation
was introduced in South Africa in 1948. As a
result, South Africa was expelled from the
Commonwealth in 1961 and not readmitted until
1994, when all South Africans won the vote. In
Britain, supporters and opponents of apartheid
clashed throughout that period.*

⬅ *Nelson Mandela, born in 1918, was a tireless campaigner
against the system of apartheid in South Africa. He was a leader
of the African National Congress (ANC) and demanded votes
for all South Africans, regardless of colour. He was imprisoned for
27 years and finally released in 1990, after a long international
campaign for his freedom. From 1994 to 1999 he served as the
first president to be elected by all the people of South Africa.*

AFTER THE EMPIRE

After independence, some former colonies became republics, but others remained monarchies, still recognising Queen Elizabeth II as head of state. Today the British monarch still reigns in 16 'Commonwealth Realms'. These are Antigua and Barbuda, Australia, the Bahamas, Barbados, Belize, Canada, Granada, Jamaica, New Zealand, Papua New Guinea, St Kitts and Nevis, St Lucia, St Vincent and the Grenadines, the Solomon Islands, Tuvalu and the United Kingdom. Australia has so far voted to remain a monarchy, but has a strong republican movement.

↑ *The Commonwealth has encouraged sporting and cultural links among its members. This Commonwealth Games was held at Victoria, British Columbia, Canada, in 1994. Winner of the men's 1500 metres was Reuben Chesang of Kenya.*

← *Elizabeth II is also Queen of Canada. Here she accompanies Brian Mulroney, Canadian Prime Minister from 1984–93.*

WINDS OF CHANGE **427**

1958
White youths attack Black immigrants in
Notting Hill, London.

1965
Race Relations Act makes discrimination illegal
(also in 1968).

New Britons

The British Isles have been settled by many different groups of people throughout their history. Black people were in Britain as early as Roman times. In the 1950s a new wave of immigration began from the lands of the former British empire. Like others before them, these immigrants came either to find work or to escape persecution in their homelands.

↑ *The golden dome of a mosque rises above Regent's Park, in central London. Islam, Sikhism and Hinduism now play an important part in modern British life, alongside Judaism and Christianity.*

ARRIVING IN HOPE

The first Caribbean immigrants to arrive in Britain came on board the *Empire Windrush*, a ship that docked at Tilbury, London, on 22 June 1948. They numbered 500, many of them ex-servicemen hoping to make use of skills they had learned while fighting for Britain during the war. The group included a dozen women and one 13 year-old boy.

◄ *Young Caribbeans came to England in search of a decent wage, but found that there was little money left to save or send home.*

THE NEWCOMERS

In the 1950s, British governments recruited many workers from the Caribbean region – where there was widespread unemployment – to staff National Health Service hospitals or to work in public transport. Others came in search of jobs and were joined by their families. Indians and Pakistanis arrived too during the 1960s. In 1972 Asians, including many who held British passports, were expelled from their homes in Uganda. Most of the new arrivals settled in large industrial cities such as London or Birmingham.

➡ *A Caribbean carnival, first held in London's Notting Hill district in 1965, soon developed into one of Europe's most popular street festivals. A love of Caribbean music and dance styles have forged links between young people for over 40 years.*

A MIXED WELCOME

It was the ancestors of the 1950s and 60s immigrants who had created the wealth of the British empire. The new arrivals were often hard-working and enterprising, Some were trained as doctors, nurses and teachers. However they were often met with a lack of understanding and racial prejudice. Some politicans stirred up trouble, but new racist political parties remained very small. Laws were passed against discrimination. Britain began to absorb new cultures, as it had throughout its history.

The Cold War

The period from 1945 to 1990 is often called the Cold War. This refers to the tension between Russia (the 'Soviet Union') and the countries of the West, led by the United States. The Soviet Union was still ruled by the Communist Party, although supporters of its ruthless leader Joseph Stalin (who died in 1953) had by now killed most of the idealists who had taken part in the revolution. The West remained capitalist. In the United States anti-Communist feelings reached fever pitch in the 1950s. The world teetered on the brink of war.

⬆ In 1948 the Allies airlifted supplies into Berlin's Tempelhof airport to beat a Russian blockade.

➡ Just before the end of the Second World War, in February 1945, the Allied leaders Winston Churchill of Britain, Franklin D Roosevelt of the USA and Joseph Stalin of the Soviet Union, met at Yalta, in the Crimea. They discussed the post-war settlement and how Europe would be divided between the great powers.

NATIONAL SERVICE

During the Second World War, young men had been called up into the armed services. Conscription continued until 1962, even though the United Kingdom was no longer at war. Some said that this National Service was good for young people, teaching them discipline and a trade.

▶ Many recruits felt that weapons drill and army routine served little use in peacetime.

THE IRON CURTAIN

After the Second World War, Europe was divided into two power blocs. Winston Churchill said it was as if an 'iron curtain' had fallen across the continent. In 1949 Western Europe and North America joined in a military alliance, the North Atlantic Treaty Organization (NATO). Eastern and Central Europe were now in the hands of Communist governments and in 1955 they united within the Warsaw Pact. The rival blocs faced each other in Germany, which was divided in two. The former capital, Berlin, was itself divided and surrounded by Communist territory. British troops were stationed in the west.

⬇ Polaris was the first missile system was developed in the United States in the 1950s and came into service in 1960. By 1968 it was being used by Britain's Royal Navy. It was the first missile to be fired from submarines.

Polaris missile
Each missile was 9.4 metres long and 1.4 metres thick. It carried a nuclear warhead. The first Polaris missile had a range of 2200 kilometres. The final model, adopted by the United Kingdom in 1969, had a range of 4800 kilometres.

WHEN THE WAR TURNED HOT

In Asia the Cold War turned hot, especially after China too became ruled by Communists in 1949. The newly formed United Nations Organization sent a multi-national force, including many British troops, to fight a Communist invasion of Korea. This war lasted from 1950 to 1953. From 1965 the United States also fought a bitter war against Communists in Vietnam, but was defeated in 1973. Cold War tensions spread around the world, preventing peaceful development in Africa, Asia, Central and South America.

British Troops arriving in Korea on 3 September 1950. They are seen marching from the quay after landing at the southern port of Pusan (now Busan).

Many British people thought that the Vietnam War was unjust and protested against it on the streets. British governments supported the United States' policy, but – unlike Australia – sent no troops.

1958
Campaign for Nuclear Disarmament (CND) founded in London.

1961
East Germans divide Berlin with fortified wall (until 1989).

BOMBS AND PROTESTS

The chief danger of the Cold War was the rapid increase in the number of nuclear bombs and missiles, just a few of which could destroy the world. Britain held nuclear weapons as a 'deterrent', so that no other country would risk an attack. The United States set up large air and naval bases in the United Kingdom. Many British people protested against nuclear weapons and a Campaign for Nuclear Disarmament (CND) was founded in 1958.

END OF THE COLD WAR

Many Western leaders believed that once one nation had turned Communist, its neighbour would soon follow, one falling after the other like so many dominoes. This did not happen, for the Communist nations were divided amongst themselves. The Soviet Union tried to bring in political reforms in the 1980s, but its economy finally collapsed. By 1991 the old Soviet Union was finished and the Cold War was over.

SPIES WHO CAME IN FROM THE COLD

Much of the conflict between the Cold War powers was secret, carried out by spies and undercover agents. Some Russian and Central European spies were secretly working for the west, while some members of the British secret service gave away secrets to the Soviet Union. These included Guy Burgess, Donald Maclean, Kim Philby and Anthony Blunt. British writers loved to create Cold War thrillers with spies as heroes, such as Ian Fleming's James Bond or Len Deighton's Harry Palmer.

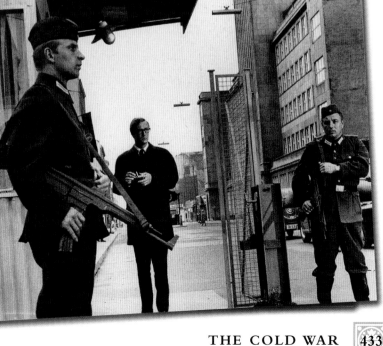

▼ Spies slip through Checkpoint Charlie on the Berlin Wall, in a scene from the film Funeral In Berlin, 1966.

Rocking and Rolling

In the second half of the 1950s, the European economy began to recover from the war years. More and more families watched television. Glossy magazine advertisements offered dreams of foreign travel or the ideal home. British car designer Alec Issigonis produced the classic Morris Minor in 1948 and the world famous Mini in 1959, the year in which England's M1 motorway opened. High-rise flats began to tower above Britain's cities in the 1960s.

↓ Four young lads from Liverpool formed a pop group in 1960. Paul McCartney, Ringo Starr, George Harrison and John Lennon made up The Beatles. During the 1960s they became the most successful band the world has ever known.

Ringo Starr
(b.1940)

George Harrison
(1943–2001)

John Lennon
(1940–80)

Paul McCartney
(b.1942)

1958
First section of motorway opens in England, M6.

1961
The first contraceptive pills go on sale in Britain.

← *Putting on the style… rock 'n' roll music took over dance halls in the years 1957–59.*

TEENAGE REBELS

It was in the post-war years that teenagers began to be seen as a separate social group. For the first time they had money and leisure, which they devoted to pop music and outrageous fashion. In the 1950s came American rock 'n' roll music, skiffle and modern jazz. Rebels were known as 'teddy boys', 'teddy girls' and 'beatniks'. They were followed in the 1960s by gangs of 'mods' and 'rockers', mini-skirted girls, long-haired 'hippies', and shaven-headed 'skinheads'. English popular music became famous all over the world.

→ *The 'punks' of the late 1970s despised the hippies for going soft. Punks listened to loud, discordant music. They pierced their bodies, dyed their hair in bright colours and wore torn clothes and metal chains.*

ROCKING AND ROLLING

→ *Television became very popular in the 1950s and colour sets became common in the 1970s. Millions of people watched 'soap operas' such as* Coronation Street *(1960),* Crossroads *(1964), and* Eastenders *(1985).*

CHANGING THE WORLD

To the older generation, it seemed that young people had lost all respect for authority. The old class system was ridiculed. In the 1940s and 50s, politicians had been listened to with deference. In the 1960s they were publicly mocked on satirical television shows such as *That Was The Week That Was*. By the late 1960s many young people were experimenting with drugs or exploring new religions. A great social upheaval was taking place – but it was hardly a revolution. The working-class pop stars were soon living in splendid mansions, just like the aristocrats had before them. Many young people did turn to revolutionary politics, but capitalist economics remained firmly in place.

→ *Look Back in Anger was a play by John Osbourne, staged at London's Royal Court Theatre in 1956. It was made into a film in 1958. This generation of writers became known as the 'Angry Young Men' because of their rebellious attitudes to society. Plays that portrayed everyday life were nicknamed 'kitchen-sink dramas'.*

WOMEN'S LIBERATION

By the late 1960s, feminists were calling for changes that went far beyond matters of voting rights and equal pay. They had a new vision of the roles of men and women in society, of how they should relate to each other and how girls and women should be empowered in a society dominated by men.

CHANGING SKYLINES

The cities of the British Isles went through great changes in the 1970s and 80s. Heavy industry was in rapid decline. Steel mills, factories and shipyards were closing down, as cheaper labour forces were employed in other parts of the world. Changes in trade patterns and shipping left great seaports such as Liverpool struggling for survival. By the 1990s, more and more people in the British Isles were moving to work in service industries, such as banking, finance or tourism. Daring new architecture now appeared in cities such as London and Manchester.

↓ *Cars such as the ever popular Mini Minor were ideal for the city – small, cheap to run, quick to nip in and out of traffic jams and easy to park. They became a symbol of 'Swinging London' in the 1960s.*

LOK 576P

MODERN ART IN BRITAIN

In the 1950s British artists explored abstract shapes and new media. Sculptors such as Henry Moore and Barbara Hepworth produced rounded, flowing figures and forms with hollows and holes. In the 1960s, 'pop artists' such as painter Peter Blake drew their inspiration from advertising and comic strips, while 'op artist' Bridget Riley played with optical illusions in paintings that seemed to twist and turn before one's eyes. Later artists turned to video, photography and light and sound installations.

◀ *Angel of the North, Antony Gormley.*

Conflict, peace and Trade

↑ *A British teacher working for Voluntary Service Overseas (VSO) talks with pupils in Thailand.*

In 1919 an international body called the League of Nations was founded, in order to prevent the outbreak of another world war. It failed completely, so in 1945 a new organisation was set up, the United Nations (UN). Its aim was to promote peace, health, human rights, economic and cultural co-operation.

WORKING FOR WORLD PEACE

The United Kingdom (from 1945) and the Republic of Ireland (from 1955) played an important part in the United Nations. Both committed troops to international peacekeeping operations and to military task forces. The blue berets of UN soldiers became a familiar sight in trouble spots around the world. Individual citizens also began to play an important part in tackling the world's problems. Volunteers from Britain and Ireland were to be seen in some of the world's poorest countries, teaching, building, distributing food, caring for the sick.

No end to the fighting

British troops served in many smaller conflicts after the Second World War. They were in Palestine before the creation of the Israeli state in 1948. From 1954 they saw action in Cyprus. In 1956 Britain and France launched a politically disastrous bid to prevent Egypt from nationalising the Suez Canal. Britain fought a war with Argentina over the Falkland, or Malvinas, Islands in 1982 and in the 1990s Britain sent troops to the Balkans and the Gulf. In 2003 Britain joined the Untied States in invading Iraq, a costly and prolonged conflict, during which Iraq plunged into chaos. Middle Eastern politics brought terrorism back to the streets of Britain at this time.

Arrest of Iraqi militiamen by British soldiers on the road to Basra in 2003.

The new europe

After the Second World War, many people wanted to safeguard the future peace of Europe. As early as 1946, Sir Winston Churchill was calling for a United States of Europe. In 1949 Britain and Ireland joined the new Council of Europe, and in 1973 both countries finally joined the European Economic Community (EEC) – an economic and political alliance known since 1993 as the European Union (EU). Many enjoyed the economic benefits of EU membership and the Irish economy was transformed. In Britain, critics nicknamed 'Eurosceptics' complained of bureaucracy and loss of national sovereignty. However supporters ('Europhiles') believed that the union was necessary in a world economy that was no longer based on nation states.

Ireland North and South

The President of the Republic of Ireland since 1997 has been Mary McAleese, a lawyer and journalist who was born in Northern Ireland in 1951. It was during her presidency that the British and Irish governments, working together, managed to bring about a more peaceful Northern Ireland.

By 1949 most of Ireland was a republic, fully independent from the United Kingdom. However six counties of the northern province of Ulster remained part of the UK. The Irish Republic still claimed those counties, and the Irish Republican Army (IRA) continued its campaign of violence against Britain during the 1950s and 60s.

IN THE REPUBLIC

In the 1950s, Ireland remained a conservative, largely agricultural society. The Roman Catholic Church dominated public and political life. The Irish language, although taught in schools, was no longer widely spoken. The pockets where it survived were called *Gaeltachtaí*. After the 1960s, the power of the Church began to lessen. Ireland opened up more to the world and tourists poured into the west. After Ireland joined the European Economic Community (EEC) in 1973, its economy began to grow rapidly and new industries were developed, such as computer assembly or food processing.

PRESIDENTS OF THE IRISH REPUBLIC	
✤ Douglas Hyde	1938–1945
✤ Séan O'Ceallaigh	1945–1959
✤ Éamon de Valera	1959–1973
✤ Erskine Childers	1973–1974
✤ Cearbhall ó Dálaigh	1974–1976
✤ Patrick Hillery	1976–1990
✤ Mary Robinson	1990–1997
✤ Mary McAleese	1997–

PRIME MINISTERS OF THE IRISH REPUBLIC

✤ Éamon de Valera (Fianna Fáil)	1932–1948
✤ John Costello (Fine Gael)	1948–1951
✤ Éamon de Valera (Fianna Fáil)	1951–1954
✤ John Costello (Fine Gael)	1954–1957
✤ Éamon de Valera (Fianna Fáil)	1957–1959
✤ Sean Lemass (Fianna Fáil)	1959–1966
✤ Jack Lynch (Fianna Fáil)	1966–1973
✤ Liam Cosgrave (Fine Gael)	1973–1977
✤ Jack Lynch (Fianna Fáil)	1977–1979
✤ Charles Haughey (Fianna Fáil)	1979–1981
✤ Garret Fitzgerald (Fine Gael)	1981–1982
✤ Charles Haughey (Fianna Fáil)	1982
✤ Garret Fitzgerald (Fine Gael)	1982–1987
✤ Albert Reynolds (Fianna Fáil)	1987–1994
✤ John Bruton (Fine Gael)	1994–1997
✤ Bertie Ahern (Fianna Fáil)	1997–

MORE TROUBLES

A new round of 'troubles' broke out in Northern Ireland in 1969, as the minority supporting the Republic, mostly Catholics, clashed with the Protestant majority who supported the union with Britain. British troops were drafted in and the situation became worse after 'Bloody Sunday' in 1972, when 13 civil rights protestors were shot dead by British troops in Derry. New paramilitary groups were formed on both sides, engaging in murder and terrorist bombing, often in English cities.

THE ROAD TO PEACE

In 1988 a peace accord known as the Good Friday Agreement was approved by all sides in Britain, Northern Ireland and the Irish Republic. The Irish Republic dropped its claim to the six counties of the north. Prisoners were to be released, weapons handed in, troops scaled down and the police force reformed and re-named. However the devolution of power to a Northern Ireland Assembly faltered, and was not resumed until 2007, when at last Ian Paisley of the Democratic Unionist party and Martin McGuinness of Sinn Féin agreed to share power in a joint administration.

 Old enemies sit side by side. The Rev. Ian Paisley (Democratic Unionist) and Gerry Adams (Sinn Féin) talk to the press at the Northern Ireland Assembly in Stormont in 2007.

Left, Right or Centre?

➡ *Harold Wilson, MP for Huyton, won three elections for Labour – in 1964, 1966 and 1974.*

After the Second World War, the three chief political parties within the United Kingdom were the Conservative Party, the Labour Party and the Liberal Party. The Liberals never achieved government during this period. It is common to talk about parties as 'right-wing' (following conservative policies) or 'left-wing' (inclined to more liberal or socialist policies). Which course would British politics follow, left or right?

'YOU'VE NEVER HAD IT SO GOOD'

In 1951 Sir Winston Churchill regained power for the Conservative Party. They kept it for 13 years. Sir Anthony Eden lost votes over the Suez Crisis. Harold Macmillan was nicknamed 'Supermac' by the press. His slogan was 'You've Never Had It So Good' – which in economic terms was probably true. Sir Alec Douglas Home, like his predecessors, came from the upper classes and lacked the common touch. By contrast Harold Wilson, who brought Labour back to power in 1964, prided himself on being a man of the people. Between 1951 and 1979 both Labour and Conservative parties moved towards the centre ground. Edward Heath, the Conservative who took Britain into Europe in 1973, was a centrist, as was Labour leader James Callaghan.

Coal miners strike against pit closures, led by Arthur Scargill.

Victory for 'New' Labour under Tony Blair.

THE THATCHER YEARS

During the 1970s, unemployment rose. Both Heath and Callaghan came under pressure from striking trade unionists. Conservative Margaret Thatcher who came to power in 1979, was Britain's first woman Prime Minister. She moved her party to the right, attacking trade union rights and defeating a national miners' strike in 1984. Nationalised industries were now privatised.

PRIME MINISTERS OF THE UNITED KINGDOM

♣ Clement Attlee (Labour)	1945–1951
♣ Sir Winston Churchill (Conservative)	1951–1955
♣ Sir Anthony Eden (Conservative)	1955–1957
♣ Harold Macmillan (Conservative)	1957–1963
♣ Sir Alec Douglas Home (Conservative)	1963–1964
♣ Harold Wilson (Labour)	1964–1970
♣ Edward Heath (Conservative)	1970–1974
♣ Harold Wilson (Labour)	1974–1976
♣ James Callaghan (Labour)	1976–1979
♣ Margaret Thatcher (Conservative)	1979–1990
♣ John Major (Conservative)	1990–1997
♣ Tony Blair (Labour)	1997–2007
♣ Gordon Brown (Labour)	2007–

MAJOR, BLAIR AND BROWN

Thatcher won support in three general elections, but introduced some unpopular social policies. She was ousted by her own party in 1990, to be replaced by a moderate, John Major. There were battles betwen left and right in the Labour Party. A breakaway faction founded the Social Democratic Party (SDP) in 1981. This merged with the Liberals in 1988. New parties such as the Greens also began to make an impact. Labour finally abandoned socialism and in 1997 was returned to power under Tony Blair, who adopted many Thatcherite policies, including a very close alliance with the United States. He was succeeded as leader of 'New' Labour ten years later, by Gordon Brown.

The Houses of Parliament were still organised into two chambers or Houses. The 1997 Labour government began to reform the House of Lords.

Wales, Scotland, England

In the 1920s and 30s more and more people in Scotland and Wales were looking at ways of reforming or abolishing the union of nations within the United Kingdom. By the 1960s they were beginning to make their mark at general elections. Devolution of power from the parliament at Westminster became an important issue. Across Europe, regional cultures were gaining more political recognition.

↑ London's City Hall rises on the South Bank of the Thames. Home of the city's new Assembly, it was opened in 2002.

A WELSH ASSEMBLY

Wales went through great social changes in the 20th century. The upheaval of the world wars disrupted towns and rural communities. The coalmining industry of the south and northeast was closed down after 1984. The Welsh Nationalist Party (later, Plaid Cymru) was founded in 1925, and after the 1960s moved leftwards in its politics. The flooding of the Tryweryn valley to make a reservoir, pushed through the Westminster Parliament against the wishes of Welsh MPs, increased support for nationalists. The unionist policies of the Conservative governments in the 1980s and 90s were also opposed by Liberals and many Labour supporters. A Welsh Assembly, based in Cardiff, was voted into existence in 1997.

A SCOTTISH PARLIAMENT

In Scotland as in Wales there was wide-scale emigration, a decline in heavy industry and a rural population which struggled to make a living. The 1990s saw extensive clearance of poor housing from cities such as Glasgow. Scotland too was a Labour party stronghold. It was not until the 1960s that the Scottish Nationalist Party (SNP, founded in 1928) began to make inroads. In 1975 oil was discovered off the Scottish coast. Many Scots wanted to control this vital resource themselves, rather than the Westminster Parliament. Scotland already had its own separate legal and education system, and in 1997 it voted in its own Parliament too.

➡ *In 1999 Scotland had its own Parliament again for the first time since the reign of Queen Anne. The state opening in Edinburgh was a grand affair.*

ENGLISH REGIONS AND CITIES

Where did the devolution of power to Wales and Scotland leave England? Some politicians proposed regional assemblies for England. Regions such as the Northeast or Cornwall certainly saw themselves as culturally different from the Southeast. Some people believed that the real problem was economic, a North–South divide based on prosperity. Some wanted to bring life back to local government. Major change was introduced in London, which gained its own Assembly. London's first elected mayor, in 2000, was a radical politician named Ken Livingstone.

WALES, SCOTLAND, ENGLAND 445

Looking to the future

↑ The ultra-modern 30 St Mary Axe building and the Tower of London give two contrasting views of London today.

People have always liked to think that there was a golden age in the past, a time when all was well with the world. Others have put their faith in progress towards a golden future. The fact is that at most times in the history of Great Britain and Ireland, there have been disasters, injustices and problems. At the same time, people are trying to make the world a better place. History helps us learn from our past so we can face the challenges of a changing world, and plan for the future.

CHANGING CLIMATE

Scientists agree that world climate is warming. There have been periods of gradual climate change before, indeed Great Britain became an island as a result of them. The difference this time is the speed of change and the claim that global warming is the result of human activities such as power generation, transportation and industry. If sea levels rise, we shall have to decide which areas of coastline can be lost to the sea, which can be defended, and how lives can best be protected.

↓ This barrier across the River Thames was built in 1983, to protect London against flooding. Global warming would make the climate of the British Isles more stormy, and sea levels would rise again.

2003
The Iraq War begins. UK joins the US invasion and occupation of Iraq.

2005
Confirmed that global temperature has risen by 0.74°C in the last century.

⬆ *Many children are adept at using computers.*

THE ELECTRONIC AGE

Electronic communications revolutionised the world, and the British Isles too, in the 21st century. By 2007, 62 percent of the United Kingdom's population was using the Internet, with 21.8 million going online each day. Ireland was a leading centre of IT (information technology) related industries. Electronic technology was also transforming broadcasting, telephones, music, shopping, and other areas of daily life.

FUEL AND POWER

Because of global warming and dwindling reserves of fuel, power generation is a major issue of this century. There are schemes for making coal and gas cleaner to use. The oilfields beneath the North Sea are running out, and western Europe is increasingly reliant on supplies from Russia and Central Asia. Nuclear power requires dangerous radioactive waste to be securely stored for hundreds of thousands of years. However the British Isles are ideally located for generation from renewable sources such as wind and. Many people are already turning their homes into centres of microgeneration, with wind turbines or solar panels.

➡ *An old house gets a modern makeover, with solar panels on the roof. These absorb energy from sunlight that is converted into electricity.*

FACTS AND FIGURES

Today, the UK has a population of 60,776,000 million, growing at the rate of nearly 0.3 percent a year. Men can expect to live to 76, women to 81. Some 99 percent of adults can read and write. Incredibly, 80.4 percent of jobs are in service industries. Only 18.2 percent of workers work in factories, and just 1.4 percent grow the food we eat. The Republic of Ireland has a population of just 4,109,000, growing at over 1 percent each year. Life expectancy and literacy are much the same as the UK. However 64 percent of Irish jobs are in services, 29 percent in manufacturing and 8 percent in farming.

▲ The next generation.

 Kelly Holmes (left) wins the Women's 1500 metres final for Britain at the 2004 Olympic Games in Athens, Greece.

QUESTIONS OF IDENTITY

Who lives in the British Isles? Over the millennia these islands have been populated by peoples from every corner of Europe and far beyond, just as peoples from these islands have populated other parts of the world. Politicians or journalists sometimes claim that issues such as immigration, emigration, asylum, or the political relationship between the various peoples and nations that occupy these islands, are peculiar to our own times. As this book has shown, they are as old as the history of the British Isles. The rich diversity of peoples and cultures should be a source of strength. That will depend on fairness, mutual respect and the ability of political institutions to adapt to change in the years to come.

CHANGING COMMUNITIES

Changing economics have altered communities in town and country across the British Isles, and this major historical change is happening worldwide. The village shop or post office, the corner shop in the suburbs or the independently owned store in the high streets of towns and cities have all come under threat in recent decades. Four or five huge supermarket chains dominate the UK market, and the commercial life of whole districts has shifted to out-of-town retail parks. Rising house prices have forced many young people to leave their villages and towns, as wealthier people move in.

⬇ *A debate in the House of Commons is interrupted by anti-war protestors in February 2004. How should Parliament be reformed in the coming century?*

A PLACE IN THE WORLD

History has shown us that political change is driven forward by economic developments. Centuries-old United Kingdom institutions such as the unelected House of Lords are already being reformed. Will Britain remain a monarchy or become a republic? Will nation states continue to exist at all if the economy is global? Even if world government is unlikely to happen in our own lifetimes, international law and a just economic system for the world as a whole will remain the only hope of securing freedom for the peoples of the British Isles from the wars and terrorist violence that have marked the start of the 21st century.

History-makers

"The farther backward you can look, the farther forward you can see…"

Adam, Robert
1728–1792
Scottish architect

Born in Scotland, Adam travelled widely in Europe, studying ancient buildings and art. On his return to Britain in 1758, he began work as an architect, in partnership with his brother James (1730–1794). Together, they designed many great country houses. Some of their most famous buildings still survive today, including Syon House near London, Harewood House in Yorkshire, and Charlotte Square in Edinburgh.

▲ *The Adams also designed fittings and furniture for their houses. This fireplace, decorated with white stucco (carved plaster) uses features from ancient Greek art.*

Alcock, Sir John
1892–1919
English aviator

Alcock had a distinguished career in the Royal Flying Corps (the forerunner of the Royal Air Force) during World War I (1914–1918). In 1919, he made the first non-stop flight across the Atlantic Ocean with Sir Arthur Whitten Brown. They flew from Newfoundland, Canada,

▶ *Alcock and Brown made their 1919 flight in a World War I bomber.*

to Ireland in 16 hours 27 minutes. Alcock was killed in a flying accident soon afterwards.

Alexander II
1198–1249; reigned 1214–1249
King of Scotland

Alexander lived at a time when Scotland was an independent kingdom, and often at war with England. After fighting off rivals to his Scottish throne, Alexander agreed a series of treaties with English kings. This began a period of peace that lasted for 80 years. During Alexander's reign, the boundary between England and Scotland was finally fixed, to where it still is today.

Alfred the Great
849–899; reigned 871–899
Anglo-Saxon king

Alfred was ruler of Wessex, in southwest England. When he came to power, England was divided into several small, rival kingdoms, and a Viking army had invaded. In AD 878, he was forced into hiding in Athelney Marshes, but used the time away from the royal court to plan his comeback. He defeated the Vikings at the Battle of Edington, and they agreed to leave Wessex. Alfred then gave orders for burghs (fortified towns) to be built

throughout Wessex to defend it from further attack. He also began a campaign to conquer all the other English kingdoms that were not occupied by the Vikings, and declared himself king of England. He took control of London.

Anderson, Elizabeth Garrett
1836–1917
English doctor

No university or hospital would accept women as medical students, so Anderson worked as a nurse and studied to be an apothecary – the old name for a pharmacist. She attended college lectures (where she was mocked by male students), and studied anatomy by cutting up dead bodies in her bedroom. She qualified as an apothecary in 1865, becoming the first woman to be listed as a doctor in England. Anderson used her skills to help sick women and children. In 1866, she opened a dispensary (chemist shop) for women in London, where she examined patients and gave advice, as well as selling medicines. It later became a major hospital, named in her honour. Anderson was appointed head of the London School of Medicine for Women. She was elected England's first woman mayor in 1908, serving the town of Aldeburgh in Suffolk.

Arkwright, Sir Richard
1732–1792
English inventor

While apprenticed to a wig-maker, Arkwright experimented with different ways of spinning and weaving thread. In 1767, he invented a water-

▶ Arkwright's spinning machine transformed the cloth-making industry in northern England.

powered machine that could spin fine cotton thread, strong enough to be used for weaving. Arkwright's invention meant that, for the first time, pure cotton cloth could be woven by machine.

Astor, Nancy
1879–1964
US-born British politician

Born in America, Astor married a wealthy newspaper owner, who was also a Member of Parliament. She helped him in his political work, and also managed his huge, luxurious home, entertaining important businessmen, political leaders, writers and journalists.

When her husband became a lord, he resigned as an MP, so Astor decided to stand for election in his place. She won, and in 1919, became the first active woman MP in Britain.

Attlee, Clement (Earl Attlee)
1883–1967
English politician

From a middle-class, professional background, Attlee trained as a lawyer, and became mayor of Stepney, east London, in 1920. He was horrified at the poverty, illness and bad housing he found there, and was determined to improve it.

He became a Labour MP in 1922, and held important posts in Churchill's wartime government.

Attlee was elected Prime Minister in 1945 – the first Labour Party leader to have an absolute majority in the House of Commons. He introduced many policies to reform British society, and to shape a new role for Britain in international politics after the end of World War II (1939–1945). These included the welfare state, and state control of major industries, including coal, gas, electricity and the railways.

▼ Attlee was Prime Minister for six years.

Austen, Jane
1775–1817
English novelist

The youngest daughter of a country clergyman, Austen never married, and spent most of her life quietly at home with her family. She began to write as a child. Austen completed her first full-length novel, *Pride and Prejudice*, when she was only 21.

One of Britain's greatest writers, Austen won little fame during her lifetime and received hardly any money. Yet her skill at observing and describing people, her insights into character and feelings, her elegant use of language and her sharp sense of humour, have delighted readers ever since her first book appeared.

Babbage, Charles
1792–1871
English mathematician

As a child, Babbage was brilliant at maths, and it became his life-long career. Today, he is remembered as the inventor of the world's first computer – a mechanical 'calculating engine' that he began to build in 1812.

Baden-Powell, Robert
1857–1941
English founder of scouting

A soldier, Baden-Powell served in India and commanded British troops during the Boer War (1899–1902).

In 1903, he returned to Britain, and began to realise that his wartime experiences could be used to train young people in fitness, self-discipline and community spirit. In 1907, he arranged the first Scout camp for boys. In 1908, a national Boy Scout organisation was formed, and the Girl Guides organisation was founded in 1909.

▼ Baden-Powell wrote many books during his lifetime, including Scouting for Boys (1908).

Baird, John Logie
1888–1946
Scottish electrical engineer

Having trained as an electrical engineer, Baird invented the first machine to transmit live pictures, in 1922. Four years later, he built the first television set. Baird's machines were supplied to the BBC in 1929 and used to make the first regular TV broadcasts in 1936. But in 1937, the BBC stopped using them, preferring a system that used a cathode-ray tube.

Barnardo, Thomas
1845–1905
Irish philanthropist

Barnardo came to London from Ireland to train as a medical missionary. He intended to work overseas, but was shocked by the poverty and disease of England's big cities. He set up more than 90 homes to care for sick, abandoned or abused children. The Barnardo organisation continues today.

Bateman, Hester
1709–1794
English silversmith

Remembered today as one of the world's great silversmiths, Bateman did not go to school or college. Instead, she learned her craft from her husband, who was a jeweller. When he died, she took over his business, helped by two of their five children. Bateman's own work soon became famous for its simple, graceful designs.

▶ *A silver seal by Bateman.*

Beale, Dorothea
1831–1906
English campaigner

Beale wanted girls to be as well-educated as boys, so that they could lead interesting, fulfilling lives. Before 1850, schoolgirls were not taught subjects such as maths, science or Latin. People said they were not 'suitable' for women's brains. Beale was determined to prove them wrong. Aged only 27, she became headmistress of a girls' school in the west of England.

Beale also campaigned for the right of women to attend university. She was supported by many other women campaigners, especially Florence Mary Buss (1827–1894).

Beatles, The
founded late 1950s
English musicians

A pop group, formed in Liverpool in the late 1950s, which transformed the British music industry. Original members were John Lennon (1940–1980), Sir Paul McCartney (born 1942) and George Harrison (1943–2002). In 1962, they were joined by Richard 'Ringo Starr' Starkey (born 1940). The Beatles wrote almost all their own songs. At first, they were based on rhythm-and-blues and rock-and-roll styles. Later, they became adventurous and experimental, using Eastern instruments and electronic techniques.

Becket, St Thomas (à)
1120?–1170
English archbishop

Becket began his career as a senior government official. King Henry II of England was so impressed by his skills that he invited him to become archbishop of Canterbury. For many years, King Henry quarrelled with the Pope in Rome. He expected Becket to support him, and was furious when he sided with the Pope.

Four knights murdered Becket in Canterbury Cathedral. The killing caused a scandal. King Henry was disgraced, and Becket became a saint.

Beckett, Samuel
1906–1989
Irish playwright

Born in Dublin, Ireland, Beckett moved to France. He wrote in both French and English. His plays, such as *Waiting for Godot* (1956), are strange yet compelling, forcing viewers to think and question. Beckett won the Nobel Prize for Literature in 1969.

Beckham, David
born 1975
English footballer

Each generation has its footballing heroes, and in the 1990s it was the turn of Beckham. He appeared for Manchester United in 1992 and in 1999 helped them to win the League, the FA Cup and the UEFA Champions League. In 2003, Beckham joined the Spanish team Real Madrid, and in 2007 he signed with US club Los Angeles Galaxy. He captained the England soccer team from 2000 to 2006. Beckham married Victoria Adams of the Spice Girls pop group, and they are known to an adoring press as 'Posh and Becks'.

Bede, St
672/3–735
Anglo-Saxon scholar

Bede lived as a monk in the northeast of England. During his lifetime, he was respected as the most learned man in Europe. Bede's most famous work was *The Ecclesiastical History of the English Church and People*. In it, he describes life in Anglo-Saxon England, and how the first Christian missionaries arrived there from Rome.

Beeton, Isabella
1837–1865
English cookery writer

Beeton was married to a publisher. She worked with him on a magazine, then became editor of her own ambitious project – a cookery book published in 30 monthly instalments. This contained more than 3000 recipes, together with helpful hints on medicine, housework, good manners and the law. In 1861, the separate instalments were bound together to make one volume: *Mrs Beeton's Book of Household Management*. It became a great success, and is still in print today.

Behn, Aphra
1640–1689
English writer

Famous as the first Englishwoman to support herself entirely by writing, Behn lived an exciting, mysterious life. As a girl, she crossed the Atlantic Ocean to Surinam (in South America), and later went to the Netherlands as a British government spy.

Returning to England, Behn began to write novels and plays. Like her, they were lively and witty, and proved very popular. Her most famous work, *Oroonoko*, tells the story of a young black prince who is transported from West Africa to the Caribbean as a slave.

Bell, Alexander Graham
1847–1922
Scottish-born US inventor

Born and educated in Scotland, Bell emigrated in 1870 to Canada, then the USA. While working as a teacher of deaf people, he experimented with different machines for transmitting sound, especially speech. He invented the telephone, which he first displayed in public in 1876. The next year, he founded a telephone company, to profit from his invention and to fund future research. In 1887, he invented the graphophone. Later, he worked on plans for travel by speedboat and aeroplane.

▲ *Adventurous and independent, Behn became known for her entertaining writing.*

Bevan, Aneurin 'Nye'
1897–1960
Welsh politician

Son of a Welsh miner, Bevan began to work as a miner himself at the age of 13. He became active in the trade union movement, and was elected as an MP in 1929. On the left wing of the Labour Party, he was a brilliant public speaker, and campaigned passionately for workers' rights. In 1946, he was made minister of health in the new Labour government, and was responsible for setting up the National Health Service.

Blake, William
1757–1827
English poet and artist

Blake was one of Britain's most original thinkers. He began to write verses while still a child, and

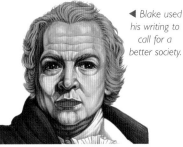

◀ *Blake used his writing to call for a better society.*

illustrated them with his own designs. After training as a print-maker, he opened a shop to sell decorative prints and his own unusual books and poems.

Blake was very critical of the society he lived in, disliking its greed and hypocrisy, and calling for a return to a simpler, purer way of life. He especially hated factories, big machines, and the inhuman demands they made on ordinary people. One of Blake's most famous poems, *Jerusalem*, was turned into a rousing hymn.

Blair, Anthony (Tony)

born 1953

English politician

Born in Edinburgh, Blair trained as a barrister. He became a Labour MP in 1983 and was Prime Minister from 1997 to 2007, winning three general elections. He moved his party away from its traditional socialist roots, re-branding it as 'New' Labour. He was a very close ally of United States President George W Bush, joining him in a controversial invasion of Iraq in 2003. He was succeeded by his longtime rival in the Labour Party, Gordon Brown.

Booth, Catherine and William

1829–1890 and 1829–1912

English religious campaigners

Catherine Mumford and William Booth met at a Methodist prayer meeting. They married and founded the Salvation Army – a religious organisation that aimed to teach the Christian faith to poor and outcast families. The Booths believed that the existing churches ignored these people, and that the way to reach them was by offering welfare help, and by preaching and singing hymns in the streets.

Brian 'Boru'

reigned 975–1014

Irish High king

Ruler of Munster (Ireland), and later Irish High King, Brian Boru fought to drive Viking invaders out of his lands. He won control of the Viking trading city of Dublin, and forced other rulers in Ireland to obey him. He was killed fighting against the Vikings and his Irish enemies at the Battle of Clontarf.

Boudicca

died AD 62

Ancient British queen

Boudicca was the wife of Prasutagus, king of the Iceni tribe of eastern England. When he died in AD 60, Roman invaders put most of his family in prison, or made them slaves. Boudicca joined with another threatened tribe, the Trinobantes, to attack Roman camps and forts. In AD 61, she led her army to attack London, where they destroyed buildings and killed many people. However, Boudicca's army was finally defeated by Roman soldiers, and she was trapped on the battlefield. Too proud to surrender, she poisoned herself.

◀ *Britten composed operas and other works.*

Britten, Benjamin (Lord Britten)

1913–1976

English musician

Born in Suffolk, Britten began to compose tunes as a child. In 1939, at the beginning of World War II (1939–1945), he left England for America. He believed strongly in peace, not war. However, he became homesick and returned. With friends, he founded a yearly music festival in Aldeburgh, Suffolk, and invited the world's best musicians to perform. One of Britten's most famous works is *Gloriana*, written for the coronation of Queen Elizabeth II.

▼ *Boudicca led her armies to war against Rome and burned down London.*

Brontë Sisters

Charlotte 1816–1855;
Emily 1818–1848;
Anne 1820–1849
English writers

Daughters of a clergyman, the Brontës lived in the wild, remote countryside of northern England. All three worked as badly paid schoolteachers in small schools, then returned home. From childhood, each sister wrote poems and, later, novels. Charlotte's novel *Jane Eyre* was the first to be published. Readers were fascinated by this romantic story of a brave, strong-minded girl and a gloomy but attractive hero. Next, Emily published *Wuthering Heights*, a passionate story of doomed love between a wilful heroine, Cathy, and Heathcliff, the man who deserted her. The public was surprised and shocked to learn that it had been written by a woman. Anne's *Agnes Grey* and *The Tenant of Wildfell Hall* were printed soon after.

▲ *Brontë sisters Anne (left), Emily (centre) and Charlotte (right).*

▼ *Statue of Robert the Bruce at Stirling Castle, Scotland.*

Bruce, Robert the (Robert I)

1274–1329; reigned 1306–1329
Scottish king

Bruce lived at a time when rival nobles and warriors were claiming the right to be king of Scotland, and when English kings Edward I and Edward II had ambitions to conquer Scotland for themselves.

After defeating his rivals and becoming king, Bruce led soldiers to recapture all the Scottish castles occupied by the English. He defeated Edward II at the Battle of Bannockburn (1314) and forced England to recognise Scotland as an independent nation.

Brunel, Isambard Kingdom

1806–1859
English engineer

Son of Sir Marc Brunel, a famous French-born engineer, Isambard Brunel also had a very successful career. He began by building bridges, including the daring Clifton Suspension Bridge at Bristol. Brunel then became chief engineer for the new Great Western Railway, surveying more than 1600 kilometres of track and designing tunnels, bridges and stations. In 1838, he designed the *Great Western*, one of the first steamships to cross the Atlantic. In 1858, he built the *Great Eastern*, the largest ship ever made (until 1899).

Bunyan, John

1628–1688
English writer

From a humble background (he trained as a tin-smith), Bunyan fought on the side of Parliament against King Charles I during the Civil War. He then became active in minority Christian groups – some of which held extreme views, such as believing that the world was soon to end.

In 1660, Bunyan was sent to prison for his beliefs. When he was released, he wrote a book based on his thoughts in prison. He called it *Pilgrim's Progress*, and it told the story of an ordinary man seeking to live a good life and reach heaven. Published in 1678, it immediately became very popular.

Burns, Robert

1759–1796
Scottish poet

The son of a poor Scottish farmer, Burns was keen to be educated, and read all he could. He also began to write poems and songs, in standard English and also in the Scottish dialect he spoke at home. Burns wrote simply and powerfully about the countryside, friendship and falling in love. He also retold many traditional Scottish stories and legends. When his first book of poems was published, it became an overnight success. Burns died aged only 37, but was not forgotten. His birthday, 25 January, is still celebrated by Scots today.

Byrd, William
1543–1623
English musician

The greatest British composer of the 16th century, Byrd wrote mostly religious music for singers and instrumentalists. He also liked to experiment with new musical techniques. In 1588, he composed the first madrigals in English. Madrigals are a type of song, invented in Italy, in which several vocalists sing the same words to a different tune, blending their voices together to create harmonies.

Byron, George (Lord Byron)
1788–1824
Anglo-Scottish poet

Son of an eccentric soldier from a noble family and an unhappy heiress, Byron had an unusual upbringing. As a young man, he cultivated a wild, romantic image, got into fights, ran up enormous debts, and had many risky adventures and scandalous love affairs. Byron loved to shock, but he also had a serious side. He worked hard, was active in politics, and was the most talented writer of his day. He wrote clever, witty pieces making fun of his enemies, beautiful short poems about life and love, and adventure stories in verse.

In 1816, Byron was forced to flee England, leaving his wife and young daughter, after it was reported that he had fallen in love with his own sister. He travelled to Europe, where he met other writers, and also freedom-fighters who were campaigning for independence for Italy and Greece. In 1823, he travelled to Greece to join the fight for independence. He died of a fever soon afterwards.

Caratacus
active around AD 40–50
Ancient British warrior

Son of Cymbeline/Cunobelinus, king of a Celtic tribe, Caratacus led the fight against the Roman invasion of Britain in AD 43. He was defeated and went into hiding, but in AD 47 formed an alliance of other Celtic tribes to fight once more. In AD 51, he was betrayed by Cartimandua, queen of a Celtic tribe who was friends with the Romans, and was taken prisoner in Rome. There, Caratacus made a speech that impressed the Roman emperor Claudius so much that he set him free.

Carroll, Lewis (Charles Dodgson)
1832–1898
English writer

Carroll spent most of his life as a mathematician at Oxford University, but he is remembered today as a writer of fantasy books for children. The best-known of these books is *Alice's Adventures in Wonderland*, published in 1865. Carroll also wrote nonsense verse for adults, and experimented with photography.

▲ *The Mad Hatter was a favourite character from Carroll's* Alice's Adventures in Wonderland*.*

▲ *Tutankhamun's death mask was found by archaeologist Howard Carter when he discovered the pharaoh's tomb in the early 20th century.*

Carter, Howard
1874–1939
English archaeologist

Carter won worldwide fame when he discovered the tomb of the pharaoh Tutankhamun in Egypt in 1922. The wonderful treasures he found encouraged public interest in archaeology.

▼ *When Carter first peered into the tomb of Tutankhamun, he exclaimed that he could see wonderful things – jewellery, a model boat and a golden throne.*

Caxton, William
*c.*1420–1491
English printer
The first printing press with movable type was built by Johan Gutenburg in Germany around 1455. Caxton learned the technique of printing whilst living in Bruges, Belgium, and printed his first book in English there in 1474. Two years later he moved to London, where he printed about 80 further volumes, including many books of poems and romances.

▲ *Caxton's press was used to create the first printed books in Britain.*

Cecil, William (Lord Burghley)
1520–1598
English politician
A lawyer, Burghley worked as an adviser to three ruling monarchs – Henry VIII, Edward VI and Elizabeth I. Wise, cautious and cunning, he helped to decide government policy. He encouraged friendship with the Netherlands and France, promoted new industries, and reformed the government's finances. At a time of great political tension, Burghley helped Queen Elizabeth to stay in power and increase her own authority and England's prestige. He ordered the execution of Mary Queen of Scots because he believed that she was a threat to peace and good government.

Chaplin, Sir Charles 'Charlie'
1889–1977
English actor
The son of music-hall performers, Chaplin grew up in an orphanage. In 1913, he travelled with a British theatre company to America, where he was spotted by a Hollywood film director, who recognised his talent. From 1914 to 1940, Chaplin made a great many films, some featuring the character he created – a bowler-hatted tramp. Most of these films were silent and Chaplin was a brilliant mime. Some of his films, such as *The Kid* (1921), were purely amusing. Others, such as *Modern Times* (1936), commented on social conditions. In these, Chaplin sympathised with ordinary people and made fun of people with power.

Charles I
1600–1649; reigned 1625–1649
King of England and Scotland
Charles I was a charming, hard-working man, interested in the arts and his family. However, he was an unhappy, unsuccessful king. Stubborn and untrustworthy, he quarrelled with Parliament, mostly about religion and finance. When Parliament refused to give in, he decided to rule alone with the help of a few chosen ministers. From 1629 to 1640, he did not summon Parliament at all and many people felt that their rights had been taken away. Charles tried to impose an Anglican prayer book on the Scots and this led to the Bishops' Wars (1639–1640). This caused so many financial problems that he was forced to recall Parliament in 1640, and to ask it to pass new laws so that he could collect more taxes. In 1641, he argued with Parliament again about rebels in Ireland. This led to the outbreak of civil war in 1642, as the Royalists fought with the forces of Parliament. The war raged around the British Isles. Charles I was eventually defeated and executed in London on 30 January 1649, an event that shocked Europe. The monarchy was not restored until 1660.

Charles II

1630–1685;
reigned 1660–1685
*King of England
and Scotland*

The eldest son of King
Charles I, Charles spent many
years in exile after his father
was executed in 1649. He was
welcomed back to England in
1660, when Richard Cromwell
proved to be a poor leader.
Shrewd, intelligent and witty,
Charles II handled the
difficult situation that faced
him with great tact and skill.
Unlike his father, he found
ways of working peacefully
with Parliament, and tried to
heal the divisions left by the
civil war. Even so, he still faced
financial problems and religious
quarrels. Famous for his love of
horse-racing, pretty women and the
theatre, he was also interested in the
latest scientific discoveries, and
encouraged new research.

Chaucer, Geoffrey

*c.*1340–1400
English writer

One of the first poets to write in
English as well as French and Latin,
Chaucer worked as a government
official and became famous for
poems written to entertain
members of the royal family at the
courts of King Edward III and King
Richard II. His best-known work is
The Canterbury Tales. This
masterpiece describes a mixed
group of travellers riding on a
pilgrimage to a holy site. Much of
the tale is a collection of stories that
Chaucer pretends were told by the
pilgrims – though, of course, he
wrote them himself.

▲ *Christie also wrote plays, including
The Mousetrap (1952), Britain's
longest-running play.*

Christie, Dame Agatha

1890–1976
English writer

Author of popular detective stories,
Christie created some memorable
characters, including Belgian
detective Hercule Poirot and
eccentric elderly sleuth Miss Jane
Marple. Her books have
complicated, clever plots and many
are set in exotic, faraway lands.
Christie often travelled abroad with
her husband, the archaeologist Max
Mallowan, and used experiences
from her travels in her work.

Churchill, John (Duke of Marlborough)

1650–1722
English soldier

A professional soldier, Churchill
led British armies to many victories
against rival European nations,
especially against France. He
pioneered new, successful battle
tactics. His most famous victories
were at Blenheim (1704) and
Ramillies (1706). At first he was
popular, but lost public support
because so many men died fighting
in his wars. Churchill was also
involved in politics – together with
his wife, Sarah Jennings. They
strongly supported the Whig party,
which called for civil and political
freedom in place of strict rule by
unreliable kings and queens.

Churchill, Sir Winston

1874–1965
English politician

Stubborn, independent,
unpredictable and sometimes
unpopular, Churchill ended his
career as a national hero, admired
by millions. He was born into a
famous political family (he was
descended from John Churchill)
and when young, showed a talent
for writing. He served as a soldier
and worked as a newspaper reporter
in Africa before becoming a
Conservative MP in 1900. Churchill
changed his views to support the
Liberal Party in 1904. He served as
a government minister, but resigned
in 1915 after a Navy attack he had
authorised went badly wrong.

During the 1920s and 1930s,
Churchill's views were often

▼ *This commemoration stamp of
Churchill was issued in 1965.*

controversial. Even so, from 1924 until 1964, he was continuously elected as an MP. He rejoined the Conservative Party in 1924, served again as a government minister, then became Prime Minister in 1940, soon after the start of the World War II (1939–1945). Although almost 70 years old and unwell, he united the nation in a courageous war effort. His rousing speeches comforted servicemen and civilians, and made them believe they could win. He lost the general election in 1945, but was back in office from 1951 to 1955. He died ten years later.

Clive 'of India', Robert (Lord Clive)
1725–1774
English soldier
A successful soldier, Clive conquered and ruled large parts of India on behalf of the British East India Company – a trading association of rich merchants who also had great political power. Although he committed suicide after being accused of corruption, his time in office in India prepared the way for Britain's later takeover of India as part of the British Empire in 1858.

Cobbett, William
1763–1835
English campaigner
Journalist and campaigner for poor people's rights, Cobbett attacked privilege and corruption among public figures. He also fiercely criticised landlords who exploited their tenants, fearing that the rapid growth of industry and big cities would ruin many ordinary people's lives.

Cockcroft, Sir John
1897–1967
English scientist
Cockcroft was the first researcher to 'split' the atom (with his colleague James Walton) in 1932. Cockcroft's experiments, using high-voltage electricity to force atoms to disintegrate, provided important information that was used by many later scientists. Cockcroft and Walton won the Nobel Prize for their work in 1951.

Cockerell, Sir Christopher
1910–1999
English engineer
Cockerell became famous as the inventor of the hovercraft, a vessel that can travel fast over land and sea, balanced on a cushion of air. Cockerell's first hovercraft was launched in 1959, and achieved speeds of 100 kilometres an hour. It successfully crossed the English Channel later the same year.

Coleridge, Samuel
1772–1834
English poet
The youngest of 13 children of a West Country clergyman, Coleridge wrote some of Britain's best-loved verse, including *The Rime of the Ancient Mariner* (1798), and *Kublai Khan* (1816).

In 1798, Coleridge worked with poet William Wordsworth to produce a book of poems called *Lyrical Ballads*. Their simple style and plain language caused a sensation, as did their subject matter – the countryside and ordinary people's lives. Coleridge later wrote about politics, literature and philosophy.

Collins, Michael (The Big Fellow)
1890–1922
Irish politician
The son of a farmer from County Cork, Collins took part in the 1916 Easter Rising, when Irish nationalists rebelled against British rule. He was imprisoned, but soon released. In 1919 and 1920, he led guerrilla attacks on British soldiers. He also took part in negotiating the treaty that set up the Irish Free State in 1921. The next year, he became Ireland's Prime Minister. Some Irish Republicans, however, did not accept the Free State arrangement, which left Britain with certain powers in Ireland. A civil war broke out, and Collins was killed in an ambush by Republicans who wanted total independence.

◀ *Coleridge's poem,* The Rime of the Ancient Mariner, *tells of a nightmare voyage after the death of an albatross.*

Columba, St (Colmcille)

c.521–597

Irish religious leader

Born into a noble Irish family, Columba became a Christian and was forced to leave his homeland. He travelled to the west of Scotland, where he founded a monastery on the island of Iona, and trained missionaries to spread the Christian faith. Iona became a great centre of prayer and learning.

Constable, John

1776–1837

English artist

Pictures of the English countryside painted by John Constable are among Britain's best-known works of art. The son of a Suffolk miller, Constable was inspired by the gentle landscape around him. He was also interested in difficult new techniques, such as painting light and shadow.

▼ Flatford Mill *(1817) by John Constable.*

▶ *Cook was one of the greatest explorers and navigators in the world.*

Cook, Captain James

1728–1779

English explorer

Cook joined the navy as a seaman, but was promoted to officer because of his navigation skills. He was also expert at surveying and recording information. Cook was chosen to command *Endeavour* on a round-the-world voyage to collect scientific and geographic data. Between 1768 and 1771, he made the first scientific maps of the coasts of New Zealand, eastern Australia and Hawaii. Cook made further voyages to explore the Pacific (1772 –1775 and 1776–1779). He was killed by local people in Hawaii.

Cooper, Anthony Ashley (Lord Shaftesbury)

1801–1885

English campaigner

Inspired by his Christian beliefs, Cooper campaigned for shorter working hours in factories, especially for women and children. Thanks to him, new laws – known as the Factory Acts – were introduced between 1833 and 1850. He also introduced laws protecting boys and girls from being sent underground to work in mines.

Cranmer, Thomas

1489–1556

English archbishop

A priest and scholar with firm but moderate Protestant views, Cranmer played an important part in arranging for King Henry VIII to divorce Catherine of Aragon, his first wife. As a reward, Henry made Cranmer Archbishop of Canterbury in 1533.

Cranmer wrote new prayer books for use in English churches, devised new kinds of church service, and drew up a list of core beliefs, the Thirty-Nine Articles, for a reorganised, Protestant Church of England. When Roman Catholic Mary I became queen in 1553, Cranmer was put in prison. He was burned to death as a heretic (person whose beliefs are thought to be wrong) in 1556.

Crick, Francis
1916–2004
English scientist

Together with American James Watson, Crick made one of the most important discoveries in biology of the 20th century. They discovered the 'double-helix' structure of DNA, the basic building block from which all living cells are made.

Crick and Watson's work allowed other scientists to make great advances in understanding genetics (the study of inherited biological features) and led to hopes of finding a cure for serious diseases.

Crompton, Samuel
1753–1827
English inventor

Son of a weaver, Crompton was put to work spinning thread as a boy. He found old-fashioned hand-spinning so slow, and early spinning machines so inefficient, that he invented a new machine of his own. It became known as a 'mule', and produced fine, strong cotton thread. It was copied and used in many factories, but Crompton got little payment from factory owners, and died poor.

Cromwell, Oliver
1599–1658
English politician

A devout Puritan (Christian with strict, simple beliefs), Cromwell became an MP, and supported Parliament against King Charles I during the English Civil War (1639–1660). When the king was defeated in 1649, Cromwell helped to arrange his trial and execution.

Cromwell was an excellent army commander. In 1649, he was sent to Ireland to lead Parliament's soldiers against rebels. He became hated and feared for his brutal tactics, but he believed he was doing God's work. In 1653, he was appointed 'Lord Protector' of Britain – head of the government that Parliament set up to replace the dead king. He ruled sensibly and tolerantly, and refused to be called 'king'. His son, Richard, ruled after him, but was not a success. When King Charles II came to power in 1660, Cromwell's body was dug up and cut into pieces.

Dafydd ap Gwilym
poet, active 1320–1370
Welsh poet

Dafydd ap Gwilym is rated by many as the greatest Welsh poet in history. Born in Llanbadarn Fawr, near Aberystwyth, he became a master of traditional Welsh verse but was also influenced by French poetic ideas. He wrote in the Welsh language, rejoicing in the beauty of women and the natural world.

Dalton, John
1766–1844
English scientist

A teacher at first, Dalton spent his later career as a scientist, investigating gases and how they behave. He discovered how gases expand when heated and his findings became known as Dalton's Law. His research into clouds and air helped other scientists who were studying the weather. He also investigated atoms – the smallest particles of matter that had been discovered at that time.

▶ *John Dalton made important scientific discoveries about gases and their behaviour.*

Darby, Abraham
1667–1717
English iron master

After a visit to study brass-working in the Netherlands, Darby set up a new metalworks in Bristol. He invented new ways of casting iron, which allowed goods to be made more quickly and cheaply, so ordinary people could afford them. He moved to Coalbrookdale in Shropshire, where he pioneered a new technique for smelting iron. His work was continued by his son (Abraham Darby, 1711–1763), who built the world's first cast-iron bridge at the Coalbrookdale works between 1776 and 1779.

Darwin, Charles Robert
1809–1882
English naturalist

After completing his university education, Darwin was appointed naturalist (biologist) on HMS *Beagle*, a ship making a pioneering voyage to South America from 1831 to 1836. On this voyage, Darwin saw and reported on many new species of plants and animals. His findings led him to work out a new theory of 'evolution', in which he described how life on Earth has developed and changed over millions of years. In 1859, Darwin

published his ideas in a book, *On the Origin of Species by Means of Natural Selection*. This was followed by *The Descent of Man* in 1871. Darwin's theories caused great controversy. Many people were shocked by the thought that humans might be related to apes, and religious leaders said Darwin's ideas were blasphemous. Today, most scientists think that he was correct.

David I
c.1082–1153; reigned 1124–1153
King of Scotland

Scottish king David I aimed to introduce French and English cultures to Scotland, as he considered these more civilised than Scottish ways. Some Scottish nobles did not agree. David was the first Scottish king to issue his own coins. He also reformed the government and the legal system, encouraged trade and built many new towns. He claimed and won the right to rule northern England from English kings.

Davies, Emily
1830–1921
English educationalist

A clergyman's daughter, Davies worked to reform society and win rights for women, especially rights to education, and to vote on equal terms with men. She trained as a teacher and in 1866 set up the London Schoolmistresses' Association, so women could work together to improve schooling for girls. In 1869, Davies founded a college for young women, which later became Girton College at Cambridge University – the first women's college at Oxford or Cambridge universities.

Davy, Sir Humphry
1778–1829
English scientist

Born in Cornwall, the son of a wood-carver, Davy conducted pioneering experiments to investigate chemistry and electricity.

In 1815, Davy invented a safety lamp, which was carried by coal miners working deep underground. Unlike earlier miners' lamps, it did not set fire to mine gases and cause dangerous explosions. Davy's invention saved many lives. He also worked to make science useful for industry, and to help ordinary people understand the latest scientific ideas.

Defoe, Daniel
c.1660–1731
English writer

Defoe fought as a soldier, set up in business as a merchant, and then became a journalist and novelist. Today, his most famous book is *The Life and Surprising Adventures of Robinson Crusoe*, which he based on the story of a real-life castaway.

Delius, Frederick
1862–1934
English musician

Born in Yorkshire of German parents, Delius composed music based on traditional English tunes, in a graceful, romantic style. He continued to compose, with the help of a devoted friend, even after he lost the ability to see and speak.

de Valois, Dame Ninette (Edris Stannus)
1898–2001
Irish dancer

Born in Ireland, de Valois danced in France before settling in London to found her own ballet school. She began to create very successful new ballets of her own, and to direct dancers in new productions of existing ballets. In 1931, she founded her own ballet company, which later became the Sadlers Wells Ballet and then, in 1956, the Royal Ballet.

She also founded the Royal Ballet School to train dancers from a very young age.

Dickens, Charles
1812–1870
English writer

Born into a poor family, 12-year-old Dickens was sent to work in a factory, but was determined to make a better life for himself. After starting as a solicitor's clerk he worked at different reporting jobs. His first novel, *The Pickwick Papers*, was published in instalments in a popular magazine when Dickens was only 24. It was a great success, and he became famous. Dickens

▲ *Dickens wrote 15 novels from 1836 to 1870. His final work, Edwin Drood, was unfinished.*

produced many more novels and short stories. All combine dramatic plots, vivid character sketches, humour and social criticism. Dickens was shocked by the miserable conditions in which many ordinary people had to live and work. He also used his skill as a popular writer to campaign for many causes.

▲ Disraeli was Prime Minister for six years in the late 19th century.

Disraeli, Benjamin
1809–1882
English politician

Disraeli trained as a lawyer and worked as a journalist, but soon became active in politics. He was a keen, ambitious Tory (Conservative) MP. In 1852, he became chancellor of the exchequer, and was Prime Minister in 1868 and from 1874 to 1880. Disraeli believed in the idea of 'one nation', in which rich and poor worked together for the country's good. His government won praise for its policies to improve housing, make factories safer, and ban the sale of harmful food and drugs. Disraeli also negotiated important treaties between Britain and other nations. He strongly supported Britain's claims to rule an Empire, and arranged for Queen Victoria (who admired him greatly) to become empress of India. His great political rival was William Gladstone.

Donald II
?–900; reigned 889–900
King of Scotland

The first Scottish ruler to be called 'king of the Scots', King Donald completed the task that many earlier Scottish leaders had failed to achieve. He succeeded in uniting almost the whole country and its many different peoples, including the Picts, Scots and Vikings, under single rule.

Donne, John
1571?–1631
English poet

A scholar, soldier, and then clergyman, Donne wrote some of the best-loved poems in the English language. Some of his lines, such as 'no man is an island' are still often quoted today. He was also a famous preacher, attracting many people to hear him at St Paul's Cathedral in London.

Doyle, Sir Arthur Conan
1859–1930
Scottish writer

Doyle trained as a doctor in Edinburgh, but is famous today as the writer of stories featuring the brilliant, eccentric detective, Sherlock Holmes. When Doyle started writing, detective stories were a new and unusual type of fiction. His work did much to make them highly popular with readers around the world.

Drake, Sir Francis
c.1542–1596
English explorer

Born in Devon to a seafaring family, Drake sailed with his cousin, Sir John Hawkyns, to West Africa and the Caribbean. Fiercely Protestant, he regarded the Spaniards as his enemies because they were Roman Catholics, and England's rivals at sea. His pirate raids on Spanish ships off the coast of America were encouraged by Queen Elizabeth I. He also claimed California as a British colony. Drake's raids made him very wealthy, and annoyed Spain. As a reward, Elizabeth I knighted him on board his ship, *The Golden Hind*. From 1577 to 1580, Drake sailed around the world – only one ship had achieved this before. The peak of his career came in 1588, when he led English ships to fight against the Spanish Armada and helped to defeat it.

Dunlop, John Boyd
1840–1921
Scottish inventor

Dunlop worked for most of his life as a vet, but was also a keen inventor. In 1888, he made the pneumatic (air-filled) tyre, which transformed transport. Without it, bicycles, cars and lorries would not have been able to travel as quickly, safely or comfortably.

Dunstan, St
c.909–988
Anglo-Saxon archbishop

Born to a noble family, Dunstan was brought up to be a monk. He soon became a leading adviser to King Edgar. Dunstan also reformed the way the Church was run in England.

▲ *Edward I earned the nickname 'Hammer of the Scots' for his wars against Scotland.*

Edward I

1239–1307; reigned 1272–1307
King of England

A famous warrior, Edward I won many battles against the Scots, but his armies were eventually driven back by Sir William Wallace. Edward was more successful in his attacks on Wales. He defeated Welsh prince Llywelyn ap Gruffudd and took control of Wales in 1284. Many of the massive castles he built to control his newly conquered lands still exist today. In England, Edward was best-known as a strong lawmaker, who reformed the way the English government was run.

Edward III

1312–1377; reigned 1327–1377
King of England

Edward III came to power at a difficult time. His father, Edward II, had been put in prison, then murdered by English nobles, because of his bad government. His mother, Isabella of France, was ruling the country with her lover, Mortimer. While still a teenager, Edward took control of the government, sent Isabella back to France, and gave orders for Mortimer to be killed. Edward's strong government brought peace and prosperity to England for the rest of his reign. Handsome, brave and popular, he encouraged chivalry among his supporters and staged many lavish tournaments. In 1337, he claimed the right to rule France, starting a long series of battles that became known as the Hundred Years War (1337–1453).

Edward IV

1422–1483; reigned 1461–1483
King of England

Edward ruled at a time when there was civil war in England. These battles – the Wars of the Roses (1455–1485) – were fought between rival nobles. All claimed the right to be the next king. Edward became king after his father, the Duke of York, was killed at the Battle of Wakefield (1460). He was immediately challenged by the Earl of Lancaster's army, but defeated them at Towton. A brave army leader, Edward was also a clever politician, famous for his intelligence and charm. This helped him to win over enemies and bring peace, though he could also be ruthless. His rule was constantly threatened by plots and rebellions, all of which he survived.

Edward VII

1841–1910; reigned 1901–1910
King of the United Kingdom

Son of Queen Victoria, Britain's longest-reigning ruler, Edward did not became king until he was 60 years old. He spent his early years enjoying life – he was famously fond of good food, lively music, pretty women, and sport – but he also helped and supported his mother after his father died. Skilled at foreign languages, especially French, he took a keen interest in overseas affairs, before and after he became king.

▼ *Edward VII gave his name to a period of British history – the 'Edwardian Age' (c.1900–1914) – when Britain was at its richest, most powerful and most confident.*

Edward, the Black Prince
1330–1376
English prince

Eldest son of Edward III, Prince Edward was his father's top army commander. He fought many battles against France during the Hundred Years War, and also in Spain. There, he caught a disease and died at a young age, so he never became king. He was famous and very popular in his own time.

Edward the Confessor
c.1005–1066; reigned 1042–1066
King of England and Saint

Edward was the eldest son of King Ethelrd II (the Redeless) and his wife, Emma. As a child, Edward had to flee to Normandy to escape the Danes. He lived there for many years. He returned to England in 1041, and became king in 1042. He ruled well, but faced many problems.

Elgar, Sir Edward
1857–1934
English composer

One of the most important English composers, Elgar wrote many works for orchestras, choirs and solo instruments that are still popular

▲ *One of Elgar's tunes was later turned into the famous song* Land of Hope and Glory.

today. His music blended the rich 'romantic' style of great European classical composers with gentler English themes. Many of Elgar's works were inspired by the beautiful countryside of the Malvern Hills, where he lived.

Eliot, George (Mary Ann Evans)
1819–1880
English novelist

Daughter of a wealthy landowner, Evans was a very clever child. She was also a talented musician, and deeply religious. When her mother died, she took over the running of their large household, but religious doubts led to quarrels with her father, so she left and spent years studying philosophy and writing for serious magazines. From 1854, Evans lived with scholar G H Lewes, who encouraged her to write fiction. As she doubted her skills and wanted no publicity, she published under a man's name. However, her books won great praise and popularity for their intelligence, skilful story-telling, understanding of how people think and feel, and perceptive comments about 19th-century life. Her major novels include *The Mill on the Floss* (1860) and *Middlemarch* (1871–1872).

Elizabeth I
1533–1603; reigned 1558–1603
Queen of England

Elizabeth came to power at a time when the country faced many problems. At home, there were serious quarrels between Catholics and Protestants. Abroad, there were threats from rival nations Spain and France, and from rival claimants to her throne.

▲ *Elizabeth I was one of England's most successful rulers.*

A clever, well-educated, cautious politician, Elizabeth arranged a moderate settlement to the religious quarrels, and worked with trusted advisers and army commanders to defend England from foreign attack. Where possible, she made peace treaties, but when war could not be avoided, she encouraged English troops with rousing speeches. She became tremendously popular after English sailors stopped the Spanish Armada from invading in 1588. During Elizabeth's reign, great achievements were seen in music, art and especially literature. She paid for many poets and writers – including Shakespeare – to perform their works at her court. She also encouraged explorers to seek treasure and claim new lands for England overseas. Elizabeth's private life was always unhappy. Her mother, Anne Bolyen, was executed by her father, Henry VIII. As a young woman, Elizabeth survived various plots against her life. Early in her reign, she decided to remain single and did so. This was the only way that she could be sure of staying in power. As a result it seems that she often felt extremely lonely, especially in older age.

Elizabeth II

born 1926; started reign 1952, crowned 1953

Queen of the United Kingdom

When Elizabeth was born, her parents, the Duke and Duchess of York, did not expect to become king and queen. In 1947, she married a distant cousin, Prince Philip of Greece, and from 1951 began to undertake royal duties on behalf of her father, who was unwell. He died in 1952, and she was crowned queen the following year. Although she has no say in government policy, Elizabeth is admired by politicians for her knowledge and judgement. She performs many royal duties and has travelled more than any previous British ruler. Some younger members of her family were criticised in the late 20th century, but Elizabeth is still widely respected for her hard work and devotion to duty.

Faraday, Michael

1791–1867

English scientist

Faraday began his career as assistant to Humphry Davy, then started his own investigations. He made many important discoveries about electricity and magnetism, and also investigated the electrical properties of atoms. A unit of electrical measurement, the farad, is named after him.

Fawcett, Dame Millicent Garrett

1847–1929

English suffragist

The sister of Elizabeth Garret Anderson, Fawcett spent most of her adult life campaigning peacefully for women's right to vote, and for laws that treated women equally with men. In 1897, she became president of the National Union of Women's Suffrage Societies – a nationwide federation of groups campaigning for women's rights.

Fawkes, Guy

1570–1606

English conspirator

One of the leaders of the Gunpowder Plot in 1605. This was a conspiracy to murder the Protestant king, James I of England (VI of Scotland) by blowing him up with gunpowder, and to replace him with a Roman Catholic ruler. The plotters believed this was the only way to win religious freedom for Catholics in England. However, most Catholics did not support the plot, and disliked the violence involved. The plotters were betrayed, and Fawkes was discovered on 5 November, hiding with barrels of gunpowder under the Houses of Parliament. With seven others, he was hanged for treason. Fawkes' plot is still remembered today, when people burn 'guys' on bonfires on 5 November.

Fielding, Henry

1705–1754

English writer

Playwright and novelist Fielding produced many satirical books, mocking other writers and criticising the way some people lived. Fielding was friends with many politicians and lawyers, and in 1748, was appointed a magistrate. Until his early death, he worked hard to reform law and order in London.

Flamsteed, John

1646–1719

English astronomer

In 1675, Flamsteed was appointed England's first Astronomer Royal, based at the Royal Greenwich Observatory in London. He was asked to help draw up accurate star-charts to guide sailors at sea. In fact, he produced the world's first star atlas, describing the carefully observed positions of almost 3000 stars. Flamsteed also observed the changing position of the Sun and Moon in the sky, and calculated tables showing the changing tides.

▼ *Henry Fielding's most famous novel is* Tom Jones.

Fleming, Alexander
1881–1955
Scottish bacteriologist

Fleming worked as a medical researcher. In 1928, he noticed that green mould growing on a dish in his laboratory was killing bacteria nearby. From this discovery, he helped create penicillin, one of the world's first antibiotic drugs. Penicillin was not widely available until 1940, when Sir Howard Florey found ways of mass-producing it. Since then, it has saved many lives. Fleming and Florey were jointly awarded the Nobel Prize for medicine in 1945.

Fonteyn, Margot (Peggy Hookham)
1919–1991
English dancer

Fonteyn was the first internationally acclaimed ballerina to be trained in England. Before her, most ballet dancers came from Russia, Italy or France. She gave her first performance in 1935, and continued to dance for many years. Fonteyn was famous for her elegance, sensitivity and charm. She performed many well-established roles, but also created new ones. In 1962, she formed one of the most famous dancing partnerships in the history of ballet, with Russian superstar Rudolf Nureyev.

Foster, Sir Norman
born 1935
English architect

Foster is famous for dramatic buildings made of glass and steel. He uses the latest engineering technology to create exciting new shapes. Well-known buildings include Headquarters of the Hongkong and Shanghai Banking Corporation, Hong Kong (1986), Stansted Airport, Essex (1991), Canary Wharf underground station, London (1999), the new German *Reichstag* (parliament building), Berlin (1999) and the Millennium Bridge, London (2000).

Fox, George
1624–1691
English Quaker

A Christian preacher, Fox, disagreed with the way the Church in England was run. He disliked elaborate ritual, and distrusted the power of priests. From 1647, he spent many years travelling the countryside, speaking to ordinary people about his religious views. He taught that God speaks directly to people's souls, and that God should be worshipped simply. Around 1650, Fox founded a religious society called 'Friends of the Truth'. It later became known as the 'Society of Friends', or the 'Quakers'. Fox was put in prison many times for his views, but continued to preach.

Franklin, Rosalind
1920–1958
English scientist

Franklin was one of the first scientists to use X-rays to study how matter is made. She began her work by investigating coal, and then started to explore living substances, including viruses and DNA – the basic 'building block' of life that is found in all human cells. Discovering how this was made was tremendously important, and laid the foundations for all future work in genetics. Franklin died of cancer aged only 38.

▼ *Frobisher's journey from England to the Arctic Circle.*

Frobisher, Sir Martin
1539–1594
English explorer

Aged 14, Frobisher left his respectable, wealthy family for an adventurous life at sea. He took part in pirate raids off Africa, and against Spain, but later decided to search for the NorthWest Passage. In 1576, he reached the Arctic Circle, but was forced to retreat by ice. He tried again in 1577 and 1578, but failed, and people mocked him. He won back his good name by fighting against the Spanish Armada in 1588.

Fry, Elizabeth
1780–1845
English prison reformer

Married to a wealthy banker, Fry could have had a comfortable, sheltered life. But as a Quaker, she believed it was her duty to help others. She began to visit women in prison and was shocked by the conditions she found. The women were in crowded, dirty cells, often without any food. Their children had to go to prison with them. Fry organised clean clothes and water and fresh food. She set up prison schools and found work, such as sewing, that the women could do to earn a little money. She also spent hours talking or reading to them, believing that most prisoners could live honest, useful lives.

Gainsborough, Thomas
1727–1788
English artist

The most famous, popular artist of his time, Gainsborough's works portray fashionable people, in beautiful landscape settings. Towards the end of his career, he turned to painting dramatic scenery and ordinary people's lives.

Gaskell, Elizabeth (Mrs Gaskell)
1810–1865
English writer

After marrying a clergyman, Gaskell devoted her life to caring for her children and sharing her husband's welfare work. She began to write to cope with her grief at the death of her baby son. Her novels, such as *North and South* (1854–1855), paint a vivid picture of life among ordinary people, and show a deep sympathy with their troubles, hopes and fears. Gaskell also supported many campaigns to improve working and housing conditions in big factory towns.

Geldof, Sir Bob
born 1954
Irish musician and campaigner

Born in Dun Laoghaire, Ireland, Geldof achieved success with a rock group called the Boomtown Rats from 1975 to 1986. In 1984 he founded a pop charity called Bandaid to raise funds for famine victims in Ethiopia, and in 1985 'Live Aid' concerts broadcast

▼ *Gainsborough painted many genteel scenes of the English countryside, including* View of Dedham.

around the world, raising millions of pounds. An outspoken lobbyist of world leaders, Geldof has continued to campaign for Africa and against global poverty.

George I
1660–1727; reigned 1714–1727
King of the United Kingdom

George was born in Germany, and became ruler of the German state of Hanover in 1698. He inherited the right to be king of Great Britain and Ireland after Queen Anne, last ruler of the Stuart Dynasty, died without children. He never learned English, and relied heavily on government ministers to help him rule. He was very unpopular throughout Britain, but is remembered today as the founder of a new dynasty, the Hanoverians.

George III
1738–1820; reigned 1760–1820
King of the United Kingdom

George III was hard-working, religious, and devoted to his family. He played an important part in politics, supporting the Tory Party and strengthening royal control of the government. However, George faced many problems that he was unable to solve. There were riots by political reformers, a long war with France, quarrels in India and Ireland, and demands for independence by Britain's colonies in America. George refused to compromise with any of them, and this led to further protests at home, and the formation of a new, independent nation in America. George also suffered from mental illness, and in 1811 was declared unfit to rule. His son, the Prince Regent (later George IV) ruled for him until he died.

George V

1865–1936; reigned 1910–1936

King of the United Kingdom

George V served in the Navy as a young man. He did not expect to rule, but became heir to the British throne in 1901 when his older brother died. He won respect for his hard work and devotion to duty, especially during World War I (1914–1918). He also tried to solve political problems in Ireland, and worked closely with politicians during the economic crisis of the 1930s. He was the first British ruler to make a broadcast to the nation.

George VI

1895–1952; reigned 1936–1952

King of the United Kingdom

The second son of George V, he became a naval officer, taking part in battles at sea during World War I (1914–1918). He also served in the Royal Air Force. Shy and quiet, he became king (and the centre of public attention) when his elder brother Edward VIII gave up the throne. His personal courage and sincerity helped to improve the image of the royal family, as did his happy family life with his wife Elizabeth and his daughters, Elizabeth and Margaret.

Gladstone, William Ewart

1809–1898

English politician

After serving as a Conservative government minister, Gladstone changed his political views and joined the Liberal Party. He campaigned for better working conditions in factories, religious tolerance, and a ban on slavery. He was Prime Minister four times between 1868 and 1894.

While in office, Gladstone reorganised government finances, the armed forces and the civil service. He also introduced many reforms. The most important were designed to improve education, make Parliament closer to the people, and remove unfairness in Irish land-owning law. He believed strongly that Ireland should have the right to rule itself. This led to a major split within the Liberal Party.

▲ *Prime Minister Gladstone was known for his rousing speeches in Parliament.*

Glyndŵr, Owain

*c.*1354–*c.*1417

Welsh rebel

Descended from Welsh princes, Owain began his political career working for the English government. However, a dispute over land, and his disgust with brutal and arrogant English rule in Wales turned him into a rebel, fighting for independence.

Owain won many Welsh supporters, and in 1400 they declared him 'Prince of Wales' – a title claimed by the sons of English kings. Owain led armies to attack English soldiers and capture English castles in Wales. This was the last and largest Welsh revolt against English rule, and it failed. By around 1416, English troops controlled all of Wales. Legend says that he will return to fight again.

Grattan, Henry

1746–1820

Irish politician

Born and educated in Dublin, at a time when Ireland was ruled from England, Grattan campaigned for Irish independence. He trained as a lawyer, then entered the Irish Parliament, where he won fame as a brilliant speaker. He campaigned, successfully, to repeal (cancel) the rule by which all laws made in Ireland also had to be approved by the English Parliament. This made him a national hero. He also opposed the union of the English and Irish Parliaments in 1801, but agreed to represent an Irish constituency in the new united Parliament. Once there, he campaigned strongly for equal rights for Roman Catholics.

Greene, Graham

1904–1991

English novelist

One of the most famous writers of the 20th century, Greene's novels combine exciting storylines with the discussion of important moral questions of sin and forgiveness, right and wrong. All Greene's work was strongly influenced by his Roman Catholic faith. His best known works include *Brighton Rock* (1938), *The Power and the Glory* (1940), *The Third Man* (1950), and *Travels with My Aunt* (1969).

Grey, Lady Jane
1537–1554
English claimant to throne
Lady Jane Grey was used by her powerful relatives to try to win power. Well-educated, and a keen supporter of the reformed Protestant Church, she was married to the son of the Duke of Northumberland, who hoped that his family would one day rule England. When sickly boy-king Edward VI died in 1553, Northumberland and his supporters declared that Jane was queen. Jane was forced to give up the throne after only nine days, and Mary came to power. Jane was imprisoned and executed the next year.

Gwyn, Nell
1650–1687
English actress
From a poor background, Gwyn started her career selling oranges to audiences in London theatres. She then became an actress, and her beauty, good humour and wit attracted many noblemen. Her most famous lover was King Charles II, and their children were given noble titles.

Halley, Edmond
1656–1742
English astronomer
Oxford mathematics professor, astronomer and friend of astronomer Isaac Newton, Halley was one of the first scientists to study nebulae – clouds of glowing gas that appear in the night

▶ *Halley's comet glows brightly in the night sky as it passes Earth. It was last seen in 1986.*

sky. He is best-known today for his observations of a bright comet, now named after him, that travels at regular intervals of 76 years across the sky.

Hardie, James Kier
1856–1915
Scottish politician
Born to a poor, unwed mother in Scotland, Hardie went out to work aged only eight years old to help his family survive. He became a coal-miner aged ten. As a young man, he began to campaign for improvements in miners' pay and

▲ *Hardie served as Labour party chairman from 1905 to 1906.*

conditions. He also studied at night school. He found work as a journalist, then became an MP. In 1893, he was a founder member of the Independent Labour Party. This later joined with other working people's organisations to form the Labour Party.

◀ *Hardy wrote many novels, including* The Mayor of Casterbridge *(1886).*

Hardy, Thomas
1840–1928
English writer
Son of a stone-mason from Dorset, in southwest England, Hardy trained as an architect but became a writer. He published a series of novels set in Dorset and the counties nearby, which he called Wessex. They became very popular.

   Hardy's novels describe the lives of ordinary people and their struggles against injustice, bad luck and misunderstandings. He also painted vivid pictures of the Wessex countryside, in which the weather and scenery often seem to mirror his characters' feelings. His most famous works include *Tess of the D'Urbervilles* (1891), *Far From the Madding Crowd* (1874), and *Jude the Obscure* (1896). Towards the end of his life, Hardy wrote poetry, which also won great praise.

Hargreaves, James
*c.*1720–1778
English inventor
Trained as a woodworker and maker of looms, Hargreaves invented a new machine that could spin several strands of thread at once. It became known as a 'Spinning Jenny', and played a great part in the Industrial Revolution that transformed the British economy during the early 19th

century. Using machines such as the Spinning Jenny meant that goods could be made much more quickly and cheaply than by hand.

Harold II
1019–1066; reigned 1066
Anglo-Saxon king

The last Anglo-Saxon king of England, Harold reigned for less than one year. Son of Earl Godwin of Wessex, the most powerful nobleman in the country, Harold was sent to France by English king Edward the Confessor in 1064. There, he promised loyalty to Duke William of Normandy, who wanted to be king of England after Edward died. Edward, however, wanted Harold to be king instead, and publicly named him as his heir. He was crowned the day after Edward died. Harold soon faced problems. Many noble families would not support him, and his own brother (Tostig), and Norwegian king Harald Hardrada invaded northern England. Harold led an army to meet them, and defeated them at Stamford Bridge. However, William was also planning an invasion. Harold hurried south to fight bravely against William at Hastings, but was killed. William became king.

Harvey, William
1578–1657
English doctor

Court physician to kings James I/VI and Charles I, Harvey was the first European to discover how the blood circulates round the body through veins and arteries, and how the heart works as a pump. He also studied how babies grow and develop in the womb, and how animals move.

Hawking, Stephen
born 1942
English scientist

Hawking is one of the youngest people ever to be elected to membership of Britain's Royal Society (an association of top scientists). Hawking has investigated the structure and origins of the Universe by combining the two most important and challenging theories of 20th-century mathematics and physics – relativity and quantum mechanics. He has also studied space objects such as black holes.

Heath, Sir Edward
1916–2005
English politician

Conservative Prime Minister from 1970 to 1974, Heath is remembered today for his lifelong wish to bring the British closer to the rest of Europe. While he was in power, Britain finally joined the European Economic Community (today known as the European Union) after many years of negotiations and uncertainty. At home, Heath was less successful. His government faced serious economic problems, and he was forced to resign after a series of major strikes by coal-miners.

Henry II
1133–1189; reigned 1154–1189
King of England

Founder of the Plantagenet Dynasty, Henry came to power as king of England after years of civil war fought between his mother, Matilda, and her rival, King Stephen. He conquered lands in Ireland and France, and forced the king of Scotland to recognise him as overlord. He also tried to reduce

the power of the Church in England, but less successfully. He had to make a public apology after the murder of Archbishop Thomas Becket.

▲ Henry II was king of England for 35 years in the 12th century.

Henry IV
1367–1413; reigned 1399–1413
King of England

Grandson of Edward III, and son of John of Gaunt, Henry married a noble heiress and became the richest man in England. Henry also had political ambitions and wanted to be king. He won fame fighting in Germany, but was accused of plotting against King Richard II of England and was exiled. His lands in northern England were taken away from him. In 1399, Henry returned to England, took back his lands, and forced Richard to give up the throne. He became king in Richard's place, founding a new dynasty – the Lancastrians. At first, his rule was successful and he defeated various riots and rebellions. However, he clashed with Parliament, and was accused of extravagance.

▲ Henry IV was king in the early 15th century. He was ill for his final years, and died aged 46 years old.

Henry VII
1457–1509; reigned 1485–1509
King of England

Born in Wales, Henry was descended from the Tudor family. He went to live in France in 1471, partly to escape the civil war that was raging in England at that time. Henry saw his chance to seize the throne and invaded England in 1485, fought against and killed King Richard III, and married the daughter of king Edward IV.

Henry spent the early years of his reign restoring law and order and putting down rebellions. He began to repair the damage to England's economy caused by years of war. Henry's style of government was cold, stern and calculating, but in private he was a loving husband and devoted son.

Henry VIII
1491–1547; reigned 1509–1547
King of England

Henry was the second son of Henry VII. Famous for his good looks when young, skill at sports, and love of music and dancing, Henry VIII was very different from his father, and seemed the ideal man to be king. While Henry was in power, the navy was rebuilt and strengthened, new law courts were set up, and new officials were appointed to help the government in London keep close control of outlying regions of the country – and of the powerful noble families who lived there.

Henry hated the day-to-day business of government, but chose capable ministers, including Thomas Cromwell and Thomas Wolsey, to help him rule. When the Pope refused to allow Henry to divorce his first wife, Spanish princess Catherine of Aragon, because she had not produced an

◀ Henry VII was the founder of the powerful Tudor Dynasty.

heir, Henry took control of the Church himself.

When Henry's second wife, Anne Boleyn, also failed to produce a son, she was accused of unfaithfulness, and beheaded. His third wife, Jane Seymour, did give birth to a boy, but she died a few days later from disease. Henry then married Anne of Cleves, a German princess, because he supported her family politically. The couple did not get along, however, and separated. Henry's fifth wife was Catherine Howard. She bore no children, was unfaithful to him, and was executed. His final wife, Catherine Parr, also had no children, but they lived contentedly together until Henry's death.

Hepworth, Dame Barbara
1903–1975
English sculptor

A pioneer of abstract art (art that does not aim to create a recognisable picture of a person, object or place), Hepworth created sculptures in metal, wood and stone. Her work was inspired by the textures and colours of the materials she worked with, and by the natural environment. It is famous for its smooth shapes, and for often being pierced with holes.

Herschel, Sir William
1738–1822
German-born astronomer

Born in Hanover, Herschel moved to Britain, where he worked as an astronomer. In 1781, using a telescope of his own design, he discovered the planet Uranus, situated between Saturn and Neptune. His observations helped to double the known size of the Solar System. He was made King's

Astronomer by George III and went on to become first president of the Royal Astronomical Society. His son John (1792–1822) and his wife Caroline (1750–1848) were also notable astronomers.

Hitchcock, Alfred
1889–1980
English film director

One of Britain's most successful film directors, Hitchcock worked in Hollywood, the centre of the 20th-century film industry, as well as in the UK. He became famous for a series of horror films, including *Psycho* (1960) and *The Birds* (1963). Hitchcock's film work combines excitement, fear and chilling thoughts about why some people's minds become evil.

Hobbes, Thomas
1588–1679
English philosopher

Political philosopher Hobbes is remembered today for his book, *Leviathan*, published in 1651. In it, he put forward his views on how society works. He believed that people were selfish by nature, and that they would only work to benefit themselves – or to escape death and danger. This led him to suggest that strict laws and powerful rulers were necessary to run society. Without them, Hobbes believed, people could not be trusted to behave well towards others and would just please themselves.

Hockney, David
born 1937
English artist

Famous for large paintings in bright colours, and for small but powerful drawings, Hockney was one of the most popular artists in late 20th-century Britain and America. His work appealed to ordinary people as well as to art experts. His much-loved works are dramatic, full of strong feelings, sometimes humorous, and brilliantly portray effects of light and shade. Hockney's designs for the theatre are also highly praised.

Hodgkin, Dorothy
1910–1994
English scientist

Using newly invented X-ray techniques, Hodgkin studied the way crystals were made. She then used this information to find out more about how chemicals combine to form new compounds, making important discoveries that helped doctors and chemists formulate new drugs. Hodgkin was awarded the Nobel Prize for Chemistry in 1964.

Holmes, Kelly
born 1970
English athlete

Holmes took up running at the age of 12 and became a physical training instructor with the British army in 1991. She achieved fame at the 2004 Olympic Games, held in Athens, Greece. She won gold medals for both the 800-metre and the 1500-metre events. She retired from athletics the following year.

Hooke, Robert
1635–1703
English scientist

After working as assistant to Robert Boyle, Hooke began to make experiments of his own. He studied many different topics, including astronomy, optics (the science of light), cell biology and the science of materials. He discovered a law (now named after him) that describes how materials bend and stretch. Hooke also invented new scientific machines, and suggested improvements to microscopes and telescopes.

Hughes, Ted
1930–1998
English poet

In his poems, Hughes used powerful, direct language to communicate his vision of the world as a beautiful but cruel and savage place. Most of his works are about animals, fish or birds. Towards the end of his life, when Hughes knew he was dying, he also wrote about his feelings for his first wife, the American poet Sylvia Plath, who committed suicide in 1963. Some people think that this was his finest work. He won many awards and was made Poet Laureate in 1984.

Hume, David
1711–1776
Scottish philosopher

Born in Edinburgh, Hume worked as a government official. However, he is remembered today for his books on politics and philosophy. In them, he described his theories about how people think and learn, how society should be governed, and how the economy should be run. At a time when almost everyone believed in God, he shocked many people by refusing to do so. Instead, he argued that people – and governments – should be guided by reason, intelligence and experience.

Hywel Dda (the Good)
?–AD 950
Welsh king and lawmaker

Hywel ap Cadell was a wise king from west Wales, who gained control over most of the country. He is remembered for introducing a body of law, which remained the legal code in Wales until (and in some cases after) the English conquest. He enjoyed good diplomatic relations with King Alfred of Wessex, and in AD 928 went on a pilgrimage to Rome.

James IV
1473–1513; reigned 1488–1513
King of Scotland

After years of civil war in Scotland, James won back control of the whole country, including the wild, lawless Highlands. He also played a leading part in European politics, making alliances with France and marrying a daughter of King Henry VII of England. When England and France went to war in 1513, however, he supported France. This led England to attack, and James was killed, along with many Scottish nobles, at the Battle of Flodden (1513).

James VI and I
1566–1625;
reigned Scotland 1567–1625;
England and Ireland 1603–1625
King of Scotland and England

Son of Mary Queen of Scots, James became king of Scotland as a child. When Queen Elizabeth I of England died in 1603, he also inherited her throne. James became the first king ever to rule England, Scotland and Ireland, although the thrones were not legally united.

Intelligent, yet quarrelsome and stubborn, James believed strongly that God had given kings a 'Divine Right' to rule, and that they should therefore be obeyed without question. This angered many nobles and MPs. His favouritism towards certain people also made him unpopular, as did his friendship with England's enemy, Spain.

▲ James VI and I ruled when Queen Elizabeth I died.

Jenner, Edward
1749–1832
English doctor

Country doctor Jenner pioneered the medical technique of vaccination. This places dead or weakened germs inside a person's body, so that it will learn to fight against them and protect them from future disease. Jenner discovered that dairymaids, who often caught a rash called cowpox from the animals they milked, never got smallpox, a similar but much more deadly human disease. So he deliberately infected patients with cowpox. Although people said this was very dangerous, Jenner's patients did not catch smallpox. He had proved that vaccination worked.

John
1165–1216; reigned 1199–1216
King of England

Nicknamed 'Lackland' because as the youngest of Henry II's sons there had been nothing left over to give him, John was not a very successful king. His reign is remembered today for a very important document that he was forced to seal in 1215. Its name was Magna Carta, meaning great charter, and for the first time ever, it introduced laws limiting the king of England's powers and guaranteeing rights to his subjects. When John broke these laws, the English nobles rebelled against him.

John, Augustus
1878–1961
Welsh artist

Born in Wales, the brother of Gwen John, Augustus was a successful painter. He was famous for his portraits, mostly of beautiful women and famous people, painted in a bold, dramatic, colourful style.

John, Gwen
1876–1939
Welsh artist

Born in Wales, John studied in London and then moved to live and work in Paris. There, she became close to many great artists, notably Rodin, while producing important paintings of her own.

Unlike much modern art, which was lively, bold and colourful,

John's work was calm, quiet and often grey-toned. Usually, it showed women or girls in peaceful rooms.

Johnson, Amy
1903–1941
English aviator

One of the first women to gain a pilot's licence, Johnson won worldwide fame when she flew solo from Britain to Australia in 1930. Her flight took 17 days and was very dangerous. Later, Johnson flew solo to India and Japan, and became the first woman to fly across the Atlantic from east to west. She volunteered to fly for the Women's Auxiliary Air Force during World War II (1939–1945), but her plane was shot down over the River Thames, and she was killed.

▲ In 1932, Amy Johnson broke the record (previously held by her husband) for the fastest flight from London to Cape Town, South Africa.

Johnson, Samuel (Dr Johnson)
1709–1784
English writer

Son of a bookseller in Lichfield, Staffordshire, Johnson began his career as a schoolmaster, but left to live and work in London. At first,

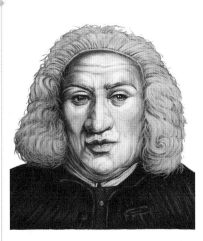

▲ Samuel Johnson compiled the first dictionary of the English language.

he wrote reports of debates in Parliament for newspapers, but in 1747 he was commissioned to produce an English dictionary. This was a great success when it was published in 1755, and Johnson became respected for his scholarship, outspoken opinions and wit.

Johnson also wrote essays, novels and biographies, and founded the famous Literary Club.

Jones, Inigo
1573–1652
English architect

After travelling in Europe to study art and architecture, Jones returned to England, where he introduced many new, Italian-style designs. He admired and copied the Italian architect Palladio, who based his own work on ancient Greek and Roman styles. Jones was employed by King James I and his family to create costumes and scenery for masques (plays with music) at the royal court. The king also asked him to design houses and palaces. The most important of these, the Banqueting House in Whitehall, London, still exists.

Joyce, James
1882–1941
Irish writer

Born in Ireland, James left home aged 21 to travel in Europe. He later settled in Paris, where he spent most of his life. Even so, many of his works, such as *Dubliners* (1914), *Ulysses* (1922) and *Finnegan's Wake* (1939) describe Ireland and Irish people. In his novels and short stories, Joyce experimented with many new ways of writing. He broke away from traditional rules of grammar, choosing instead to use words in long strings or short bursts, or to imitate the jumble of thoughts and feelings experienced by the characters in his books.

▲ James Joyce wrote the semi-autobiographical novel A Portrait of the Artist as a Young Man (1916).

Julian of Norwich
c.1342–c.1413
English mystic

Julian was an anchoress – a religious woman who decides to shut herself away from the rest of the world to devote her life to God. She spent most of her life in a small room attached to a church in Norwich, in eastern England. During an illness, Julian reported seeing visions from God. She described these to priests at the church, along with the thoughts and feelings they had inspired in her. Julian's words were later written down in a book. During her life, Julian became well-known for her wise advice and spiritual counselling. After her death, her book gave comfort and hope to many readers.

Kay, John
1704–*c*.1764
English inventor
Son of a factory owner, Kay invented machines to replace traditional methods of producing cloth by hand. In 1730, he made a hand-operated twisting machine, producing yarn that was stronger and smoother than hand-spun thread. In 1733, he invented a weaving machine that made wide cloth much more quickly and cheaply than hand-workers could. It became known as 'the flying shuttle'.

▲ *Kay's weaving machine was used in many factories during the Industrial Revolution.*

Keats, John
1792–1821
English poet
One of Britain's best-loved poets, Keats was born to a poor family in London, and trained as an apothecary. However, Keats was determined to be a writer and in 1816 gave up his medical work. In 1818 and 1819, he produced a series

of brilliant poems, including *Ode to a Nightingale, To Autumn, The Eve of St Agnes,* and *Ode to a Grecian Urn.* However, he was already seriously ill with tuberculosis. Keats left England in 1820 to escape the cold winter weather. He died in Italy, aged only 25, the next year. Keats' work was, and still is, admired for its rich language, which he used to create vivid pictures and to conjure up powerful feelings.

Kenneth I (MacAlpine)
died *c*.859; reigned *c*.843–858
Scottish king of Alba
Kenneth lived at a time when Scotland was divided into several different kingdoms. A famous warrior, he became ruler of Dal Ríada in the Highlands, around 841. Two years later, he conquered other Scottish kingdoms and declared himself the first king of 'Alba'.

Kingsley, Mary
1862–1900
English explorer
Kingsley spent the first 30 years of her life quietly at home with her parents. When they died, she decided to travel. She made two long journeys through West Africa, travelling along rivers by canoe, and meeting dangerous animals along the way. She also climbed to the top of Mount Cameroon, the highest point in West Africa. Unlike many Europeans, she was sensitive to the cultures and traditions of African people, and did not try to force her beliefs on them. Back home in Britain, she campaigned on behalf of Africans who were unhappy with British rule. She died of fever, aged 38, in South Africa, while working as a volunteer nurse.

Kipling, J Rudyard
1865–1936
English writer
Born in India, Kipling worked as a journalist in Lahore (now in Pakistan) and published many poems and stories there. His books described everyday life in the sub-continent, and among members of the British Raj (ruling class). From 1889, Kipling lived in Britain and earned his living as a full-time writer. His most successful works were for children, and included *The Jungle Book* (1894) and *Just So Stories* (1902).

Kipling's work was remarkable for including ordinary speech and soldiers' slang. He had a gift for creating memorable phrases, which were widely copied in Britain, India and elsewhere. In 1907, Kipling became the first British writer to win the Nobel Prize for literature.

Knox, John
c.1513–1572
Scottish Protestant
Scholar and church lawyer, Knox was a leading Protestant during the early years of the Reformation (a reform movement that divided the Christian Church in the 16th century). As a young man in Scotland, he was captured by the French (who wrongly suspected that he had been involved in murdering a Roman Catholic cardinal) and sent to work as a slave, rowing galleys. Knox was set free in 1549, travelled to England, and then studied with Protestant scholars in Switzerland. In 1559, he returned to Scotland. There, he became a famous preacher, encouraging Protestant reforms. He also protested against his country

being ruled by a woman, Mary Queen of Scots.

Lawrence, D H
1885–1930
English writer

Lawrence was born in the English Midlands. Its mines, factories, busy cities and wooded countryside form the setting for several of his books. Encouraged by his ambitious mother, Lawrence trained as a teacher. In 1912, just a few years after he started work, he eloped with Frieda von Richtofen, the headstrong, aristocratic, German wife of one of his college professors. Lawrence spent the rest of his life travelling with Frieda, and writing. Many of Lawrence's novels are based on his own feelings or experiences. In *Sons and Lovers* (1913), he explored his love–hate relationship with his mother. In *Women in Love* (1921), he described the uncertain, confused feelings of many young people after the end of World War I (1914–1918). His last novel, *Lady Chatterley's Lover* (1928), was banned in Britain until 1960 because it described sex, and used swear words. Lawrence did intend to shock, but he also wanted to break down old rules that stopped people from different classes and different backgrounds living happily together.

Lawrence, T E (Lawrence of Arabia)
1888–1935
Anglo-Irish soldier

After working as an archaeologist in the Middle East, Lawrence volunteered to help the British government's allies during World War I (1914–1918). He was employed by Prince Faisal, leader of an Arab rebellion against the Turks. Turkey was an ally of Germany, Britain's chief enemy in the war. Lawrence helped to train Arab soldiers to fight against Turkey. Later, he described his desert adventures in a book. After the war was over, Lawrence helped Arabs who were campaigning for independence, but the British government did not agree with his views. Unable to settle in peacetime, Lawrence joined the Royal Air Force in 1922 under a false name. He also began to write. He was killed in a motorbike accident near his home in 1935.

▲ *Dressed in Arab costume, Lawrence became the most famous of several British officers working with the Arabs in World War I (1914–1918).*

◄ *Skull of Australopithecus boiseii, discovered by Mary and Louis Leakey.*

Leakey, Louis
1903–1972
English anthropologist

Leakey was born in Kenya to British parents, who were missionaries. After being educated in England, he returned to Africa to study Stone Age remains. In 1948, he discovered the skull of an ancestor of modern apes, from 25–40 million years ago. In 1959, his wife Mary discovered another ancient skull. Leakey used this skull to prove that human beings had evolved from ape-like creatures about one million years earlier than anyone had previously thought. The Leakeys found many other important remains, mostly in Olduvai Gorge, now in Tanzania.

Leakey, Mary
1913–1996
English anthropologist

Wife of Louis Leakey, Mary helped her husband, and later her son, Richard, excavate very ancient sites at Olduvai Gorge, Tanzania. After her husband's death, Mary continued his work. She also published many books and papers. She was a respected expert on prehistoric rock paintings and ancient technology.

Lessing, Doris
born 1919
English writer

Lessing spent her childhood in Rhodesia (now Zimbabwe). In 1949, she moved to England and began to write. For many years, Lessing was active in politics, at first as a Communist, later as a feminist and supporter of human rights. Her novels deal with important political issues in a thoughtful, perceptive way. *The Grass is Singing* (1949) is about racial prejudice in southern Africa.

Leverhulme, Lord William
1851–1925
English industrialist and philanthropist

Factory-owner Leverhulme won fame in two separate ways. With his brother, he began to make soap from vegetable oil, rather than tallow (sheep's fat). To sell this new product, he gave it an attractive brand name, Sunlight, and launched an advertising campaign. Today, this is commonplace, but it was new and unusual at the time. Leverhulme also pioneered ways of providing good housing and welfare benefits for his employees. Close to his factory on Merseyside, he built a new town called Port Sunlight, with pleasant homes for workers, and arranged medical care, pensions, and profit-sharing schemes for his staff.

Lister, Lord Joseph
1827–1912
English surgeon

Lister was a surgeon who pioneered a new technique that saved countless lives. In the past, many patients died from infections after operations. In 1865, Lister read that French chemist Pasteur had discovered that infection was caused by bacteria (germs). So he decided to try to kill any germs before they could infect his patients. He covered wounds with dressings soaked in strong

◀ *Lister used a spray-pump to disinfect hospitals with carbolic acid.*

disinfectant, and sterilised his operating theatre with a fine mist of disinfectant sprayed in the air. Lister's technique, which he called 'antisepsis', worked well.

Livingstone, David
1813–1873
Scottish explorer

Born in southern Scotland, Livingstone worked in a cotton mill until he had saved enough money to study medicine. As soon as he qualified as a doctor in 1840, he sailed for southern Africa. Here, he worked as a medical missionary, set up schools and simple hospitals, and earned the respect and affection of many of the African people he worked with and trained. Livingstone also made several long journeys of exploration. He explored the Zambezi River, and became the first European to see Lake Nyasa and the Victoria Falls. In 1865, he set off to search for the source of the Nile River. Nothing was heard of him for more than five years, until American journalist H M Stanley went in search of the explorer, finding him in 1871 and greeting him with the words, 'Dr Livingstone, I presume?'.

▶ *Livingstone was the first European to see Victoria Falls, naming them after Queen Victoria.*

Lloyd, Marie
(Matilda Alice Victoria Wood)
1870–1922
English entertainer

Daughter of a waiter with 11 children, Lloyd was born in poverty. As a child, she began performing in London music halls (popular theatres where comedians, singers and dancers entertained crowds of workers). She also played leading parts in pantomimes. Lloyd became famous for her outspoken stage personality and for her witty songs, which she performed with great style and skill. Some of these are still well-known today, such as *My Old Man Said Follow The Van*, and *Oh Mister Porter*. Lloyd was known as 'the Queen of the Music Hall'.

Lloyd George, Lord David
1863–1945
Welsh politician

Trained as a solicitor, Lloyd George aimed for a political career. He became Liberal Party MP for Caernarfon, and was soon appointed to government posts. From 1908 to 1915, he was chancellor of the exchequer, and introduced many important social reforms. He provided government money to pay the first Old Age Pensions, and started a National Insurance scheme, where working people contributed a share of their wages to pay for welfare benefits. In 1916, Lloyd George challenged his fellow Liberal,

Herbert Asquith, for power, and became Prime Minister. Lloyd George proved a strong, capable leader during World War I (1914–1918). But his decision to work closely with Conservative politicians angered many Liberal supporters, and left the Liberal party weakened and divided. After the war was over, he planned large government housing schemes, to provide 'homes fit for heroes' – the soldiers returning from battle. However, his government ran short of money in 1921, and many of the schemes were halted. He was forced to resign in 1923.

Llywelyn ap Gruffudd
*c.*1225–1282
Welsh ruler of Gwynedd

The last Welsh prince came to the throne of Gwynedd in 1245. He won back large areas of North Wales that had been seized by the English. He brought most of Wales under his rule and in 1267 was recognised as Prince of Wales by Henry III of England. However, new wars against the English king Edward I, sparked off by his brother Dafydd, resulted in Llywelyn's death in a skirmish at Cilmeri in 1282. His head was sent to London for public display, while his body was buried at the Abbey of Cwm Hir. His death marked the end of Welsh independence.

Llywelyn ap Iorwerth (the Great)
1173–1240
Welsh ruler of Gwynedd

Prince of Gwynedd (North Wales), Llywelyn became the most powerful ruler in Wales, and was accepted as leader by all the other rulers of Welsh kingdoms, although he never claimed the title 'Prince of Wales'. In 1205, he married Joan, daughter of King John of England. However, the two kings fell out, and Llywelyn was soon fighting against an English invasion. He also made an alliance with powerful marcher lords, who owned vast estates on the Welsh borders, and were often hostile to English kings.

Locke, John
1632–1704
English philosopher

Locke lived during a time of political unrest and civil war in England. In his writings, he discussed the nature of political power. Locke argued that kings and governments had no absolute right to power. Instead, it was given to them by the citizens they ruled, because citizens needed someone to make laws and enforce public order. If a king or government made bad laws or failed to protect citizens from war and crime, they lost the right to rule, and should be replaced. Locke also wrote about how humans gather knowledge. He believed that we are born knowing nothing, and have to learn everything though our five senses, or by experience. Locke's ideas about government and about human learning were seen as dangerous and revolutionary.

Lovell, Sir (A C) Bernard
born 1913
English astronomer

Lovell is a pioneer of radio astronomy, the study of stars and other heavenly bodies using the faint radio waves they give off. He spent many years raising funds to build the world's first large steerable radio telescope, at Jodrell Bank in northwest England. It was completed in 1955, and demonstrated its power and usefulness by tracking *Sputnik*, the first satellite launched into space in 1957.

Lowry, L S
1887–1976
English artist

Born in Manchester, Lowry worked as a clerk and studied art at night school. His paintings – in a deliberately childish, 'matchstick-figure' style – portray people and their everyday activities in the industrial city of Salford, where Lowry spent most of his life.

Lynn, Dame Vera (born Vera Margaret Lewis)
born 1917
English singer

With a charming smile, warm personality and soft, attractive singing voice, Lynn became known as 'the Forces' Sweetheart' during World War II (1939–1945). She gave many concerts and broadcasts for troops, and also recorded patriotic songs such as *The White Cliffs of Dover*. After the war, Lynn continued to support charities that offered help to former servicemen and their families.

MacAdam, John
1756–1836
Scottish engineer

MacAdam moved to America, where he worked in business, and became very rich. In 1783, he returned to Scotland, and used some of his money to pay for experiments in road design. Five years later, he moved to Cornwall and continued his road research, funded by the government. MacAdam's experiments showed that several things were needed to create a smooth, long-lasting road. It needed to be well-drained, waterproof, and laid on top of layers of well-packed soil. MacAdam also developed a new, long-lasting road surface, made of small rocks and stone chips, bound together with gravel or slag (waste from iron-smelting factories).

Macbeth
c.1005–1057; reigned 1040–1057
King of Scotland
Today, Macbeth is remembered as the hero – or villain – of one of Shakespeare's most dramatic plays, Macbeth. The real Macbeth was a nobleman who became king after killing his cousin Duncan I. King Duncan had attacked him, as part of a long-standing feud. Macbeth ruled peacefully until Scotland was attacked by the Earl of Northumberland, who wanted to help Duncan's son, Malcolm III, seize the throne. Macbeth was defeated, but survived for a further three years. He was killed in another battle against members of Duncan's family, who were determined to continue their feud.

MacDonald, Flora
1722–1790
Scottish heroine
Flora MacDonald was born on the island of South Uist in the Hebrides. She was adopted by a Scottish noblewoman, travelled to Edinburgh to be educated, then went to live in Skye.

In 1746, Flora was asked to help Jacobite leader Charles Edward Stuart, who was trying to escape from English soldiers. She disguised

him as her Irish woman servant, 'Betty Burke', and smuggled him to safety on a waiting French warship. Later, the English government found out what she had done, and put her in prison. Within a year, she was set free. She later married and lived in America and Scotland.

▲ *MacDonald was a Labour MP and was elected Prime Minister in 1929.*

MacDonald, J Ramsay
1866–1937
Scottish politician
Born to a very poor unwed mother who was a servant on a Scottish farm, MacDonald worked hard at school, found a job as a Labour Party official, then became a Labour MP in 1906. He was a pacifist (someone who believes that all war is wrong), and could not support Britain fighting in World War I (1914–1918). His views angered many voters, and he lost his seat in Parliament in 1918. He was re-elected in 1922. A moderate, he aimed to make Labour 'responsible'

and fit for government. He was Prime Minister for a few months in 1924, and from 1929 to 1931. During the economic crisis of the early 1930s, MacDonald headed a national government from 1931 to 1935, with members from Labour, Conservative and Liberal Parties. He believed that this would be best for the country, but many Labour Party supporters saw him as a traitor, and he was expelled from the party.

Mackintosh, Charles
1766–1843
Scottish chemist
Remembered today for coats made of waterproof fabric, named after him, Mackintosh studied dyestuffs and other chemicals used in industry. In 1823, he invented a way of coating cloth with rubber solution. Later, he also developed a vulcanisation (strengthening) process for rubber tyres.

Mackintosh, Charles Rennie
1868–1928
Scottish designer
Creator of a distinctive new style, based on flowing lines and tall, slender shapes, Mackintosh was one of the main exponents of the Art Nouveau style in Scotland. He trained as an architect, and designed many buildings in and around Glasgow, including a stylish new School of Art.

Macmillan, Harold
1894–1986
English politician
Grandson of a Scottish crofter, and son of a successful publisher, Macmillian came from a family that had moved rapidly from poverty to

wealth. Educated as a 'gentleman', he fought bravely during World War I (1914–1918), then went into politics, as a Conservative. He was first elected MP in 1924 and went on to become a government minister, responsible for housing (1951–1954). He later served as chancellor of the exchequer, then Prime Minister from 1957 to 1963. Macmillan held power at a time when Britain's economy was booming, and he proudly declared, 'Most of our people have never had it so good!'. In foreign affairs, he worked with leaders in many British colonies who wanted independence from British rule.

Macmillan, Kirkpatrick
1813–1878
Scottish inventor

Blacksmith Macmillan invented the world's first pedal-driven bicycle in 1839. The pedals were very hard to use, putting great strain on the knees. However, when copies of Macmillan's invention were made by Gavin Dalzell, in 1846, cycling began to grow more popular.

▼ *The first pedal-driven bicycle in the world, invented by Macmillan.*

Malcolm III 'Canmore'
c.1031–1093; reigned 1058–1093
King of Scotland

Malcolm became king after killing Macbeth in battle. He worked to try to unite the different peoples of Scotland into a single kingdom, but had to spend much of his reign defending Scotland against English attack. He was killed in battle in Northumberland.

Malthus, Thomas Robert
1766–1834
English economist

A clergyman and scholar, Malthus investigated the way that a population grows. He believed that each population would naturally go on increasing until it grew too big for its local food supply. Then there would be famine, people would die and the population would fall. There would be enough for everyone to eat until the population grew too big again. Malthus argued that it was possible to stop this miserable cycle of events. If people had fewer children, populations would remain the same size, and might even fall. Then there would be no danger of famine. Malthus believed that people could be encouraged to have fewer children by stopping charity and welfare payments.

Margaret, St
c.1046–1093
Queen of Scotland

A member of the Anglo-Saxon royal family, Margaret was married to King Malcolm III as a way of making peace between two countries, England and Scotland, that were often at war. She introduced many English words and customs to Scotland. For example, she gave all eight of her children non-Scottish names (many were taken from the Bible). Margaret was reported to be very religious, kind and charitable. She also encouraged leaders of the Church in Scotland to obey Roman Church laws. She collapsed and died when she heard the news that her husband and eldest son had been killed in battle. Margaret was buried in a beautiful church at Dunfermline, and made a saint in 1250.

Markova, Dame Alicia (Lilian Marks)
1910–2004
English dancer

Born in London, Marks studied with leading French and Russian ballet teachers before going to dance with a famous international company, the *Ballets Russes*, aged only 14. Her name was changed to Markova, since almost all other top dancers had Russian names. In 1929, Markova returned to England, becoming a prima ballerina at 19 years old. She performed many star parts, becoming the first English ballerina to dance difficult roles in famous classical ballets, such as *Swan Lake*. In 1935, Markova founded her own ballet company with male dancer Anton Dolin, which later became the London Festival Ballet.

Marlowe, Christopher (Kit)
1564–1593
English writer

Creator of several successful plays in blank (non-rhyming) verse, such as *Dr Faustus* and *Tamburlaine the Great*, Marlowe's lines are still quoted today. He also wrote many poems, mostly about love. He died young, in a tavern brawl. William Shakespeare borrowed ideas from Marlowe's work to use in his early plays.

▲ *Mary I reigned for five years until her death in 1558.*

Mary I
1516–1558; reigned 1553–1558
Queen of England

Daughter of Henry VIII and his first wife, Catherine of Aragon, Mary was intelligent and very well educated. As an only child, she was brought up to expect that she would one day rule England. In 1527, however, when she was 11 years old, her life changed completely. Henry VIII demanded a divorce from Mary's mother, so that he could marry his new love, Anne Boleyn. Henry hoped that Anne would bear him a male child to be his heir. Mary sided with her mother and remained loyal to her mother's Roman Catholic faith. Henry took Mary away from Catherine, and they never saw each other again. Mary was proclaimed queen in 1553. Aged 37, and needing an heir, Mary arranged a marriage with King Phillip II of Spain. Like her, he was Catholic. However, the marriage was very unpopular. Mary became hated further still after she began to persecute Protestants who refused to accept her Catholic faith.

Countless ordinary people were hanged as rebels, and over 300 well-known figures were burnt as heretics. People called her 'Bloody Mary'. She died in 1558 of cancer.

Mary, Queen of Scots
1542–1587; reigned 1542–1567
Queen of Scotland

Daughter of King James V and the French princess, Mary of Guise, Mary became queen of Scotland aged just six days old. She was sent to France to be educated, while her mother ruled Scotland on her behalf. As a child, Mary married the French crown prince. He became King François II in 1559, but died one year later, and Mary was sent back to Scotland in 1561. She faced a difficult situation. She was young, in an unknown country, at a time when many people thought that women were unfit to rule. She was a Roman Catholic, but most Scots were Protestants. She also had to find a suitable husband, so she could produce an heir. She ignored all advice, and wed her cousin, nobleman Henry Darnley. Darnley was ambitious, but stupid and jealous of Mary's power. He was accused of planning the murder of her friend, musician David Rizzio. Soon afterwards, Darnley was found dead. Mary then scandalised Europe by eloping with one of the chief suspects, a violent noble named Bothwell. After this, the Scottish people no longer wanted Mary as queen. They locked her up in a castle, but she escaped, and fled to England in 1558. There, she became a serious problem for Queen Elizabeth, because England's enemies in Spain and France wanted Mary to be queen. Some Roman Catholics in England

wanted this, too. For almost 20 years, Elizabeth kept Mary shut up in remote country houses, as it was too risky to set her free. Finally, she accepted senior ministers' advice and had Mary executed, after Mary was accused of taking part in several plots.

Matthews, Sir Stanley
1915–1999
English footballer

A professional footballer since the age of 17, Matthews played in 886 first-class matches, and in 54 internationals for England. Usually playing at right wing, he became known as 'the wizard of the dribble'. Few players before or since have shown such balance or control. His career lasted for a remarkable 33 years, until he was 50.

Maxwell, James Clerk
1831–1879
Scottish scientist

A physicist, Maxwell studied electricity and magnetism. He was the first to realise that electromagnetic radiation existed, and to realise that light is a form of electromagnetic energy. He worked out mathematical equations to describe how electromagnetic forces work. He was also a capable administrator, setting up and running the Cavendish research laboratory at Cambridge University for many years.

Mill, John Stuart
1806–1873
English philosopher

A civil servant and later an MP, Mill is remembered today for his writings on liberty, justice, women's rights and economics.

He supported individual freedom, and was suspicious of state control and of 'free market' forces. He believed that neither would create a good environment for all citizens. Mill campaigned for ordinary men and women to get the vote, and for workers to have the right to help run factories.

Milton, John
1608–1674
English poet

Milton lived at a time when England was divided by religious disputes and civil war. Both these are reflected in his writings. During the civil war, he wrote poems and pamphlets calling for England to become a republic, and defending the right to express an opinion in print without fear of prosecution. Milton's greatest work, *Paradise Lost* (1667), is a long epic that re-tells the Bible story of Adam and Eve. Milton went blind in middle age, but this did not stop him writing or studying as his wife and daughters read to him.

Montfort, Simon de
c.1208–1265
English nobleman

Born into a noble family in Leicester, and married to the sister of Henry III, de Montfort won fame as a soldier. Brave, energetic and clever, but also greedy, ruthless and self-satisfied, he won both admirers and enemies. He quarrelled with Henry over the running of royal government and in 1263 started a civil war. In 1264, de Montfort captured the king and his eldest son, Prince Edward, on the battlefield. He forced Henry to summon parliament, which had not assembled for many years, believing that its members would help the king rule. However, Edward escaped from prison, de Montfort's enemies attacked, and he was killed at the Battle of Evesham in 1265.

▼ *Bronze statue by Henry Moore.*

Moore, Henry
1898–1986
English sculptor

Moore created massive single figures and family groups, mostly of stone. His work stands in front of many important public buildings, in Britain and around the world. Unlike earlier sculptors, Moore did not make small-scale models of his designs. Instead, he carved straight into wood or stone, believing that he would create a more truthful image that way. Moore was also a skilled draughtsman. During World War II (1939–1945), he worked as an official war artist, creating many memorable drawings of ordinary people sheltering from bomb attacks.

More, Sir (or St) Thomas
1478–1535
English politician

A famous scholar and government minister at the court of King Henry VIII, More was a Roman Catholic, who opposed Protestant Church reforms. He resigned as chancellor when Henry announced his decision to seek a divorce from Catherine of Aragon, and was put in prison in 1534 for refusing to accept Henry's marriage to Anne Boleyn. Henry gave orders for More to be executed. More's writings ensured that his fame survived his death. He is still remembered for his book *Utopia*, in which he discussed the best way of running society, and criticised the governments of his time.

Morris, William
1834–1896
English designer

Morris planned a career as a clergyman, but gave up religion to devote his life to arts and crafts. He believed that hand-made, individually designed goods were better than items mass-produced in factories. Morris was a brilliant designer, especially of fabrics and printed books. He also wrote many stories, poems and political works, putting forward his socialist ideas. He greatly admired medieval art and architecture, and helped found the Society for the Protection of Ancient Buildings to preserve Britain's heritage.

Napier, John
1550–1617
Scottish mathematician

Napier is remembered today as the inventor of logarithms – sets of tables where numbers are shown as functions (forms) of different bases (number used as units for multiplying or dividing). For example, 2 is the logarithm of 100 to base 10, because 100 = 10 x 10. Before calculators or computers were invented, logarithms were used by mathematicians to perform complicated calculations quickly and accurately. Today they are still used to measure and describe natural phenomena, for example, the way our ears respond to sound, in precise mathematical ways.

Nash, John
1752–1835
English designer

One of the earliest architects to plan whole streets and towns, Nash worked for the Prince Regent (later King George IV) to design elegant new buildings, especially in London. He planned Regent Street and Trafalgar Square (both 1826–1835), rebuilt Buckingham Palace and designed Marble Arch (both 1821–1830). In Brighton, he created a fantastic, Eastern-style pavilion for the Prince Regent.

Nasmyth, James
1818–1890
Scottish engineer

Designer of several experimental steam-powered machines and railway locomotives, Nasmyth was most famous for the huge, steam-powered hammer that he invented in 1839. It became widely used in metal-working factories and iron forges. Towards the end of his life, Nasmyth became interested in astronomy, producing one of the first detailed maps of the Moon.

Nelson, Lord Horatio
1758–1805
English admiral

Nelson joined the Navy aged 12, and served on ships sailing to the Arctic and the Caribbean. His skill as a seaman and leader was soon recognised, and he was given his first ship to command while still in his twenties. Although small and slight, he showed great physical courage. He lost his right eye fighting against the French in 1793, and his right arm in 1797. The following year, he defeated the French at the Battle of the Nile (1798) and became a national hero. He also became friends with Lady Emma Hamilton, whose husband was British ambassador in southern Italy. They had a daughter, Horatia, and remained deeply in love for the rest of Nelson's life. Promoted to admiral in 1801, Nelson ignored orders given by a cautious senior officer to win a daring victory at the Battle of Copenhagen. It was said that he held his telescope to his blind eye, and so could not see the flags sending messages from the senior officer's ship. His greatest success came at the Battle of Trafalgar in 1805, where his ships destroyed the French fleet. Nelson was killed in the fighting, but his victory made Britain the greatest naval power in the world.

Newcomen, Thomas
1663–1729
English engineer

Newcomen invented the first steam-powered engine that was strong and reliable enough for industrial use. Made to pump water out of deep coal mines, it was first installed in 1712. Newcomen's design was later adapted and improved by inventor James Watt.

Newton, Sir Isaac
1642–1727
English scientist

One of the greatest scientists in the world, Cambridge professor Newton was a mathematician and physicist. He made many key mathematical discoveries. He also discovered, and explained in mathematical terms, the natural laws that rule the Universe. Newton's Laws of Motion describe the forces at work when movement happens. His Law of Gravitation describes terms such as weight and mass, and explains why objects fall to Earth, and why the Earth orbits the Sun. Newton also studied optics (the science of light and vision) and was the first to show that white light is made up of many different colours. In 1703, he was elected president of the Royal Society, the highest scientific honour of his day.

▼ *Newton developed many important scientific theories, including how gravity works.*

▲ *Florence Nightingale became known as 'the Lady with the Lamp' because of her habit of checking the wards every evening.*

Nightingale, Florence
1820–1910
English nurse

Born in Florence, Italy, Nightingale received a strict academic education from her father, and accompanied her mother on visits to sick and poor people. She wanted to become a nurse, but her parents would not allow it – nursing was not a well-trained or respectable career at that time. In 1854, British troops were sent to fight in the Crimea, southern Russia. Nightingale volunteered to lead a group of nurses there, and a family friend (who was a government minister) obtained official permission for her to go. Nightingale and her nurses found that conditions in army hospitals were dreadful, and set about improving them, with great success. Nightingale proved to be a formidable organiser, who cared deeply about the wounded men in her charge. She was honoured as a heroine back in Britain. To thank her, the British public raised large sums of money to set up a school of nursing at a London hospital, where Nightingale taught other women to care for patients and to manage hospitals and nursing homes of their own.

Offa
?–796
Anglo-Saxon king of Mercia

Warrior and ruler of the English kingdom of Mercia, in the West Midlands, Offa took control of weaker English kingdoms and declared himself king of the English. He ordered the building of a massive earthwork, known as Offa's Dyke, to mark the boundary between his kingdom and Wales, and to display his wealth and power. Offa's Dyke was around 193 kilometres in length and 7.6 metres in height. Most of it still exists today.

Olivier, Baron Laurence
1907–1989
English actor

Son of a clergyman, Olivier became a professional actor aged 17. With a powerful presence and a commanding voice, he achieved great success in many classic plays and films. He was famous for playing Shakespeare's heroic Henry V – the film that he starred in and directed became one of the best-known British films ever.

Oliver also directed many stage plays, and led the British National Theatre Company from 1963 to 1973. A theatre on London's Southbank is named after him.

▲ *Olivier won an Oscar for Best Actor in* Hamlet *(1948).*

Orwell, George (Eric Blair)
1903–1950
English writer

The son of a senior British government official working in India, Orwell served in the British police force in Burma, then returned to England to become a novelist and political writer. To support himself while finishing his first books, he worked at miserable, low-paid jobs, and met many unemployed people. This led him to sympathise with working-class

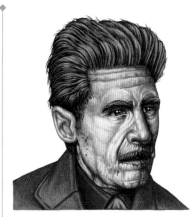

▲ Orwell's two most famous books, Animal Farm (1945) and Nineteen Eighty-Four (1949), are fierce attacks on all governments that control and manipulate their citizens.

protests, and to fight on the Republican side against Fascists, in the Spanish Civil War. Although Orwell was a socialist, he strongly disliked Communist governments, because they abused their power.

Owen, Robert
1771–1858
Welsh social reformer

Remembered today as a pioneer of the co-operative movement (which encouraged workers to join together to improve their lives), Owen was the son of a Welsh draper. He believed that people's character was shaped by the conditions they lived and worked in, and that ordinary people could only be 'good' if they were provided with fair wages and decent places to live. Owen trained as a master-spinner, then took over cloth mills at New Lanark, in Scotland. He ran them as a model factory, building new houses, schools, shops and water supplies for his workers.

▶ Robert Owen campaigned to improve the lives of factory workers.

He hoped others would follow his example. Owen also campaigned for new laws to make factories safer and healthier, and supported some of the first trade unions in Britain.

Owen, Wilfred
1893–1918
English poet

One of the most important poets who took part in, and wrote about, World War I (1914–1918). Owen had already produced several fine poems by 1914 – the year the War began. He fought as a British soldier in France, turning his horrific experiences and those of his comrades into bleak, bitter verses, full of anger at the tragic waste of young men's lives. Owen was killed in action one week before the end of the war. His poems still have the power to shock and move readers, and have been set to music by major composers, including Benjamin Britten in his *War Requiem*.

Paine, Thomas
1737–1809
English political writer

The son of a farmer from the east of England, Paine worked as a customs officer, before being dismissed for writing a pamphlet calling for higher pay. He emigrated to America, where he edited a newspaper and wrote a book supporting the American colonists' demands for independence from British rule. After America

became independent in 1776, Paine was sent to France on business, and supported anti-government protesters there. Next, Paine travelled to London, where he published his most famous work, *The Rights of Man* (1791–1792). In it, he argued that kings and queens should not govern, but that all countries should be republics. He also supported the Revolution that had started in France in 1789, and had overthrown the royal government. Paine's work outraged many people in Britain. He was accused of encouraging rebellion, and people burnt effigies (models) of him on bonfires. Paine fled to France, where he joined the revolutionary government. He returned to America in 1802.

Palmerston, Lord
1784–1865
English politician

Palmerston began his political career as a Conservative MP, but changed his views and became a Liberal. He served as an MP for an astonishing 58 years, and was a government minister for 48 of them. His first interest was in foreign affairs, where he strengthened Britain's influence in Europe, and supported independence movements in Greece and Turkey because he thought it would benefit Britain. He also began the Opium Wars – battles to protect English merchants (many of whom sold the deadly drug opium) – in China. In 1852, he became home secretary. He introduced laws to improve working conditions in factories. In 1855, Palmerston became Prime Minister. He ended Britain's war with Russia because it was too costly, and ordered British soldiers in India to put down a rebellion by Indian troops. His government was defeated in 1858, but Palmerston was soon back in power in 1859 with a strong team of politicians to help him introduce many new policies. These included cutting government spending, reducing taxes, and encouraging free trade (without limits or tolls) with other countries. Palmerston became unpopular when he refused to improve education for ordinary children, or to reform Parliament – at this time, few ordinary men, and no women, had the right to vote.

▲ Lord Palmerston became Prime Minister in 1855.

Pankhurst, Emmeline
1858–1928
English suffragette
Leader of the Suffragette movement, which demanded votes for women, Pankhurst, and her daughters Christabel (1880–1958) and Sylvia (1882–1960), are remembered today for taking direct, sometimes violent, action in their campaigns. They did this because they felt that peaceful, legal demands for women's right to vote would never succeed. In 1903, with her daughter Christabel, Pankhurst founded the Women's Social and Political Union. From 1905, Pankhurst, her daughters, and many other women staged dramatic protests – chaining themselves to railings, throwing bricks through windows, interrupting debates in Parliament, and damaging men's sports facilities such as football grounds. They were arrested and put in prison, where they went on hunger-strike, and were brutally force-fed. During World War I (1914–1918), Pankhurst called for the Suffragettes to stop their protest and to work hard for their country instead. Many Suffragettes and other women became volunteer nurses, drove ambulances or worked in factories, taking over essential jobs done by men who had joined the army. They proved to be hard-working and reliable, and when the war ended in 1918, the government allowed women over 30 years old the right to vote. The Suffragettes welcomed this, but said it was not enough. They continued to campaign, peacefully, until women were granted the right to vote on equal terms with men in 1928 – the year Pankhurst died.

Parnell, Charles Stewart
1846–1891
Irish politician
Parnell's father came from a distinguished Anglo-Irish family. His mother was American. Determined to help Ireland win independence, Parnell went into politics, and was elected as a British MP in 1875. In 1879, he became president of the Irish Land League, a body that campaigned for lower rents and better property rights for Irish people. The next year, he was elected leader of the Irish Home Rule party. In 1885, he helped persuade Prime Minister Gladstone to support calls for Irish independence. Five years later, in 1891, Parnell's political career ended after a scandal involving Irish actress, Kitty O'Shea, and he was forced to resign.

Parsons, Sir Charles
1854–1931
English engineer
In 1884, Parsons designed and built the world's first industrial steam-turbine engine. It used power from coal and water to generate electricity. Soon, steam turbines were installed in many power stations. Parsons' invention transformed the way many goods were made, and also revolutionised home heating and lighting. He also designed steam-turbine engines for ships, and an experimental vessel, the *Turbinia* (1894), which used steam-power.

Patrick, St
5th century AD
British missionary
Remembered today as the patron (guardian) saint of Ireland, Patrick was born in Britain, and spent his life as a Christian missionary. Very little is known for certain about Patrick's work in Ireland, although many stories and legends have been told about it. For example, he drove all poisonous snakes from the land and told them never to return. There were probably Christian communities in Ireland before Patrick arrived. He may have been sent there by the Christian Church in Britain to help strengthen them.

Peel, Sir Robert
1788–1850
English politician

Son of a factory-owner, Peel became a Conservative MP, home secretary (1834–1835) and Prime Minister (1841–1846). He is remembered today chiefly for founding the Metropolitan Police force to combat crime in London. For many years, policemen were nicknamed 'bobbies' after him. Peel also supported free trade between Britain and other nations, and moderate reform of Parliament, although he did not agree that all adult citizens should be allowed to vote. After a quarrel within the Conservative Party, Peel and his supporters formed a third party, most of whom later joined the Liberals.

Penn, William
1644–1718
English Quaker

A member of the Society of Friends (Quakers), Penn was imprisoned in the Tower of London in 1668 for publishing writings about Quaker beliefs. They were illegal in England at that time. Penn was put on trial, but the jury refused to convict him, and he was set free in 1670. In 1681, the English government granted him a charter (licence) to found a settlement in North America, where he and other Quakers would be free to worship in the way they wanted. It was named Pennsylvania, after him, and its capital was Philadelphia (founded 1682) – 'the city of brotherly love'.

Pepys, Samuel
1633–1703
English diarist

A senior government official who worked for the Royal Navy, Pepys is remembered today for the diary that he kept between 1660 and 1669. In it, he recorded many national events, including the Great Plague (1665) and the Great Fire of London (1666), and descriptions of new scientific discoveries.

The diary also includes a detailed account of Pepys's private life. He wrote in a secret code, so Pepys felt safe to include in the diary his innermost thoughts about politics and the powerful people he worked for. He also revealed all kinds of information about the clothes he bought, the food he enjoyed, the music he liked to play, outings with his friends, money worries – and even quarrels with his wife, and love-affairs with his women servants.

Percy, Henry 'Hotspur'
1364–1403
English soldier

A famous warrior, Percy was the eldest son of the Earl of Northumberland, the most powerful nobleman in northern England. He was given the nickname 'Hotspur' for his reckless courage in battle. Together with his father, he plotted against King Richard II and helped King Henry IV to seize power in 1399. As a reward, Henry gave Hotspur and his father important army commands, patrolling England's border with Scotland. However, Henry failed to pay their wages, or let them keep the ransom money from Scottish prisoners they captured in battle. So they joined forces with the Welsh under Owain Glyndŵr to rebel against Henry. Hotspur was killed at the Battle of Shrewsbury in 1403. His father was killed five years later, also fighting against the king.

Pitt, Lord William (Pitt the Elder)
1708–1778
English politician

Pitt became a Whig MP in 1735. Although disliked by the king and many politicians for his cold but powerful personality, he served as a government minister, proving to be capable and fair at a time when many other ministers were accused of self-seeking ambition and corruption. Pitt successfully shaped government policy during the Seven Years War (1756–1763). From 1766 until 1768, he was Prime Minister. However, ill health (possibly a nervous breakdown) caused him to resign.

Pitt, William (Pitt the Younger)
1759–1806
English politician

Son of Pitt the Elder, Pitt trained as a lawyer, then became an MP in 1781. Unlike his father, he supported the Tory Party. Clever and ambitious, he was soon made a government minister, then Prime Minister in 1783. He was only 24 years old, the youngest man ever to be chosen for the job. The young Prime Minister reformed government finances, reduced the national debt, changed the way British merchants and soldiers ran their lands in India, and increased people's respect for Parliament.

After the French Revolution of 1789, Pitt acted swiftly to stop any British people supporting the rebels in France, or discussing revolutionary ideas. Pitt also worked to unite Ireland with the other countries of Britain. The law to set up this union was passed in 1800. The year after that, Pitt resigned because George III refused to give the Catholic people of Ireland equal religious freedom and political rights to the rest of the British people who were mostly Protestant. Pitt returned to power in 1804 to help lead the war against Napoleon's France. He died in office before the war ended.

Pope, Alexander
1688–1744
English poet

After a childhood illness, Pope was left physically disabled, and was often mentally depressed. However, he had a powerful intelligence and quick wit, which he used to criticise people who he found foolish or pompous, especially governments and fashion-leaders. His most successful works were translations of ancient Greek epics. They were scholarly yet readable and enjoyable, and remained popular for more than 100 years. They also made Pope very rich.

Priestley, Sir Joseph
1733–1804
English scientist

A pioneer researcher, Priestley investigated the chemistry of gases and was one of the discoverers of oxygen in 1774. Priestley's enquiring mind led him to question many accepted religious beliefs. He became leader of a breakaway Christian church in Birmingham in 1779. Priestley was also a great supporter of political reform, and backed American colonists' demands for freedom from British rule. He also supported the French Revolution. Because of this, his house was attacked by mobs in 1791, and destroyed. Priestley fled to America, where he spent the rest of his life.

Purcell, Henry
c.1659–1695
English composer

Son of a singer in the royal chapel in London, Purcell also joined the choir, but became more famous as an organist and composer. He wrote many works especially for the royal court, such as birthday odes (songs) for the queen, and impressive pieces for choir and organ to be performed at royal coronations.

Purcell also composed many religious works, and music for the theatre. He is remembered today as the composer of the first opera in English in 1689. Called *Dido and Aeneas*, it is a tragic love story and was written for young students at a girls' school.

Raleigh, Sir Walter
1552–1618
English explorer

Born in Devon, Raleigh fought as a soldier in France, then became a courtier, serving Queen Elizabeth I. He became one of her favourites. However, he was restless at court, planned overseas voyages, and took part in wars in Ireland. He encouraged British explorer Humphrey Gilbert to explore Newfoundland, and explored the northeast coast of America himself, although unsuccessfully. After quarrelling with the queen, Raleigh tried to win back her favour by sailing to South America in search of treasure, and by fighting against Spanish settlers there. After Queen Elizabeth's death, Raleigh plotted against the new king, James I, and was imprisoned in the Tower of London for several years. He passed the time by writing *History of the World*. He was freed in 1616, but angered the king by attacking his allies overseas. He was executed as soon as he returned to Britain.

▲ Raleigh was a writer, poet and explorer. He founded the first English colony in 1584 in the New World (North Carolina, USA).

Rogers, Lord Richard

born 1933

English architect

Born in Florence, Italy, and then trained in Britain and the USA, Rogers won great fame with one of his earliest projects – the startlingly new *Centre National d'Art et de Culture Georges Pompidou*, in Paris. Rogers designed this with Renzo Piano between 1971 and 1977. Built like an industrial structure of glass and metal, 'the Pompidou Centre' was revolutionary at the time because it had all of its structural parts, such as stairs and drains, displayed on the outside instead of being neatly hidden away. Since then, Rogers has designed many more high-tech buildings. These include the new headquarters for Lloyds of London (an insurance company) and the European Court of Human Rights in Strasbourg.

Rossetti, Christina

1830–1894

English writer

Daughter of an Italian political refugee and an English governess, Rossetti published her first poems aged 12. After her father became ill, she had to find work to help support her family. She taught Italian, and opened private girls' schools. Shy, nervous and deeply religious, she refused offers of marriage, preferring to live quietly at home. However, her poetry revealed a different side of her nature. It was technically very clever, rich and dramatic, and full of passionate feelings of love and loss. She was the sister of Dante Gabriel Rossetti.

▲ *Rosetti's* La Ghirlandaia, *1873.*

Rossetti, Dante Gabriel

1828–1882

English artist

Brother of Christina, Rossetti became famous for his paintings in glowing colours and deliberately old-fashioned style. He was a founder-member of the Pre-Raphaelite Brotherhood – a group of artists and writers who admired the creative work produced in the Middle Ages in Europe. They painted pictures and wrote poems on medieval topics, and copied medieval designs in their work and in their clothes, furniture and house decoration. Towards the end of his life, Rossetti concentrated on painting portraits of women in dreamy, brooding style.

Rowntree, family

Joseph I (1801–1859);
Henry Isaac (1838–1883);
Joseph II (1871–1954);
Benjamin Seebohm (1871–1954)

English philanthropists

For three generations, members of the Rowntree family were leading businessmen and social welfare pioneers. Inspired by his Quaker beliefs, Joseph I built up a grocery business, and used the profits to set up schools for poor children. His son Henry Isaac set up a very profitable chocolate-making factory. Henry's brother Joseph II used some of the profits to found three Rowntree trusts, which paid for research into social welfare schemes. Joseph's son, Benjamin Seebohm, ran the family company, but also became famous for carrying out surveys into poverty and its causes.

Roy, Rob (Robert MacGregor)

1671–1734

Scottish outlaw

Born in central Scotland, Rob Roy was a cattle-dealer, a skilled sword-fighter, and a supporter of the Jacobites – people who wanted the Stuart Dynasty to rule Britain. In 1712, Rob Roy quarrelled with some of the men who worked for him. They ran away, taking money he owed to the powerful Duke of Montrose. In return, the Duke seized Rob Roy's lands, and made him an outlaw. For several years, Rob Roy lived by stealing sheep and cattle, and by blackmailing

▶ *'Rob Roy' was a nickname meaning 'Red Robert' in Gaelic.*

wealthy families. He managed never to be caught. Even though he broke the law, he became a hero to many ordinary Scottish people. Rob Roy was finally arrested in 1727, but was pardoned and set free. He spent the last years of his life peacefully at home.

Royce, Sir (Frederick) Henry
1863–1933
English engineer
In 1898, Royce designed and built his first automobile – one of the earliest in Britain. In 1906, he formed a business partnership with Charles Rolls (1877–1910), a fellow motoring enthusiast who had helped to set up the RAC (Royal Automobile Club) in 1897. The Rolls-Royce company designed powerful, luxurious cars that became very famous. Rolls and Royce were also pioneers of flight.

▲ *The Rolls Royce was a symbol of power and luxury.*

Russell, Earl Bertrand
1872–1970
English philosopher
Russell won fame as a young man for his brilliant mind. He was a mathematician and philosopher, specialising in logic. However, he lost his job as a university lecturer during World War I (1914–1918) because he believed all fighting was

wrong, and because he supported other men, known as conscientious objectors, with the same views. They were all seen as traitors at that time. From around 1920 to 1940, Russell earned his living as a writer. His *History of Western Philosophy*, which explained the subject to ordinary readers, was widely praised, and he won the Nobel Prize for Literature in 1950. He also supported many controversial 'progressive' causes, from votes for women to nuclear disarmament and educational reform. In 1958, he became the first president of the British Campaign for Nuclear Disarmament. In 1961, he was imprisoned, aged 90, for organising 'ban the bomb' campaigns.

Russell, Dora
1894–1986
English campaigner
Daughter of a senior civil servant, Russell graduated from university with a first-class degree. She worked as her father's secretary when the British government sent him to New York, then returned to Britain, where she fell in love with Bertrand Russell. They travelled to China, wrote books together on politics and society, and married in 1921. Although many married women at that time spent their lives at home, Russell continued her feminist and socialist campaigns after she was wed. She was one of the first people to demand maternity leave and affordable birth control. She also ran a progressive school, where pupils made the rules and helped plan lessons. Independent and free-spirited, she separated from Bertrand Russell in 1935. In the 1950s and 1960s, she helped set up campaigning organisations,

including the National Council for Civil Liberties, and the Campaign for Nuclear Disarmament.

Scott, Sir Robert Falcon
1868–1912
English explorer
Scott served in the Royal Navy for 20 years, then successfully commanded the British National Antarctic Expedition of 1900–1904, which explored the Antarctic territory known as King Edward VII Land. In 1911, he led a second expedition, this time to the South Pole. He arrived there in 1912, but found that the Norwegian explorer, Roald Amundsen, had reached it before him. Together with all his team, Scott died on the return journey to base camp, after struggling bravely against cold, hunger and exhaustion.

▶ *In the race to the South Pole, Scott and his team came second, behind Roald Amundsen.*

Scott, Sir Walter
1771–1832
Scottish writer
Scott spent his childhood in the Scottish countryside. He became fascinated by traditional songs and stories, and decided that he would become a writer one day. He worked as a lawyer in Edinburgh, but also wrote in his spare time. The first collection of his poems,

The Minstrelsy of the Scottish Border, was published in 1802–1803, and others soon followed.

After 1814, Scott began to write novels. These proved very popular. Some, such as *Ivanhoe* and *Rob Roy*, are still enjoyed today. Scott became rich, and invested money in a new publishing company. However, the company failed, leaving vast debts, and Scott was declared bankrupt.

Shackleton, Sir Ernest Henry
1874–1922
Irish explorer

A member of Robert Scott's 1900 expedition, Shackleton led a team towards the South Pole in 1909, getting closer to it than anyone had ever been before. During Shackleton's next expedition, from 1914 to 1916, his ship *Endeavour* was trapped and crushed by ice. Shackleton and his crew escaped by rowing 1300 kilometres across icy seas in an open boat. After a long, dangerous journey, they found shelter on South Georgia, an island off Antarctica.

Shakespeare, William
1564–1616
English playwright

The most famous English writer of all time, Shakespeare was born in the town of Stratford-upon-Avon. His father was a merchant and Shakespeare could have joined his business. Instead, he left home as a young man to work as an actor, then a writer, in London. He also became part-owner of two of London's most popular theatres and staged performances at the royal court.

His plays are admired as classics today, and are performed all over the world. They include love stories such as *Romeo and Juliet*, historical epics such as *Henry V*, and tragedies such as *Hamlet*. As well as plays, Shakespeare also wrote magnificent poetry, mostly about love and death. So many lines from Shakespeare's plays have been 'borrowed' for everyday speech, that he has shaped the way the English language has developed.

Shaw, George Bernard
1856–1950
Irish writer

Famous for his left-wing political views, Shaw wrote many plays about key social issues of his own time, such as women's rights, freedom and war. He was also one of the first vegetarians to campaign for healthier food and animal welfare. Although Shaw's works had a serious purpose, they were often very witty and entertaining, and are still popular today. One of his best-known plays, *Pygmalion*, was turned into the very successful musical, *My Fair Lady*.

Shelley, Mary
1797–1851
English writer

Shelley was the daughter of two radical writers, William Godwin and Mary Wollstonecraft. She had an unhappy childhood after her mother died. Aged only 16, she ran away to Europe with the poet Percy Bysshe Shelley. One summer, they shared a house in Switzerland with other writers and thinkers, including Lord Byron. While there, Mary Shelley wrote one of the most famous horror stories of all time, about a student called Frankenstein and the terrible monster that he created.

Shelley, Percy Bysshe
1792–1822
English poet

The son of an MP, Shelley quarrelled with his family because of his radical views on politics and religion. He refused to believe in God, and argued that politics should be guided by people's individual feelings, rather than by strict laws or governments. He published all these ideas in his poems, which outraged many readers. Shelley's private life was also criticised. He ran away twice with very young women (his second wife was Mary Shelley) and he was often in debt. He drowned, aged only 30, in a boating accident in Italy.

▲ *Percy Bysshe Shelley was a Romantic poet. His major works include* To a Skylark, *and* Prometheus Unbound.

Smith, Adam
1723–1790
Scottish economist

Smith is famous today for his theories on economics, which have inspired right-wing politicians in many parts of the world. A brilliant scholar, he was a professor at Glasgow University before becoming tutor to the sons of a rich and powerful Scottish nobleman. Smith spent years travelling with his pupils in Europe, meeting many famous writers and thinkers. In 1766, he returned to Scotland, and spent the next ten years writing his most important book, *An Inquiry into the Nature and Causes of the Wealth of Nations*. In it, he discussed what made people, and countries, rich, and how wealth could be created.

Stanhope, Lady Hester
1776–1839
English explorer

Born to a wealthy noble family, Stanhope was intelligent, capable and eccentric. As a young woman, she lived with William Pitt the Younger, her uncle and Prime Minister, and acted as his official companion, meeting many famous people and taking an active part in politics. After he died in 1806, she became bored with life in Britain, and decided to seek adventure abroad. She never returned home. Dressed in Arab men's clothes, Stanhope travelled through Greece to Turkey, Syria and Egypt, and became the first European woman to visit many remote areas, and to explore many ancient monuments. She also became passionately involved in desert wars and feuds. The letters she wrote about her adventures still provide useful evidence for historians today.

Stephenson, George
1781–1848
English engineer

Stephenson began his working life in coal mines. He was one of the first people to realise how steam power and railways could help the coal industry develop. He built his first steam locomotive to haul coal trucks in 1814. Soon afterwards, he became engineer to the pioneering Stockton and Darlington Railway Company, and drove the world's first steam-powered train along its tracks in 1825. He worked closely with his son Robert (1803–1859) to build more new steam locomotives, including the famous *Rocket* in 1829. It became the standard design on which all later steam locomotives were based. Stephenson also designed many bridges in Britain, Canada and Egypt.

Stevenson, Robert Louis
1850–1894
Scottish writer

Stevenson studied engineering and law, but wanted to be a writer. After leaving university, he travelled in Europe, and wrote two books about his experiences. He also met an American woman traveller, who he followed to California, and married. From then on, he made his living as a writer. Some of his stories, such as *Treasure Island* and *Kidnapped*, told of exciting adventures. Others, such as *The Strange Case of Dr Jekyll and Mr Hyde*, were sinister and mysterious. For most of his life, Stevenson was unwell. In 1888, with his wife, he travelled to Samoa, a tropical island in the Pacific Ocean, hoping its climate would cure him but he died there six years later, aged only 44.

Stuart, Charles Edward (Bonnie Prince Charlie)
1720–1788
Claimant to the crown of the United Kingdom

Charles was the eldest grandson of James VII and II of Scotland and England. In 1688, James had been forced by Parliament to give up the throne because of his religious beliefs – it was illegal for the king or queen of Britain to be a Roman Catholic. Charles was also a Catholic, so, in law, he had no right to rule. However, he still claimed to be the rightful king of Britain, and many people who did not like the Hanoverian Dynasty supported him. In 1744, King Louis XV of France encouraged Charles to invade Britain. He hoped this would make it difficult for British troops to defend their country against French attack. Charles landed in Scotland in 1745, and led an army into England. They reached Derby, but were forced to retreat. Charles' supporters (known as Jacobites, from the Latin version of 'James') were massacred at the Battle of Culloden in Scotland in 1746. Charles spent five months on the run in the Scottish Highlands before Flora MacDonald helped him to escape.

Stuart, James Edward
1688–1766
Claimant to the crown of the United Kingdom

Father of Charles Edward Stewart, and eldest son of King James VII and II, James Edward was forced to flee to France when his father gave up the throne. As a Roman Catholic, he could not become king in his father's place. Instead, his Protestant sister Mary became queen, and ruled jointly with her husband, William of Orange, a Protestant ruler from the Netherlands. As a young man, James Edward fought in the French army. Then, in 1715, he led an invasion of Britain to claim his right to rule. He hoped to join forces with a rebellion, led by a Scottish nobleman, the Earl of Mar. However, he was soon defeated, and escaped, first to France and then to Spain. In 1719, he organised a second invasion, but his fleet was wrecked by storms at sea.

Stuart, Miranda (James Barry)

1795?–1865

English doctor and soldier

Born in Edinburgh, and orphaned by the time she was 15, Stuart hoped for a career in medicine. However, women were not allowed to become doctors by law. So Stuart disguised herself as a man, studied at medical college, and qualified in 1812. She was the first woman in Britain to do this – even though, at the time no one knew what she had achieved. Barry then joined the army, and served as a doctor in Canada, South Africa, southern Russia and the Caribbean. She was a good, but very strict, organiser, and was given many important and responsible posts. Stuart spent the whole of her life as a man. However, one of her army comrades suspected that she might be a woman, and after her death, rumours started to spread. Her body was dug up and examined. When she was found to be female,

the army cancelled the grand military funeral it had planned for 'James Barry'.

Swift, Jonathan

1667–1745

Irish writer

Remembered today for his novel *Gulliver's Travels*, Swift was a Protestant dean who spent most of his life in Dublin. He wrote many books and pamphlets on politics and society. Some, such as *Gulliver's Travels*, comment on people's behaviour through fantasy and humour; others are more savage and critical.

Tallis, Thomas

*c.*1505–1585

English composer

Tallis devoted his entire career to composing music to be sung in churches, by choirs of young boys and men. A skilful organist, he was employed for many years at the Chapel Royal, in London, where the royal family and courtiers went to pray. His music wove several different parts (tunes) together within one piece to create a rich, mysterious and holy sound. Tallis' work influenced other British composers for hundreds of years, and is still performed today.

Telford, Thomas

1757–1834

Scottish engineer

Trained as a stone-mason, Telford also studied architecture. In 1788, he was appointed surveyor of public works in Shropshire. There, he supervised the construction of canals and aqueducts, including some of the most important and difficult building projects of his

time. In 1802, he returned to Scotland to begin a massive survey of roads and communications. He planned and designed the Caledonian Canal, which cuts right across the country, plus 1400 kilometres of road, more than 1200 bridges, large public buildings and new harbours. He also designed roads and bridges in England, Sweden and Wales.

Tennyson, Lord Alfred

1809–1892

English writer

Appointed Poet Laureate in 1850, Tennyson was one of the most famous writers of the Victorian age, and a great favourite with Queen Victoria herself. After leaving university and travelling in Europe, he composed many poems in fashionable mock-medieval style. Many featured ancient legends, such as the story of British hero King Arthur. However, he also took an interest in new, scientific ideas. His poem, *In Memoriam*, was written after one of his friends died young. It deals with difficult subjects such as bereavement, change and memory, and links them to ideas about evolution – one of the most controversial scientific discoveries of Tennyson's day.

Terry, Dame Ellen

1848–1928

English actress

From a well-known theatrical family, Terry became famous for her own acting skills, and for her beautiful speaking voice. She played most of Shakespeare's great heroines, such as Juliet and Cleopatra, and also performed in many new plays – some contained roles written especially for her.

In 1878, she began a stage partnership with another famous actor, Henry Irving. Together they achieved many successes.

Thackeray, William Makepeace
1811–1863
English writer

Famous for witty novels that describe and criticise fashionable society, Thackeray started his career as a journalist. He began writing stories when he was faced with a financial crisis, after the savings bank where his family inheritance was kept collapsed. He also wrote satirical columns for magazines and newspapers, and gave public lectures. Thackeray's best-known novel, *Vanity Fair*, shocked many people when it first appeared, because its beautiful, fascinating heroine was also deceitful and unscrupulous.

Thatcher, Baroness Margaret
born 1925
English politician

The daughter of a grocer in a country town, Thatcher was intelligent and hard-working. She won a place at Oxford University, where she studied science, but decided to make a career in law. At the same time, she became passionately involved in politics. She was first elected to Parliament in 1959 as a member of the Conservative Party. Displaying ambition and ability, she was appointed a junior government minister within two years. She became Prime Minister in 1979 – the first British woman to lead a government. Thatcher stayed in power until 1990. Her policies were admired by some and hated by others. She reorganised Britain's welfare system, privatised state-owned industries, and attacked trade unions. She also led Britain into a controversial war with Argentina. She was unsympathetic to feminist ideas, preferring to use old-fashioned charm combined with iron-willed determination to get her own way.

▲ *Thatcher became Prime Minister in 1979 – the only woman ever to lead the British government.*

Thomas, Dylan
1914–1953
Welsh writer

Born in Wales, Thomas moved to London as a young man to work as a broadcaster and journalist. He also wrote and recited poetry. He was an intense, dramatic performer, and was highly praised. His most famous work, *Under Milk Wood*, is a picture in words of a small Welsh town. As in all Dylan's work, the writing is passionate, vivid, playful and very powerful.

Thomson, Sir William (Lord Kelvin)
1824–1907
Scottish scientist

Born in Belfast to a famous family of scientists, Thomson began studying mathematics and physics at Glasgow University when he was only 11 years old. He became professor there aged 22. At 24, he developed one of his brightest ideas – a new scale for measuring temperature. It is still used today, and is named after him. The same year, with a colleague, he discovered one of the fundamental laws of physics – the second law of thermodynamics. It explains how and why heat always flows from something warm to something colder.

Tippet, Sir Michael
1905–1997
English composer

A passionate, mystical character, Tippett created unique music that blended European classics with early English songs and American jazz and blues. Tippett was also well-known for his political views. A keen pacifist, he believed that all war was wrong. One of his best-known works, *A Child of our Time*, was inspired by his concern for the suffering of ordinary families in war.

Trevithick, Richard
1771–1833
English engineer

One of the pioneers of railway transport, Trevithick worked as a mining engineer. He invented a steam-powered engine and used it in locomotives to transport miners and coal along roads. In 1803, he was the first person to design a steam locomotive that could run on rails. It appeared in 1804 at Penydarren in South Wales.

Trollope, Anthony
1815–1882
English writer

Remembered today for his shrewd, sly novels about middle-class life in cathedral towns, Trollope also had a successful career as a civil servant. He worked for the Post Office, and arranged for the first pillar-boxes to be built in British streets. He wrote most of his 47 novels after he had retired. The most famous include those in the Barsetshire chronicles series.

Tull, Jethro
1647–1741
English inventor

An Oxfordshire landowner, Tull invented some of the first farm machines in the western world. Before his inventions, almost all work on British farms, except

▲ Turner was one of the great masters of landscape art as shown in The Grand Canal, Venice.

ploughing, was done using human muscle-power and hand-tools. Around 1701, Tull invented a seed drill (machine for planting seeds). Soon after, he travelled to Europe to study farming there. This led him to develop a horse-drawn hoe (machine for uprooting weeds) and schemes for manuring the soil to fertilise it, and to rotate crops to stop the build-up of pests and plant diseases.

Turner, J M W (Joseph Mallord William)
1775–1851
English artist

Turner showed artistic talent even as a child. He began to study at art college aged 14, then spent many years travelling and sketching in Britain and Europe. His early works were pictures of landscapes, in watercolours and oil

▼ Tull invented the seed drill, which made farming crops much easier.

paint. Towards the end of his life, Turner lost interest in accurately recording the views he saw, and became much more concerned with portraying dramatic effects of light and shade. In many of his works, such as the famous *Rain, Steam and Speed*, sunlight and clouds make abstract patterns, and it is hard to see any precise details at all. His work was so original that some people have called him 'the greatest British-born artist'.

Tyler, Wat
?–1381
English rebel

Leader of the Peasants' Revolt in 1381, Tyler organised farmers and craftsmen to march in protest against taxes and government corruption. He came face to face with King Richard II in London, and tried to force the king to give in to the rioters' demands. However, Tyler was stabbed to death by one of the king's supporters, and the protest collapsed.

Vaughan Williams, Ralph
1872–1958
English composer

One of the most important British composers of the 20th century, Vaughan Williams began to write music when he was only six years old. He studied with leading European composers, but decided that his own music should be based on traditional British tunes, or inspired by British landscape, folklore and poetry. He wrote many beautiful works for singers and for orchestras, in a haunting, romantic style, and was a respected teacher and choir-master. Vaughan Williams also worked hard to preserve ancient British folk songs and instrumental works, which he feared would vanish as new 20th-century music, played on radios and gramophones, became more popular.

Victoria
1819–1901; reigned 1837–1901
Queen of the United Kingdom

The longest-reigning British ruler, and one of the most successful, Victoria became queen when she was only 18 years old. Her youth and innocence won many admirers, as did her public declaration of her wish 'to do what is right'. People hoped that her reign would mark a new start for many British enterprises. Victoria was intelligent, practical, very determined and had a strong sense of duty. She took an active interest in politics, although she did not support any one party. In 1840, she married her cousin Albert, a German prince. Extremely happy together, they had nine children. Albert was also her chief adviser, as well as developing his many interests, from art to new technology. Victoria was devastated when he died in 1861, and withdrew from public life for some years. Persuaded to take up her duties again by Prime Minister Disraeli, she became a popular symbol of Britain's fast-growing power and prosperity, at home and abroad. In 1876, the British government declared her 'Empress of India'.

▲ *Queen Victoria's reign lasted for 63 years, longer than any other British monarch.*

Wallace, Sir William
*c.*1274–1305
Scottish soldier

A famous soldier, Wallace led the Scots to fight against King Edward I of England, who invaded their homeland. He was appointed guardian of Scotland after his troops defeated the English at the Battle of Stirling Bridge in 1297. The next year, he lost a battle against the English at Falkirk in central Scotland, and was forced to flee. He escaped to France, where he recruited more soldiers. Wallace returned to Scotland in 1303, even though the English had declared him an outlaw, and offered a prize for his capture. He was betrayed to the English and put in prison. Soon after, he was taken to London, tried for treason, and executed.

Walpole, Sir Robert
1676–1745
English politician

Walpole came from a family of country landowners. A supporter of the Whig party, he held many senior government positions, at a time when Parliament and ministers were rapidly becoming more important in deciding policy than kings or queens. He was leader of the Cabinet (group of top government ministers) for many years during the reigns of George I and George II. For this reason, he is known as 'Britain's first Prime Minister' (prime meaning first). His policies aimed to increase British prosperity and maintain peace.

Watson Watt, Sir Robert
1892–1973
Scottish scientist

Watson Watt began his career as a meteorologist (a scientist who studies the weather). After investigating radio waves given off by thunderstorms, he realised that radio signals could be used to identify the position of aircraft in the sky, even when it could not be seen – for example, at night – and built a machine to prove this. He called his invention RADAR (RAdio Detection And Ranging). He completed the first proper RADAR machine in 1935, which could detect moving objects 160 kilometres away. When World

War II (1939–1945) broke out four years later, RADAR proved extremely useful to Britain, giving warning of approaching enemy planes. Later, RADAR was developed for use on board aircraft and on ships at sea.

Watt, James
1736–1819
Scottish engineer

Remembered today as one of the founders of the Industrial Revolution, Watt began his career as a scientific instrument-maker. In 1763, he saw a model of Newcomen's steam engine, and realised that it could be improved. Around the same time, he also began experiments with steam and heat. In 1774, he began a business partnership with wealthy factory-owner Matthew Boulton. Together, they produced new steam-powered engines. Watt also designed new gears, new cylinders and many other devices, all of which made steam engines more efficient and more useful. Boulton and Watt's engines were used to power machines in British factories.

Wedgwood, Josiah
1730–1795
English manufacturer

Factory-owner Wedgwood started a new pottery-making business in Staffordshire in 1759. Working with artists, staff in his factories produced useful and ornamental types of pottery in striking new designs. Many were based on ancient Greek and Roman styles. Unlike many early factory-owners, Wedgwood aimed to produce very high-quality goods, even though he was using mass-production techniques. Today, examples of early

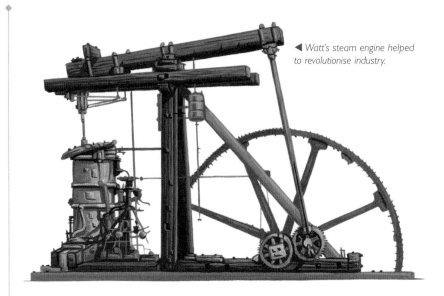

◄ *Watt's steam engine helped to revolutionise industry.*

Wedgwood pottery – typically pale-blue, with raised white designs – are highly prized by collectors.

Wellington, Duke of (Arthur Wellesley)
1769–1852
English soldier

A brilliant army commander, Wellington was famous for his strict discipline (he was known as 'the Iron Duke'), ruthless intelligence and dry wit.

Wellington led British troops to fight against Napoleon's France. His most famous victory was the Battle of Waterloo (1815), which ended French hopes of taking control of Europe. After he retired from active fighting, Wellington became a Tory (Conservative) politician, serving as Prime Minister from 1828 to 1830, and in 1834. He did not support many of the campaigns for social and political reform at that time, but gave Roman Catholics in England full civil and political rights for the first time in hundreds of years.

Wells, H G (Herbert George)
1866–1946
English writer

Trained as a scientist, Wells became a pioneer writer of science fiction, blending his expert knowledge with exciting stories in works such as *War of the Worlds* (1898). He hoped that these would make people think about the society they lived in, politics, and the benefits and dangers that science might bring. Wells was a keen member of the moderate socialist Fabian Society.

▼ *The political hopes and fears of Wells are reflected in his work.*

Wesley, John
1703–1791
English preacher

A scholar at Oxford University, Wesley became leader of a small group with keen religious ideas. They became known as 'methodists' – a name that is still preserved today, in the church Wesley founded. After a profound religious experience in 1738, Wesley decided to devote the rest of his life to preaching the Christian faith. However, many members of the established Church of England disliked his views, and were suspicious of his hopes of contacting people on the margins of society. So Wesley began to travel round the countryside, preaching in the open air to anyone who would listen. He was helped and supported by his brother Charles and their friends. The Wesleys attracted many followers. He hoped they would remain within the Church of England, but this proved impossible so he founded the Society of Methodists in 1784.

Whittle, Sir Frank
1907–1996
English engineer

Father of jet propulsion, Whittle revolutionised transport in the 20th century. He spent his whole career in aviation, joining the Royal Air Force as a teenage apprentice, then working as a pilot and test-pilot. His first jet-engined plane flew experimentally in 1941, and began regular flights in 1944.

Wilberforce, William
1759–1833
English reformer

Son of a wealthy merchant, Wilberforce served as an MP. In 1785, he experienced a conversion to Christianity and became deeply committed to social reform. He became convinced that slavery was wicked and started to campaign against it. In 1807, he persuaded Parliament to ban the slave trade in Britain. After this great success, he continued to work for slavery to be abolished throughout the world. He also supported many schemes to help poor people, and to improve religious education.

Wilde, Oscar
1854–1900
English writer

Born to a cultured, well-educated family, Wilde grew up to be a flamboyant and extravagant young man, keenly interested in art and literature. Living and working in London, where he became a fashionable – although shocking – public figure, he published poems, children's stories, and a spine-chilling novel. Wilde was most famous for his plays, and for his brilliant, witty conversation. Although married, with sons, he was also attracted to young men. In 1895, he was put on trial for homosexual behaviour. At that time, this was against the law, and he was sent to prison. On his release, many of Wilde's former friends no longer wanted to know him. Unwell, poor and unhappy, Wilde sought refuge in France, where he died.

▶ Oscar Wilde's most famous play is The Importance of Being Earnest.

▲ William the Conquerer claimed the English throne after Edward the Confessor died.

William I (the Conqueror)
1027–1087
King of England

The son of Robert, Duke of Normandy, William was descended from Viking invaders who settled in northern France after *c.*AD 900.

After the English king Edward the Confessor died, William claimed the right to rule England, saying that Edward had promised it to him in return for his help. However, other rivals also claimed the throne, so William invaded England in 1066. He landed on the south coast, fought a battle at Hastings, where Harold was killed, and took control of the kingdom. He put down a series of uprisings against foreign rule – the most important was led by an East Anglian outlaw named Hereward the Wake – then began to reform the English government. William introduced French laws and methods of working, and also 'feudalism' – a way of rewarding powerful nobles with large estates, so long as they promised to help the king and fight for him in battle. Probably his most famous memorial is the Domesday Book, a massive survey of England and its wealth, prepared for him in 1086, so that he could collect more taxes.

William III (of Orange)
1650–1702; reigned 1689–1702
King of England and Scotland

A grandson of King Charles I, William was a member of the Orange dynasty, which ruled the Netherlands. He married Mary, daughter of King James II/VII, in 1677. When James was forced to give up the throne, William and Mary ruled jointly as king and queen. At first, they faced opposition. There were rebellions in Scotland and Ireland between 1689 and 1690. However, William and Mary won support in England, because, unlike King James, they agreed to let Parliament decide government policy.

Wilson, Lord Harold
1916–1995
English politician

Determined to make a career in politics, Wilson became a Labour Party MP in 1945. He became a government minister just two years later – one of the youngest ever. In 1963, he was elected leader of the Labour Party, and was Prime Minister 1964–1970 and 1974–1976. Throughout Wilson's time in office, Britain faced serious economic problems and trade union conflicts, which he was unable to solve. He also failed to settle problems in the colony of Rhodesia (now Zimbabwe) after the white government there declared itself independent from Britain and refused to accept black majority rule. However, Wilson's governments did introduce important reforms in education, welfare, and civil rights, especially women's rights, and divorce.

Wollstonecraft, Mary
1759–1797
English writer

An intelligent, original thinker, Wollstonecraft was unable to have an interesting career because she was a woman. At the time she lived, women could not go to university or join any of the professions. Instead, she worked as a governess and nurse, writing in her spare time. Wollstonecraft was sympathetic to the radical ideas of the French Revolution of 1789, and became an outspoken campaigner for equal rights for women. Her most famous book *A Vindication of the Rights of Women* (1792) called for women's complete equality with men. It inspired many campaigners throughout the 19th century.

In 1797, Wollstonecraft married a famous revolutionary journalist, William Godwin. She died the same year, after giving birth to their daughter, Mary Shelley.

Wolsey, Thomas (Cardinal)
1472?–1530
English priest and politician

Wolsey (right) was a Roman Catholic priest who went to work as a government official. He held many senior positions, including lord chancellor. He helped shape England's relations with other European countries and with the leaders of the Roman Catholic Church in Rome. But after he failed to win King Henry VIII a divorce from his first wife, Catherine of Aragon, the king came to hate him and accused him of treason. He died on his way to the trial.

Woolf, Virginia
1882–1941
English writer

Born into a remarkable, intellectual family, Woolf became famous as a novelist and critic, and also as a member of the 'Bloomsbury Group' – a collection of writers and artists who lived in the Bloomsbury district of central London and who shared many experimental, unconventional ideas about life and creative work of all kinds. Together with her husband Leonard Woolf, she ran a well-known company, the Hogarth Press, which published new work by unknown writers. Her own books won praise for their 'stream of consciousness' technique (written as if inside the mind of their characters) and for their feminist ideas. Throughout her life, Woolf suffered from mental illness.

She committed suicide soon after completing her final novel.

Wordsworth, William
1770–1850
English poet

One of Britain's most famous writers, Wordsworth's poems are still popular today. He was born and brought up in the Lake District, in northwest England, and spent most of his life there. Its magnificent mountain scenery is described in many of his works, and strongly influenced his thoughts and feelings. He was one of the first writers to suggest that people's surroundings can affect their character and their behaviour, for good or ill. As a young man, Wordsworth had revolutionary ideas about writing and politics. He deliberately used simple, natural-sounding language that did not rhyme. This marked a great change from other poetry of the time, which was full of grand, complicated words arranged in strict verse patterns. He travelled to France to show support for the French Revolution of 1789, but later changed his opinions and held conservative political views. He was made Poet Laureate in 1843.

Wren, Sir Christopher
1632–1732
English architect

Trained as a scientist, Wren changed careers to become an architect. After the Great Fire of London (1666) he drew up plans to rebuild the large area of the city that had been destroyed in the blaze. These were never used, but were greatly admired. As a result, Wren was

▶ *Wren's new St Paul's Cathedral.*

given an important position by King Charles II, and asked to build many new London churches to replace the ones damaged in the Great Fire, including St Paul's Cathedral. This was a massive project, which took many years (1675–1711) to complete. Wren's design for St Paul's included advanced technical features such a huge, domed roof supported on a drum-shaped stone base, wrapped in iron chains for support.

Wyclif, John
*c.*1330–1384
English reformer

A scholar at Oxford University, Wyclif wrote many books criticising the wealth and power of the Roman Catholic Church. Wyclif called for reforms in Church government, simpler ways of worshipping, and for the Bible to be translated from Latin into English so that ordinary people could understand it. He also said that priests and Church leaders should live purer, more holy lives.

Wyclif's ideas were spread by wandering preachers, and won many supporters, who were known by the nickname 'Lollards'. Wyclif himself, however, and the Lollards, were attacked by Church leaders and the government. Wyclif was forced to give up his job, and after 1401, many Lollards were burned as heretics (people with dangerous beliefs).

Yeats, William Butler
1865–1939
Irish poet

Yeats was a keen supporter of Irish independence and very knowledgeable about Irish history, folklore and traditional culture. While working as a poet and dramatist, he helped to set up societies to study Irish literature, and was co-founder of the Irish National Theatre Company. His play, *The Countess Cathleen*, inspired many other writers to create works set in, or about, Ireland. Some of his poems – such as the well-known *The Lake Isle of Innisfree* – are on Irish topics, others are on universal themes such as love, or growing old. From 1922 to 1928, Yeats served as a senator in the newly formed Irish Free State. He was awarded the Nobel Prize for Literature in 1923.

Index

Entries in **bold** refer to main subject entries. Entries in *italics* refer to illustrations.

Acknowledgements

All artworks are from the Miles Kelly Artwork Bank

The publishers would like to thank the following picture sources whose photographs appear in this book:

Page 16 © Alun Bull, English Heritage and Cresswell Heritage Trust; 17 t Photolibrary Group Ltd; 27 t/r Richard Hannington/Fotolia.com; 35 b/r Steve Peake; 42 b/c Courtesy Vale of White Horse District Council; 76 Hulton-Deutsch Collection/Corbis; 92 William McKelvie/Fotolia.com; 106 © Ted Spiegel/Corbis; 125 david hughes/Fotolia.com; 126 © Douglas McGilviray/Fotolia.com; 132 Jaspal Bahra/Fotolia.com; 145 t/r Topham Picturepoint TopFoto.co.uk; 167 Hulton-Deutsch Collection/Corbis; 170 Adam Woolfitt/Corbis; 175 t/r Fotolia; 175 b David Woods/Fotolia.com; 178 t Richard Cummins/Corbis; 183 b Private Collection/Bridgeman Art Library; 207 t/r Historical Picture Archive/Corbis; 210 Richard Steinberg/Fotolia.com; 213 t/r Jaroslaw Grudzinski/Fotolia.com; 214 Johnny Lye/Fotolia.com; 216 t/r Robert Williams (Magma) 219 t/r Adam Woolfitt/Corbis; 221 b/l Portrait of Queen Elizabeth I, when a princess, c.1547–58 (oil on panel), Anglo-Italian School, (16th century)/Private Collection, © Philip Mould Ltd, London/The Bridgeman Art Library; 224 t/r The Art Archive; 227 t/r Lance Bellers/Fotolia.com; 238 b/l Mary Evans Picture Library; 245 b/r Bettmann/Corbis; 256 b/r jean philippe NAPPEY/Fotolia.com; 261 b Historical Picture Archive/Corbis; 281 Phillips, The International Fine Art Auctioneers/Private Collection/Bridgeman Art Library; 287 b/r Handel Corbis; 290 James Francis Philip Mould Ltd, London/ The Bridgeman Art Library; 305 t/r Pleasure gardens Historical Picture Archive/Corbis; 313 River Liffey Artur Bogacki/Fotolia.com; 314 t/r Henry Grattan Corbis; 315 Vinegar hill Mary Evans Picture Library; 321 t/l Cartoon George and Caroline Public Record Office/HIP TopFoto.co.uk; 326 t Royal Albert Bridge Hulton-Deutsch Collection/Corbis; 332 b/l Child in mines Mary Evans Picture Library; 333 Cotton manufacture TopFoto.co.uk; 338 Peterloo Massacre Mary Evans Picture Library; 342 b/r Kew Gardens Tao Pang/Fotolia.com; 348 b/r Keir Hardie Topham Picturepoint/TopFoto.co.uk; 353 b courtesy of the Gaelic Athletic Association; 380 TopFoto.co.uk; 396 b Hulton Deutsch Collection/Corbis; 397 t/r Hulton Deutsch Collection/Corbis; 397 b Crawford Municipal Art Gallery, Cork, Ireland/Bridgeman Art Library; 399 c/r Hulton Deutsch Collection/Corbis; 399 b Hulton Deutsch Collection/Corbis; 401 b Hulton Deutsch Collection/Corbis; 402 b Bettman/Corbis; 405 b Bettman/Corbis; 406 t photograph by Ken Lambert, Camera Press London; 406 b Hulton Deutsch Collection/Corbis; 408 t Topham Picturepoint; 411 b/l Stephen Coburn/Fotolia.com; 412 Bettman/Corbis; 418 t TopFoto.co.uk; 420 b/r Topham Picturepoint; 421 t/r Hulton-Deutsch Collection/Corbis; 421 b/r Hulton-Deutsch Collection/Corbis; 422 t/r Hulton-Deutsch Collection/Corbis; 423 Hulton-Deutsch Collection/Corbis; 425 t/r Bettmann/Corbis; 425 b/r Bettmann/Corbis; 426 t/r Bernard Bisson/Corbis SYGMA; 428 c/l Topham Picturepoint; 428 t/r jeff gynane/Fotolia.com; 430 t/r Topham Picturepoint TopFoto.co.uk; 432 t Topham/AP; 432 b Topham Picturepoint; 433 Paramount/Kobal Collection/Art Archive; 435 t Bettmann/Corbis; 436 t ArenaPAL/TopFoto.co.uk; 436 B Woodfall/Associated British/The Kobal Collection 437 b Mike Shannon/Fotolia.com; 438 © Antoine Gyori/AGP/Corbis; 440 TopFoto/EMPICS; 441 EMPICS/TopFoto; 442 t Topham Picturepoint; 444 © david hughes Fotolia.com; 448 b/l National Pictures TopFoto.co.uk; 449 PA/TopFoto

All other photographs are from:

Castrol, Corel, digitalSTOCK, digitalvision, John Foxx, PhotoAlto,
PhotoDisc, PhotoEssentials, PhotoPro, Stockbyte